THE BLACK PHARAOHS

For
Margaret S. Drower and Robert D. Anderson

THE BLACK PHARAOHS

Egypt's Nubian Rulers

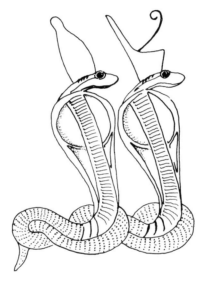

ROBERT G. MORKOT

The Rubicon Press

The Rubicon Press
57 Cornwall Gardens
London SW7 4BE

British Library Cataloguing-in-Publication Data

A catalogue record for this book is available from the
British Library

ISBN 0-948695-23-4 (hbk)
ISBN 0-948695-24-2 (pbk)

Designed by The Rubicon Press
Printed and bound in Great Britain by Biddles Limited
of Guildford and King's Lynn

CONTENTS

List of Illustrations

All drawings are by the author unless otherwise stated.

Acknowledgements

Over the years, I have incurred enormous debts of gratitude to many colleagues who have willingly shared information and ideas on ancient Nubia and the Kushites in Egypt. I would particularly like to mention Lisa Heidorn, Raymond Johnson, Peter Lacovara, Christian Loeben, and Stephen Quirke. My thanks also go to Professor Jean Jacquet and Dr. Helen Jacquet-Gordon for information on their excavations at Medinet Habu. The late Professor Ricardo Caminos willingly discussed his copy of the Karimala inscription at Semna, its text and interpretation, as well as many other obscure points. To Irene Vincentelli Liverani my thanks go for sharing information on the material from the site of el Arab; and to Mario Liverani for numerous offprints; and to both for their generous hospitality in Rome. I am also deeply grateful to Alison Roberts, whose wide knowledge in the area of religion has long been a stimulus and whose gentle criticisms caused me to rethink and recast a previous study.

Peter James has constantly acted as a sounding-board and supplier of numerous references and ideas. Many years ago Peter jumped on one of my cavalier remarks and introduced me to the chronological debate. As a conventionally trained Egyptologist, I was initially sceptical, but gradually I saw that there was a case to answer, and this resulted in the chapter on Nubia in *Centuries of Darkness* (James *et al.* 1991). The ideas expressed here are more developed than those in *Centuries* and if I have not chosen to be dogmatic on chronological revision, it is not because I have abandoned the idea: I still see it as the most convincing explanation of the problems of the Nubian (and other) "Dark Age".

I also owe much to a group of friends who have encouraged me and, over the past twelve years carried me off to look at antiquities in the remotest corners of Egypt, Syria and Libya.

For photographic permissions I would like to thank Sue Carney, the Committee of the Egypt Exploration Society, Dr. Rita Freed and the Boston Museum of Fine Arts. My thanks also go to Patricia Spencer for assistance in the Egypt Exploration Society's Library and Archives over many years. Full acknowledgements for the sources will be found in the list of illustrations.

This book has been long in production, and my thanks go to Anthea Page, Juanita Homan and Robin Page of The Rubicon Press for asking me to write it, and for their assistance and forbearance.

I am grateful to Robert Anderson and Margaret Drower (Mrs. Hackworth-Jones) for accepting the dedication. Both encouraged me to pursue the study of Nubian and Meroitic archaeology when it was almost totally neglected by British Egyptology. From Robert I have received much encouragement and sound advice ever since I first wrote on the 25th Dynasty in 1975. I also envy his ability to modulate with ease between Egyptology and music. Margaret Drower's command of the vast field of Near Eastern history has always been an inspiration. It was she who taught me that the ancient world was as complex and dynamic as ours, and not just a group of societies – Egypt, Assyria, Persia – which can be treated in isolation. Ever since my undergraduate days, Margaret Drower has offered constant encouragement, both practical and moral. It came as no great surprise to me, to find on an undergraduate essay unearthed in the late stages of editing this volume, a comment from her which quite possibly was the seed from which this whole volume grew, rather slowly.

I   Bow-Land

For around one hundred years, between 750 and 650 BC, two great powers, Egypt and Assyria, vied for control of western Asia. At the centre of the conflict stood the kingdoms of Israel and Judah. This was the age of the Jewish prophets and their legacy has characterised the protagonists – the Assyrian emperors and the Kushite pharaohs of Egypt – for posterity. Inveighing against the Assyrian kings "who shook the earth, who made realms tremble, who made the world like a waste and wrecked its towns", they were equally hostile to their own rulers' reliance on the Kushite pharaoh, the proverbial "broken reed".

The Kushite pharaohs are known to Egyptology as the "25th Dynasty". The dynasty and its Kushite successors are also called "Napatan" from the city of Napata near the 4th Cataract of the Nile, which was one of the Kushite kingdom's principal cities. Although their rule in Egypt was brought to an end by Assyrian invasions and the intrigues of the Libyan dynasts who ruled the Delta, the Kushite kingdom continued through phases of prosperity and recession for another 800 years before it fragmented and eventually metamorphosed into the Christian kingdoms of Nubia. This later phase (from *c.* 200 BC) is known as the Meroitic period from the southern Kushite city of Meroe. It was as rulers of Egypt that these Kushite pharaohs were drawn into the politics of western Asia; their original kingdom lay far to the south. In the words of the Israelite prophet Isaiah, it was "a land shadowing with wings beyond the rivers of Kush". To the Assyrians, Kush was a "far and inapproachable region". Even the Egyptians regarded the southern limits of Kush as the "horns of the earth". This image of a remote and exotic land, the source of ivory, gold, incense and slaves, was perpetuated through Greek and Roman literature into the writing of modern Egyptology.

The original centres of Kushite power lay in the southern part of the land known today as Nubia. Nubia is the middle Nile valley spanning the northern part of the modern state of Sudan and the southernmost part of Egypt. Many countries and political states within this region are listed in ancient Egyptian records, but, despite the theories and attempts of Egyptologists, it is very difficult to place these names on a map, or tie them to the archaeological remains.[1]

1

Numerous names have been given to the whole region or to various states which existed there. Although some of these names have an indigenous origin, many of them were imposed by people from outside. The most ancient names known are Egyptian: Ta-Seti and Ta-Nehesy. Ta-Seti, "the Land of the Bow" was that region between Aswan and Edfu which was later part of the Egyptian state, the first of the *nomes* of Upper Egypt. Ta-Nehesy was "the land of the *nehesyu*-Nubians": Nehesyu was a name given to both settled peoples of the river valley and to the nomadic peoples of the surrounding deserts. *Wawat* was the indigenous name of a state which covered part of the valley south of Aswan, and was later used as a term for the administrative district between Aswan and the 2nd Nile Cataract. The other important indigenous power was Kush which lay south of the 3rd Cataract. Again this name was taken by the Egyptians and used for the whole of the southern part of Nubia. It became the name applied by not only the Egyptians, but the Assyrians and other peoples of western Asia to the whole of Nubia. So it is found in the biblical, Assyrian (as *Kusu*) and the Persian (*Kushiya*) texts.

To the Greeks, Nubia and Kush were included in a much wider region, *Aithiopia*. As the Greeks became more familiar with the peoples of the region, the name Aithiopia came to be understood as meaning "the land of the burnt-faced people", but originally it seems to have meant those who lived closest to the rising sun.[2]

Aithiopia was a vaguely defined region on the southern fringes of the Greek world, but, with greater knowledge of both India and Egypt, the Greeks of the classical and hellenistic periods divided Aithiopia into many different areas. There were thus regions of Aithiopia which had contacts with the Greek world and other further off and still ill-defined regions beyond them. Of these Aithiopian lands, the most important was the kingdom of Meroe. Meroe maintained strong contacts with Egypt under the rule of the Ptolemies, and became firstly a formidable adversary of Rome and later an important trading partner. The earliest archaeological remains from Meroe have been dated to the early years of the Kushite kingdom of the 8th century, but the city's origins are certainly very much more ancient. Its name first appears in Kushite texts of the later Napatan period, as Barua(t). The decline of Meroe was in part due to the rising importance of trade along the Red Sea which developed in the first centuries AD and the consequent rising power of the kingdom of Aksum in the highlands of Ethiopia. Nubia was a relatively late name, first found in the 3rd century BC. Its origin is uncertain. Some scholars have associated it with the Egyptian word *nub*, meaning "gold", but others have suggested a connection with the Noubai, a people who came into the Nile valley from the region of Darfur and Kordofan. In this book, "Nubian" is

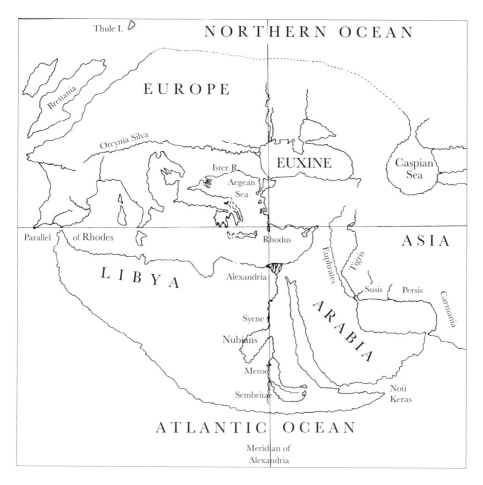

Map of the world according to Eratosthenes. Eratosthenes placed Rhodes, Alexandria, Aswan and Meroe all on the same meridian. (Fig. 1)

used in a geographical sense, without ethnic connotations. The ancient populations of Nubia are now usually referred to as Kushite, thereby avoiding confusion with the modern Nubian population and Nubian language speakers.[3]

Inevitably, this large number of names causes some confusion. The older literature used the classical "Ethiopia" to designate the Nubian and Sudanese civilizations, and also for the Egyptian "25th Dynasty". This was dropped by the 1970s, and here, to avoid confusion with the modern state of Ethiopia, any reference to the classical designation is as *Aithiopia*.

Nubia itself is divided into two regions. Lower Nubia, the northern part, between the 1st Cataract of the Nile at Aswan and the 2nd Cataract, now lies beneath the waters of Lake Nasser. Lower Nubia was a barren

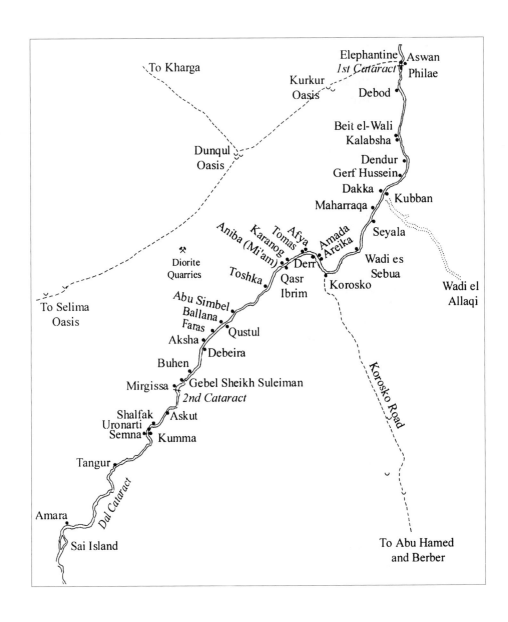

Map of Lower Nubia (Fig. 2)

country, but admired for its austere beauty. The river cut easily through the soft sandstone, leaving only a narrow valley with high banks and a narrow fertile strip along the water's edge. The cultivation broadened where wadis opened onto the river. In recent centuries the region was renowned for its date plantations, their richness contrasting with the stark surrounding desert. Although best known for the great New Kingdom temples, such as Abu Simbel, built by Ramesses II, and those of the Ptolemaic and Roman periods, Lower Nubia was the home to important Kushite states from the very earliest times until the kingdoms of Ballana and Nobadia in the 4th-6th centuries AD.

The *Batn el Hagar*, the Belly of Rock, and the 2nd Cataract formed a natural southern frontier which was at times (notably the Middle Kingdom) exploited by the Egyptians. Upper Nubia has its northern limit at the 2nd Cataract, but a rather flexible southern boundary – it is often used in literature to cover the whole of the region as far south as Khartoum. Here, Upper Nubia designates the region as far south as the 4th Cataract. Upper Nubia is divided into zones by further cataracts, the most fertile region lying south of the 3rd Cataract. This stretch of the river, the Dongola Reach, is the most fertile part of the river valley south of Thebes. Recent survey in this area has shown that at some periods of antiquity, notably during the Kerma kingdom, the river had up to three channels which would have made it immensely fertile. Because of its natural wealth, and its key position to control the southern trade routes, the earliest major Nubian power, the Kushite kingdom of Kerma, developed here. The later Kushite kingdom also had its origins in this reach of the Nile, but further south, at the foot of the 4th Cataract.

Although the desert roads from Lower Nubia regain the river between the 4th and 5th Cataracts, the river is unnavigable and the banks barren. No ancient signs of permanent settlement have yet been identified here, and the main routes between the Dongola Reach and the central Sudan seem always to have crossed the Bayuda Desert. These desert roads, passing the wells at Fura, strike the Nile in the Shendi Reach, in the region of Meroe.

This southern region, the heartland of the Meroitic state, was known to the Greek and Roman writers as the "Island of Meroe", since it was bordered by the rivers Nile and Atbara. Here, after its period of rule in Egypt, the Kushite state flourished until the 4th century AD, before fragmenting into a number of new kingdoms. The region's importance stretches far back into the earliest periods, but we know little of its archaeology before the rise of the Kushite state in the 8th century BC. It must, however, have been the focus of important kingdoms – perhaps those recorded in the Egyptian sources as Miu and Irem. Lying between the Nile

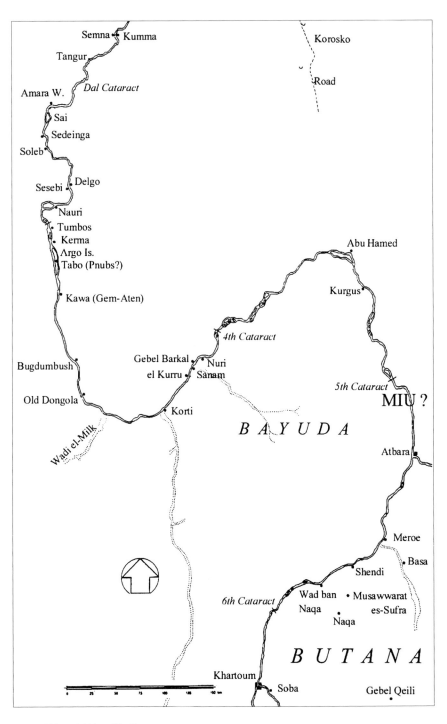

Semna • Kumma
Tangur
Dal Cataract
Amara W.
Sai
Sedeinga
Soleb
Sesebi • Delgo
Nauri
Tumbos
Kerma
Argo Is.
Tabo (Pnubs?)
Kawa (Gem-Aten)
Korosko
Road
Abu Hamed
Kurgus
4th Cataract
Bugdumbush
Gebel Barkal • Nuri
el Kurru • Sanam
5th Cataract
MIU ?
Old Dongola
Korti
Wadi el-Milk
B A Y U D A
Atbara
Meroe
Basa
Shendi
6th Cataract
Wad ban • Musawwarat
Naqa   es-Sufra
Naqa
B U T A N A
Khartoum
Soba
Gebel Qeili

Map of Upper Nubia. (Fig. 3)

and the Atbara, and within the seasonal rain belt, this was in ancient times a savanna land, probably quite densely wooded in places. It was rich in the wildlife now found only much farther south in eastern Africa, such as giraffes, elephants, lions and leopards. The country inland from Meroe is also called the Butana. This savanna land, stretching to the Ethiopian foothills, supplied the luxuries – ebony, ivory, animal skins and incense – on which Kushite trade depended.

To the west of the Nile lie Darfur and Kordofan, both significant in the mediaeval period. Our knowledge of these regions in earlier times is still very limited. Recent surveys in the Wadi Howar have suggested that it may have been able to support a small settled population into Meroitic times, and there are some indications of Meroitic activity. Remains from earlier periods suggest strong cultural contacts with the Kerma and C-Group peoples.

Equally problematic is the land to the east, modern Ethiopia. Here lay the land of Punt. Visited by the Egyptians from very early times, Punt was a principal source of incense. The Egyptians sailed to "Punt" for two thousand or so years, and, although they doubtless visited much the same geographical region, its political and cultural, and possibly ethnic, composition would have changed. Recent excavations in eastern Sudan have identified a series of cultures and archaeological sites which might be associated with the Punt of the Late Bronze Age (c. 1500-1100 BC). In the 1st millennium BC a new situation began to develop in Ethiopia. Cultural influences, and probably population movements, from south Arabia led to the gradual development of new powers in the Ethiopian highlands, culminating in the kingdom of Aksum. Aksum came to dominate the Red Sea trade in the early centuries AD, and this was probably one factor in the decline of the Meroitic state.[4]

To the south of the Kushite and Meroitic kingdoms, our knowledge of the ancient southern Sudan is very patchy. Archaeology has been limited, although objects carrying the names of the 25th dynasty pharaohs have been found in the cemeteries at Sennar and Gebel Moya. While we are forced to focus on contacts with Egypt and western Asia we should remember that the Kushite world reached out to the south, the east and the west.

II Beyond the Rivers of Kush

Our understanding of the history of Nubia and its importance is vastly different from how it was understood a hundred years ago, and even more radically different from how it was perceived fifty years before then. These changes are due to the development of archaeology, Egyptology and Assyriology.

Before 1800, few Europeans had travelled further south than Aswan. Nevertheless, on early maps which included the region, the "Island" and city of Meroe may be found, and the city of Napata. Both were known from the Greek and Roman writers, Meroe being particularly renowned. Those Europeans who had visited the Sudanese kingdom of Sennar, or Darfur in the west, were mostly missionary priests, principally Jesuits. They had travelled, not along the river, but by the desert roads.

For James Bruce (1730-1794), the motive was to find the source of the Nile.[1] In 1772, Bruce returned from Ethiopia along the Blue Nile via the Funj kingdom of Sennar, to the confluence of the two rivers (present-day Khartoum). Travelling northwards he passed the village of Begarawiya, where he saw "heaps of broken pedestals and pieces of obelisks". He commented that it "is impossible to avoid risking a guess that this is the ancient city of Meroe". He was right, but made no more detailed observations. Bruce returned, not along the river, but across the desert road from Berber to Daraw, so the great temples scattered along the river's length, such as Barkal, Soleb and Abu Simbel, were to remain "unknown" for a further forty years.

Following the events of 1798, European interest in Egypt intensified. The scholars who accompanied Napoleon's expedition recorded monuments throughout Egypt, but did not venture south of the 1st Cataract. The first European to travel extensively in Nubia was the Swiss, John Lewis Burckhardt (1784-1817), who, in the employ of the British "Association for promoting the discovery of the interior parts of Africa", made two journeys through Nubia in 1813 and 1814. On the first, he travelled along the river, through the hostile landscape of the 2nd cataract as far as Soleb. His second journey accompanied the caravan from Daraw, near Kom Ombo, across the Eastern Desert, striking the river again at Berber. From Berber the caravan followed the Nile to Shendi and then the river Atbara to the Ethiopian mountains, before branching north-east to Suakin on the Red Sea. Burckhardt noted many ancient monuments, and he was the first European in modern times to enter the temple of Abu Simbel. He passed Meroe, as Bruce had done, but did not pay particular attention to the ruins: archaeology was not his main purpose. Burckhardt died from dysentry on his return to Cairo, but the narrative of his journeys was swiftly published and contained much valuable information on the ancient remains which he had seen.

The Pyramids at Meroe as they appeared to George Hoskins. (Fig. 4)

As Egypt came under greater European influence, more antiquarians came to draw the monuments and copy the reliefs and inscriptions, as well as to remove antiquities to European museums. More people travelled in Nubia also, but few went farther south than the 2nd cataract. A considerable number of Europeans went to Egypt to join the service of the Turkish Viceroy, Mohammed Ali Pasha. They ranged from doctors and geologists to engineers and plain adventurers. The most renowned was Belzoni, the great acquisitor of antiquities, but others, such as Giovanni Finati, Louis Linant de Bellefonds and Frédéric Cailliaud, also began their Egyptian careers in the Viceroy's service.

The second and third decades of the 19th century were the time of rich travellers such as the Englishman, William Bankes of Kingston Lacy in Dorset. Bankes graduated from Cambridge University and immediately became an MP. Between 1815 and 1818 he travelled in the Near East and Egypt. At this time, the whole region seems to have been swarming with such young men. At Jerusalem, Bankes had met up, and travelled briefly in

The temple of Semna as seen by Hoskins. The relief of Queen Karimala is on the façade. (Fig. 5)

Transjordan, with another such, James Silk Buckingham, who was on his way to take up a position in India.[2] The two men met up again a few months later in Syria. Parting company in Aleppo, Bankes continued to Egypt, Buckingham to Baghdad and then to Calcutta. Buckingham's publication of the narrative of his eventful journey and stay in Baghdad included one of the first European accounts of the monuments of Mesopotamia. Bankes was later described as a "conceited, self-opinionated young man" who travelled with "a gold-fitted dressing-case laden with perfumes". He was perhaps an extreme example, but his travels were not entirely without purpose: he was interested in the decipherment of hieroglyphics, and he acquired an important collection of Egyptian antiquities, including an obelisk with a bilingual inscription. Bankes was also wealthy enough to hire the services of others to accompany him. One was Giovanni Finati who, having left the service of Mohammed Ali, became a professional dragoman and interpreter. In Egypt, Bankes employed a young Frenchman, Louis Linant de Bellefonds (1799-1883), as a draughtsman. On their return to Egypt from Dongola, Bankes asked Linant to undertake another journey into Nubia and locate Meroe.[3] As a result, Linant was the first European to visit the ruins of Naqa and Musawwarat es-Sufra, although his plans and drawings were not published. He was later (1827) employed by the Association for promoting the discovery of the interior parts of Africa, for whom he made a journey into southern Sudan. Linant spent the rest of his life in the service of the Egyptian government.

In 1820, the aspirations of Mohammed Ali drew him into Sudan. Mohammed Ali had driven the Mamelukes out of Egypt in 1811, but they had established Dongola as their stronghold. In order to crush them, and also to reopen the slave route from southern Sudan, Mohammed Ali despatched an army under the command of his son, Ismail Pasha. Various Europeans attached themselves to this military expedition, in a distinctly non-military capacity. Two young clergymen, George Waddington and Barnard Hanbury, accompanied it as far as Merawe where they were ordered back by Ismail Pasha. They published an account of their travels and the Nubian monuments in 1822.[4] Another member of the expedition was Frédéric Cailliaud (1787-1869) who had been employed by Mohammed Ali to find the emerald mines of the Eastern Desert. Cailliaud went on to Sennar, visiting Naqa and Musawwarat on his return journey. He met Linant near Meroe, and travelled with him as far as Soleb. Cailliaud's publication (1826) of his plans and drawings in folio volumes of plates, with an extensive text, under the title *Voyage à Méroé*, made, for the first time, the monuments of the Meroitic civilization available to European antiquarians.

The largest and most systematic of the surveys to record monuments was the joint Franco-Tuscan expedition led by Jean François Champollion (1790-1832) and Ippolito Rosellini (1800-1843) in 1828-1829. They copied monuments throughout Egypt and Lower Nubia, travelling as far south as Semna. Champollion's initial speculations on the decipherment of hieroglyphics had been published in 1822 and 1824, and, although it was not yet possible to read the inscriptions, the importance of the cartouches which contained royal names was recognised. Champollion died suddenly, whilst preparing the publication of the survey, and his advances in the understanding of the ancient language were not revealed until his grammar and dictionary were published by his brother. Because of Champollion's sudden death, it was Rosellini's publication that was the principal record of the survey. This hugely important work, appearing between 1832-1844, amounted to over 3,000 pages of text and nearly 400 folio plates. In his vastly influential text volumes, Rosellini drew together all of the available evidence, not only from Egypt, but also from European museum collections.

Nubia south of the 2nd Cataract was not visited by the Franco-Tuscan expedition, but it still attracted small private groups. In 1829, Lord Prudhoe (later 4th Duke of Northumberland) accompanied by Major

Orlando Felix and the ubiquitous Giovanni Finati, travelled as far as Gebel Barkal at the 4th Cataract (they had met Champollion *en route*, at Semna). At Gebel Barkal, Felix made some important sketches of monuments and cartouches,[5] and Prudhoe himself acquired the two red granite lions which were later presented to the British Museum.

Another wealthy Englishman, George Hoskins (1802-1863), travelled as far south as Musawwarat and Meroe, in 1833. He could not visit Naqa because lions were reported in the region, and his artist refused to go there. Hoskins published the account of his travels in 1835 (see *figs*. 4, 5, 7, 12, 62), and included in it chapters on the history of Nubia.

The copying of inscriptions and reliefs was of enormous importance to the newly developing science of Egyptology. It was hoped that, through the means of texts and depictions, the gaps in history and religion, which had been sketched from the writings of the Greeks and Romans, and, to a lesser extent from the Bible, could be filled in.

Following the work of Champollion on the decipherment of hieroglyphics, a number of travellers made collections of cartouches. As a result of his travels in Egypt and Nubia, Orlando Felix had published a volume of cartouches in 1830. In this he urged the writing of history "from the monuments", rather than from the classical tradition. But, desirable as that might be, the number of texts available, and understanding of them, was still insufficient to make it practicable. All studies of the 25th Dynasty (as for the rest of Egyptian history) continued to be based on classical and biblical texts.

The foundation of Egyptian chronology was the *Aigyptiaka* of Manetho, a priest who had written a history of Egypt in the reign of Ptolemy II (*c*. 280 BC). Manetho's text actually survived only in excerpts and summaries in the works of the jewish historian Josephos (b.AD 37) and the early christian writer, Eusebius (AD 263-339) and in the king-lists copied by a Byzantine monk, George Syncellus (d. *c*. AD 812) from Eusebius and Julius Africanus. Syncellus's version of the king-lists had been used by the chronologer, Joseph Scaliger, in 1606, and other editions were published in the 17th and 18th centuries. To this framework, historical episodes were added from many other Greek and Roman sources, notably the *Histories* of Herodotos, and the encyclopædists Diodoros of Sicily (*fl*. 60-30 BC) and Strabon (*c*. 63 BC-AD 21).

Although the classical sources were limited in their specific information on the kings Manetho called the 25th Dynasty, and even more so on their Meroitic successors, there was much on Aithiopia and its customs. Indeed, so important was the classical tradition regarding law and religion in Aithiopia that the Rev. Michael Russell writing in 1833 began his book with the comment:

There is no country in the world more interesting to the antiquary and scholar than that which was known to the ancients as "Ethiopia above Egypt," the Nubia and Abyssinia of the present day. It was universally regarded by the poets and philosophers of Greece as the cradle of those arts, which at a later period covered the kingdom of the Pharaohs with so many wonderful monuments, as also of those religious rites which, after being slightly modified by the priests of Thebes, were adopted by the ancestors of Homer and Virgil as the basis of their mythology.

Russell, in common with the views of his time, and following the classical tradition, believed that civilization originated in Aithiopia and from there was passed to Egypt.

The other important tradition was the bible. Although there were numerous references to Egypt in those books, there was little that could be specifically considered historical. Even today, the important Egyptian episodes – the stories of Joseph and the Exodus – remain unattested in the Egyptian archaeological or historical record, and their precise relation to Egyptian kings continues to provide grounds for speculation and argument. It was only a very few of the later pharaohs who were actually named in the biblical record, but, of these, one was the "Aithiopian" king Tirhaka (Taharqo) who is said to have aided Hezekiah, king of Judah, at the time of the Assyrian invasion led by Sennacherib.

Already in 1835, Hoskins, although relying extensively on the classical and biblical sources, supplemented these with observations on the surviving monuments. He also included some of the evidence presented by Rosellini in the first part of his monumental publication. Rosellini's work resolved many of the confusions which had come about through trying to reconcile the classical tradition and monumental record.

The Græco-Roman tradition attributed the Kushite conquest of Egypt to a king named *Sabbakon* (*Sabacon*) whom we now call Shabaqo (or Shabaka). His name had been incorrectly equated by Orlando Felix and others with the cartouches of a king, Ankh-ka-re Sebekhotep, who actually reigned over one thousand years before, in about 1750 BC. The next king in Manetho, *Sevechus*, was identified with a pharaoh whose cartouches were known from the temple of Luxor and a statue in the Villa Albani collection in Rome. *Sevechus* was also thought to be the same as "So, king of Egypt" who sent aid to Hoshea, king of Israel, when the Assyrian king Shalmaneser V invaded and besieged Samaria. The third of Manetho's kings was *Taracos*. There was no doubt that this was the same as the "Taharka, king of Aithiopia" who aided Hezekiah of Judah against the Assyrian, Sennacherib. The events of the conflict, culminating in the battle

The small votive figure of Monthu in the Anastasi collection, as it appeared in Rosellini's publication. It is now in the British Museum. (Fig. 6)

of Eltekeh and siege of Jerusalem, were narrated in the second *Book of Kings*. This was the occasion when the Assyrians warned that:

> Egypt is a broken reed that will run into a man's hand and pierce it if he leans on it. That is what Pharaoh king of Egypt proves to all who rely on him.

The conflict with Sennacherib was also recorded by Josephos and, in a more garbled form, by Herodotos. The name of *Taracos* was preserved on monuments at Thebes and he had been recognised by Cailliaud, Hoskins and others as the king who had commissioned the rock-cut temple at Gebel Barkal.

Rosellini correctly identified the cartouches of Shabaqo, Shebitqo and Taharqo. The incorrect equation of Shabaqo and Sebekhotep was, however, perpetuated in some English literature (notably the work of Samuel Sharpe who still sustained the error in 1859). Rosellini also recognised that all of the monuments previously attributed to *Sevechus*, such as the Villa Albani statue, were actually works of Shabaqo.

Two other "Ethiopian" kings were also identified from cartouches copied by Orlando Felix on monuments at Gebel Barkal. These were "Aspel(t)", or "Ospher(t)" (Aspelta) and Amonasô (Amanislo). The latter king was tentatively identified with "Ammeris the Aithiops" referred to by

The rock-cut temple of Taharqo at Gebel Barkal, as illustrated by Hoskins. (Fig. 7)

Manetho. Known only from a cartouche on one of the Prudhoe lions, Amonasô received little further attention in the historical reconstructions. He was not, however, completely neglected. The name, read as Amonasro, was used by Mariette for that of the Kushite king in his plot for Verdi's opera, *Aida*, which was first performed in Cairo in 1871.

The fourth text-volume of Rosellini's *Monumenti Storici* (1841) devotes a brief chapter to the three kings of the 25th Dynasty and their known monuments. These monuments were still very few. To *Sciabak* (our Shabaqo) could be ascribed the reliefs in the "palazzo" (ie temple) of Luxor and those on the gateway of the 4th Pylon at Karnak. Two statues carrying his name were also known. The statue in the collection of the Villa Albani had been excavated in Rome (or at Hadrian's Villa at Tivoli) and published in the middle of the 18th century. A small statuette of "Amon-Chnuphis" (actually of the god Monthu) was noted as being in the possession of the collector, Giovanni Anastasi. The next king, *Sciabatok*, was to be equated with the *Sevechus* of Manethon. His name is now read as Shebitqo, Shebitku, or Shabataka. The third king, *Tahraka*, was, following the biblical record, the opponent of Sennacherib. Reliefs with his cartouche could be identified at Medinet-Habu, Karnak and Barkal. The name is now read as Taharqo, or Taharka.

The last of the large-scale surveys to copy reliefs and inscriptions was that of the Royal Prussian expedition between 1842 and 1844, led by Karl-Richard Lepsius (1810-1884). The enormous folio volumes of plates which resulted are still valuable today as a record of monuments since damaged or destroyed. The expedition also acquired important objects for the Berlin Museum, including part of a chapel of Shebitqo from Karnak, a wall from the pyramid chapel of king Amanitenmomide at Meroe, granite sculptures from the temple of Gebel Barkal and the stela of king Nastaseñ.

Rosellini had achieved much in ordering the mass of material that had been recorded and establishing an historical framework. At the same time, enormous advances were being made in the understanding of the hieroglyphic script, which were to be crucial for the development of Egyptology in the succeeding decades. Foremost amongst those philologists who transformed hieroglyphic studies from decipherment into translation were the Vicomte Emmanuel de Rougé (1811-1872), from 1860 Professor of Egyptology at Paris, and Heinrich Brugsch (1827-1894).

Egyptian hieroglyphic was not the only ancient script which was now being read by European scholars: the cuneiform scripts of Mesopotamia were also beginning to yield their secrets. A number of scholars was attempting to decipher the different languages written in cuneiform, but it was an army officer, Major-General Sir Henry Rawlinson (1810-1895), who, in 1847, published a translation of a text in Babylonian. The next decade saw advances in the decipherment and the reading of Assyrian texts by such notable scholars as Edward Hincks and Jules Oppert. More strikingly, from the point of view of the general public, the monuments of Assyria were being revealed. In 1845, Austen Henry Layard (1817-1894) began excavations at Tell Nimrud where he discovered the remains of the palace of Assurnasirpal II, in the city of Kalkhu, the biblical Calah. The next year, 1846, Layard began work at Nineveh where he unearthed the palace of Sennacherib. Amongst the 3 km (1.8 miles) of stone reliefs were the magnificent scenes of the storming of the city of Lachish. The British were not alone in Mesopotamia; the French consul, Paul Émile Botta (1802-1870), had dug at Nineveh in 1842. Finding nothing, he had transferred his attentions to Khorsabad where he was much more successful, striking upon the palace and capital of Sargon II. With their resonances of episodes in the biblical narratives, these discoveries excited enormous interest.[6]

Whilst study of ancient Egypt was entering a new phase in European academic institutions, the middle decades of the century also saw important changes in the attitude to ancient monuments by the rulers of Egypt. Mohammed Ali died in 1848, but Egypt remained virtually independent of the Turkish sultan under the rule of his descendants. One of the most influential Europeans in Egypt at this time was Ferdinand de

Lesseps, later to be granted the concession for the construction of the Suez canal (completed 1869). With the help of de Lesseps, Auguste Mariette (1821-1881), persuaded Said Pasha to establish an Antiquities Service for the preservation of the monuments, and to prevent their theft and destruction. Mariette was appointed Director of monuments in 1858. His tenure of office saw many monuments cleared of sand and of the villages which, in many cases, were built on their roofs and in their courts. This revealed enormous numbers of new reliefs and inscriptions, even whole monuments, which had been inaccessible to the earlier epigraphic expeditions. Mariette also established an Egyptian national collection, the origin of the present Cairo Museum.

The first major challenge to the interpretation of the "Ethiopian" dynasty as based upon the classical and biblical sources was the discovery of the "Victory Stela" of Piye at Gebel Barkal in 1862. The stela was found along with four others by an Egyptian army officer, but the exact circumstances of the discovery are not clear. The officer, whose name is not known, seems to have made some small excavation in the temple at Gebel

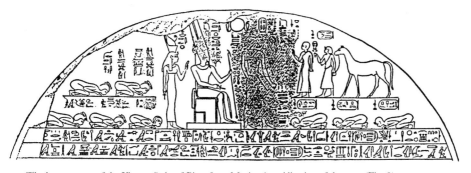

The lunette scene of the Victory Stela of Piye, from Mariette's publication of the text. (Fig. 8)

Barkal near the 4th Cataract of the Nile. The monuments he uncovered had not been noted by any of the European scholars who had visited the temples in the preceding decades, and certainly Richard Lepsius would have removed them in 1844, had they been visible. The Egyptian officer recognised the importance of the inscriptions and attempted to make copies which he sent to Mariette. Immediately realising the significance of the find, Mariette sent orders to the governor of Dongola that the stelae should be seized for the government and sent to Cairo. The stelae were loaded onto a barge and sailed as far as Kerma, but, when they arrived there, the flood waters were already falling, and the Cataract could not be passed. The flood of 1863 saw the stelae moved as far as the 2nd Cataract, but it was not until the end of the next year, 1864, that they finally arrived in Cairo.

By the time of the Piye stela's arrival in Cairo, it had already been published. Mariette had written an open letter to the Vicomte de Rougé, and had sent him the officer's copy of the text. De Rougé had promptly published a translation in 1863. De Rougé, referring to cartouches of a king "Piankhi" (as the name Piye was read) recorded at Barkal by Richard Lepsius, concluded that there were, in fact, two kings named "Piankhi". Piankhi-meriamon was to be dated between 770 and 725 (about 742), and Piankhi, the husband of Amenirdis, about 667/6. Mariette identified the king of the stela with the latter ruler, and placed the campaign *after* the reign of Taharqo, around 660 BC.

Along with the stela of Piye, the new Cairo Museum received four other almost perfectly preserved Kushite royal inscriptions: the "Dream Stela" of Tanwetamani, the "Election Stela" and the "Banishment Stela", both of the reign of king Aspelta, and the stela of king Harsiyotef. With the arrival of the five stelae in Cairo, Mariette published, in 1865, resumés of all of their contents, and over the next few years translations appeared in French, German and English.

Another fundamental contribution to the history of the 25th Dynasty was made in 1869 when Jules Oppert (1825-1905), one of the foremost Assyriologists of the day, published a study based upon his translations of the Assyrian historical texts. These recorded the conflict of Taharqo and the Assyrian king Assurbanipal, and the accession of Taharqo's successor whose name was read in the Assyrian as *Urdamaneh*.

The new evidence was rapidly incorporated into historical studies, most notably in the enormously influential history of Egypt by Heinrich Brugsch. This work, first published (in German) in 1877, was translated into English in 1879, then again, in a revised and condensed edition, in 1891.[7]

Brugsch's reconstruction of the history of the 25th Dynasty was based upon the Victory stela of Piye, the Dream stela of Tanwetamani and the Assyrian records published by Jules Oppert. The evidence of statuary and temple reliefs is also noted. The classical sources, particularly Manetho, are cited, but are now subordinated to the Egyptian hieroglyphic record. The writing of history "from the monuments" urged in 1830 by Orlando Felix had indeed come to pass. Ironically, this historical reconstruction strikes us today as less satisfactory than that of Rosellini, based upon Manetho and the bible! Some considerable confusions entered the interpretations at this time, and, although some were corrected in academic journals, they were not incorporated into the English translation of 1891, thus perpetuating the errors for at least two decades.

The principal source of error came with the use of the Assyrian texts. The conquest of Egypt was attributed to Piankhi (Piye), but it was assumed that he was swiftly driven out by the Assyrians. His successor was identified with the king of the Dream Stela, Tanwetamani. The name we read today as Tanwetamani (or Tanutamun) was read by Brugsch and others as "Meri-Amen Nut", "Nut" for short. Not altogether surprisingly, Brugsch and Oppert failed to identify this "Nut" with the "Urdamaneh" of the Assyrian texts, who was equated with an entirely different Egyptian ruler, Rudamen. Brugsch placed the reign of Taharqo after that of "Nut", and the confusion was further increased by the introduction of a second Piankhi. Brugsch made this second Piankhi, along with Shabaqo and Shebitqo, a contemporary of Taharqo. This interpretation, which to us is decidedly bizarre, was influenced by the monuments of the royal women who held the office God's Wife of Amun. A number of their inscriptions and statues, notably the splendid alabaster statue of Amenirdis I, had recently been uncovered at Karnak, and it was generally assumed that they were royal wives, rather than priestesses.[8]

Relief portrait of the God's Wife of Amun, Amenirdis I, from her tomb chapel at Medinet Habu. (Fig. 9)

Although some of the errors of interpretation which are to be found in Brugsch's work were soon corrected, many of the basic assumptions were retained until George Reisner's excavations in the royal cemeteries of Kush. Notable amongst these was the existence of more than one king called "Piankhi". Indeed, Piankhis proliferated in the succeeding years, until Petrie acknowledged five and Henri Gauthier seven (both conceding that some of them might be the same). The reasons for this are considered later (Chapter 12).

Brugsch's history reveals another fundamental difference to earlier 19th century reconstructions, which was also the result of writing history "from the monuments": the importance of Aithiopia – still advocated by Hoskins and Russell amongst others in the 1830s – was now completely displaced.

At the very beginning of his work, Brugsch cites the view of Greek literature that Egyptian civilization was brought from Meroe by a band of priests. He dismisses this and comments that the Egyptians:

> ... ascended the river to found in Ethiopia temples, cities, and fortified places, and to diffuse the blessings of a civilised state among the rude dark-coloured population.[9]

Brugsch invokes the monuments that were then known and, observing the chronological progression southwards, concludes that all of the Kushite monuments are late. Brugsch's view that civilization did not begin in Nubia should not be overly criticised, as it was formed on the evidence which Egyptologists of his time considered to be the most important – the stone-built temples and their inscriptions. When Brugsch wrote his history, there was nothing resembling what we would term archaeological evidence from Egypt, much less Nubia. Civilization was synonymous with stone buildings and writing.

When Brugsch turns to the rise of the Kushite state, he proposes that Piye was descended from the High Priest of Amun, Herihor. After the death of the last Ramesses:

> The whole South ... recovered its freedom, and the Ethiopians began to enjoy a state of independence. Meanwhile, if the power of Egypt was no longer felt, Egyptian civilization had survived. All that was wanting was a leader. Nothing could have appeared more opportune for the priests of Amen than this state of things in Nubia and Ethiopia, where the minds of an imperfectly developed people must needs, under skilful guidance, soon show themselves pliable and submissive to the dominant priestly caste.[10]

So, the powerful new independent Kushite state was ruled by the descendants of Egyptian priests. This view remained popular for many decades. Repeated in the classic histories of Egypt by Wiedemann, Rawlinson and Breasted, amongst others, it almost acquired the status of a fact. So great is its allure that it has recently been revived in a slightly modified form. In this passage, as in the earlier one, Brugsch has introduced a racial note: the Egyptians were the civilizers and the rulers of a "rude dark-coloured" Nubian population, and Brugsch has already classified who the Egyptians were at the beginning of his work:

> ... according to ethnology, the Egyptians appear to form a third branch of the Caucasian race, the family called Cushite; and this much may be regarded as certain, that in the earliest ages of humanity, far beyond all historical remembrance, the Egyptians, for reasons unknown to us, left the soil of their early home, took their way towards the setting sun, and finally crossed that bridge of nations the Isthmus of Suez, to find a new fatherland on the banks of the Nile.[11]

Brugsch's influential history thus encapsulated two trends in European academic development. The first was to replace the traditions

The influential German Egyptologist, Heinrich Brugsch. (Fig. 10)

21

preserved in the Greek and Roman literature with a history derived from the Egyptian monumental record, supplemented, in the case of the 25th Dynasty, with the Assyrian record. This move was entirely reasonable: the classical traditions, such as Manetho, were fragmentary and quite clearly corrupt. The other trend, expressing a view of what race the Egyptians were, and the relative importance of Egypt and Kush, reflected a number of preoccupations of 19th century academics.[12]

These views were now to be developed, and apparently supported, by excavations in Nubia itself.

III   Rescuing Nubia's History

The later years of the 19th century saw an enormous amount of activity on the monuments of Egypt. The antiquities organisation, firstly under Mariette and later under Gaston Maspero (1846-1916), began the clearance and consolidation of the temples. Academic journals devoted to Egyptology increased in number, and scholars published dozens of new texts which the greater understanding of the language made available.

In Egypt itself, there was a considerable amount of excavation, and the development of more precise methods of archaeology. Inscriptions, statues and other works of art continued to be highly prized, but the importance of smaller artefacts, objects of daily use, and, particularly, pottery was now recognized.

In Nubia and Sudan, political events again played an important role. In 1881 the Mahdi "uprising" began, culminating with the fall of Khartoum and death of General Gordon in 1885. The British sent a military expedition to Sudan in 1896, and, in 1898, following the defeat of the Khalifa at the battle of Omdurman, Sudan was brought under British rule, nominally with Egypt.

In the wake of Britain's imperial expansion into Sudan came that Egyptological manifestation of British imperialism, Wallis Budge of the British Museum. Budge was an unscrupulous operator, his archaeological work being far from scientific, but he was also a prolific writer, and author of numerous volumes aimed at the interested public. For all of the criticisms which can, with justification, be levelled at Budge from the academic standpoint, it has to be conceded that he produced some useful works. In a period when, despite the British involvement in Sudan, there was scant interest in its archaeology expressed by other British Egyptologists, Budge wrote *The Egyptian Sudan*, a two-volume work which detailed the country's history and monuments. He also produced *The Annals of the Nubian kings* which had translations and commentaries on the five stelae found at Gebel Barkal in 1862, and those which had found their way to the Paris and Berlin Museums. For all its failings, this remained the only English-language translation to contain all of these inscriptions until very recently.

The turning-point in archaeology in Nubia came with the building of a dam at Aswan. The dam was constructed between 1898 and 1902, but there was no attempt to survey the monuments or conduct excavations of endangered sites.

Gaston Maspero, Director-General of the Antiquities Department, made a visit to Nubia, and, seeing the neglected state of the monuments, asked Arthur Weigall to make a tour of inspection. Weigall (1880-1934) made three tours of Nubia during 1905 and 1906, copying inscriptions and noting places which should be examined properly. Weigall also observed not only the pillage of many graves and cemetery sites, but also that sites had already been lost beneath the rising waters of the reservoir.

In the winter of 1905-06, James Henry Breasted (1865-1935), founder of Egyptology in the United States, also spent a season in Nubia, recording monuments, primarily the New Kingdom temples. Distressed by the destruction of monuments in Egypt, and aware of the inaccuracies of many of the early copies, Breasted's intention was largely epigraphic: the accurate recording of reliefs and inscriptions. The following year, he made an important record of sites in Upper Nubia and Sudan. Although the results of his work were published only in preliminary form, the photographs and notes he made are still of the utmost importance. Breasted's *History of Egypt*, first published in 1905, as well as being enormously popular, was one of the most influential of histories.

In 1906, the decision was made to raise the 130 foot high Aswan Dam by a further $16^1/2$ feet, the work being carried out between 1908 and 1910. Weigall's report formed the basis for the first major examination of all Nubian sites in the region to be flooded. This, the First Archaeological Survey, operated between 1907 and 1911, and was put in the hands of George Andrew Reisner and Cecil Firth whose work still forms the backbone of Nubian studies.

Born in Indianapolis in 1867, Reisner first read Law at Harvard, and then, as a travelling Fellow of Harvard University, went to Berlin for three years (1893-96), where he took up Semitic Languages. He studied cuneiform Assyrian and Egyptian hieroglyphic under Kurt Sethe, and also worked as an assistant in the Berlin Museum. On his return to the U.S.A., Reisner's archaeological career began as Director of the Hearst expedition to Egypt (1899-1905), in which he adopted a systematic approach to excavation, recording and publication. It was because of this experience excavating Egyptian predynastic material that Reisner was selected, in 1907, to lead the Nubian Survey.

Reisner worked in Nubia only for the first season, Cecil Firth (1878-1931) taking responsibility for completing the work and the publication of much of the material. That first season, however, recovered so much

*The American
Archaeologist,
George Reisner,
admiring a pot.
(Fig. 11)*

hitherto unknown material that Reisner was able to construct a Nubian cultural sequence which he correlated with Egyptian history. In Egypt, the predynastic culture had been named after the first site where their remains had been noted - so they had names such as "Naqada" or "Badarian". In trying to name his Nubian cultures, Reisner opted for the easiest solution and named the cultures from the earliest "A", "B", "C" and so on to the latest phase (equivalent to the Byzantine period) which he designated "X". Reisner equated the Nubian A-Group with the Egyptian Early Dynastic, B-Group with the Old Kingdom, and so-on. Unfortunately, Reisner's terminology which was intended only as a preliminary classification has become firmly established and, with some revision, is still in use, although recognised as a totally inadequate way to describe this complex group of cultures.

In 1910 Reisner was appointed Curator of Egyptian Art at Boston Museum of Fine Arts and Assistant Professor of Egyptology at Harvard University. Shortly afterwards he initiated the Harvard-Boston joint expeditions to Nubia, which began with the excavation of the site of Kerma (1913-16). A wealth of fascinating material led Reisner to interpret the site as an Egyptian trading centre. This is now discounted, but Kerma's importance has increased since it has been recognised as the capital of a major Kushite kingdom. After a season working on a late Nubian site at Gamai, the expedition transferred to the temples and royal cemeteries of the Napatan and Meroitic periods, firstly at Gebel Barkal, el-Kurru and Nuri, near the 4th Cataract (1916-1919), and then to the cemeteries of

The deffufa at Kerma as seen by George Hoskins who thought that it was a fortress. (Fig. 12)

Meroe itself (1922-1925). Reisner's final Nubian seasons, 1924-1932, were spent in the 2nd Cataract fortresses of Middle and New Kingdom date.

Reisner's work in the royal cemeteries has been as significant for the history and chronology of the Napatan and Meroitic periods as his work with the Archaeological Survey was for the broader foundations of Nubian studies. In all of the royal cemeteries that he excavated Reisner established a sequence for the burials based upon a number of criteria – such as position in the cemetery and type of burial. This enabled him to draw up a preliminary king-list and form a loose chronological background for the Meroitic state. Reisner's original outline was published as a series of articles, and later considerably refined by Dows Dunham in his publications of Reisner's excavations.

In addition to his Nubian work, Reisner excavated in Egypt and in Palestine where he led the excavations at Samaria, the early capital of Israel.

The work of Reisner and Firth during the First Survey laid the foundations of Nubian studies, and, although their archaeological technique was quite sophisticated for its time, it was based upon a number of influential premises. Firstly, they paid considerably more attention to the earlier than the later phases, because they believed that literary sources would fill those in: still archaeology was thought to be of most use when there were no texts. Also, even though they were carrying out a salvage operation, they were still interested in acquiring objects which could be displayed in museums. Emphasis therefore was still very much on the clearance of cemeteries, rather than settlement sites. Firth himself lamented the lack of time the survey had for examination of settlement sites. Indeed, the archaeology of death remained the major element in the later Surveys, so much so that W.Y. Adams has commented "we often seem to know more about how the early Nubians died than about how they lived".[1]

In his interpretations, Reisner reveals the prejudices of his age and his education. Most notably, Reisner associated cultural change with an influx of new peoples. So, he suggested that his different "Groups", A, C, X, were new peoples coming into the Nubian Nile valley. Combined with the anatomical work of his colleagues, Elliot Smith and Douglas Derry, this led to a cyclical view of Nubian history, with new populations eventually declining and being replaced. These interpretations were typical of the period, but are nowadays totally rejected, because of the inadequate methodology used and the assumptions which governed them.

Reisner had been trained in Egyptology in Berlin, and it was the Institute founded by Lepsius that dominated Egyptology in the later 19th and early 20th centuries. Under Lepsius's successor, Adolf Erman (1854-1937), Berlin was renowned for its philological studies. Erman's influence has been described as "cyclonic", and his rigorous methodology influenced all those who studied in Berlin, whether philologists or archaeologists. Erman's students came not only from the German-speaking world, but also from abroad, notably George Reisner and Henry Breasted from the USA, Henri Gauthier from France and Alan Gardiner from England.

Amongst Erman's students was Heinrich Schäfer (1868-1957), who became director of the Egyptian Museum in Berlin and Professor at the University. Between 1908 and 1910 Schäfer directed the expedition sent by the Royal Prussian Academy of Sciences to study Nubian monuments. Schäfer later produced the first complete edition of the major texts of the Napatan period, then still referred to as "Ethiopian".

One of Erman's first pupils was Georg Steindorff (1861-1951), who served as Professor at Leipzig University (1893-1938) before being forced to leave for the USA. Between 1912 and 1914 and again between 1929 and 1933, Steindorff excavated at Aniba, the ancient Miam, a major site in Lower Nubia. He uncovered the New Kingdom temple, fortified town and cemeteries, and a large C-group cemetery. His work brought a fine collection of antiquities to the Leipzig museum.

Hermann Junker (1877-1962) who had also studied in Berlin accompanied Schäfer during the expedition of 1908-1910 and then led a series of excavations of his own, at the important sites of el-Kubania,

Arminna and Toshka (1910-12). From 1912 Junker was Professor at Vienna where he helped to found the Institute of Egyptology and African Studies which is still a focus for Meroitic studies.

Concurrently with the Archaeological Survey and the Harvard-Boston expedition, there were other teams working in Nubia. At Maspero's instigation, the major Nubian temples were recorded photographically. Their inscriptions were copied by two of Erman's former students, Günther Roeder and Henri Gauthier, and published in a series entitled *Les temples immergés de la Nubie*. For some monuments these still remain the fundamental publication. The Eckley B.Coxe Expedition of 1907-1911 excavated a number of sites in Lower Nubia for the University Museum in Philadelphia. Under the direction of David Randall MacIver (1873-1945), the expedition dug the first large Meroitic cemetery known, at Karanog, another Meroitic cemetery at Areika, and the fortress of Buhen. MacIver had earlier shocked the academic establishment by suggesting that the great stone structures at Zimbabwe were built by indigenous African people and not by foreigners. MacIver was assisted by C.L. (afterwards Sir Leonard) Woolley (1880-1960), who is best-known for his later work in the Royal Cemetery of Ur.

Excavation as military campaign: Reisner's team at Meroe. (Fig. 13)

John Garstang (1876-1956) had trained in excavation with Flinders Petrie and was later appointed as Professor of Archaeological Method and Practice at Liverpool University. Much of his later excavation was in Palestine and Anatolia, but between 1909-1914 he directed the first major excavations at Meroe. This concentrated on what was called the Royal City, a large enclosed area with the enormous temple of Amun adjacent to it. Despite the vast quantity of objects revealing the richness of Meroitic culture, which Garstang recovered from the ruins, these excavations are still published only in preliminary form.

One of the sponsors of Garstang's excavations was the wealthy chemicals and pharmaceutical manufacturer, Sir Henry Wellcome. Wellcome also funded his own excavations at Gebel Moya and Abu Geili – still amongst the most southerly of excavations in Sudan.[2]

The only expedition to approach Reisner's in geographical and historical range was that of the Oxford Excavations in Nubia, led by F.Ll.Griffith. Griffith (1862-1934), a brilliant philologist, was the founder of Nubian studies in Britain. Griffith excavated at Faras, a C-Group, New Kingdom and Meroitic site straddling the modern Egyptian and Sudanese borders. He then moved to Sanam downstream from Gebel Barkal and the 4th Cataract (1912-1913). Here he uncovered a large cemetery, the only non-royal cemetery of Napatan date to be excavated until recently, as well as a temple and a building which was dubbed the "treasury".[3] Another Napatan site, Kawa, was dug by the Oxford expedition between 1929 and 1936, the work being completed, after Griffith's death in 1934, by M.F.L. Macadam and L.P. Kirwan.[4] Only a part of the vast site was excavated, and that part, as was usual at the time, the temple precinct. Griffith was primarily a philologist, making enormous contributions to the difficult fields of Egyptian hieratic and demotic; his catalogue of the demotic inscriptions from Nubia being completed and published by his wife after his death. His major contribution was undoubtedly the decipherment of the Meroitic script and the publication of a large corpus of texts. It is fair to say that today we have little more ability to actually translate the Meroitic language than Griffith did. As an excavator, Griffith certainly does not stand comparison with Reisner. Nevertheless, he excavated important sites, and, at a time when British Egyptology was showing remarkably little interest in Nubia, Griffith was making one of the most significant contributions to the development of the study. The objects from Griffith's excavations have endowed the Ashmolean Museum in Oxford with the finest Nubian collection in Britain.

The decision was made to raise the height of the Aswan Dam yet again, and in 1929 Bryan Emery was appointed to direct an Archaeological Survey between Sebua and Adindan. This new heightening of the Dam was to raise water levels through the whole of Egyptian Nubia, and destroy all ancient sites on either side of the river below River level 130, over a stretch of 90 miles. Emery worked with his wife, Molly, Laurence Kirwan and five Egyptians from 1929 until 1934. The material which was excavated confirmed and enlarged upon Reisner's work in the First Survey. Of major significance was the excavation, at the very end of the survey, and under the most difficult circumstances, of the great X-Group cemeteries at Ballana and Qustul. These proved to be the immensely rich burials of Nubian rulers after the fragmentation of the Meroitic state in the 4th century AD.[5]

In 1935 Emery was asked to take over the work of Cecil Firth at Saqqara, and he continued to excavate in the necropolis until his own, sudden, death, in 1971. A break in these excavations, caused by the Suez crisis in 1956, saw Emery return to Nubia to dig at the vast fortress of Buhen, already partially cleared by MacIver and Woolley. The excavation, under the auspices of the Egypt Exploration Society, eventually became part of the UNESCO campaign.[6]

The focus of Egyptology at Berlin under Hermann Grapow (1885-1967) remained philology. The Swedish scholar, Torgny Säve-Söderbergh studied both with Grapow in Berlin and with Hermann Kees in Göttingen. His doctoral thesis, completed and published in Sweden, remains a standard work on the relations between Egypt and Nubia from the Old Kingdom until the end of the New Kingom.[7] Säve-Söderbergh later played a leading role in the UNESCO campaign, and the joint Scandinavian Expedition was the largest single mission to work in Nubia. Excavating a large number of sites of all periods, the publication of the results has included some fundamental reassessments of Nubian history.[8]

The years following the 2nd World war saw some dramatic developments in Nubian studies, forced largely by political circumstances. Notably, both Egypt and Sudan ceased to be under colonial rule, and, in different ways, self-determination affected archaeology.

In Berlin, Fritz Hintze (1915-1993), another of Grapow's pupils, succeeded him to the chair created for Lepsius at the Berlin (now called the Humboldt) University, in the newly-created GDR. Hintze established the Humboldt University, and the GDR, as the leading centre for Meroitic studies, and was instrumental in developing Meroitic as a discipline in its own right, not merely an adjunct of Egyptology. Fritz Hintze, and his wife Ursula, an Africanist, conducted a survey of sites in the Butana (1957-58), followed by a series of excavations at Musawwarat es-Sufra and the recording of inscriptions of Sudanese Nubia threatened by the building of the new Aswan Dam (1960-70).

Changes in Sudan itself, had a radical effect on the study of its archaeology. Peter Shinnie succeeded A.J.Arkell as Commissioner for Archaeology in 1948. The department was enlarged, but with the transition of Sudan to full independence in 1956, the antiquities department too passed from British control. To effect the move to a Sudanese service, a new Commissioner was appointed, a Frenchman, Jean Vercoutter. Vercoutter had been working in Sudan since 1953, first at the fortress of Kor, at the 2nd Cataract, and then on the island of Sai. Vercoutter was already a renowned Egyptologist with a special interest in the broader connections of the ancient world: he published studies on Egyptian objects and connections with Carthage and the Aegean world. During his five years in Khartoum, Vercoutter trained a new generation of Sudanese archaeologists and planned the new National Museum in Khartoum, which opened in 1972.

Between 1957 and 1963 a team from the University of Pisa excavated at Soleb and Sedeinga, two of the most important sites of the Egyptian New Kingdom in Upper Nubia. Amongst the collaborators was the French Egyptogist, Jean Leclant, who had already published fundamental studies of the 25th Dynasty monuments of the Theban region.[9] Leclant has continued to promote Nubian and Meroitic studies, and has made further important contributions to the study of the 25th Dynasty and Napatan period. Excavations continue at the site of Sedeinga.

Soon after Vercoutter's appointment, came the announcement of the intention to build a new High Dam at Aswan. Vercoutter immediately prepared a report on the endangered monuments of Sudanese Nubia, and played a vital role in getting UNESCO to recognise that they were as important as the more obvious monuments of Egyptian Nubia. Having placed the antiquities organisation on a firm, Sudanese, footing, Vercoutter transferred as Professor to Lille in 1960, but continued to work extensively in Nubia during the UNESCO campaign. The small 19th Dynasty temple and town of Aksha was dug (1960-62) and parts of the temple removed to the Khartoum Museum. He also undertoook the re-excavation of the vast fortress of Mirgissa (1963-67).

The decision to build the new Aswan Dam was the most important of all post-war developments. The reservoir (Lake Nasser or Lake Nubia) flooded the whole of Egyptian Nubia and part of Sudanese Nubia. The story of the UNESCO campaign to record and salvage the monuments – most famously, Abu Simbel – is well-known. The work of the international expeditions has contributed a vast amount to Nubian studies, and the process of publishing and synthesising the material has continued since the archaeological work in the field ceased. One important feature of the Nubian campaign was the work of anthropologists and archaeologists who

The great rock-cut temple of Ramesses II at Abu Simbel, as it appeared at the beginning of the 20th century. (Fig. 14)

were not, by training, Egyptologists. This has helped Nubian studies to move away from a perspective dominated entirely by Egyptology. The campaign saw the development of archaeological techniques and a much greater interest in settlement archaeology. As all sites of all periods had to be investigated, there was not the luxury of choice as had been the case in Egypt. This has resulted in a more balanced view of the archaeology of the Nile valley between the 1st and Dal Cataracts.

Despite the enormous activity and interest generated during the UNESCO campaign, most archaeologists preferred to return to Egypt after its completion, with only a small number of foreign missions choosing to continue their work in Sudan. Vercoutter and his team returned to Sai, and also inaugurated a survey in the region immediately south of the Lake. A Swiss team began work at the island of Argo, and have since moved to Kerma. The excavation of the Kerma culture cemetery at Sai, and in Kerma city itself, have radically revised Reisner's interpretations, revealing Kerma to have been a powerful Kushite kingdom of great wealth (Chapter 5).

At Gebel Barkal, the excavations of the University of Rome, directed by Sergio Donadoni, have revealed a number of Meroitic temples and palaces. More recently, investigations of the cemeteries in the region of Barkal have been undertaken by Irene Liverani Vincentelli.

Survey and excavation outside of the Nile valley has radically changed our perceptions of the desert regions and of the interconnections between different cultures and movements of peoples. Many of the most important recent excavations have been concerned with the prehistoric or post-Meroitic phases of Sudanese history, and, the excavations of Irene Liverani apart, there has been less attention paid to the Napatan period.

With the flooding of Nubia, only one site remained accessible between Aswan and the southern end of the lake, the fortress of Qasr Ibrim. On its rocky eminence, the fortress became an island as the waters of the lake rose around it. Excavation has continued here, and in 1990 revealed the earliest phases of the fortifications, which raise many new questions about the history of Nubia in the early Napatan period.[10]

The enormous amount of excavation and survey in Lower Nubia has made it one of the most intensively studied regions of the world. This, alas, is not yet balanced by excavation in Upper Nubia and the central Sudan. Neverthless, the history of Nubia has been radically rewritten, first by Reisner and again in the light of the UNESCO campaign. More recently, re-examination of some of the material from the cemetery at el-Kurru and from Kawa has led to renewed debate about the origins of the Kushite kingdom of Napata. It has to be emphasised that new excavations, or the more detailed analysis of objects from earlier excavations, can still radically alter our understanding of phases of Kushite history.

Reisner's key works established a sequence of Nubian cultures from the prehistoric to the Christian periods. Reisner, understandably, linked his sequence closely with Egypt's history, and consequently interpreted his material in the light of that, and with a set of views current in the early years of the century. Reisner was educated very much in the Darwinian evolutionary model dominant in academic schools, which saw European *man* as the epitome of evolution. The analysis of the anatomical material from the cemeteries, particularly the skull measurements, was influenced by preoccupations of the period. Sir Grafton Elliot Smith, and his pupil

Winifred Brunton's portrait of Taharqo used the black granite head of the king from Karnak as its model, but adds a leopard skin for ethnic effect.(Fig. 15)

Douglas Derry, both worked on material from the First Archaeological Survey.[11] Reisner's interpretation of Nubian cultures owed a lot to these skull measurements. Nubian history was seen as a cyclical process, with "decline" of the different phases blamed on miscegenation - admixture with "Negroes" from further south. For example, the A-Group were seen as essentially the same as the Predynastic Egyptians, but, in the B-Group, supposedly the latest and declining phase of the A-Group, Smith and Derry perceived a stronger "negroid element". Similarly they supposed that the C-Group, although containing some "negroid element", had had a new admixture from the north. The general view of Egyptian ethnicity was that propounded by Brugsch some thirty years before – essentially Caucasian. So the early interpretation of the Nubian cultures postulated waves of immigration, either from the north or from the south, and associated these movements with cultural rise and decline. This interpretation has parallels with the general interpretation of the later, Meroitic, culture which attributed cultural decline to the increasingly "negroid" population. As W.Y. Adams commented "the racist point of view which was shared by nearly all the early students of Nubian history condemns the age more than the men".[12]

Recently, in a highly controversial study, Martin Bernal has examined some aspects of nineteenth century academic development, which led to this view.[13] Bernal's interpretation has been widely discussed in Classical studies, but less so in Egyptology.[14] One important factor which Bernal

The God's Wife of Amun, Amenirdis I. Although Winifred Brunton used the alabaster statue from Karnak as her model, she chose to show Amenirdis white rather than black. (Fig. 16)

emphasises is that Egyptology was open to many influences from other academic fields, and was not, nor is, a purely empirical, scientific, discipline.

Whilst many of these prejudiced views have gradually been abandoned, Reisner's cultural sequence still forms the backbone of Nubian history. So too, his work in the royal cemeteries at Kurru, Nuri and Meroe established the chronological framework for the Napatan and Meroitic periods. Reisner's work also established the direction for the writing of Nubian history: cultural, rather than political or royal.

In more general history-writing, Breasted's immensely popular and influential volume essentially canonised the views of the late 19th and early-20th centuries.[15] The increasing emphasis placed upon archaeology has, to some extent, seen a decline in the writing of history at a general level, the *Cambridge Ancient History* and Sir Alan Gardiner's *Egypt of the Pharaohs* being the principal contributions of recent decades. Gardiner himself acknowledged that his history was that of a scholar whose preoccupation was philology, rather than archaeology. Whilst the writing of general histories has declined, there has, of course, been much more detailed analysis of specific periods and individual reigns. For the Kushite pharaohs, Jean Leclant's seminal studies of Kushite monuments at Thebes have considerably increased our understanding. One of the most significant developments of recent decades has been the attention devoted to Egypt under the Libyan pharaohs. Whilst, to some extent, the older views of a period of decline have been preserved, the historical studies of the "Third Intermediate Period", firstly in the epoch-making works of Jean Yoyotte and Kenneth Kitchen, have analysed the vast quantity of material from the period and offered many new interpretations. These works have paved the way for some quite radical new propositions, most of which are, as yet, still only available in the specialist literature.[16]

The historical and archaeological work of this century allows a new appraisal of the history and significance of the Kushite dynasty in Egypt. Numerous historical problems still remain, but we have a much clearer view of the Egypt which was conquered by the Kushites and of the genesis of the Kushite kingdom which enabled that conquest to take place.

IV   The Elephant

The conquest of Egypt by the Kushite kings in the 8th century BC is often portrayed as an unexpected event by historians. It happened, it is recorded by the Victory Stela of Piye, but apparently has no prologue. Early Egyptologists were certainly influenced by 19th century views of Africa in this interpretation, but the archaeological record – made so much clearer in the past 90 years – has done little to change the accepted view. The period between the end of Egyptian "colonial" rule and the emergence of the independent state has been baffling. There were – it seemed to Egyptologists – no historical records from this time nor, apparently, much archaeological evidence which fitted here. Nubia was in a Dark Age – "a perplexing historical void"[1] and the general conclusion was that "it took some time for the lesson of the pharaohs to sink in".[2]

No recent writers have actually ignored the existence of earlier organised states in Nubia, but the "gap", estimated by some at 200 years, others 300, and by the most extreme, at 400 years, divorced them from the "Napatan" kingdom of the 8th century.[3] No clear succession from earlier Kushite states or the Egyptian viceregal period was visible. An earlier generation of Egyptologists had a rather different, if equally unsatisfactory, interpretation of this period, as we shall see.

The tradition of rulership in Nubia extends back as far as it does in Egypt, for over two thousand years before the emergence of the "Napatan" state. These traditions continued during periods of Egyptian rule and were inevitably influenced by the Egyptian style of kingship. Throughout the ancient Near East – certainly during the Late Bronze Age (c. 1500-1050 BC) and Iron Age – the Egyptian, Assyrian and Persian monarchies stood as models to be emulated by the rulers of western Asia. How far this emulation was able to extend beyond adopting styles of regalia and iconography is difficult to assess: the internal political and religious structures of individual states would have served as a bar on some of the aspects of kingship practised in the great empires. But there certainly were influences, and, in the same way, the rulers of Nubia were doubtless deeply influenced by Egypt, combining aspects of the pharaonic kingship with their own traditions.

To understand the time when the Kushites dominated Egypt, we must look back to the development of states and rulership within Nubia itself and the complex history of its relationship with Egypt.

The terms used to identify the main cultural phases in Lower Nubia were first employed by George Reisner. It has to be admitted that, practical as they are, terms such as "A-Group" and "C-Group" make the cultures sound extremely dull, but they have now become so firmly established that

Nubian rock drawing of a man hunting an ostrich. (Fig. 17)

attempts to substitute others have generally failed. Bruce Trigger attempted to introduce Early Nubian, Middle Nubian and Late Nubian, but with only limited success. The form "A-Horizon" and "C-Horizon" suggested by W.Y. Adams similarly did not achieve any lasting impact. As the complexity of these early Nubian cultures is increasingly recognised, so the difficulty of categorising them also increases. In Egypt (and in Nubia, with Kerma) prehistoric cultural phases are usually designated by the "type-site", usually the first place where the archaeological material is recognised.

The early culture of Lower Nubia, called by Reisner the "A Group", is first identified in the late fourth millennium BC, and reached its peak around 3100-3000 BC, which was also the time of the unification of Egypt into a state under one ruler. The A-Group phase lasted for about 1,000 years and in range extended from el-Kubania, north of Aswan, to the 2nd Cataract. It had strong contacts with the regions south of the 2nd Cataract, and its cultural influence can be seen as far south as Sedeinga and Kerma in the Dongola Reach.[4]

The archaeological surveys of Nubia have produced enormous quantities of material datable to this phase, mostly from cemetery sites, but our knowledge of the archaeology of the regions to the south is much more limited. Excavations in the Dongola Reach, at Kerma, have now revealed the antiquity of that site and considerably increased our knowledge of its early development. Other surveys in the Dal, Delgo and Dongola reaches of the river have also identified early sites. Far less archaeological work has been carried out in the central Sudan, but there must have been strong contacts with the northern regions of Nubia.

The archaeological evidence of the A-Group provides a good lesson in the changes in the historical interpretation of Nubian culture. Because the earliest sites were found in the north of Nubia, and the culture gradually extended southwards, Reisner believed that the A-Group expansion represented a gradual southward migration of predynastic Egyptians. Seeing that the culture peaked at the same time as the unification of Egypt, Reisner called the following phase which, in his interpretation, was a decline lasting throughout the Egyptian Old Kingdom, "B-Group". Reisner's "B-Group" has now been shown not to exist, at least in the way in which he perceived it. The evidence belongs to robbed and poor graves, and to graves which actually *precede* the A-Group. In Reisner's interpretation the order was partially reversed. His treatment of the Kerma culture was the same, and this reveals one of the key intellectual tenets behind Reisner's archaeological interpretation: the 19th century theory of decline, usually associated with miscegenation (racial admixture).

Archaeologists regarded A-Group society as loosely structured, and relatively unstratified. They also assumed that it was not sufficiently centralised for us to talk about "states". The UNESCO Nubian campaign identified many more A-Group sites, and their publication and analysis has radically changed our perceptions. It is now possible to see developments over the thousand years of the A-group, from a loosely structured society into a group of "chiefdoms" or "kingdoms". One major factor in this development was undoubtedly the growth of trade with Egypt and its control by a small elite.

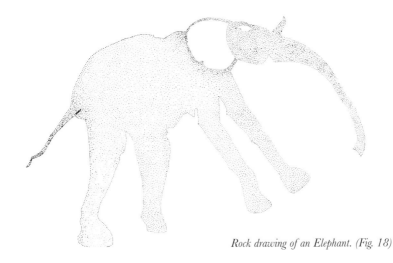

Rock drawing of an Elephant. (Fig. 18)

Environmentally, Nubia during this Early Nubian phase was probably very different to the later periods. Throughout history, the climate of the Sahara region has fluctuated between dry and wet phases. In the prehistoric period, Nubia enjoyed a wetter phase, and both sides of the river valley were covered for a considerable distance with savanna-type vegetation which supported a great variety of wildlife. The earliest rock-drawings show herds of giraffe, antelope, gazelle and ibex, wild ass or zebra, and large wild ox. Hippopotami and crocodiles lived both in the Nile and in the lakes which existed in the surrounding regions, and there are many rock-drawings of elephants *(Fig. 18)*. Such a wide variety of wildlife supported a hunting population, both animal – lions, hyenas and wild dogs – and human. These rock-drawings also provide evidence of the domestication and herding of cattle *(Fig.* 19) The desiccation of the region has gradually forced this abundant wildlife much further south. Human activity has doubtless had an impact also, although this is much more difficult to assess. Crocodiles and hippopotami remained abundant in Egypt and Nubia until Europeans hunted them beyond the 2nd Cataract in the middle of the 19th century AD.

During the A-Group phase, the process of desiccation had doubtless already begun, but it is uncertain how far it had advanced. We might assume that, even with an increase in aridity, there were seasonal pastures, notably in the wadis of the mountainous region between the Nile and the Red Sea (today's Eastern Desert).

The A-Group, like many of the succeeding cultures of Nubia and Sudan, was an early manifestation of the East African cattle cultures, such

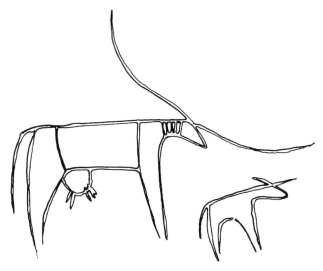

One of many rock drawings showing a long-horned cow and calf. (Fig. 19)

as the Maasai, which still exist.[5] The few habitation sites which have been excavated, and the majority of graves, do not give signs of any great affluence. For much of the year, the people lived near the river probably in small settlements strung out along the narrow cultivable strip. Their houses were hemispherical huts of straw or grasses on a frame. They grew wheat and barley, peas and lentils. Hunting, fowling and fishing supplemented their diet. During the flood season they moved to the desert margin where there was probably still sufficient grazing land for their herds. Their clothing was of dyed leather, and consisted of a loin-cloth or penis-sheath, and they practised body painting. Their jewellery consisted of bracelets and anklets of stone and bone, or occasionally ostrich egg shell and ivory; their necklaces were beads of shell, ivory, bone and stone, with some made of faience imported from Egypt. Such a description does lend support to the interpretation of the A-Group as a relatively simple society, loosely structured, with scattered settlement and perhaps little more than subsistence agriculture.

The artefacts excavated in some of the cemeteries, however, present a very different picture. Objects of limestone, cylinder seals and stone vessels, painted pottery and faience, slate palettes, combs and hairpins can all be identified as imports from Egypt. The pottery vessels were probably used for the import of foodstuffs which could not be produced in Nubia, notably wine. Beer, oil and perhaps wheat and barley may also have been imported in these vessels. The main exchange must have been for valuable raw materials. The Nubians may already have been acquiring gold and semi-precious stones from the deserts, but, to judge from the Egyptian cemeteries, the bulk of the trade would have been ebony, incense, vegetable oils, animal skins, and, perhaps most importantly, ivory. It is possible that there were still elephants in Lower Nubia or the Dongola Reach, but some of the commodities, notably the ebony and incense, must have come from much further south.

This trade was carried out with the emergent kingdom of Upper Egypt, based upon Nekhen (*Hierakonpolis*).[6] The kingdom of Nekhen had its southern boundary in the area of Gebel Silsila, the narrowest point on the river and the northern limit of Nubia.

The main trading centre was probably the island of *Abu* (Elephantine), at the foot of the 1st Cataract, within Nubian territory. Meaning "the elephant" or "ivory", its name reflects its importance as a trading place for that most valuable of the commodities of the south, ivory.

There is also evidence that the Egyptians traded further south along the river. Rock-drawings of boats of Egyptian Predynastic type have been found as far south as Sabu at the 2nd Cataract. One site, Khor Daud, north of Dakka, has been identified as an Egyptian trading centre. Here

500 Egyptian vessels were excavated, giving some impression of the scale of the trade.[7]

The final phase of the Early A-Group saw expansion southwards to the 2nd Cataract and strong contacts with the region immediately to the south. This resulted in changes in the cultures of both regions, notably in the development of pottery styles. The most notable product of the later A-Group (called "Classic") were very fine "eggshell" wares, sometimes painted inside and out in dark red on an orange ground. The patterns often imitated basket work.

The Classic period saw the emergence of "chiefdoms" or "kingdoms" in Lower Nubia. To judge from the evidence of the cemeteries, these were centred upon Dakka, Seyala and Qustul. A stone-built settlement at Afiya, near Tomas, might have been the residence of one of the chiefs of this period, and the evidence of the graves suggests that they had a standard of living as high as that of the elite in Egypt at the same time. Wine jars and stone cosmetic vases were imported from the north in large quantities. A particular type of vase with wavy handles suggests that there were long-range contacts (through Upper Egypt) with the Delta and Syria-Palestine. Cylinder seals and their impressions show that the chiefs maintained some form of communication with their Egyptian counterparts.

The first of the "chiefly" graves was excavated near Seyala by Cecil Firth during the First Archaeological Survey.[8] Typical of the period, the graves were large pits dug into the alluvium and roofed with massive sandstone slabs. They served as family graves, with several individuals being interred over the years. In the most important of the Seyala graves, copper axes, chisels and bar-ingots were found, along with a lion's head of quartz covered with faience glaze, a mica mirror, two large double-bird shaped palettes and two maces with gold-plated handles (*Fig.20*). One of the most outstanding of the artefacts was the handle of one of the maces, decorated with animals in low relief, including an elephant on top of two serpents, a giraffe, lion and types of antelope. The style of these animals is the same as that found on slate palettes of the time of Narmer. The other objects too belong to the early part of the 1st Dynasty.

The University of Chicago excavations at Qustul between 1962 and 1964, during the UNESCO campaign, found comparable graves in the cemetery designated "L".[9] Here, eight extraordinarily large graves were attributed to rulers. These graves had been ransacked in ancient times, and the remaining contents were dispersed, making it almost impossible to assign some artifacts to their original tombs. Nevertheless, the remains were striking.

The pottery belongs to the Terminal A-Group phase, and the objects of Egyptian origin can be dated to the 1st Dynasty. If found in Egyptian

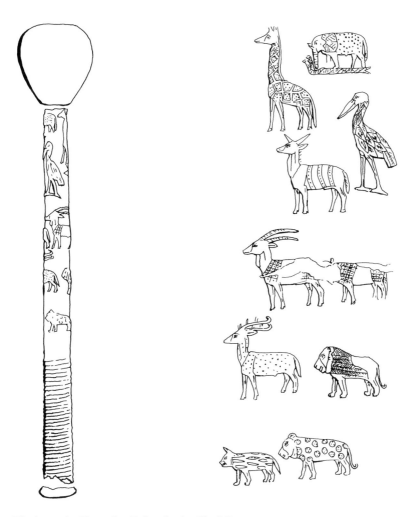

The decorated gold mace handle from Seyala. (Fig. 20)

graves, they would be dated to the reigns preceding that of the pharaoh Djer, the closest parallels for the objects actually being from the reigns of Aha and his predecessors.

Bruce Williams, who published the excavations, argued that these graves were "royal", on the basis of their size and construction, and the abundance and variety of the objects associated with them. Williams is undoubtedly right that the graves represent an important centre of power in the Qustul region. Williams, however, went further than suggesting that this was a powerful Nubian monarchy which had strong contacts with Egypt. He proposed firstly that this was the first "pharaonic" royal cemetery, predating those of Upper Egypt, and secondly that these Nubian kings actually conquered Upper Egypt. Williams argued that the Upper Egyptian monarchy was, in fact, of Nubian origin.[10]

Williams's theory was immediately refuted by another leading Nubian archaeologist, W.Y. Adams, who insisted that there was no evidence that the Qustul Cemetery represented the nascent pharaonic monarchy.[11]

The arguments focussed on a number of objects which were argued to be local products and which displayed "pharaonic" motifs. It is certain that these objects are actually imported from Egypt. One of the most significant was a limestone incense burner, with sunk relief decoration showing a seated royal figure wearing the white crown of Upper Egypt (*Fig. 21*).

The Qustul incense burner, with its scene of an Upper Egyptian ruler in a boat. (Fig. 21)

Since Bruce Williams published his ideas, excavations at Abydos have now found "royal" Egyptian graves which actually predate the Qustul burials. Nevertheless, the Qustul cemetery is good evidence that the rapid development of powerful states in the period around 3100 BC was not confined to Egypt, and that there was a mutual influence.

Although it was not the origin of the Egyptian monarchy, Nubia itself was undergoing some form of political cohesion, with states and powerful individual rulers emerging. The process by which the unified pharaonic state emerged is still poorly understood. Current excavations in the Delta are showing that there were strong contacts between that region and western Asia. Rather than a development confined to the Egyptian Nile valley, the unified state arose in a context of cultural and trading relations extending from Sudan to Mesopotamia. The role of Nubia in this process was doubtless enormously important, certainly as a supplier of "luxury" goods and perhaps also of soldiers. Nubian soldiers played an important role in the Egyptian armies in many later phases of Egyptian history, and they may also have played a part in the armies which brought about the united Egyptian state. Recent anthropological work on skeletal material from Predynastic Upper Egyptian sites has shown that the population was ethnically the same as the Nubian and upper Nile populations.[12]

Reisner identified a group of material which he designated "B-Group" and attributed to the period following the unification of Egypt. In this he saw a gradual decline of the A-Group, caused by an increased "negroid" element in the population moving into Nubia from the south. This intepretation is now recognised as wrong, and it is clear that, instead of slow decline, the A-Group kingdoms came to a sudden end.[13]

All of the evidence gathered by the surveys of Nubia convinced archaeologists that Lower Nubia was depopulated during the period of the Egyptian Old Kingdom. Although there were climatic changes and variations in flood level, this does not provide a sufficient explanation for the disappearence of the people and end of the powerful kingdoms. What then did cause the collapse of the A-Group monarchies and the depopulation of the country?

The emergence of Egypt as a united state is undoubtedly a key factor. Some archaeologists suggested that there was a break in trade relations between the new state and Nubia. Undoubtedly, this would have undermined the prosperity of local society, but it is unlikely to have been the sole reason for the end of settled population. Once the kings of Nekhen had united Egypt, the "luxuries" of the south would have been even more vital than before, and the termination of trade is hardly to be expected. On the contrary, an increase in trade is more likely than a cessation. What appears to have been decisive is a change in attitude on the part of the Egyptian pharaohs. No longer content simply to exchange goods, they moved to gain direct control of the Nile route to the south, and to exploit Nubia's natural resources themselves. In order to do that, the local powers had to be crushed. The success of the Nubian rulers as suppliers of gold and controllers of the Nile traffic was to be their downfall. Rather than a decline through miscegenation, as Reisner had suggested, the end of the A-Group was the result of direct, and ruthless, intervention.

The earliest evidence of military activities by the pharaohs is an ebony plaque with the name of Hor Aha from Abydos, and a rock inscription at Gebel Sheikh Suleiman, near Wadi Halfa (*Fig. 22*). The Hor Aha plaque shows a prisoner designated by the *Seti*-symbol, but may refer to the region between Aswan and Gebel Silsila, which carried the same name. There has been some academic dispute about the dating and interpretation of the Gebel Sheikh Suleiman inscription, but it is generally accepted that it shows an Egyptian boat and Nubian captives. The military action it records must belong to the reign of one of the early 1st Dynasty pharaohs, most probably Djer.

The archaeological evidence also suggests that the Egyptians had achieved their purpose by the reign of Djer. There must have been intensive military activities by the pharaohs and their armies in Lower

The Gebel Sheikh Suleiman rock inscription. The inscription probably dates from the reign of the pharaoh Djer, and records the defeat of the Kushites by the Egyptians.(Fig. 22)

Nubia. This resulted in the kingdoms which posed a threat to Egyptian supremacy in Lower Nubia being crushed, the settlements destroyed and the majority of the people being forced to take up a nomadic existence.

The Nubian people must have been driven into the regions flanking the Nubian Nile valley, possibly the eastern hills, which appear to have retained their trees, at least in the wadis, until the end of this phase. The Egyptians themselves did not maintain a large, permanently settled population in Nubia, and it must have been possible for the Nubians to come to the river seasonally, perhaps even to raise some crops.

There are few indications of major Egyptian military activity during the Old Kingdom, although there were doubtless occasional campaigns to prevent people moving back permanently into the valley. An inscription referring to the reign of the pharaoh Sneferu designates one year as that of the "Hacking up the Nehesyu, bringing 7,000 prisoners and 200,000 cattle". This action could have been launched against the A-Group descendants in the region of the Wadi Allaqi or Wadi Korosko, although it is perhaps more likely that it was despatched from Buhen southwards into the 3rd Cataract and Dongola Reach to secure the control of the trade routes.

The pharaohs of the Old Kingdom exploited Nubia's available resources, and seem to have done it directly through the use of Egyptian rather than local labour. The Egyptians did not confine themselves to the valley, and graffiti have been found in the Wadi el-Allaqi, although it is uncertain whether the gold mines were being exploited. The diorite quarries 80 km west of Toshka were a major focus of attention during the 4th and 5th Dynasties, and the inscriptions there name Re-Djedef, Sahure and Djedkare-Isesi. The most renowned monuments quarried here are the statues of Khaefre (Khephren) found at the valley temple of the king's Pyramid at Giza. The distance of the Toshka quarries from the river shows quite clearly that the Egyptians were actively prospecting for desirable minerals and stones.

The largest Egyptian settlement in Nubia was at Buhen at the foot of the 2nd Cataract. It may have been founded as early as the 2nd Dynasty, but it is not certain that it was continuously occupied. Buhen's most important period seems to have been the 4th and 5th Dynasties, and the names of the pharaohs Khufu, Khaefre, Menkaure, Userkaf, Sahure, Neferirkare and Niuserre were found there. A walled enclosure surrounded a terraced town with magazines and workshops. Copper may have been smelted here, brought from Egypt, then traded further south.

Djedkare-Isesi, second but last king of the 5th Dynasty, is the last of the Old Kingdom pharaohs attested in Nubia. A new situation was rapidly developing there, as we learn from Egyptian texts of the 6th Dynasty.

It is impossible to know whether the return of people to the valley was the cause, or the result, of the Egyptian withdrawal. During the time of the later Old Kingdom, the climate deteriorated throughout north-east Africa, resulting, in the 6th Dynasty, in conditions very similar to those of the present-day. Rhinoceros, elephant and giraffe which had existed much earlier in Egypt and Lower Nubia had, by this time, disappeared. In the future, they would be found only in Upper Nubia and further south. This desiccation must have affected the hilly regions to the east of the Nile and forced people back into the valley. Famine scenes in the pyramid complex of the 5th-dynasty pharaoh, Unas, at Saqqara show starving people from Libya forced into the Nile valley in search of food. The abandonment of Egyptian settlement in Nubia may have been due to the increased numbers of people moving back into the Nubian Nile valley, as well as pressures exerted on the central authority elsewhere. Maintaining direct control of the Nile traffic from bases in Nubia might have placed too much pressure on the resources now available.

The new culture which now appears in Nubia is known to archaeology, rather uninspiringly, as the "C-Group", and was to be the dominant culture of Lower Nubia for the next thousand years. The C-Group presents us with the same problems of interpretation as the A-Group. Despite its enormous span of time, it is difficult to analyse historically. We can describe the cultural phases and their development, we can speculate on the way of life, but it is far more difficult to assess the social, political and religious lives of the people.

The culture of the C-Group is so similar in many ways to that of the A-Group that most archaeologists have agreed that it was in some way descended from it. Presumably, during the years of the Old Kingdom, the people had been forced into the valleys of the eastern hills or perhaps in the western desert which was beginning to become more arid. They may originally have been able to sustain themselves, but if they were large herders of cattle this must have become increasingly difficult, or involved them in wide-ranging seasonal migrations. C-Group affinities with cultures over a wide range of Upper Nubia are now noted. In the Nile Valley, pottery of types closely similar to that of the C-Group is found in association with the early sites at Kerma in the Dongola Reach. In the west, similar pottery types have been found in the Wadi Howar. Whatever the origins of the C-Group, the presence of settled people in the Lower Nubian Nile Valley resulted in the emergence of new political powers.

Records of trading expeditions from Egypt into Nubia during the 5th and 6th Dynasties incidentally illuminate the growth of states there. The interpretation of these texts has, inevitably, been the focus of considerable academic controversy. There are two major problems relating to them. The first, common with Egyptian texts concerning Nubia, is trying to locate the various place-names mentioned.

The second is the problem of relating the historical record of Egyptian origin to the archaeological evidence.

The texts come from a number of different sources, but notably from the tombs of Egyptian officials at Aswan. These officials served during the reigns of Pepy I, Mernere and Pepy II.[14]

In the early years of the pharaoh Mernere, the Governor of Upper Egypt, Uni, was sent to Aswan to quarry granite, and the chiefs of Irtjet, Wawat, Yam and Medja all cut wood for the transport ships. Later Mernere visited the southern frontier himself, and a relief on the rocks above the 1st Cataract depicted the rulers of Irtjet and Wawat, and of the Medja, doing obeisance to him. Apart from the political import of these texts, they show that, despite the climatic changes, there were still considerable amounts of timber to be felled in Nubia, and of good enough quality to be used for barges to transport large blocks of granite.

The texts in the tomb of Harkhuf at Aswan are especially important for our understanding of the changing political patterns in Nubia. On his first journey, Harkhuf found Nubia divided into three "chiefdoms", Wawat, Irtjet and Satju. By the time of his second journey, Irtjet and Satju had both been joined under the rule of one chief, and by the time of third journey, Wawat had been added to them, creating one large kingdom.

Harkhuf's destination was Yam which lay south of the other three states. When Harkhuf arrived in Yam, he learnt that its ruler had left on a military expedition against the Libyans.

Wawat, Irtjet and Satju are thought to be regions of Lower Nubia. Lower Nubia itself falls naturally into three agricultural zones, separated by less productive regions. The archaeological evidence conforms to these three zones, and it has been assumed that the political structure also followed the same pattern. The northernmost, Wawat, lay south of the cataract, extending perhaps as far as Seyala. Irtjet may have been the

Korosko bend of the river, from Wadi es-Sebua to Toshka, and Satju, the Abu Simbel to Buhen region. The Medja are later well-documented as the peoples of the hilly regions between the Nile valley and the Red Sea hills. Yam, the focus of Harkhuf's journey, was situated further south. The next major productive regions are around the island of Sai and then the Dongola Reach. At the very northern end of the Dongola Reach lies the Kerma basin. In recent years, Nubian scholars reached a consensus that the kingdom of Yam was probably to be identified with the early phases of the Kerma culture.

This view of Nubia was recently challenged by the Egyptologist, David O'Connor, who argued that the named powers were actually much larger in extent. Wawat, he proposes, covered the whole of Lower Nubia, Irtjet and Satju filled the Dongola Reach, and Yam lay much farther to the south, in the Berber-Shendi Reach of the central Sudan. When Wawat became united with Irtjet and Satju, O'Connor submits, it became a formidable power extending over much of Nubia from Aswan to the 4th Cataract.[15]

O'Connor has successfully highlighted a number of problems: the difficulty of interpreting very sparse information, and also the academic assumptions about how Nubia functioned. The information about the political state of Nubia contained in the Harkhuf texts is incidental to their purpose, Harkhuf's life and royal service. It has generally been assumed that "states" in Nubia would be smaller and less organised than Egypt. At present, the problem is irresolvable. There were certainly important powers in the Berber-Shendi Reach, but our knowledge of the archaeology of the region in this early period is virtually non-existent.

The inscriptional evidence can support either the conventional interpretation of Nubia's political geography or O'Connor's more radical version. The archaeology does not help resolve the problems. The implications of these texts do, however, warn us about the social and political complexities which may lie behind what might otherwise be dismissed as a relatively simple material culture.

By the 6th Dynasty the Egyptian pharaohs no longer had direct control of Lower Nubia, and they had to treat with the local Nubian rulers to acquire the products of the south. The inscription of Harkhuf shows that either they had to pay dues to the rulers through whose territory they passed, or they had to intimidate them with large forces: Harkhuf returned with an escort from the ruler of Yam. It is also clear that the Egyptians chose to support certain local rulers against others, for their own benefit. If Yam is to be identified with Kerma, then the control of trade had moved from Lower Nubia into the Dongola Reach.

Although we have evidence in these Egyptian texts for local rulers in Nubia, we have no images of how they displayed their power, no representations to indicate what type of regalia they wore, and no burials have yet been identified which might belong to them.

The latter years of the long reign of Pepy II (*c.*2278-2184 BC) seem to have witnessed the increased power of the local elites in Egypt, and the period following the king's death saw the breakdown of centralised control in Egypt, but much of this process remains obscure. There had been famines in the 5th Dynasty, and this problem recurred during the succeeding decades (the First Intermediate Period).

With long-distance trade in the hands of the king and central government, the collapse of that authority and the breakdown of Egypt would have resulted in a serious disruption of trade. What effect this would have had on the Nubian suppliers is, of course, hard to estimate, although there is some suggestion that there were political changes in Upper Nubia, the Kerma region, during the same period.

Although there were still kings in Memphis, the *nomarchs* were establishing greater authority in their own districts (*nomes*). Nevertheless, the local officials continued to acknowledge the Memphite kings who were still recognised as the source of legitimate power. Eventually, the nomarchs began to arrogate many of the epithets and trappings of monarchy, expand their spheres of influence and assume royal titles. The major powers to emerge during the so-called First Intermediate Period were *Nen-nesut* (*Herakleopolis*) south of Memphis, where the next line of kings reigned, and the Upper Egyptian city of *Waset* (*Thebes*). Inevitably, with the traditional centre of Egyptian power in the north weakened, the more remote districts of Upper Egypt exerted their autonomy. The nomarchs of Waset began to bring the whole of Upper Egypt under their control, and eventually adopted the pharaonic style. Ultimately these Theban rulers, in the person of Nebhepetre Menthuhotep II, reunited the whole of Egypt (*c.*2040), inaugurating a new period of stability (the Middle Kingdom).

The breakdown of a centralised Egypt during the First Intermediate Period undoubtedly affected Nubia, at least the ruling elites. Trade must have been disrupted, even if it did not cease. Textual sources no longer mention Yam, and, in later documents, Shaat and Kush have replaced it as the most important territories. A smaller state, Yam-nas, might represent a fragment of the earlier power. Archaeology too suggests that there were changes in Upper Nubia about this time, but as yet their nature is unclear.

Throughout the First Intermediate Period the nomarchs controlled their own local armies, and frequently there was armed conflict between districts. Already in the 6th Dynasty, Mernere had included contingents from Irtjet, Wawat, Yam, Kaau and the Medja in his army, now many of the nomarchs' armies included Nubians. There are many scenes of conflict in the tombs of this period, particularly those of the nomarchs of the Oryx nome (at Beni Hasan) and the Hare nome (at el Bersha). Both districts owed their allegiance to the Herakleopolitan pharaohs. Sauty (Asyut) was also under northern control, and the finest and best-known representation of Nubian mercenaries comes from there. The wooden model of a contingent of Nubian bowmen, with its companion contingent of Egyptian spearmen, was found in the tomb of Mesehti. Although Nubian mercenaries seem to have been employed throughout Middle Egypt, it is not surprising that the evidence from Upper Egypt is even richer.

From the time of the Theban expansion in the later years of the First Intermediate Period, a significant group of monuments records Nubian mercenaries who lived and worked in Upper Egypt. Mostly from the region of Gebelein, these funerary stelae depict the soldiers with members of their families. Some of the soldiers may have married Egyptian women. The soldiers also had Egyptian servants, indicating their high status.[16]

Surprisingly, since the Upper Egyptian nomes were under the control of Thebes, Nubians are depicted on none of the many soldiers' funerary stelae known from that vicinity. With the expansion of Theban power, conflict with Nubia was inevitable. A stela of Menthuhotep II states that Wawat and the Oasis (Kharga) were annexed to Egypt. Nubian mercenaries were employed in these campaigns, although they would not have been sent to attack their own regions.

Although these texts record that the Theban rulers were leading their armies into the northern part of Nubia, there are no large records of their successes. There is evidence that the earliest stages of a number of the major fortresses, Aniba, Kubban and Ikkur, were begun earlier than the reign of king Senusret I, but they cannot be ascribed with certainty to Menthuhotep II.

With the reunification of Egypt, and the consolidation of his power, Menthuhotep set about building a splendid tomb and temple opposite his native city of Waset (Thebes). Standing in the bay of the cliffs at Deir el-Bahari, it was a striking building, decorated with elegant reliefs.

A number of the king's consorts had chapels and burial places in the complex, and some Egyptologists have seen in the way in which they are represented a Nubian origin for the dynasty. One of the royal ladies, Kemsit, is painted a dark pink in some reliefs, but in others is painted black. Edouard Naville, the excavator of the shrines and temple of Menthuhotep and his family, thought that there was little doubt that Kemsit was of Kushite origin. Others have pointed out that, in Egyptian practice, this is not a necessary implication of a figure painted black: black was a colour associated with fertility and rebirth. As such it was appropriate in a funerary context. Colour symbolism, amply attested in Egyptian art, has caused many problems of interpretation, and no single rule can be applied.[17] Later, in the New Kingdom, there are examples of Kushite princes being coloured red-brown, in the conventional manner of the Egyptian elite, in their own tombs, but coloured black in Egyptian contexts where they appear as foreign subjects of the pharaoh. In addition to fragments of a fine sarcophagus, Naville also recovered a skull from the burial of Kemsit, which was considered to be of "negroid type". In his identification of the skeletal remains as "negroid", Naville may well have been influenced by his understanding of the relief decoration. The arguments in favour of a Kushite origin for Kemsit might thus be seen as circular, but she is not alone amongst Menthuhotep's consorts.

Queen Kawit was also painted black, and again this has been interpreted as funerary symbolism. Kawit, however, as well as being painted black on the inside of her sarcophagus, has the distinguishing characteristics of a Kushite in Egyptian art, notably the so-called "Kushite fold" (*Fig. 23*). The lady Ashayt, yet another of Menthuhotep's consorts, is shown on her sarcophagus attended by two black women who are described as from the land of the Medja. One is called Fedtyt and the other Mekhenet. Ashayt is also shown black, as is a fourth consort, Sadhe.

It is possible that all of these women were of Kushite origin, and in the case of Ashayt, perhaps more specifically of Medja descent. Yet a further problem arises. It was quite customary for images of royal consorts

Queen Kawit, shown on the exterior of her sarcophagus having her hair dressed. (Fig. 23)

and of officials to reflect the features of the reigning monarch. It could be argued that the women were not necessarily Nubian, but perhaps the king was. A seated statue of the king, painted black, was found mummified and buried at Deir el-Bahari. This statue and its colouring has been cited as evidence for a Nubian origin for the pharaoh. In this instance it seems quite certain that the statue is connected with fertility: the king wears the robe of the *sed*-festival, when he was reborn. Other relief fragments from the temple, however, do seem to show him with features that would elsewhere be suggestive of a Kushite descent. Our knowledge of Menthuhotep's ancestors, the princes and kings of Thebes, many of them called Antef, does not indicate that they were Nubian, but the prominence of Nubian militia in Upper Egypt during the ascendancy of the Theban princes may well have led to marriage alliances with the ruling families of Nubia and the Eastern desert.

As with representations of the 11th-dynasty rulers, some writers have seen indications of a Kushite origin in the portrait sculpture of the 12th-dynasty kings. For such an origin there is also some literary support, in the *Prophecies of Neferti*, a document written in the reign of Amenemhat I but given an historical setting some six hundred years before, in the reign of Sneferu. Here we read of a time of turmoil which is put to an end with the accession of a new king, Amenemhat I.[18]

> Then a king will come from the South,
> Ameny, the justified, by name,
> Son of a woman of Bow-Land (*Ta-Seti*), a child of Upper Egypt.
> He will take the White Crown,
> He will wear the Red Crown.

Amenemhat, probably to be identified with the one-time Vizier to Nebtawyre Menthuhotep IV, seized the kingship and founded a new dynasty. Bow-Land, *Ta-Seti*, was the name for the 1st *nome* of Upper Egypt (stretching from Elephantine to Edfu) as well as for Nubia. There is thus a strong suggestion that Amenemhat may have had some Kushite blood. But even if they were, at least partially, of Nubian descent, these 12th-dynasty pharaohs showed little compassion for that country in the conquest of the Nile valley south of the 1st Cataract.

Although Menthuhotep II had taken the Egyptian army into Nubia, and may have begun to build fortifications, Nubia had regained its independence by the time of Amenemhat I's accession. During the later years of the 11th Dynasty, Nubia had come under the rule of local kings who adopted the style of pharaohs.[19]

The 12th Dynasty kings were forced into prolonged and intensive campaigning in Nubia. Once they had established their suzerainty, they constructed a series of massive fortifications to protect the Nile traffic, and to act as depots and staging posts. All of this suggests that they faced a formidable opposition in the Nubians. This, of course, is not surprising – the Egyptians had used Nubian troops in their armies because they were highly skilled. Now the Egyptian army had to face the Nubian troops on their home ground.

This is strangely at variance with the usual interpretation of the archaeological record which paints a picture of C-Group society, as it had of the A-Group, as relatively loosely knit and uncentralised.

The emergence of a kingdom in Lower Nubia might have been in opposition to the expansion of the Theban kingdom southwards under Menthuhotep II. The evidence is limited to a series of rock drawings and inscriptions scattered throughout Lower Nubia. Some of the rulers emulated the pharaonic style.

The rock-inscriptions name three kings who are attested only in Nubia and who cannot be identified with any known Egyptian pharaohs. Although the date of these Nubian kings is still uncertain, most Egyptologists have suggested that they ruled in the period preceding the re-unification of Egypt by Menthuhotep II, or in the period following that king's death and before the campaigns of Amenemhat I and Senusret I.

The best-documented of the three kings is Qakare In, who was attested by thirteen rock-cut inscriptions throughout Lower Nubia, ranging from Gudhi, north of the rapids of Bab el-Kalabsha, to Abu Simbel. Qakare is known from no record in Egypt, and cannot be identified with

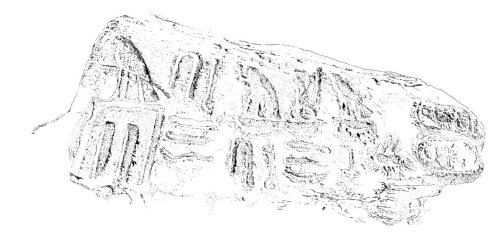

The rock inscription of Qakare In(y) at Khor Midargi. (Fig. 24)

54

any of the ancestors of Menthuhotep II, who carried the name Antef. Qakare probably ruled in Nubia at the end of the 11th Dynasty and through the early years of Amenemhat I, perhaps with that king's consent, until mutual relations deteriorated, and Amenemhat declared war on Nubia. An inscription of the Vizier Antefoqer might contain a veiled reference to Qakare as "him who rebelled against the king".

Another king, Iy-ib-khent-re left an inscription at Gebel Agg, close to one of Qakare, and the relative positions of the inscriptions suggest that Iy-ib-khent-re was later, perhaps the direct successor to Qakare.[20] The third king, Wadjkare Segerseni, was once thought to be identical with one of the Heraklopolitan rulers of the 8th Dynasty, because of the identical throne-names, but is now recognised as a local Nubian ruler.

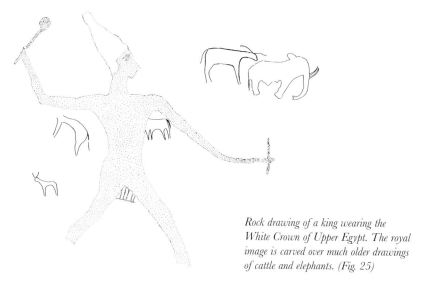

Rock drawing of a king wearing the White Crown of Upper Egypt. The royal image is carved over much older drawings of cattle and elephants. (Fig. 25)

In addition to the rock-drawings of figures in the pharaonic style associated with the inscriptions, there are others which are much less sophisticated, and another group which, although similar, shows distinctly Kushite figures. The pharaonic type usually shows the king wearing the White Crown, the crown of Upper Egypt, and brandishing a mace. Many of these drawings have been assumed by Egyptologists to be of Egyptian pharaohs, but quite probably depict Nubian rulers, either those who left their names, or others who chose to be represented in the Egyptian fashion.

The distribution of the inscriptions of king Qakare make it very likely that, at the time of the 12th Dynasty expansion, Lower Nubia was a united kingdom which presented a formidable obstacle to Egyptian aspirations. Such a situation would explain the intensity of Egyptian military activity.

It took a series of major campaigns during the co-reign of Amenemhat I and his son Senusret I to bring Nubia firmly under Egyptian domination. Most of the records of the military action are dated by the reign of the younger pharaoh, and he probably led the campaigns himself.

Building work in the fortress of Buhen was well under way by year 5 of Senusret I, his father's 25th year. Two years later an expedition was sent into Nubia, but is explicitly stated to have been without fighting or the taking of captives. The major campaign was in year 29 of Amenemhat I (equivalent to year 9 of Senusret I) and both kings may have been present in Nubia. The purpose of this expedition was "to vanquish Wawat". A rock stela of the Vizier Antefoqer probably belongs to the end of this same campaign. Taking to his flagship, called the "Great Oar", Antefoqer led the fleet:

> Then the Nubians of the entire remaining part of Wawat were slaughtered. I sailed victoriously upstream, slaughtering the Nubian on his river-banks and then I sailed downstream plucking corn and cutting down their remaining trees.[21]

A later inscription of Antefoqer states that he had been sending forces on behalf of the pharaoh for 20 years in order to destroy Wawat. By year 18 of Senusret I, all opposition in Wawat had been reduced, and a stela of the same year from Buhen suggests that all later campaigns were directed south of the 2nd Cataract.

The expansion of Egyptian might in Nubia, and the monuments raised for its continuance, are well-known. The great scale and extent of the defences of the 2nd Cataract region, built to control the safe transit of trade and to secure the southern frontier, must, as has been emphasised in recent years, indicate that the Kushite opponents to the south and from the east presented a formidable opposition to the Egyptians.

Although the 12th Dynasty pharaohs did not succeed in driving out the population, as had happened at the beginning of the 1st Dynasty, their prolonged campaigning, which involved the devastation of villages and agriculture, subjugated Nubia. Yet once their object was achieved, there seems to have been little attempt to integrate the C-Group population of Nubia into the Egyptian state: the main concern of the Egyptians was securing the trade routes to the south.

The Egyptians built a number of forts in Lower Nubia, to ensure control of the river, to act as staging posts and, as at Kubban, to protect access to gold-mining regions. The major building operations were confined to a 65-kilometre (40 mile) stretch of the barren 2nd Cataract. A series of forts was built on islands and the west bank, within sight of each

The great Middle Kingdom fortress of Buhen. (Fig. 26)

other, or linked by lookouts and signalling posts. Senusret III established Semna as the permanent southern frontier of Egypt. Here was a natural control point, where the river passed through a narrow channel, dominated by two forts, Semna and Kumma, with a southerly outpost at Semna south, connected to the fort by a massive wall.

Senusret III campaigned in Nubia in his 10th, 12th, 16th and possibly 19th regnal years. In the first of these, his scribe left an inscription on the rocks at Dal, some 60 kilometres (37 miles) south of Semna. Yet, it seems that most of the military activity may have been directed against the Eastern desert, rather than the kingdom of Kush to the south. There was certainly a significant two-way trade between the Egyptians and the emergent power of Kush, based on Kerma. This strong Egyptian presence at the Cataract and the action to the south was not directed against Kush, but was to protect the Nile route and assist in the exchange of goods. Perhaps in the early years of its ascendancy, Kush was not militarily strong enough to safeguard the route, and required Egyptian help and protection through the barren and difficult region between Kerma and the 2nd Cataract. Here the river passed through the Dal cataract and was probably open to attack from the desert.

The fortresses doubtless had a military function, and were not, as W.Y.Adams, in one of his more bizarre interpretations, proposed, "examples of the material hypertrophy which is characteristic of Egyptian civilisation" in which "the size of the fortresses might be less a reflection of the pharaoh's will than of his inability to curb his architect's ambitions".[22]

Names such as "Subduer of Nubia" (Semna south), "Warding off the Bows" (Kumma), "Repelling the Inu" (Uronarti), "Curbing the Foreign Countries" (Shalfak) and "Repulse of the Medja" (Serra East) show quite clearly who the Egyptians thought their enemies were. The location of most of the forts on islands in the river, or on the west bank, points to the east bank as the major threat.

In the latter years of the Middle Kingdom however, the forts acquired a new function: as a defence against the south. The Egyptians had bolstered and encouraged the power of the Kushite kingdom, as the main supplier of the luxuries of the south. They had probably encouraged the development of its military strength to protect the Nile route south of the Cataract, and aid the transit of goods. Now the power of Kush was to become the major threat to the security of Egyptian Nubia.

V The Kingdom of Kush

The political powers which flourished in Nubia in the years of the 12th Dynasty are named in a remarkable group of documents known as the "Execration texts".[1] These were written either on pottery jars or on figures in the form of a bound captive. Their texts are spells against hostile forces, including elements of the Egyptian population as well as foreign rulers and their subjects. They give the names of the most important territories of Nubia at this time, and the names of their rulers.

Many of the Nubian places mentioned in these texts cannot be precisely located, but we know that some were in the Eastern Desert, and that some of those in riverine Nubia lay between the Dal and 4th Cataracts. Lower Nubia seems not to be referred to at all in the Middle Kingdom texts, although one of the earliest examples, of the 6th Dynasty, lists Irtjet, Wawat, Yam, Medja and Satju. Presumably the campaigns of the early 12th Dynasty had so effectively reduced the power of the Lower Nubian kings that they no longer posed any threat.

The Execration texts name rulers of the different Nubian territories, and sometimes their father or mother as well. These texts show that the various Nubian states, however structured, had recognised leaders. Egyptian knowledge about the names of rulers and their parents shows that there were diplomatic contacts between Egypt and these regions, and that the rulers engaged in some form of treaty with the Egyptians.

A papyrus document (called Papyrus Bulaq) mentions the payment of *inu*-tribute, indicative of some sort of alliance between these Nubian rulers and the pharaoh. In the case of the Papyrus Bulaq, these were probably the chiefs of Aushek and the Medja, whose people were so often recruited into the Egyptian army. Beyond giving the names of rulers and their territories, none of these texts aids further understanding of the practice and institution of kingship in Nubia at this time. Nothing has yet been discovered in sculpture or statuary, which represents any of these rulers. Again, the disparity between the archaeological record and the texts is enormous. The structure of society remains elusive, although it may be presumed to have been hierarchically organised.

It is only after the Egyptian withdrawal from Nubia in the early 13th Dynasty that we get any idea of how the Kushite rulers chose to be depicted. The powerful pharaonic monarchy *might* have served as a model, but, as yet, we have no clear evidence that it did. For Lower Nubia, there is little chance of further information becoming available, although some scholars are reappraising material excavated in the earlier campaigns. In Upper Nubia, archaeology is now yielding much more information. At Kerma, the "palace" of the last kings has recently been discovered and may well provide information on the role and functions of kingship and court life.

The Medja lands of the Eastern Desert harboured formidable chiefdoms or kingdoms, but, due to the relatively small amount of archaeological work, our knowledge of them is still severely limited. The Medja were divided into different groups, or principalities. Aushek occurs in two texts, with princes named Tjeghedju and Kui. A later papyrus (P.Bulaq, already referred to), of the reign of a king named Sobekhotep (perhaps the third, *c*.1745 BC) records that two chiefs of Aushek were on a diplomatic visit to Thebes where they were later joined by a third chief. Two rulers of another locality, probably also in the Eastern Desert, Webat -sepet, are named in different documents. One was called Itjaw. The parents of the other ruler, Iunai, are also named: his mother was Tjehufi and his father Kehaubi.

The peoples of this region were certainly nomadic, or semi-nomadic, and the recent excavations by Rodolfo Fattovich and Karim Sadr in the Atbai region of the eastern Sudan have shown that there were strong cultural similarities extending over a very wide area. These similarities could be caused by seasonal movements of peoples over large territories, or they might indicate a cultural horizon extending over the whole region. Whatever the ultimate explanation, it is now clear that the desert regions were far more important than we have hitherto readily acknowledged.

Amongst other rulers were the prince of Irsyk, called Menenkia; Saktuy, prince of Rukiyt; and Wai of Makia. These regions may have been in the Upper Nubian Nile valley or the central Sudan. Of particular interest, the state of Yam-nas had a female ruler, called Satjyt, whose mother is also named, *suggesting* that this part of Nubia may have had an influential matrilineal system. Yam-nas itself might be a last fragment of the state of Yam which had been so important in the time of the 5th and 6th Dynasties.

The most important places in the Middle Kingdom texts were those which lay on the river immediately to the south of the Egyptian frontier at the 2nd Cataract: Shaat and Kush.

Shaat, we know from the excavations directed by Jean Vercoutter, was the island of Sai and a major centre of the Kerma culture. A ruler of Shaat, Aktui, was the son of a woman named Rehai and of Setikkhi, perhaps himself an earlier ruler. Shaat itself may have been a subject state of the Kushite ruler of Kerma. It certainly served as a useful buffer on the northern border of that kingdom.

Kush was based upon Kerma itself, and was to become the most important and powerful of the states after the Egyptian withdrawal from Nubia in the 13th Dynasty. The name of one ruler of Kush is preserved in the Execration texts, perhaps to be read as Wetetereress. Others are known from the monuments set up by their officials when they seized Lower Nubia.

Kerma lies on the east bank of the Nile south of the 3rd Cataract. The site was first excavated by George Reisner between 1913 and 1916, and in recent years has been the focus of further excavations by a joint Swiss-Sudanese team under the direction of Charles Bonnet. The recent excavations have uncovered a town site and have added considerably to our understanding of the monuments already studied by Reisner.

Reisner interpreted the remains as evidence of an Egyptian trading settlement which eventually, due to the admixture of the Egyptian and local populations, degenerated. Reisner's interpretation, so typical of its time, is now of course rightly rejected, and the site of Kerma recognised as the centre of a major Kushite state.

The Eastern Deffufa at Kerma. (Fig. 27)

Another important cemetery of the Kerma culture, on the island of Sai, was excavated by Vercoutter's team, and the evidence that it provided for the chronology of the site was analysed by Brigitte Gratien in a study which completely overturned the work of Reisner. Gratien's conclusions, supported by recent excavation, essentially inverted Reisner's sequence. What Reisner had interpreted as "decline" is now recognised as the earliest phases, the origins of the culture. Once again, the prejudices of Reisner's time led him to draw the wrong conclusions.

At Kerma, the excavation of the town and cemetery site produced large quantities of objects demonstrating the high artistic attainments of the people. It is likely that some Egyptian artisans were employed by the rulers, since the massive brick structures, although unique in design, owe much to Egyptian techniques. Other Egyptian crafts, such as faience manufacture, were practised, and combine both Egyptian and Kushite motifs. Many imported objects are found in Kerma sites.

It is possible, even likely, that the Kerma region was the same as the kingdom of Yam, goal of Harkhuf's journeys, but, from the time of the Middle Kingdom, the region is called "Kush" in Egyptian texts. There had certainly been political changes in the region, but they remain elusive.

Amongst the Egyptian objects excavated at Kerma was a large group of stone vessels carrying the names of Pepy I and Pepy II. Identical types have been found at Byblos, and it is known that the 6th Dynasty pharaohs had strong commercial contacts with the Levantine sea port. It is not certain, however, that the vessels found at Kerma were actually taken there during his reign. They were discovered in a much later context and might have arrived at the site many years after the reign of the pharaoh whose name was carved on them.[2] Whether or not the region's commercial importance began in the 6th Dynasty, at its height Kerma was certainly an African counterpart to Byblos and active in the transfer of rare commodities over vast distances.

The "Kerma culture", so-called because it was first known to archaeology through Reisner's excavations of the "type site", seems to develop about the time of the Egyptian First Intermediate Period, although its origins are now becoming clearer through the excavations of Charles Bonnet and his team. During the Egyptian Middle Kingdom it was the rulers of Kerma who acted as the main intermediaries for the transmission of the produce from the south.

Initially supported by the Egyptians, the power of the Kerma state increased, reaching its zenith in the late Second Intermediate Period. At its height, the Kushite state extended throughout Nubia. It may have reached as far north as Aswan; it certainly controlled the Dongola Reach of the Nile. The kings of Kush, with their capital at Kerma, were the principal rulers, but they also had their own vassals; Shaat was probably one of these. In Lower Nubia too, there were local rulers who acknowledged the suzerainty of the Kushite kings.

Reisner and the succeeding generation of Egyptologists believed that political development in Nubia was less advanced than in Egypt. The rise of powerful states in Nubia was seen as dependent on Egypt's phases of internal weakness and hence inability to interfere. So, it became customary to say that when Egypt was weak, Nubia *became* strong. Nubia's strength has rarely, if ever, been seen as a contributory factor in Egypt's weakness, as David O'Connor has complained. Certainly Egypt's relative strength or weakness was important: Egypt, compared with Nubia, was agriculturally rich, with a large population and a highly centralised administration. This model was based very largely on the vast quantity of archaeological material from Lower Nubia. As that has been published and synthesised, we have begun to formulate new models. Even with the limited agricultural potential of Lower Nubia, we increasingly recognise that the peoples of Nubia were able to develop and maintain complex chiefdoms and states that had the ability to withstand Egyptian pressure. There must have been major and intensive military campaigns by the Egyptians over long periods to subjugate Nubia at the beginning of the Old Kingdom and again at the beginning of the Middle Kingdom.

Survey and excavation south of the 3rd Cataract have radically altered our perception of that region. Brigitte Gratien's reassessment of the Kerma culture material from Sai and the extensive work of Charles Bonnet's team at Kerma itself have ensured that the power and importance of the Kushite kingdom is now acknowledged. But even more startling evidence has emerged in recent surveys in the region around Kerma. This shows that during the period of Kerma's prosperity, the broad alluvial basins had two, or perhaps even three, river channels.[3] This must have made the region immensely rich in agricultural terms. The power of Kerma was thus based on the ability to support a large population and allow the expansion of the state. The commercial activities of the elite were thus far from being the sole reason for the state's wealth. The strength of the Kerma kingdom is clearly shown in the eventual conflict with Egypt; it was to take the Egyptians a full century to impose their authority and subdue Kushite opposition.

In the past, Egyptologists believed that the internal divisions and weakness of Egypt following the 12th Dynasty allowed the Kushite rulers to take the opportunity and expand their kingdom. Rather than being opportunist, it may actually have been the growing power of the Kushite state which brought about the end of the Egyptian domination of Nubia, and for some considerable time prevented the Theban state expanding.

Harry Smith, who published the excavations at Buhen, suggests that with the breakdown of central administration in Egypt by the reign of Khasekhemre Neferhotep (*c*.1730 BC), the 2nd Cataract forts became virtually independent of the central authority.[4] Evidence from the forts, notably from Uronarti, is plentiful and suggests that by the early 13th Dynasty they were controlled by commanders, perhaps of Egyptian descent, whose offices became hereditary. The garrisons, which seem to have remained quite large, were now permanent. Formerly, soldiers had been sent to the forts for limited periods of service. Undoubtedly, there was intermarriage with the local Nubian population.

The Kushite expansion into Lower Nubia began in the 13th Dynasty. Fortresses were attacked, burned and looted. At Kor, the evidence indicates that there were two or three Kushite attacks, the Egyptians regaining and refortifying the fortress in between. At Buhen, the Kushites managed to penetrate the formidable outer defences and capture the Inner fort which was then burnt in a massive conflagration. This was followed by extensive destruction. The fort was stripped and looted, the cemeteries pillaged and the temple destroyed. Semna also shows signs of having been burnt.

There may have been a period when the forts were deserted, but this was very short. When they were reoccupied, the residents were using Kerma-ware pottery. Kerma settlements are known at Mirgissa and at Buhen, and there were doubtless others. In this phase, the administrators were still Egyptians, but now working for the ruler of Kush. It is idle to speculate whether these Egyptians had betrayed their forts, or simply bowed to events. For the next hundred years, Kush was to dominate Lower Nubia.

Having brought the fortresses under their control, the Kushite kings allowed, possibly encouraged, their Egyptian administrators to rebuild the temples. At Buhen, the fortress commander, Sepedher, left an inscription informing us that he "built the temple of Horus, lord of Buhen, in the day of the Ruler of Kush".

Two families of officials from Buhen are particularly well-documented, those of Dedusobek and Sobekemhab. The crocodile god Sobek, lord of Sumenu was particularly popular amongst these families (reflected in their names), and it is likely that many of the Egyptian settlers in the fortresses came from er-Rizeiqat (ancient Sumenu). Rizeiqat lies only a little way to the north of Gebelein, and some of the troops who settled at Buhen may well have been descended from those Nubian mercenaries who had gone north a few generations before.

In Lower Nubia the C-Group culture continued to flourish, reaching its peak even though it was under the political sway of the Kerma kingdom.[5] One notable feature of C-Group villages during this period is their defences. At Wadi es-Sebua, a large village of over one hundred houses was arranged so that its eastern side was a cliff falling to the river. A rough stone wall with archers' loopholes protected the other sides. This type of defence may reflect the local insecurity caused by the expansion of the Kerma state.

This insecurity, forcing the people from their strung out villages into closer, more easily defended, settlements probably contributed to the emergence of powerful local chiefs in opposition to the Kerma kings or supported by them against any Egyptian attempts to regain control.

One of the large C-group graves at Aniba. Similar types of grave have been found in the Eastern Desert of Nubia and may also have existed at el-Kurru. (Fig. 28)

Deriving their wealth from the control of the African trade, the command of Lower Nubia gave the Kushite kings access to both the desert roads and the river route to Upper Egypt. They may have had contacts with Thebes, but eventually they traded directly with the new rulers of the Delta, the Hyksos kings of Avaris. Numerous mud seal-impressions discovered at Kerma carry the names of the Hyksos rulers Jakeb-her, Sheshi, Maatibra and queen Ineni. These Delta pharaohs must have been the major recipients of Kushite produce which was probably conveyed by the desert road, perhaps as far as Middle Egypt. It is hardly likely that the Nile route was used to carry the goods, even though relations between Thebes and the Hyksos appear to have remained amicable until a fairly late date. The comparative poverty of the royal burials at Thebes would support the idea that the Kushite control of gold and other luxuries by-passed the Upper Egyptian kingdom.

The Kerma kingdom was a court-based and wealthy one. There must have been considerable Egyptianisation, some of it no doubt due to the presence of the Egyptian officials at Buhen and other forts. The Hyksos ruler observed normal diplomatic protocol in his letters, and presumably wrote in Egyptian, which itself indicates the presence of Egyptian speakers and scribes at the Kushite court.

Kerma itself must have been an impressive city.[6] An enclosed royal and ceremonial city stood on high ground close to the river, surrounded by habitations of the ordinary people. A vast cemetery lay in the desert some 3 km (1.8 miles) to the east of the city.

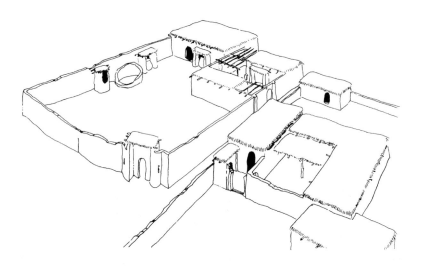

A reconstruction of houses at Kerma. (Fig. 29)

The royal city was an irregular area surrounded by substantial fortifications, including a wall some 10 m (33 feet) high. Four gateways gave access to this city, and roadways linked the gates and main structures, all of which would have been visible above the city walls. At its centre stood a temple, its remains (known as the *Western Deffufa*) still preserved to a height of 19 metres (62 feet). Built of mud-brick, it has similarities with Egyptian temples. A massive pylon formed the facade, but the actual entrance was in the side-wall. Internally it was almost solid, with sanctuary rooms and staircases leading to the roof. The town site lay around and to the west of the temple. Many of the houses were of the traditional circular plan, of grass on a wooden frame, but others were rectangular of the same construction, and some of mud-brick. Charles Bonnet has estimated that there were some 150 or 200 households, perhaps as many as 2,000 people, living here. The audience hall of the king was a circular hut, apparently rebuilt many times. It had a conical roof which rose some 14 metres (46 feet) high. If Kerma pottery can be used as a guide, the roof was brightly coloured.

The cemetery to the north-east of the settlement spans a period of 500 years. The most notable remains, and those which particularly attracted Reisner, were the great tumuli at the southern end of the site. The tumuli had brick substructures, over which the earth was raised. These tombs contained large numbers of servants killed at the time of the main interment. In Tumulus "K X", there were over 300 such burials. Reisner placed the large tumuli in the early phases of the town's history, but it is now known that they belong to the very latest phase, around 1650-1600 BC when the Kushite state was at its richest and most powerful.

Kerma, the excavated remains of the Great Hut. (Fig. 30)

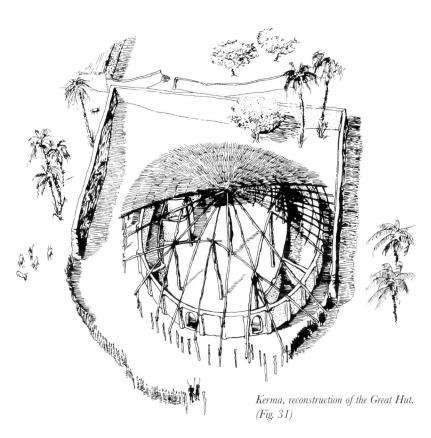

Kerma, reconstruction of the Great Hut.
(Fig. 31)

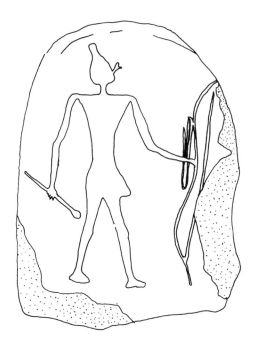

Stela from Buhen showing a Kushite ruler. (Fig. 32)

A large quantity of Egyptian sculpture was excavated at Kerma, and much of it was undoubtedly pillaged from the temples in the forts. Two of the largest and most notable pieces, however, came from much further away. They represent Hepdjefa, the nomarch of Asyut in Middle Egypt, and his wife. When he discovered these statues, Reisner proposed that Hepdjefa had been the Egyptian governor of Kerma who had "gone native" and been buried in Kushite fashion, in a massive tumulus grave with his servants slaughtered around him. This interpretation was soon dropped, and more recently it has been suggested that the statues were looted from a temple at Aswan. The statues are typical funerary monuments and undoubtedly came from Hepdjefa's tomb in the cliffs near Asyut. Asyut itself lies at the end of the desert roads from Nubia through Kharga. Were these statues items of trade, or is it possible that the Kushites were raiding so far north?

Although the excavations at Kerma have not yet produced any images of the Kushite kings, they are depicted on a number of monuments from Buhen. The most remarkable is a stela which shows a king with a mace, bow and arrows, but wearing the White Crown of Upper Egypt, with the uraeus. This king could be Nedjeh who is named in some inscriptions. It seems likely that Nedjeh was a contemporary of the Hyksos king, Aweserre Apepy, and the Theban ruler, Senakhtenre Tao. The Theban pharaohs, trapped between the Kushite and Hyksos kingdoms, now moved to reunite Egypt under their own rule.

VI Gold is as dust

The war waged by the princes of Thebes to reunite Egypt under their own rule was long and difficult. If the origins of the Theban expansion and conflict with the Hyksos are obscure, its triumphant conclusion is well-documented. Seqenenre Tao II was killed, it seems, in the thick of battle, his hastily embalmed mummy bearing the grisly wounds of the axes and spears which felled him.[1] Soon after his accession, Seqenenre's son and successor, Kamose, attempted to complete his father's work. Calling a council of war he asked:

> Why do I still contemplate my strength while there is yet one *Wer*-ruler in Avaris and another in Kush, sitting (here idle) united with an Alam and a Kushite while each man possesses his slice of Egypt, dividing the land with me?[2]

Events moved quickly when Kamose's desert patrol intercepted a letter from the Hyksos king Apepy to the new ruler of Kush indicating that he wished to continue their alliance against Thebes.

> From the hand of the ruler of Avaris, Aweserre, the Son of Re, Apepy greets the son of the ruler of Kush. Why do you ascend the throne without letting me know? Do you see what Egypt has done against me? The ruler who is there, Kamose ... is attacking me on my own territory, although I have not attacked him... Come, journey northward. Do not fear, he is here in my grasp and there is no one who will stand up to you in this Egypt ... we will share the towns of Egypt ....

Kamose led his army into Nubia in his 1st or 2nd year, and re-occupied the fortress of Buhen. No record of this campaign survives, but it must have been a major offensive to regain control of the 2nd Cataract. The success marked the limit of Kamose's ambitions in Nubia. It created a buffer zone between the Kushite kingdom and the frontier of Upper Egypt, and provided a protection while the king was engaged in his major offensive against the Delta. In the face of the Egyptian attack, the

Egyptians working for the Kushite ruler must have fled south or been captured and no doubt executed.

The Theban princes seem to have regarded Lower Nubia as a part of Egypt, and they probably wished to regain control of the territories ruled by the Middle Kingdom pharaohs. Kamose died after little more than three years of rule. He too may have been killed in battle. He was probably quite young, and his brother, Ahmose, who succeeded him, does not appear to have led any campaigns until he had been on the throne for at least ten years, suggesting that he was little more than a child at his accession.[3] Ahmose was victorious against both the Hyksos and the Kushites. Reuniting the country under Theban rule, his reign heralded a new "imperial" age.

The expansion of the Theban kingdom, resulting in the reunification of Egypt, brought extensive military conflict to Nubia. Control of Lower Nubia was achieved by Kamose, at least temporarily, and consolidated by Ahmose. The fortress of Buhen was re-occupied and its defences renewed. Whilst they were engaged in conflict with the Hyksos, the Cataract frontier seems to have held, but the continuing threat of the Kushite state, presumably in the form of attacks on Lower Nubia, drew the Egyptians south of the 2nd Cataract.

The historical events of the rise of the Theban kingdom are documented by autobiographical texts of a number of officials.[4] At el-Kab, an inscription in the tomb of Ahmose son of Abana recounts the campaigns against the Hyksos and in Nubia, but also the two "rebellions", one probably by a Lower Nubian ruler and one in Egypt itself.

It was either Ahmose or his successor, Amenhotep I who first pushed south of the 2nd Cataract. One of these kings established the island fortress of Sai in the Abri-Delgo Reach. Sai had been the seat of the Kushite kingdom of Shaat, and this must have been defeated by the Egyptians, if it had not already been absorbed into the expanding Kerma state. The Theban kings now strove to consolidate their southern frontier, which led to extensive military action in Nubia; the decisive invasion being that of Thutmose I, in the 2nd year of his reign. Thutmose I probably established his frontier at Tumbos, the northern end of the 3rd Cataract, where he built a fortress. The Egyptian border was now immediately to the north of Kerma, but there seems to have been no attempt to settle the region between the 2nd and 3rd Cataracts. The Egyptians may have been more concerned with protecting their interests in Lower Nubia than expanding farther south.

Problems always occur in attempting to interpret the Egyptian records. The locations and peoples are not always easily identified and the terms used can frequently be archaic. "Historical" records also combine the universal aspects of the role of the divine king with the specifics of the historical moment, and it is not always easy to disentangle the two.

The king's record of events, carved on the rocks at Tumbos, describes the slaughter with typical relish:

> He has overthrown the *Wer*-chief of the Nubians ... there are none who have escaped death among those who came to attack him; not a single survivor amongst them ... The Iuntiu-Setiu are laid low throughout their lands; their gore floods their valleys, ... the pieces hacked from them are too much for the birds carrying off the prey to another place.

Further details of the campaign are recorded by Ahmose son of Abana:

> Then I conveyed king Aakheperkare [Thutmose I] ... when he sailed south ... to crush rebellion throughout the lands, to repel the intruders from the desert region. I was brave in his presence in the bad water, in towing the ship over the cataract...

> ... his majesty became enraged like a leopard. His majesty shot and his first arrow pierced the chest of that foe ...

This last event is depicted on a royal scarab (*Fig. 33*).

This campaign inflicted a major defeat on the Kushite state. Kerma itself was attacked: the temple (the western Deffufa) was burned and pillaged. But recent excavations at the site have shown that the attack was soon followed by restoration in the main temple and that the city was not abandoned, as was once assumed. Despite this major setback, the

Scene on the reverse of a scarab of Thutmose I depicting the king firing arrows at a Kushite who falls, pierced in the chest. (Fig. 33)

authority of the rulers was not destroyed, and their resistance to the Egyptians continued. A monumental princely tomb of early 18th dynasty date has been excavated and is in a different part of the town from the great tumuli. The confusion following the events may well have seen a struggle for power amongst the elite of Kerma itself.

The army of Thutmose I also reached the great bend of the Nile in the 5th Cataract region, leaving a rock inscription at Hagar el-Merwa (Kurgus).[5] Although the army had reached Kerma, they probably did not sail through the hostile Kushite territories of the Dongola Reach, but crossed the desert – perhaps from Korosko. The purpose of this expedition must have been to exert Egyptian control over the gold mining regions of the Wadi el-Allaqi and Wadi Cabgaba. The appearance of the Egyptians in the Abu Hamed district must also have served to present a show of strength towards the rulers of the Berber-Shendi Reach.

Thutmose I and his army returned northwards, leaving several rock inscriptions recording the victories. Over a year after it had set out, the army arrived back at Elephantine. The king then ordered the canal through the Cataract to be cleared, and proceeded in triumph to Thebes:

> His Majesty journeyed northward, all foreign lands in his grasp, with the defeated Nubian Bowman hanged, head downward, at the bow of his majesty's ship "Falcon".[6]

Thutmose I followed his Nubian victories with military action in western Asia. There is no evidence that the king returned to Nubia, and the remaining 13 years of his reign may have allowed the Kushites to recoup their strength.

When the news of Thutmose I's death reached Nubia, the "sons of the ruler of Kush" launched an attack against the Egyptian presence in the 3rd Cataract. The new pharaoh, Thutmose II, despatched an army to suppress the "rebellion".

> This army of His Majesty overthrew these foreigners without letting anyone among their men live, just as His Majesty had ordered, except one of these children of the *wer*-prince of vile Kush, brought alive as a prisoner ... to the place of His Majesty and placed under the feet of the Good God.[7]

This Kushite prince, his life spared, would have been educated as a vassal at the Egyptian court. This new policy of taking the sons of foreign rulers served two purposes: the princes were hostages for parental loyalty, but also, and doubtless more importantly, it ensured that the next generation was educated in Egyptian ways. When they returned to rule in their homelands, they would, theoretically, be pro-Egyptian, supported in their positions by the benefits of Egyptian military assistance.

Thutmose II's reign was brief, and, shortly after the accession of his son, Thutmose III, the king's widow, the regent Hatshepsut, assumed the kingship herself. The Kushites had responded to the hostilities of Thutmose I and Thutmose II, and were making a desperate attempt to preserve their state from Egyptian subjugation. During the joint reign of Thutmose III and Hatshepsut, there were three or four campaigns into Nubia. The first was almost certainly led by Hatshepsut in person; the second, in year 12, by Thutmose III. This reached Tangur, where the king left an inscription. A third campaign in year 20 was closely followed by another, in year 21 or 22 (shortly before the death of Hatshepsut).[8]

The early years (23-31) of Thutmose III's sole reign were dominated by his Asiatic wars which brought much of Syria-Palestine into Egypt's empire.

Although the official border was to be drawn at the 4th Cataract, and the actual limit of direct control at the 3rd, Egyptian influence stretched much farther. Thutmose III reached the land of Miu where a rhinoceros was captured. Miu may have been somewhere in the Berber-Shendi reach of the river, the savanna lands of the central Sudan.[9] This was a major and far-ranging expedition. Only now did the Kushite rulers of Upper Nubia finally bow to the Egyptian authority, and the "tax" and "tribute" of Upper Nubia flowed into the treasury: it is first recorded in year 31. Following the actions led by the kings, there may have been continuous campaigning by the armies garrisoned in the fortresses and under the command of the Viceroy.

In year 34 the sons of the prince of Irem were sent to Egypt, although no military conflict is associated, and the policy of educating such princes in Egypt may now have been accepted enthusiastically by the Kushite kings. The exact location of Irem, like so many Nubian countries, is uncertain. Generally thought to have been in the Dongola Reach (where Areme was located in the Meroitic period), it might actually have been much farther south, in the central Sudan. As we shall see, Irem was later to become one of the most important and – from the Egyptian point of view – troublesome of Kushite princedoms.

His Asiatic wars completed, and Egypt's supremacy acknowledged throughout western Asia, Thutmose III returned to Nubia in his 47th year. The record of this visit gives no hint of opposition, and the king sailed through the Dongola Reach as far as the 4th Cataract. The king says that this was the first time that any pharaoh had visited the flat-topped mountain which dominates the landscape of that region, Gebel Barkal.[10]

A fortress was established somewhere here, at Egypt's official southern frontier on the river. Called *Sema-khasetiu*, "hacking up the foreign lands", it has not been located. It is not recorded again, and the next time this far frontier of Kush is mentioned in an Egyptian text (the stela of year 3 of Amenhotep II), the name of the fortress or town has changed to *Napata*.

In the last two years of his long reign, Thutmose III associated his son, Amenhotep II, with him as co-ruler. After 54 years of rule, the elder king died.

Although the Kushites seem to have acknowledged the supremacy of the pharaoh, graphic warnings were still deemed necessary. In his first year of sole rule, Amenhotep II marched into Asia, and defeated a coalition of Syrian princes. He determined to impress upon the Kushites the fate of those who broke their alliance treaties:

> When his majesty returned ... he slew with his own weapon the seven princes who had been in the land of Takhsy, and had been placed head downward at the head of his majesty's barge, the name of which is "Aakheperure-is-the-Establisher-of-the-Two-Lands". [His majesty] hanged six of the fallen ones before the walls of Thebes ... Then the other fallen one was taken up-river to Nubia and hanged on the wall of Napata, to manifest the victories of his majesty, for ever and for eternity, in the lands of the Kushites.[11]

Under the Assyrian empire, similar treatment was frequently meted out and has given the Assyrians a reputation for cruelty. In fact, the many treaties which survive from the ancient world were sworn on binding religious oaths: in breaking them, justice and right demanded such retribution.

This grisly episode actually heralded a change in Egyptian policy. Egypt's supremacy was apparently unquestioned, and the reign of Amenhotep II saw the increased use of diplomacy over war. Those princes from Kush and Asia who had been educated in Egypt were probably now assuming their thrones. The ruthless treatment of rebels would have been weighed against the enormous benefits of loyalty. In this new world, Nubia was to play a vital economic role.

The surviving ancient records indicate that there were apparently few military actions in the Nile valley for the next hundred years. Fortresses were no longer the mainstay of Egyptian power, and a number of new temple-centred towns was now built throughout Nubia. The main opposition to Egyptian rule now came from the Eastern Desert, and perhaps the far south.

The death of a king and the accession of a new one was always a difficult time in the ancient monarchies, frequently bringing rebellion throughout their dependencies. Most oaths of allegiance were regarded as binding only for one reign, so the accession of a new king saw many vassals making a bid for independence. A new king often claims military activities in his first or second year. Whilst these may have been to counter insurrections, they were frequently shows of strength to impress the subject rulers that the new king was as valorous as his predecessor.

A few military forays in Nubia are recorded for the later 18th Dynasty. Thutmose IV did not even lead his army in person. Amenhotep III may have directed two campaigns, one against the land of Ibhet, the other against Ikayta, both somewhere in the gold mining regions of the Eastern Desert.[12] The protection of these gold-producing regions was of paramount importance to the Egyptians, since upon them relied Egypt's supremacy in the world of the Late Bronze Age eastern Mediterranean.

The Late Bronze Age in Nubia, as in Egypt, appears to have been peaceful and prosperous. With the prolonged wars of the reigns of Thutmose I, II and III and Hatshepsut, the opposition of the Kushite kingdom of Kerma had been crushed. It had taken 100 years to achieve this supremacy, but the Egyptians were to dominate Nubia for the next four hundred years. There were major differences between this occupation of Nubia and those of the Old and Middle Kingdoms. Firstly, the territory which came under Egyptian control was far more extensive, stretching as far as the 4th Cataract, and the method of control was also very different. The Old Kingdom had apparently driven out the local population; the Middle Kingdom seems to have subdued it, then ignored it; the New Kingdom, to a very large degree, absorbed it.

The administration of the newly reclaimed territories had been placed under the control of a Viceroy by Kamose. The duties of the official were, at first, partly military, but, as control became more effective, they became concerned primarily with the civil administration of the territories ruled by Egypt, and with the collection of tax and tribute.[13]

In the reign of Amenhotep II or Thutmose IV, after 150 years of Egyptian presence in Nubia, the administration was reorganised along dual lines paralleling that of Egypt itself. Two provinces were created, Wawat (Lower Nubia), and Kush (Upper Nubia). These each came under the control of an official directly responsible to the Viceroy, just as the two Viziers were subordinate to pharaoh. By the time of Tutankhamun, the authority of the Viceroy stretched from Nekhen (*Hierakonpolis*) in Upper Egypt to the 4th Cataract, probably in order to include the gold mines of southern Egypt as well as those of Nubia.

Although the limit of Egyptian control was Napata and the 4th Cataract, the region between the 3rd and 4th Cataracts seems to have been left in the hands of Kushite princes who owed their allegiance to the pharaoh.[14] The major Egyptian towns and viceregal administrative centres lay to the north of the 3rd Cataract.

The agricultural production of Nubia was always limited by the narrow alluvial strip which could be cultivated, even with intensive production. Documents from the period of viceregal control record many types of fruit and vegetable products which were exported to Egypt from Nubia. Yet these must have been at least balanced by the foodstuffs imported. Further south, the pastures of the Dongola Reach were probably given over to cattle rearing. The scenes in the tomb of Tutankhamun's Viceroy, Huy, show cattle being transported to Egypt, and they also appear in large numbers in the records of the tribute. The export of these agricultural products certainly did not repay the enormous investment of the Egyptians in Nubia. What then, was the importance of Nubia to Egypt?

Cattle boat from a painting in the tomb of the Viceroy Huy. (Fig. 34)

There were two distinct aspects to the wealth of Kush: the mineral wealth and the trade routes. Both had been important in earlier periods. During the Egyptian New Kingdom they, and their significance, are far more fully documented.[15]

All of the literature on New Kingdom Nubia emphasises the importance of gold, but it remains difficult to actually quantify this. The gold of the deserts of Lower Nubia, and to a much lesser extent those of Kush, enabled Egypt to maintain her political dominance in western Asia.

Gold was mined far out in the Eastern Desert, in the Wadi Allaqi and the Wadi Cabgaba. There were also gold-producing regions closer to the

Part of a scene in the tomb of the Viceroy Huy showing the Scribe of the Gold Accounts, Hor-nefer, overseeing the weighing of gold rings. (Fig. 35)

river, in the Abri-Delgo Reach and in the 4th Cataract and Abu Hamed reaches of the Nile.

The Annals of Thutmose III, carved on the walls of the temple of Amun at Karnak, record the amount of gold produced by the mines of Wawat for years 34, 38, 41 and 42 of the king's reign. This averages at a yearly production of around 248 kilogrammes. The gold production of Kush for a roughly corresponding period (between years 34 and 41) gives an average yearly production of only around 15 kilogrammes. This gives us some idea of the relative importance of the two districts. Unfortunately, there are no corresponding figures for us to estimate the production of the Eastern Desert of Egypt, although it is possible that the Nubian mines were as important, if not more so.

During his reign, Thutmose III gave to the temple of Amun at Karnak over 152,107 *deben*, which is 13,840 kilogrammes, in lumps or rings, plus various other smaller specified quantities and golden objects. Altogether, the king's gifts to the temple reached a total of at least 15,000 kilogrammes (14.76 tons). This probably represents only a fraction of the total gold production of the reign, and donations would have been made to many other temples, to foreign rulers, and of course used by the palace itself.

Whilst there are no corresponding figures for the later 18th Dynasty, the evidence does not suggest a decline in production – if anything, perhaps the opposite.

Nubians bringing gold to Overseer of Chariotry, Hati. (Fig. 36)

An inscription from the Monthu temple at Karnak records that Amenhotep III made donations of 31,485 $^1/_3$ *deben* of electrum (= 2,865 kg) and 25,182 $^3/_4$ *deben* of gold (= 2,292 kg) to that temple, which seems to be in accord with larger amounts given to the Amun sanctuary by Thutmose III. From this and the succeeding reigns, we also have the evidence of the Amarna letters.

Amongst much other immensely valuable information, the Amarna archive details the gifts exchanged by the pharaohs Amenhotep III, Akhenaten and Tutankhamun with various rulers of western Asia and Mesopotamia. The regular "greeting-gift" which accompanied each exchange of letters was usually quite modest, but the inventories of gifts sent for the jubilee festivals, or for the furnishing of a new palace, and, most importantly of all, at the time of marriage, list a huge quantity of objects. When we consider how little of the total correspondence is actually preserved in the archive, the quantities of precious metals, ivory, ebony, along with furniture and other items are quite staggering.

Assur-uballit, king of Assyria, sent with his letter a greeting gift of two chariots and two white horses. A previous gift from Amenhotep III had clearly not been equal to expectations:

> Is such a present that of a Great King? Gold in your country is dirt; one simply gathers it up. Why are you so sparing of it? I am engaged in building a new palace. Send me as much gold as is needed for its adornment.
> When Assur-nadin-ahhe, my ancestor, wrote to Egypt, 20 talents of gold were sent to him.

When the king of Hanigalbat wrote to your father in Egypt, he sent
20 talents of gold to him.[16]

The 20 talents of gold referred to is quite probably the bride price
paid when pharaoh married a foreign princess.

The lists of objects sent to the pharaoh at the time of his marriage to
Tadu-Heba, daughter of Tushratta, king of Mitanni, gives considerable
detail, including the weight of the amount of gold and silver used in each
object. It is clear that the gift-exchange was not simply a question of
sending something nice, it was carefully judged to be of equal value to a gift
received, or not, depending on the status of the recipient. A letter from the
king of Alashiya (Cyprus) to pharaoh, enlarges on how these transactions
would have benefitted the Egyptians.[17] The Cypriot ruler sent 500 talents
of copper, but is compelled to remark:

> You have not been put (on the same level) with the king of Hatti or
> the king of Shankhar. Whatever greeting-gift (my brother) sends me,
> I, for my part, send back to you double.

So, Egyptian control of Lower Nubia gave them access to the gold
mines, and every attempt seems to have been made to exploit them to the
fullest. Large numbers of New Kingdom inscriptions are known from the
gold mining regions, and even now are being rediscovered in increasingly
remote areas. Any investment in Lower Nubia was probably considered to
be amply repaid.

If the gold production of Kush was considerably less than that of
Wawat, its importance was assured by the long-distance trade network with
the regions to south. These networks had been the basis for the power of
the Kushite kingdom of Kerma, perhaps also of the A-Group monarchs.
During the later 18th Dynasty, the produce of the savanna lands of the
central Sudan and the Ethiopian foothills seems to have been exploited on
a larger scale than ever before. It is far more difficult to quantify the
amounts of ebony and ivory brought: these commodities are hardly ever
recorded in the same way as gold. We do, however, get the occasional hint
at the vast wealth flowing from the south.

The two main materials were, as for so long, ivory and ebony. These
substances were frequently used together, along with gold, in the
production of elaborate palace furniture, splendidly exemplified by the
objects from the tomb of Yuya, father of Amenhotep III's chief wife, Tiy,
and from that of Tutankhamun.

A letter from Amenhotep III to Tarhundaradu, king of Arzawa in
Anatolia, relating to a marriage with the king's daughter, also documents

the lavish gifts sent by the pharaoh. These included 20 *minas* of gold, many garments of linen, 3 chairs of ebony overlaid with gold and 10 chairs of ebony inlaid with ivory. There were also 100 beams of ebony. This is one of the few occasions on which the raw substance is actually documented, although, to judge by the lists of gifts sent to Egypt, it must have been a frequent item of trade.

Amongst the numerous gifts sent by Akhenaten to Burra-Buriash, king of Babylon were:[18]

11 boxes of ebony, inlaid with ivory
6 pairs of animals paws of stained ivory
9 plants of stained ivory ...
10 plants of various sorts in stained ivory
29 "cucumbers", containers for oil, of stained ivory
44 oil containers decorated with apples, pomegranates and dates ...
    of stained ivory
375 containers of oil, of stained ivory
19 combs of stained ivory
19 toggle pins of stained ivory
3 headrests of stained ivory
3 *kukkubu*-containers of stained ivory
3 oxen, containers of oil, of stained ivory

This is just a brief selection of items, from one list.

Few of the surviving letters actually record the sending of raw materials from Egypt, the 100 beams of ebony sent to the king of Arzawa being one of the few examples. Another is found in one of the letters of the king of Alashiya (Cyprus) to pharaoh.[19] The king sent 100 talents of copper, and sought as a return one ebony bed mounted with gold, one chariot and a team of horses, 14 beams of ebony and various quantities of cloth (linen and *byssos*).

Apart from the items so important to international relations, the southlands provided commodities which were essential to Egypt itself. Notable amongst these was incense, gathered in the Ethiopian highlands. Used in temple and royal rituals, it was also important as a fumigant. Animal skins had a variety of uses, the most familiar being the skins of leopard or cheetah worn by the chief priests.

The influence of Egypt's trade was thus far-reaching. But who controlled this trade? There are no records of trading expeditions comparable to that of Harkhuf in the Old Kingdom, and it seems likely that the Kushite princes were responsible. In return for the goods of the south, they would have received Egyptian foodstuffs, cloth and manufactured objects, military and political support.

Throughout Nubia, indigenous princes continued to hold an important position in the Viceregal system, and the elite of Lower Nubia was rapidly absorbed into the administration.[20] Wawat itself fell naturally into three regions, each of which seems to have had its own prince. In Egyptian texts they are called *wer*, a term applied to all foreign rulers, Asiatic, Libyan or Kushite. In one instance the word used is *kwr*, the same as the later Meroitic title *qore*. This was the indigenous word for "king" and suggests that the Meroitic language was being spoken in parts of Kush at this time, and that there were scribes at the Egyptian court able to speak the language.

These princes were educated at the Egyptian court and often adopted Egyptian names, but they retained their local titles. In Egyptian scenes, such as those in the tomb of Tutankhamun's Viceroy, Huy, the princes were shown wearing their traditional costumes, but, in their own tombs, they had themselves depicted as any other member of the Egyptian elite. Their main residences seem to have been in their old local centres, as were their burial places. The style of their tombs was identical to that found in Egypt at this time, particularly in the Theban region: a decorated chapel and subterranean burial chamber, the whole surmounted by a pyramid. The funerary equipment was also typically Egyptian, with coffins, funerary masks and shabti figures. Their statues were the product of the royal workshops in Nubia, and sometimes made of imported stone.

Egyptologists once thought that, apart from the princes, the Viceregal administration largely comprised colonial Egyptians. This is certainly wrong, the administration was left mostly in the hands of the local elite families. As early as the joint reign of Thutmose III and Hatshepsut, members of princely families had adopted Egyptian names and were working in high positions in the Viceregal bureaucracy. Some of them moved from their home territory and worked in other parts of Nubia, others were appointed to offices in Egypt itself.

The cemetery at Miam (Aniba), one of the main viceregal centres in Wawat, amply demonstrates the power of the local elite families.[21] The ancestors of the "Deputy of Wawat" (*idnw*), Pennut, who served Ramesses VI, had held the offices of "Overseer of the Treasury" in Wawat and "Deputy of Wawat", along with priesthoods and stewardships for several generations. The women of the family were Chantresses of Horus, Lord of Miam.

Although most of the Viceroys seem to have belonged to noble Egyptian families, some may have had a Nubian origin. Because they were depicted as Egyptians, and there is usually only a limited amount of information about their families or origins, it is extremely difficult to be certain. The Viceroy Iuny, who served during the later years of the reign of

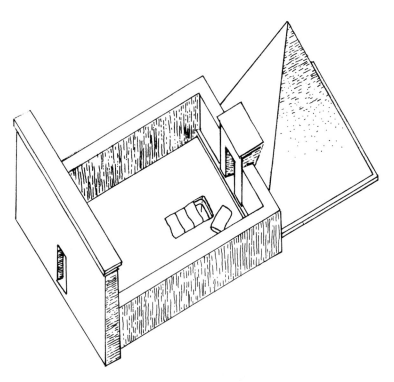

One of the New Kingdom tombs with a pyramid at Aniba. (Fig.37)

Sety I and the earliest of Ramesses II, also carried the title "*wer*-prince of the Medjayu". As the only Viceroy to hold this title, it *might* suggest that he was of Medja origin, rather than a commander of Medja troops. The name of the last Viceroy of the 20th Dynasty, Panehesy, means "the Nubian", but was common throughout the New Kingdom and can hardly be seen as a evidence for Kushite origins.

The documentation of the elite families of Nubia is richest in the later New Kingdom, the Ramesside period, but our knowledge of the princely Nubian families is greatest from the earlier New Kingdom. This is for obvious reasons: at this time they used both Nubian and Egyptian names and a mixture of titles. Later Nubians with Egyptian names and titles are indistinguishable from Egyptians. There is most information about the two southern princedoms of Wawat, Miam and Teh-khet. The northernmost would have embraced the region between Kalabsha and Seyala with the fortress of Baki (Kubban) and the entrance to the Wadi el-Allaqi at its heart. Although there is no direct inscriptional evidence, the princes may have been buried at Dehmit (Bogga) just to the north of Kubban. Here a tomb of the early 19th Dynasty was carved for a Royal Steward, named Nakhtmin. This was just the sort of title that was given to high-ranking foreigners.

Miam embraced the rich bend in the river between Wadi es-Sebua and Arminna, in later times renowned for its date plantations. At its heart lay the town of Miam (Aniba) one of the main seats of the Viceroy. The Princes of Miam were buried in tombs a little south of the town, at Toshka. Of these, the best-documented is Heqa-nefer whose tomb was decorated with finely painted scenes and contained Egyptian burial goods.[22] Heqa-nefer enjoyed a long reign, probably over 30 years, and left records over a wide area. He accompanied Merymose, the Viceroy of Amenhotep III, on various tours of duty to inspect the gold mines of the Eastern Desert. His name and titles are carved on the rocks of the Wadi Abbad as well as in the Nile valley itself, and he was depicted and named in the tomb of Tutankhamun's Viceroy, Huy.

To the south of Miam lay Teh-khet. This territory embraced the region from Abu Simbel to Buhen, and its ruling family was buried at Debeira.[23] The princes of this family are well-documented in the reigns of Hatshepsut and Thutmose III. A later prince, Ipy, lived in the reign of Ramesses II.

Heqanefer, prince of Miam, with the other princes of Wawat. (Fig. 38)

Upper Nubia, Kush, came under Egyptian sway much later than the north; the Kerma kingdom and its successor offering resistance for a full century after the first attack by Kamose. The transition must have begun with the removal of the Kushite prince to Egypt by Thutmose II followed by the intensive and wide-ranging campaigns of Hatshepsut and Thutmose III. Kush retained its princes and in the tomb of the Viceroy Huy six *weru* of Kush are depicted, alongside the three (including Heqa-nefer) from Wawat.

There has been little excavation of settlements or cemeteries of this period in the region where their domains lay, between Amara and Napata. It is likely that there were princedoms based on the old Kerma centres of Sai and Kerma, and perhaps others further south near Kawa, Bugdumbush and near Napata, at the end of the desert road to the savanna.

The great bend in the Nile between Kerma and the 4th Cataract was under the control of the "Overseers of the Southern Foreign Lands". These included the two senior officials of the administration, the Viceroy and the Overseer of the Bowmen of Kush (the head of the military), and the local Kushite princes.

One such prince, named Heqa-em-sasen, lived in the reign of Amenhotep II.[24] He was raised at the Egyptian court and had a tomb at Thebes. In addition to the traditional Egyptian titles of nobility "hereditary prince and count" he was one of the few officials to hold the rank of "Fan bearer on the right hand of the king". Heqa-em-sasen's close connection with the palace was further emphasised by his office of "Director of the Antechamber". Although he was an important personage in the Egyptian court, Heqa-em-sasen retained connections with his homeland. He was one of the "Overseers of Southern Foreign Lands", and left an inscription carved on the rocks at Tumbos. A statue of him was found in the temple at Gebel Barkal, although it was probably taken there from another Kushite temple at a later date.

Many of these foreign princes adopted an Egyptian name which included the word *heqa* "ruler" in honour of the pharaoh, such as Heqa-nefer "the perfect ruler". Others were given, or assumed, names which honoured the reigning pharaoh, such as Menkheperre-sonb, "Menkheperre (Thutmose III) is healthy". Such names were also carried by members of the Egyptian elite, and it is not always easy to identify those of foreign extraction.

As well as the princes of the Nile valley and those from the far south, the rulers of the eastern desert were also included within the Egyptian hierarchy. The Medja had long been employed as mercenaries and police in Egypt, to the extent that "Medja" was the term used for the police force, and "*wer* Medjayu" can mean both "chief of police" and "*wer*-ruler of the Medja". Despite this confusion, a family of Medja princes may be identified. An official of the reign of Thutmose III is called the "*wer*-ruler of the Medjayu". This man, Neferkhat, carries only this title, suggesting that he did indeed come from the Eastern Desert. His wife's name, Ruiu-resety, is similar to names found amongst the princely families of Lower Nubia. Neferkhat is said to have been a "follower of his Lord on his campaigns in the southern and northern foreign countries", and may have been the leader of a contingent of Medja troops. He is, like other Nubian princes, depicted as a typical member of the Egyptian elite. Neferkhat's son, Menkheperresonb, was educated in the palace and given the conventional titles of the Egyptian nobility, "hereditary prince and count" along with designators of high rank such "Great in his office, a noble in the forefront of the people". The titles which relate to his actual functions were "Overseer of the deserts of the Good God", "Prince of the Medjayu" and "Overseer of the hunters".

Another Chief of the Medjayu, Neby, lived in the reign of Thutmose IV. In this case it is difficult to know whether this man was of Medja origin, or was one of the officials who were appointed as "Chiefs" of the police. His father was a priest of Amun, and may have been Egyptian. However, his mother's name, Tatjuia, is not Egyptian, and is probably Nubian. Neby was educated at the Egyptian court, and then appointed to a high military office "Overseer of the forts of Wawat". Later he was made governor of the frontier fortress of Tjel, at the opposite end of the kingdom in the north-eastern Delta. Two other Medja princes, Ruru (a name found in the Nubian princely families) and Nefer-abet, were buried in the Theban necropolis.

The high honour accorded to Kushite princes at the Egyptian court is demonstrated by the burial of Maiherpri in the Valley of the Kings.[25] This young man – his age at death has been estimated as being about 20 years – was probably a contemporary of Thutmose IV. His burial furniture gives him the titles "child of the *kap*" and "Fanbearer on the right hand of the King", but he has no titles designating a specific office. The *kap* is widely assumed to have been a palace school which included the children of high officials and foreign princes brought to be educated at the Egyptian court. The burial furniture includes many items of military equipment, particularly that associated with the chariotry. The prince was certainly a Kushite, perhaps a Medja. His funerary papyrus is unusual in that, unlike most other foreigners in Egypt, Maiherpri was painted black with very distinctive hair.

It was not only the sons of the Kushite rulers who were taken to Egypt: in the tomb of the Viceroy Huy, two Kushite princesses are also shown.

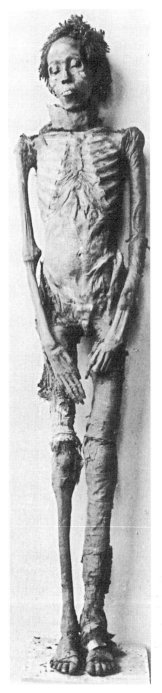

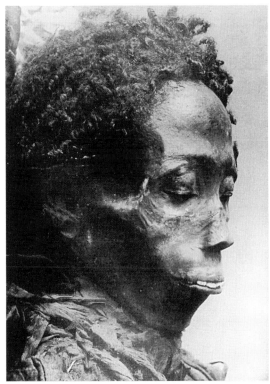

Head of Maiherpri. (Fig. 40)

Mummy of Maiherpri. (Fig. 39)

Elsewhere, references to the "children of the *weru*-rulers" imply that both male and female were taken to the court. Diplomatic marriages between the pharaohs and the daughters of the rulers of the Asiatic states are well-documented, particularly from the Amarna archive. Princesses from Mitanni in north Syria, Hatti (the Hittite kingdom of Anatolia), Babylon and the coastal cities of the Lebanon were sent to Egypt, but, in the view of most Egyptologists, Kushite princesses did not marry the pharaoh. The evidence, as ever, is difficult to find, since foreign princesses would have been given Egyptian names (the daughter of the Hittite king became Maat-Hor-neferu-re) and depicted as Egyptians. It must be emphasised that knowledge of royal wives is so limited that we rarely know who their parents

Kushite Princess in a chariot drawn by cattle. (Fig. 41)

were. It should also be said that the claims made in some literature that Tiy, the chief wife of Amenhotep III, Nefertiti, the wife of Akhenaten, and Nefertari, chief wife of Ramesses II, were Kushites, are based upon superficial evidence. A foreign origin for Tiy has often been proposed, but some Egyptologists suggested she was of Nubian ancestry, whilst others thought that she was Asiatic.[26] The almost-intact burial of her parents has nothing suggestive of a foreign origin, and their mummified remains and their titles indicate that they were members of the Egyptian elite.[27]

Although the positive evidence for Kushite royal wives is limited, the too frequently repeated view that there were none is another residue from the earlier years of Egyptology, when contemporary assumptions were imposed on the past. There is no evidence that the Egyptian attitude to Kushites was different to their attitude to Asiatics, Libyans or any of the other foreigners they had contact with. Antipathy to foreigners was a characteristic of many ancient (as, unfortunately, most modern) civilizations, but was not based on "race". Kushites, Asiatics and Libyans were all depicted *as* Egyptians when they had been absorbed into the Egyptian system. Until then, they were representatives, along with the people of Egypt themselves, of the chaotic forces which it was pharaoh's duty to control.

It is not only through the idea of royal marriages that the prejudices of an earlier age have become rooted in Egyptology. The political relationship between Egypt and the Kushite rulers has been treated in a very similar way. Nubian gold was the basis of the diplomatic exchange which now, rather than military action, maintained Egypt's supremacy in the Near East. Nevertheless, Egyptologists frequently portray the pharaoh as depleting Nubia of its gold resources and luxury goods, which then entered into a reciprocal gift cycle with the rulers of Asia, the Kushites themselves being excluded from this. There is actually no reason to believe that Egyptian relations with Nubia were essentially different from those with Asia. The Egyptian texts use the same term, *wer*, for all foreign rulers whether Asiatic, Libyan or Kushite. The Egyptians must have maintained strong contacts with the rulers who controlled the commodities they desired, even if they preferred to leave their acquisition to their subject rulers in the Kushite Marches. These rulers would have received gifts from pharaoh in just the same way as the Asiatic rulers, and probably the same types of things. Undoubtedly Egyptian linen and manufactured goods were important, as were foodstuffs, such as grain and wine, and, less tangibly, military and political support for their regimes. Another important item, chariots, is recorded amongst the "tribute" of Kush presented by the Viceroy Usersatet to Amenhotep II. The text is unclear how many were brought, but it required 50 men (perhaps two per chariot). These chariots may have been captured in battle. If so, it demonstrates that the Egyptians had given chariots and horses to the Kushite rulers. Both are frequently recorded as part of the gift exchange in the Amarna archive. So, the military developments of Late Bronze Age western Asia were rapidly introduced into Nubia.

The education of Kushite princes at the Egyptian court, the supply of Egyptian luxuries and support for their regimes were no guarantee that they would not revolt when the opportunity arose. Indeed, the presence of foreign princes and royal envoys from Nubia, Libya and Asia may well have led to intrigue and alliances against Egypt being formed by states which otherwise would not have had direct contact with each other. Such, at least, seems to have been the case in the Ramesside period.

The Ramesside period also witnessed the frequent "rebellion" of states which had been in close contact with Egypt for many decades. Irem was notable in this respect. As early as year 34 of Thutmose III, four sons

Kushite women from a scene in the tomb of the Viceroy Huy. (Pl. 42)

of the ruler of Irem were taken to Egypt, yet Irem was one of the Kushite states most frequently "in rebellion".

Most Egyptologists have supposed that Irem was the same as the earlier kingdom of Yam which Harkhuf had visited in the 6th Dynasty. A Meroitic place-name *Armi*, was located in the vicinity of Kerma, and it is tempting to equate all three places: Yam, Irem and Armi.

The location of Irem is important, since it to some extent dictates how we interpret Egyptian control of Upper Nubia. The problems of locating Irem, and the various implications, have been extensively discussed by David O'Connor.[28] If Irem was in the Nile valley somewhere around Kerma and the Dongola Reach, Egyptian control of that region was considerably less secure than has usually been accepted. There were sporadic rebellions by Irem throughout the 18th and 19th Dynasties. But, if Irem was in the central Sudan, the pharaonic military activity was far more wide-ranging and aggressive than we had previously thought. In terms of geographical range, it would compare with the campaigns in Asia. Significantly, this alternative view also suggests a much more aggressive reaction by the kingdoms of the central Sudan towards Egypt and its Nubian possessions. Irrespective of Irem's actual location, it is now clear that our interpretation has been rather complacent in its attitudes. It has been assumed for too long that the New Kingdom pharaohs easily maintained their control over a backward and loosely-structured periphery. Any kingdoms in Upper Nubia and the central Sudan must have posed a *potential* threat to the Egyptian frontiers. Any sign of weakness in the militia would have presented an opportunity to throw off Egyptian sovereignty, or attack the Viceregal centres to the north. Those signs of weakness now began to appear. For one hundred and fifty years, Pharaoh had been worshipped in Nubia as the "Lord of Bow-Land" and the "Lion over the South Country", but Egypt's dazzling sun had passed its zenith.

VII   The Crisis Years

Nubia in the later New Kingdom, the 19th and 20th Dynasties, has to some extent baffled scholars. Many have assumed that it was in decline. The archaeologists of the First Survey proposed that low Nile floods over many years affected the crop production and brought about a gradual decrease in the population. Yet, many of the largest of Nubia's temples were built during this period. Reconciling these apparent contradictions proved difficult, and Cecil Firth was compelled to remark:

> It is difficult to avoid the conclusion that Nubia had become a sort of no man's land ruled by the gods and peopled by the ghosts of the dead.[1]

The problems which affected Egypt during this period, and which had repercussions in Nubia, were not low Niles, but were even more catastrophic.

Egypt during the middle and later 18th Dynasty was the dominant power of the Late Bronze Age world, maintaining her position by use of the products of Nubia, notably gold, ivory, ebony and incense. These years of relative peace were now over, and, from about the time of the death of Amenhotep III, changes began throughout western Asia, which were to totally alter its political complexion, and eventually lead to the "collapse" of the Late Bronze Age states. The rise of the Hittite empire in Anatolia, and of Assyria, resulted in the breakdown of Egypt's ally in north Syria, the kingdom of Mitanni, whilst Hittite campaigns into Syria made it the most influential of the great powers in that region and brought it into conflict with Egypt. Closer to home, the Egyptians now faced a major threat on their western border.

Libya had always been one of the traditional enemies of Egypt, but little is known about the Libyans during the earlier 18th Dynasty as there are no records of campaigns against them comparable with those against the Nubians and Asiatics. Libyan ambassadors appear in scenes of the reign of Akhenaten, and Libyans served as members of that king's military escort. Although still depicted as one of Egypt's traditional enemies, it is with the reign of Horemheb that they first reappear in the record as actual enemies.[2]

In Egyptian terms, Libya stretched along the Mediterranean littoral, as far as Cyrenaica in the west. Egyptian settlement itself was confined to the Nile Valley and the Delta, extending probably as far as Raqote (later Alexandria). Little is known of the Oases during the New Kingdom, but it is probable that any Libyans settled there owed their allegiance to the pharaoh and his governors.

Recent excavations at Bates's Island in the bay of Mersa Matruh have yielded some significant results which suggest that this island was a centre for trade between the Libyans and the Cretans or Cypriots.[3] Minoan and Cypriot pottery found there date the Bates's Island site to the late 18th Dynasty. The Libyan settlement was on the mainland where the town of Mersa Matruh now stands, but no Egyptian objects have been found there. The excavators suggest that the island served as a place to collect fresh food and water on the route running from Eastern Crete to the Nile Delta, then on to Palestine and back to Cyprus. It is also probable that these Cretans or Cypriots were casting bronze weapons on the island, which were then exchanged with the Libyans on the mainland. In later scenes of battles between Libyans and Egyptians (such as those at Medinet Habu) the Libyans are shown using weapons of Asiatic types. Bates's Island may have been only one of a number of points of contact with western Asia, since the booty captured by the Egyptians from the Libyans suggests a high level of material culture and extensive trade contacts. Objects of gold and silver, bronze swords, and chariots are amongst the items captured by the Egyptians, which must have been of foreign, probably western Asiatic, origin. Such trade contacts also suggest that there were political contacts. Both of these could have been fostered through the Egyptian court. There were representatives of many foreign powers constantly at the court, and this must have led to the expansion of contacts amongst themselves as well as with Egypt. As events were soon to show, it also led to intrigues amongst Egypt's neighbouring rulers.

The Libyans with whom Ramesses II and his successors came into conflict were divided into a number of groups, the most important being the Libu, the Meshwesh (a name later abbreviated to "Ma") and the Seped. They were herders of cattle, sheep and goats, but not purely nomadic. References to the "towns" of the Meshwesh and to the town of the Chief of the Libu indicate that they also possessed permanent settlements.[4]

Sety I and Ramesses II marched their armies into western Asia to secure Egypt's sphere of influence, but they were also forced to take them westward, against Libya. Reliefs depicting Sety I's campaign against the chiefs of Tjehenu (Libya) were carved alongside others showing the king's major Asiatic victories, an indicator of the importance that Sety accorded them.

The captive Libyan chief, Mesher, being brought to Ramesses III. From a scene in the temple at Medinet Habu. (Fig. 43)

In the early years of his reign, Ramesses II focused his attention on Asia and the Hittite threat. The stalemate of the battle of Kadesh, followed by a palace coup in Hatti itself, led to the peace treaty of year 21. Although the Hittite front was now secured, Ramesses II faced danger on both his Nubian and Libyan borders.

A series of forts was built along the Delta margin from Memphis to the south of Raqote (Alexandria), and then along the coast as far as Mersa Matruh, a distance of 139 miles (225 km). These forts seem to have been situated every 50 miles (31 km), although only those at Alamein and Zawiyet Umm el-Rakham, to the west of Mersa Matruh, have so far been identified.[5] It was probably due to this westward thrust that the Bates's Island site was abandoned. Such evidence as there is from these forts is from the reign of Ramesses II, there is nothing later. They were either neglected, or, as seems more likely, the Egyptians were unable to resist the Libyan drive eastwards.

The Libyans posed a threat not only on the Mediterranean coast but much farther south. In Ramesses II's 44th year, the Viceroy of Kush, Setau, led a small contingent to one of the Nubian oases - probably Dunqul or Kurkur - and captured Libyans. These people were then put to work on the construction of the temple of Wadi es-Sebua. To have reached the Nubian oases, this group of Libyans must have moved southward through the Oases of Bahariyah, Dakhla and Kharga. Less than thirty years later, in the

5th year of Ramesses II's son and successor Merneptah, the Libyans had again "reached the hills of (Bahariyah) Oasis". By these Oasis routes they established contacts with the Kushite princes (perhaps already fostered at the Egyptian court). Together, the Libyans and Kushites planned a joint attack on Egypt.

The offensive is reminiscent of the joint attack proposed by the ruler of the Hyksos to the Kushites some 350 years before. Communication between the two allies was again by the desert routes, but, as on the earlier occasion, was intercepted by the Egyptians. It seems that the intention was to time a Libyan invasion of the Delta to coincide with a rebellion in Nubia, but the attack was not well co-ordinated, and the Egyptians, well warned, were able to react swiftly.

The invasion of the Delta was dominated by the Libu and was on a massive scale. Merneptah's victory inscription claims that over 9,300 Libyans and their allies were killed, and there may have been over 16,000 Libyans involved in this operation.[6] The Libyans were no mere bands of marauding nomads, but a large and highly organised force. Merneptah records that they had been forced towards Egypt's borders by famine. They were assisted by other groups, the Sherden, the Sheklesh and the Ekwesh, the Terresh and the Lukki. These people are usually grouped together under the term "Sea Peoples", and have been blamed for the destructions associated with the end of the Late Bronze Age empires. In this particular instance, it seems most likely that the named groups were mercenary soldiers.

Although the Libyans and their allies were defeated and apparently driven back, Egypt was not free for long.

The two decades between Merneptah's death and the accession of Ramesses III saw dynastic problems in Egypt, and have often been portrayed as a period of "decline". The death of the young king Siptah was followed by the rule of queen Tawosret, who had acted as regent. During these brief reigns, the most influential courtier was the Chancellor Bay who was of Syrian origin. Earlier Egyptologists regarded this combination of factors - a child pharaoh, a ruling woman and a foreign high official – as the inevitable prelude to catastrophe![7]

Increased numbers of Libyans moved into Egypt during the later 19th Dynasty and throughout the 20th. The western Delta was particularly vulnerable, since it was not as densely settled as the east, large tracts being given over to cattle grazing. Once established in this part of Egypt, the Libyans seem to have conducted raids on other towns, notably Per-Bastet (*Bubastis*) in the eastern Delta and even Memphis itself. The Egyptian administration seems to have tried to accommodate large numbers of Libyans to pre-empt problems. Ramesses II settled many of the Libyans he had captured in military camps in the Delta, and a similar policy was adopted by Ramesses III. They may have been settled around Per-Bastet which was later to become one of the major Libyan strongholds. This policy of incorporation soon saw Libyan commanders achieving high positions. Libyans also found their way into the palace staff and doubtless into the civil bureaucracy.

Egyptologists often refer to Ramesses III as the "last great pharaoh", which tells us more about their attitude to the last 1,000 years of pharaonic history than it does about the reign itself.[8] Ramesses III certainly did emulate Ramesses II – but in no superficial way. Archaeology is now showing that Ramesses III did, in fact, manage to renew Egyptian control over parts of western Asia, and that this control continued for some decades more after his death. Despite these successes, the world was in transition, and the great empires of the Late Bronze Age were soon to be fragmented.

Ramesses III had to face two major waves of Libyan invasion. The first, in his 5th year, was from a coalition of Libu, Seped and Meshwesh. The king claimed to have killed some 28,000. Later, in year 11, he forestalled a Meshwesh invasion, killing 2,175 and capturing a further 2,052. This could indicate a tribe size approaching 17,000.[9] The Libyans were again forced back from the borders of the Delta, but they may now have turned south and moved toward the Oases of Bahariyah, Dakhla and Kharga. They may even have penetrated the Oases of Nubia.

Apart from these major waves, there was a constant movement of smaller groups into the Nile valley. Ramesses III built walls around some

Shardana and Peleset mercenaries fighting with Libyans, from the scenes of the Libyan wars of Ramesses III in the temple at Medinet Habu. (Fig. 44)

of the major temples of Upper Egypt to keep the Libyans out. Abdju (Abydos), Khemenu (Hermopolis), Tjeni (Thinis) and Sauty (Asyut), all towns close to the end of the desert roads from Kharga, were defended in this way. The Theban region was also seriously affected. The earliest evidence is from year 28 of Ramesses III, but there was an increasing frequency of Libyan incursions in the succeeding reigns, particularly those of Ramesses, IX, X and XI.

The rule of the later Ramessides has often been characterised as a period of decline, the kings nothing more than a succession of elderly and ineffectual nonentities, their country afflicted by invasion, rising prices and a corrupt administration.[10] There is undoubtedly some evidence to support this view, but the picture has been overdrawn. By chance, this period is rich in administrative documents which record maladministration and also the trials of the members of the court involved in the, perhaps successful, attempt on the life of Ramesses III, and the trials of the tomb robbers. These documents relate to Thebes and Upper Egypt, and, although they reveal serious problems in the Southern City, should not be used to create a generalised picture of decadence. If anything, these archives highlight the lack of comparable documents from other periods.

Rather than simply fading away, Egypt under the later Ramessides seems to have suffered a number of violent crises. The first of these catastrophes was the loss of the empire in western Asia. This probably occurred during the reign of Ramesses VI.[11] There are signs of violent destruction in the Egyptian garrison and administrative towns of Aphek, Tell Mor and Beth Shean in Palestine. In Egypt, Ramesses VI may have led some sort of military expedition against the Libyans, perhaps from Thebes.

An ink sketch on an ostracon showing a late 20th Dynasty pharaoh, probably Ramesses VI. (Fig. 45)

Apart from a campaign of Ramesses III in Nubia, of which there is scant detail (some scholars even doubt its ocurrence), there is little record of crisis. The tomb of the Viceroy's deputy, Pennut, at Aniba gave details of the donations of land made by the official to a statue cult of the reigning pharaoh, Ramesses VI.[12] Descended from a long line of officials, Pennut was one of the most influential men in Nubia, and his donation was rewarded by the king. It was not entirely disinterested, since land donated in this way was inalienable and received tax benefits. The revenues would accrue to Pennut's descendants as priests of the cult. This endowment in itself suggests that Lower Nubia was not suffering grave crisis. That crisis, when it came, was swift.

The most detailed evidence from the late 20th dynasty comes from the Theban region, particularly from the archives relating to the workers involved in constructing the royal tombs.[13] These men lived in a village – known today as Deir el-Medina – on the west bank of the Nile, in the low hills behind the temple of Ramesses III (Medinet Habu). The village had been founded in the early 18th Dynasty and had been the home of the workmen's families over many generations. In the late 20th Dynasty, the workmen received their rations from the temple of Medinet Habu, and the village journal records how often these rations were late, forcing the workers to go on strike. Work on the royal tombs was frequently interrupted, due to non-payment of rations, and also to the presence of Libyans in the region. Throughout the reign of Ramesses XI, numbers of

The temple of Ramesses III, Medinet Habu, at Thebes. (Fig. 46)

workmen were conscripted to serve in the army, or abandoned their posts to avoid conscription.

Sometime during the reign of Ramesses XI, the villagers removed from their village to the precinct of the temple of Ramesses III, where a new village was built within the massive fortified walls. At the western end, behind the temple, the house of the village scribe, Butehamun, has been excavated. In this area a large archive of letters was discovered, which gives tantalising details of the events in the city during the closing years of the reign of Ramesses XI. The letters were written by, and to, the chief scribes Butehamun and his father Dhutmose, also called Tjaroy.

The beginning of serious trouble at Thebes was the incident known as the "suppression of the High Priest".[14] The chronology and detail of events are obscure, but it seems that the High Priest of Amun, a man

The house of the necropolis scribe, Butehamun, within the precinct of Medinet Habu. (Fig. 47)

named Amenhotep, was ousted by a rival, and spent eight months petitioning Amun and the pharaoh for redress. Amenhotep had been in office since the reign of Ramesses IX and came from a distinguished Theban family; his father had also been High Priest. Who his rival was is unknown. This event cannot be dated precisely, but it is generally thought to have occurred during years 8 and 9 of Ramesses XI. In year 8 there was a reduction in the number of workers employed on the royal tomb, and it is possible that they were conscripted by the rival High Priest to oppose the Viceroy of Kush, Panehesy, who now appeared in Thebes with an army.

Panehesy's appearance in Upper Egypt at the head of an army has been interpreted by Egyptologists in several ways. It was once thought that he was responsible for removing Amenhotep from office, but the evidence seems to support the opposite view, that Panehesy was, at least initially, acting as the king's agent in restoring the High Priest, and attempting to bring order to an anarchical Thebes. Papyri recording the trials of people involved in robbing the royal tombs refer back to this time. There was considerable disturbance in western Thebes; the temples were broken into and looters carried off the precious metal which covered doors and statues.

Medinet Habu was captured by the Nubian troops of Panehesy in the sixth month of the suppression of the High Priest Amenhotep, and the Viceroy was severe in his attempts to restore order. Summary executions were carried out, and some local people, sheltering in Medinet Habu, were taken into slavery. Others, such as a priest of the temple, named Peison, fled when their superiors were dismissed. Panehesy employed the village scribe, Dhutmose-Tjaroy, to set up an investigation into the robberies. It was found that more than 80 pounds of gold and silver had been stripped from the doorways of the temple of Ramesses II (the Ramesseum), and, in Medinet Habu, the palace had been looted and some of the temple furnishings taken. Also from Medinet Habu, 540 pounds of copper had been stripped from the palace and temple doors – but this may have been done by the Nubian soldiers themselves in order to tip their spears and arrows.

Panehesy remained in Thebes until year 12 of Ramesses XI, and he was probably still there in year 17. There were food shortages in the city, one year being referred to retrospectively as the "year of the Hyenas", but Panehesy seems to have tried to alleviate deprivation, and the scribe Dhutmose was sent to Esna, a little way to the south, in order to collect corn.

The progress of events between years 12 and 17 is undocumented, but something of significance was certainly happening in the north where Ramesses XI resided at Memphis or Per-Ramesses.

Towards the end of Panehesy's time in Egypt, he conducted a campaign into the north and attacked the city of Hardai in Middle Egypt (its location is uncertain, but lay somewhere north of el-Minya) and seems to have reached the Delta. Whilst Panehesy was in the north, there was a breakdown in order amongst the Nubian militia left in Thebes. There were robberies in the Valley of the Kings, and the type of destruction suggests that it was the work of people who were not professional tomb robbers. The sarcophagus of Ramesses VI – a massive block of granite – was destroyed, and some of the royal mummies were damaged in the attempts to remove jewellery.

Was it Ramesses XI who now wanted to remove Panehesy from office? Or did Panehesy remain loyal to the pharaoh in the face of the ambitions of the general who now appeared in Thebes to force him back to Nubia?

Ramesses XI himself probably went to Thebes in year 19, perhaps to see the destruction wrought by Panehesy's force, and at the same time to institute a new era of order. Monuments were now dated as if the king had begun his reign again, from year 1. The era was termed *wehem mesut* "the Repeating of Births" (Renaissance) and its first year was equivalent to Ramesses XI's year 19.[15]

The Renaissance saw Egypt apparently divided between two powerful officials, one of whom was the Generalissimo Herihor, ruler of the whole of the Nile valley from el-Hiba to Aswan. In addition to his military command, Herihor was appointed to, or assumed, the offices of High Priest of Amun at Thebes and Viceroy of Nubia.[16] This was the first time that these three key offices had been held by one man. His northern counterpart was Nesubanebdjed (usually referred to in literature by the Greek form of his name, "Smendes").[17] He controlled the Delta, Memphis and the Nile valley as far south as el-Hiba, near the entrance to the Faiyum.

Herihor's ambition did not stop with three major offices; within the precinct of Amun, and on his funerary objects, he assumed the royal style, placing the title "High Priest of Amun" within a cartouche, as his prenomen. It must be emphasised that Herihor was "king" *only* within the Karnak precinct; and, similarly, his position as Viceroy can never have

Herihor, as High Priest of Amun, offers flowers to Amun. His name and title are written within cartouches and are preceded with the titles Lord of the Two Lands and Lord of Appearances. (Fig. 48)

been more than titular, since Panehesy still controlled Nubia. It is impossible to be certain of the allegiances of the different parties involved. Some suspect that it might have been Panehesy and his Nubian army who were the loyalists, and this is certainly the impression given by some of the Dhutmose and Butehamun correspondence. Herihor was not alone in arrogating royal style; Nesubanebdjed also did, but, it has always been assumed by Egyptologists, only *after* the death of Ramesses XI.

Who were these two great officials? Neither of them is, so far, documented earlier than the Renaissance era, but they must have been amongst the most powerful of the nobility. Of Nesubanebdjed ("Smendes") little can be said, even after his assumption of the kingship, but he does appear in one well-known document of the period, the *Report of Wenamun*.[18] The events recorded in this papyrus begin in year 5 of the Renaissance when Wenamun, an official of Karnak temple, was sent at the command of Herihor to bring timber from Byblos for the building of a new sacred barque for Amun. In the *Report* Wenamun sails from Thebes to the Delta city of Djanet (Tanis) "where Nesubanebdjed and Tentamun are". It is to them, and not to Ramesses XI (who is not mentioned), that he presents his credentials, and it is they who commission a ship for his voyage to Syria. Tentamun is given equal prominence with Nesubanebdjed, which has led to speculation that she was a royal heiress, perhaps the daughter of Ramesses XI.

Of Herihor there is much more evidence, from the Karnak temples and from the burials of his family. At Karnak, Herihor completed the decoration of the temple of Khonsu, initially in his role of High Priest of Amun, but later assuming the style and titles of a king. In the first court of this temple, a scene depicts Herihor and his wife Nodjmet, with their family.[19] The scene is clearly modelled on the earlier processions of the sons and daughters of Ramesses II and Ramesses III, at the Ramesseum and Medinet Habu. These kings had many children, but there is no evidence that Herihor had more than one wife, and it seems unlikely that the seventeen "sons" and nineteen "daughters" are all children of his. It is more likely that this scene shows the wider ramifications of this new quasi-royal family. Herihor was probably a mature man at the time of his appointments, and the relatives probably include his sons-in-law and grandchildren. Herihor and Nodjmet, are familiar Egyptian names, as many other names of the family are, and there is no reason to doubt that the family was Egyptian. Strikingly, however, some of the "sons" in the Karnak procession have Libyan names: Masaharta, Masaqaharta, Mawasun, Madanen and Osorkon.[20] Whatever the family connections, the relief shows that Libyans were now related to the most influential people in Egypt.

The pylon of the temple of Khonsu at Karnak, with the bases of Taharqo's columned porch. (Fig. 49)

With the appearance of Herihor in Thebes, there are signs of antipathy towards Panehesy. Texts of the period write his name with a sign meaning "bad", but it may not have been until some years later that conflict between Thebes and Nubia actually manifested itself in war, since, as late as year 4 or 5 of the Renaissance, the tribute of Kush was still being paid.

It is with the Renaissance era that the letters of Dhutmose and Butehamun become particularly valuable. Having worked for Panehesy during his rule in Thebes, the father and son soon became adherents of Herihor and his family. In year 6 of the Renaissance, we find Dhutmose travelling north on the business of Herihor, at least as far as el-Hiba, and he later accompanied Paiankh to Nubia.

In year 2 of the Renaissance, Dhutmose wrote to the scribe Hori telling him to send the workmen back to the west bank from the city on the east bank. He was evidently one of the few people still resident in Medinet Habu. In another letter, Dhutmose responds to a question, saying that he does not know of any arrival of Meshwesh Libyans yet, but it is unclear whether he is referring to troops, or to nomadic groups. In later letters, of year 10, Dhutmose is asked why he has prevented bread-rations being given to the Meshwesh and is ordered to recommence them.

Herihor died in year 6 or 7 of the Renaissance. His successor as Viceroy of Nubia and High Priest of Amun, General and Army Leader, was Paiankh. Paiankh's relationship with Herihor is uncertain. He was formerly thought to have been a son, but was probably a son-in-law, married to Hrere, the daughter of Herihor and Nodjmet.[21]

Letters from the Butehamun archive show that the close relationship between Dhutmose and Butehamun and the ruling family in Thebes continued after Herihor's death. From year 7 of the Renaissance, there are letters from the 2nd Prophet of Amun, Heqanefer (a son of Paiankh), to Dhutmose. The trust placed in Dhutmose is shown by a group of letters, dated to year 10, which all relate to a serious and confidential matter.[22] One letter, from Paiankh himself, who was campaigning against Panehesy in Nubia, is addressed to Dhutmose:

> I've taken note of all of the matters you wrote to me about. As for mention you made of this matter of these two policemen saying, "They spoke all these charges", join up with Nodjmet and Payshuben as well, and they shall send word and have these two policemen brought to my house and get to the bottom of their charges in short order. If they determine that they are true, you shall put them in two baskets and they shall be thrown into the water at night – but don't let anybody in the land find out!

Paiankh's letters to his agent, named Payshuben, and to Nodjmet, the widow of Herihor, also survive, and are more explicit; they are not required to find out if the charges are true, but to:

> get to the bottom of their charges in short order and kill them, and throw them into the water by night.

In response to an unknown question or comment of Dhutmose, Paiankh is scathing:

> As for Pharaoh, life! prosperity! health!, how will he ever reach this land (Nubia)? And as for Pharaoh, life! prosperity! health!, whose superior is he after all?

Further letters suggest that the policemen had been dealt with as Paiankh wished. The tone of these letters indicates a certain contempt on the part of Paiankh for the Pharaoh.

It is with Paiankh's rise to power that hostility towards Panehesy increases. In the first year of the Renaissance, the oaths sworn by witnesses at the tomb robbery trials include the threat that they may be sent to Kush or to join the battalion of Kush. This would hardly have been the case if Kush was in open rebellion. The *inu*-tribute of Kush was still being sent to Egypt in year 4 of the Renaissance, but, in year 10, Paiankh led his army against the Viceroy.

A number of the letters written by Dhutmose from Nubia is dated to year 10 of the Renaissance, and refer to Panehesy by name, apparently as the opponent of Paiankh. Dhutmose refers to Nubia as a "hell-hole", but he had written the same of his journey through Middle Egypt! There are no details of the military activities involved in this attempt to defeat Panehesy, and it remains uncertain exactly how far into Nubia Paiankh's army penetrated. Panehesy himself held Miam where his tomb was discovered. The letters of Dhutmose invoke Horus of Baki and Horus of Miam, and we might presume that Paiankh had established his base at Baki (Kubban). Panehesy's names and titles suffered no desecration at Miam, so it seems unlikely that the town was captured.

The return of "the General", presumably Paiankh, to Thebes is recorded in a rock inscription of Butehamun on the western mountains.[23] It is dated to the 3rd month of *Shomu*, day 23, and, although there is no year given, probably belongs to the 29th year of Ramesses XI. The three leading protagonists, Paiankh, Panehesy and the pharaoh himself, are never heard of again.

And so Nubia vanishes into a "perplexing historical void".[24]

VIII Libya in Egypt

Exactly how the palace-centred civilizations of the Late Bronze Age came to an end is still a matter of great controversy. Following the collapse of the great empires, many areas of the Near East went through a Dark Age. The new world of the Iron Age was dominated by different powers.

Archaeologists have argued about the problems within this period – the causes of the collapse of Late Bronze Age society, and the specific problems of particular sites. Recently, the issue has been further confused by a debate over the length of the period involved.[1] The matter is extremely complex and involves problems in the archaeology of the whole of the Near East from the end of the Late Bronze Age to the Early Iron Age, a period generally believed to span from the 11th to 8th centuries BC. This exactly conforms to the Third Intermediate Period in Egypt. While many Egyptologists see no reason to reduce the length of time that has been allotted to this period, some think that it should be shortened, the most radical wishing to take over two hundred years out, whilst a number of archaeologists thinks that the period has been overlengthened by at least one hundred years. Effectively this would mean that the death of Ramesses XI occurred not in 1069 BC, but in 969 or even as late as 820 BC.[2]

For most Egyptologists, the minutiae of chronology does not matter. This point of view can, to an extent, be justified. For periods such as the New Kingdom, when the relative sequence of kings is certain, and their reign-lengths fairly certainly known, the absolute dates BC do not, perhaps, matter. For that reason, there are "High", "Middle" and "Low" chronologies based upon 1304, 1290 and 1279 for the accession of Ramesses II. Nor does the chronology particularly matter if Egypt is regarded in isolation, as it usually is. However, for the history of western Asia, the Aegean and Nubia, an exact chronology is of fundamental importance. In Nubia, the chronological framework dictates how we interpret the origins and rise of the Kushite state which eventually conquered Egypt.

This is not the place to argue detailed new interpretations of the Third Intermediate Period in Egypt – and the problem as it affects Nubia will be discussed later. What is significant here is the basic nature of late Libyan Egypt, its internal problems and its contacts with Western Asia in the later 8th century BC at the time of the Kushite invasions.

With the death of Ramesses XI, the relatives of Herihor were able to take legitimate control of the whole of Egypt, as kings in Djanet (Greek: *Tanis*; Biblical: *Zoan*), and as High Priests of Amun at Thebes. The accession of Nesubanebdjed (*Smendes*) as pharaoh marks the beginning of the 21st Dynasty. Unfortunately, there is still much that is obscure about the history of the 21st to 24th Dynasties.

The 21st Dynasty ruled from Djanet and Memphis, with relatives as High Priests of Amun at Thebes. An inscription of Nesubanebdjed states that the king was in his palace in Memphis when news was brought of a high Nile which flooded Luxor temple. There is, however, little evidence of building work by the Libyan pharaohs in Memphis and their attention seems to have been concentrated on Djanet.

Djanet, on the shores of Lake Manzala, now replaced Per-Ramesses as the major royal residence city in the Delta. The great temples of the older city were dismantled and their blocks and statues removed to build and adorn the newer town, its one-time port. Most of the vast mud-brick mound which hides the remains of Djanet remains unexcavated, but the vestiges of the main temple complex have been exposed. Here the Tanite kings, notably Psibkhanno ("Psusennes"), constructed a massive temple dedicated to Amun, its entrance guarded by colossi of Ramesses II brought from Per-Ramesses, its avenues flanked by at least 15 obelisks.

The tombs of some of these Libyan kings were discovered in 1940 in the outer part of the great temple of Amun in Djanet. Royal burials in this period were subterranean vaults with a chapel above. At Djanet – and probably also at Sau (*Sais*), later – the tombs stood in a precinct off the first court of the main temple. The Tanite tombs were built from massive re-used blocks from Per-Ramesses.

In Thebes, the mummies of many of the members of the royal family were discovered in a secret burial place at Deir el-Bahari. There, High Priests of Amun had collected the bodies of the 18th to 20th Dynasty kings and other members of their families from their plundered tombs, had had them rewrapped and placed in coffins, sometimes their own, sometimes borrowed. They were buried in two main groups, one in the tomb of Amenhotep II in the Valley of the Kings, the other in the Great Cache at Deir el-Bahari.

The history of the 21st Dynasty otherwise remains obscure: the names of pharaohs are known, but virtually nothing about them. There are very few recorded historical events in this period. It is an abrupt shift from the richness of the latter years of the 20th Dynasty. In part, of course, this is due to the importance of Djanet and the Delta. The excavations there may ultimately yield more information, but the nature of the region makes it unlikely that it will preserve the wealth of documents that the Theban desert has.

The family of Herihor had certainly intermarried with Libyans before the end of the reign of Ramesses XI, and the Libyans rose to the supreme position with a military leader named Sheshonq. Later tradition associates Sheshonq with the eastern Delta city of Per-Bastet (*Bubastis*, modern Zagazig) where Libyans had been settled from the time of Ramesses II.

Sheshonq gradually extended his rule over the whole of Egypt, although an inscription at Karnak still refers to him by his traditional Libyan title, the Great Chief of the Ma, in his 2nd year. He eventually

Relief on the Bubastite Gate at Karnak, showing Sheshonq I suckled by the goddess Hathor. He is accompanied by his son, the High Priest of Amun, Iuwelot. (Fig. 50)

installed one of his sons as High Priest of Amun at Thebes, and contracted marriages with the noble families of the southern city. By the end of his reign, which lasted at least 21 years, he was acknowledged as pharaoh throughout Egypt and the oases of Kharga and Dakhla.

Sheshonq I began the construction of a great court in front of the temple of Amun at Karnak, but, although it was completed, its decoration remained unfinished. Sheshonq reasserted Egyptian influence in Western

Asia, campaigning in Palestine. This was celebrated by a large relief at Karnak, which shows him smiting his enemies before Amun who holds rows of figures representing the cities which Sheshonq claimed to have subdued. Ever since Champollion deciphered Egyptian royal names, Sheshonq has been identified by Egyptologists and biblical scholars with "Shishak, king of Egypt" who, according to the biblical Book of Kings (I.14:35-36), sacked Jerusalem in the reign of Rehoboam (c.925 BC).[3]

The descendants of Sheshonq I are known to Egyptology as the 22nd Dynasty.[4] Their main seats were at Djanet, Per-Bastet and Memphis. These Libyan pharaohs appointed their sons to some of the chief benefices to act as their representatives in different parts of the country. This was eventually to cause political problems. At Thebes, the office of High Priest of Amun was usually held by the Crown Prince. At Memphis, the High Priesthood of Ptah became hereditary in one branch of the family. Also at Thebes, royal daughters were appointed as God's Wife of Amun, a religious function which was to become immensely important in the late Libyan and Kushite periods. The kings further secured their position by arranging marriages between their sons, daughters and grandchildren with the noble Egyptian families. Many major offices now became hereditary in those families, which meant that they acquired the estates and revenues attached to the offices. It is possible to view Egypt during this period as a form of feudal state, with a fairly small number of extremely wealthy and powerful families controlling the state institutions and tied by marriage to the royal house.

Egypt was divided into two main provinces, with the frontier at Teudjoi (El-Hiba), a strategic point on the river. This region, near to the entrance to the Faiyum, was to remain of key importance throughout the Libyan period. The ancient city of Nen-nesut (*Herakleopolis*) and, a little to its north, the fortress Per-Sekhemkheperre, built by Osorkon I, were both governed by royal princes. The first problems began barely four decades after Sheshonq I had assumed the kingship. Osorkon II ascended the throne of his ancestors, but the scions of the royal house held offices throughout Egypt, and some clearly felt they had as good a claim on the kingship as the pharaoh himself. A statue of the king, of a type associated with the coronation, carries a text with a prayer which presages the crisis.[5]

> [You will fashion my issue, the seed which comes forth from my limbs [to be] great [rulers] of Egypt, Princes, High Priests of Amen-Re-the-King-of-the-Gods, Great Chiefs of the Ma, [Great Chiefs] of the Foreign Peoples, Prophets of Herishef "King of the Two Lands", after I have commanded it ... You will cause them [to walk] [upon my] paths. You will confirm my children in the [positions] [which] I have given them (so that) brother is not resentful of brother.

The king's prayer was not to be granted. In Thebes the pontificate was held by a cousin of Osorkon's, named Harsiese. It is unclear whether Harsiese was appointed by Osorkon II or had seized the office. There are no indications of hostility towards the pharaoh, but the High Priest had his own name written inside a cartouche, and eventually assumed a full titulary. Harsiese, directly descended from the Libyan kings, the older Tanite royal house and the High Priests of Amun (certainly through his grandmother, and perhaps also through his mother), may well have considered himself as possessing better claims to the throne than his cousin, Osorkon II. The seeds of this crisis had been sown when Sheshonq I arranged the marriage of his son, later Osorkon I, to the heiress of the 21st Dynasty. Maatkare was the daughter of king Psibkhanno (Psusennes), and represented the line of Theban High Priests of Amun as well as Tanite pharaohs. She may also have had Ramesside blood. Sheshonq's desire to ensure the legitimacy of his descendants was to create problems in Thebes. Osorkon I appointed his son by Maatkare, the Crown Prince Sheshonq, usually designated "Sheshonq II", to the southern benefice. Sheshonq was proud of his maternal ancestry and proclaimed it on statues of a Nile-god. His own wife, Nesitanebtasheru, might be identical with the like-named daughter of the High Priest Pinudjem II (himself a direct descendant of the High Priest Paiankh).[6] Sheshonq II predeceased his father and Osorkon I was succeeded by one of his younger sons by a different wife, Takeloth I, who probably reigned only very briefly, before the accession of his own son, Osorkon II. The High Priest Sheshonq had left several sons, one of whom was Harsiese.

We do not know how independent Harsiese was. Nor what Osorkon's response to the situation was. But even if the situation remained amicable, it was to have repercussions in the future. Harsiese died sometime during Osorkon's reign and was buried at Medinet Habu in a tomb close to the small Thutmoside temple of Amun of Djeme. His children played a part in later events.

By year 16, Osorkon II's apparently last-surviving son, Nimlot, combined the office of High Priest of Amun with that of Governor of Per-Sekhemkheperre.

The end of Osorkon's reign seems to have been overshadowed by the impending crisis, although he celebrated a jubilee festival in his 22nd year, building a magnificent granite hall at Per-Bastet for the occasion.[7] Most of Osorkon's sons seem to have predeceased him. The Crown Prince had been named Sheshonq, and appointed as High Priest of Ptah at Memphis: he was already dead. A young prince, Harnakht, had been interred in the king's own tomb at Tanis, and, before the reign had closed, Nimlot, the High Priest of Amun, had been succeeded in that office by his own son, Takeloth.

The crisis came swiftly. It was probably the son of Nimlot, the High Priest of Amun, Takeloth, who now ascended the throne as Takeloth II,[8] but shortly afterwards new kings were to appear, Sheshonq III in Tanis and Pedubast in Thebes. It is uncertain what claims, if any, these new kings had.[9]

Before his 11th year, Takeloth had appointed his own son, the Crown Prince Osorkon, as High Priest of Amun at Thebes, Governor of the South (Upper Egypt), General and Army Leader. But the Prince resided at his northern fortress, Per-Sekhemkheperre, as yet unacknowledged in the south. Osorkon has left a record of his troubled pontificate, carved high on the Bubastite Portal in the temple of Karnak.[10]

In year 11 of Takeloth II, the Crown Prince sailed south, for Thebes. He defeated some opposition *en route* and entered Khemenu (*Hermopolis*), which was cleansed, indicating some violent conflict. Osorkon says that his arrival in Thebes was greeted with joy, but this must have been muted. Osorkon proceeded to examine charges of irregularities in the temple administration and cult. The guilty were arraigned, executed and burnt.[11] He reinstated sons in the places of their fathers. The implication is of some chaos in the southern city. In year 12 he sailed for Thebes three times, his ships laden with offerings to the deity. All seemed well.

Then, in year 15, the cataclysm came, "a great convulsion broke out in this land". The text is unfortunately fragmentary, but there are

Takeloth III, from a scene in the chapel of Osiris Heqa-Djet at Karnak. (Fig. 51)

references to "the children of rebellion" who "stirred up strife in both South and North". Osorkon "did not weary of fighting in their midst even as Horus following his father; years passed in which one preyed another unimpeded". Attempts at suppression failed, and eventually conciliation seems to have been the only path. Osorkon sailed for Thebes with rich offerings, going as far as to reproach Amun for the long conflict.

But soon the land fell back into rebellion. Osorkon was "quite alone, such that there was not one friend with him".

For some reason unknown to us, on the death of his father, Takeloth II, after 25 years of reign, the Crown Prince Osorkon did not ascend the throne. He now dated his inscriptions by the years of Sheshonq III.

The Karnak inscription lists the High Priest's benefactions from years 22 to 28 of Sheshonq III. Also in year 28, in Memphis, an Apis bull was buried. The funeral rites were presided over by a scion of the royal house, the Chief of the Ma and High Priest of Ptah, Peftjauawybast. Rather intriguingly, Peftjauawybast's father who also held the titles, Chief of the Ma and High Priest of Ptah, seems to have been still alive. Indeed, Pediese is also depicted on the stela recording the death of the successor bull some 26 years later, although Peftjauawybast had by then been succeeded by a younger brother. Pediese was himself a great-grandson of Osorkon II.

The next decade of Sheshonq's reign is undocumented, and it is uncertain whether Thebes was still in rebellion. This seems likely, since the final appearance of the High Priest Osorkon was in year 39 of Sheshonq III when the Karnak inscription tells us that he was with his brother, the General of Nen-nesut and Army Leader, Bakenptah, in Thebes, celebrating the festival of Amun: "then they overthrew everyone who fought against them." The rebels were, finally, defeated, but now, in the moment of his glory, Osorkon vanishes.

It was assumed by an earlier generation of Egyptologists that the Crown Prince Osorkon now ascended the throne as Osorkon III, and this view is again being favoured.[12] It seems most likely that, shortly after the 39th year of his reign, Sheshonq III died, and Osorkon assumed the throne, to reign for a further 29 years. One of the monuments which supports the identification of the king as the former High Priest is a stela found in Middle Egypt, on which Osorkon enclosed the title High Priest of Amun within his cartouche.

At Thebes, Osorkon III followed tradition and installed his own son, another Takeloth, as High Priest of Amun, and his daughter, Shepenwepet, as God's Wife of Amun. A number of small monuments was erected by the new king and his High Priest. In his 23rd regnal year, the now elderly Osorkon appointed his son, the High Priest Takeloth, as his co-regent. Jointly, they dedicated a temple to Osiris-Ruler-of-Eternity

Relief depicting the God's Wife, Shepenwepet I, being suckled by the goddess Hathor, in the chapel of Osiris Heqa-Djet at Karnak. (Fig. 52)

(Heqa-Djet), near the Eastern Gate of the temple of Amun at Karnak. This small shrine stood within a courtyard close to the boundary walls of the great temple of Amun, at the north-eastern end of the enclosure. The two kings are both depicted there, as if crowned at the same time. Another coronation is also shown, that of the elder pharaoh's daughter, Shepenwepet, as God's Wife of Amun. Rather strikingly, the princess is shown suckled by a goddess in the same way as the pharaohs themselves, and she is crowned with two crowns at the same time. These images were to be influential in the representation of later Kushite royal women.

So, on the eve of the Kushite invasions, Egypt had been convulsed by civil war in the south. The exact detail and chronology of the events immediately preceding the Kushite appearance in Egypt is unclear, but by the time of Piye's campaign there were four pharaohs ruling in different parts of the country. In addition, there was a fifth power, the ruler of the city of Sau and the whole of the western Delta. The era of Kushite rule in Egypt began with two major conficts with the rulers of Sau, and it was the rulers of Sau who eventually emerged as the beneficiaries of the Kushite and Assyrian struggle.

IX   The Hand of Assur

Egypt's period of Libyan rule saw dramatic changes throughout the Near Eastern world. The collapse of the Hittite empire led to fragmentation and the emergence of many smaller kingdoms in north Syria and Anatolia. Further south, throughout Syria, Palestine and Transjordan, powerful new kingdoms emerged.[1]

With the appearance of these new powers, there were also changes in the trade routes. Whether these were a result of Egypt's "decline", or a contributory factor to it, remains a subject of academic dispute.

Until recently, archaeologists thought that it was the "waves" of the so-called "Sea Peoples" that had actually been instrumental in the destruction of cities and in destabilising the major powers of the Late Bronze Age. This is certainly wrong. The idea of the "Sea Peoples" as a massive population movement operating together is a myth which developed in academic literature in the 19th century, principally the historical works of Gaston Maspero.[2] There certainly were movements of population at this time, but these may have been caused by the crisis. It is also certain that some cities, such as Ugarit, were destroyed and never recovered their former importance; others retained, even increased, their power. The destructions extended throughout Anatolia, Cyprus and along the coast of Syria into southern Palestine; they did not reach Mesopotamia.

The crisis cannot be ignored: its repercussions were far-reaching. People were uprooted, states collapsed and new ones emerged. In this period of change, two groups of people rose to prominence, the Aramaeans and the Arabs.[3] Both were groups which had occupied the margins of the Syrian steppe. They now began to gain control of the north-south trade routes coming from the Red Sea coast of Arabia through the Jordan valley.

This route was first dominated by the united kingdom of Israel and Judah, in the reigns of David and Solomon. This was short-lived, and the sundering of their kingdom saw the increasing economic and political power of the Aramaean kingdom of Damascus.[4] Throughout the 9th and 8th centuries BC there were periods in which Damascus, Israel and Judah were all variously allied or at war.

While the inland states fought for control of the north-south traffic, the sea-borne trade remained in the hands of the Phoenician city-states of the coast. The thickly forested mountains of the Lebanon range left only a narrow strip between mountain and sea, so many of the Phoenician cities were built on islands or promontories. This made them more easily defensible: in Assyrian reliefs they are shown, surrounded by battlemented walls, rising from the sea, their small space tightly packed with houses. This location, between the mountains and the sea, allowed little opportunity for the cities to gain large hinterland territories and they had long relied on commerce for their wealth. Important as trading centres from the Early Bronze Age onwards, they now entered their most glorious period, dominating the sea-borne trade, and acting as suppliers to the inland kingdoms.

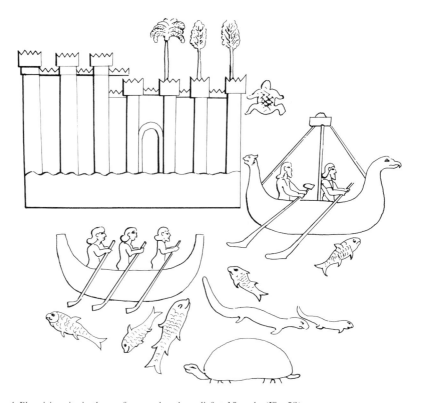

A Phoenician city in the sea from an Assyrian relief at Nineveh. (Fig. 53)

Timber from the Lebanon mountains remained one of the major exports of the cities, but their ships brought raw materials from east and north Africa, and increasingly farther afield. The cities came to specialise in the production of luxuries. Egypt continued to supply many of the raw materials and some manufactures, which were then transformed in the workshops. In Tyre, fine linen from Egypt was coloured with dye from the local *murex* (a type of mollusc). Generally called "Tyrian purple", it gave a range from rose pink to blue. Ivory furniture was made from imported tusks, the elaborately carved panels deriving many of their designs from Egyptian iconography. Papyrus was also imported from Egypt and became increasingly important as Aramaic, written in ink on paper, replaced Akkadian (written on clay tablets) as the international diplomatic language. Egyptian objects traded by the Phoenicians have been found all around the Mediterranean. In Spain, Egyptian alabaster vessels with the cartouches of Libyan pharaohs were used as cinerary urns. Egyptian faience vessels have been found in Sicily and in Etruscan graves in central Italy.

As ever, precious metals were prized, and the search for new supplies led to the expansion of Phoenician trade networks to the western Mediterranean. The Phoenicians exploited the silver mines of the Rio Tinto in Spain, and may have reached Cornwall in their search for tin. In the wake of these merchant ships, the Phoenician cities began to establish colonies. The most famous of these, Carthage (*qarthadast* "New Town"), was founded in the late-9th or 8th century BC.[5]

In Israel, the rise to power of the Omride dynasty saw the founding of a new capital, at Samaria.[6] Omri (885-874 BC) entered into alliance

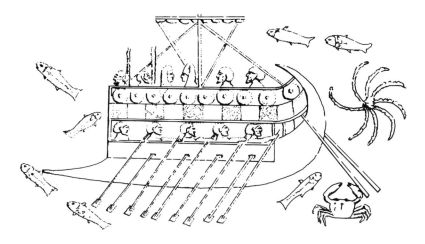

A Phoenician ship, from an Assyrian relief at Nineveh. (Fig. 54)

with the Phoenician city of Tyre, his son Ahab (874-853 BC) marrying Jezebel, daughter of Ittobaal of Tyre. There followed a period of royal patronage of the Phoenician cults in Israel. A little later, Israel also formed an alliance (again cemented by dynastic marriage) with Judah, and the two powers attempted to re-open the Red Sea trade with "Ophir" from the port of Ezion-geber. Tyrian ships must have been important in this. The

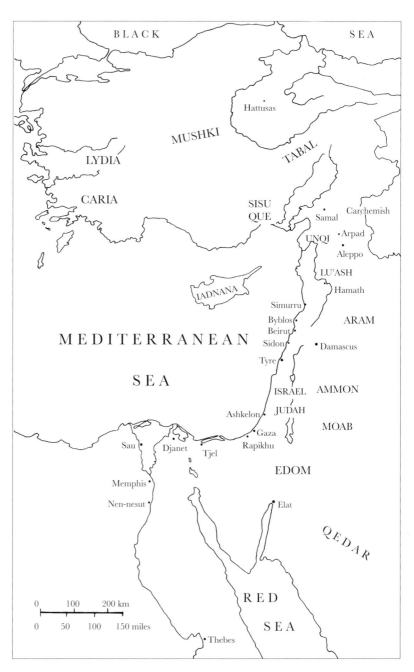

Assyrian Empire. (Fig. 55)

The Assyrian god Assur, wearing the characteristic horned and feathered crown. From a glazed tile. (Fig. 56)

location of "Ophir" has long been a focus of controversy, some scholars suggesting India or even further east. It is most likely to be the same region of east Africa as the Egyptian Punt, somewhere in northern Ethiopia.[7]

It is the Assyrian intervention in the West – Syria, Palestine, north Arabia and Egypt – which is of paramount importance in this narrative, but the ambitions of Assyria's emperors were continually checked by events on their other frontiers. The campaigns they were forced to make diverted them from the West and allowed intrigue and rebellion to develop there. Although Assyria was the ascendant power, she was surrounded by strong states and peoples which, particularly when they chose to form alliances, proved formidable opponents. The most significant of these powers lay immediately to the south, the kingdom of Babylon. Culturally, the two kingdoms had much in common, and the many ancient cities and shrines of the south were revered by the Assyrians. Although there were periods of peace between the two kingdoms, Babylon frequently allied itself with its own immediate neighbours against Assyria. These neighbours were the kingdom of Elam to the south-east, and the Sea Land, the southern marshes where the Tigris and Euphrates debouched into the Gulf. This region was the home of Chaldaean and Aramaean tribes. To the north of Assyria, the principal threat came from the mountain kingdom of Urartu, between Lake Van in the west, Lake Urmia and Lake Sevan (parts of modern Turkey, Armenia and Iran).[8]

There was a brief Assyrian intervention in the West when Tiglath-pileser I "washed his weapons in the Great Sea" (c.1100 BC). The king's campaign established an Assyrian sphere of influence in the region, perhaps at the expense of Egypt, but it was not followed up by further military action. It was around 900 BC that Assyria began to expand its power to become the dominant political force in the whole of western Asia.

Of all the ancient empires, the Late Assyrian has probably suffered the worst press. A highly specialised military machine, Assyria's policies of deportation and apparently ruthless impalation and flaying of rebels have led to its characterisation as a sinister and cruel regime. The world which the Assyrians conquered was that of the jewish Prophets, and their damnation of the Assyrian oppressor has rung down the ages.

Isaiah condemned Assyria as "the rod of tyrants that smote peoples in wrath with stroke unceasing" and her rulers as men "who shook the earth, who made realms tremble, who made the world like a waste and wrecked its towns, who never released prisoners to their homes".[9] It is an image which has dominated European perceptions of Assyria and is hard to eradicate.

The rise of Assyria began around 900 BC with the reigns of Adad-nerari II (911-891 BC) and Tukulti-ninurta II (890-884 BC).[10] Having consolidated rule over the Assyrian heartland and safeguarded the frontiers, political and marriage alliances were concluded with Assyria's powerful southern neighbour, Babylon. Assyria's westward expansion began with the accession of Assurnasirpal II (883-859 BC). Assurnasirpal was the first of the Late Assyrian emperors to "wash his weapons in the Great Sea" and receive the tribute of the Sea Coast. This included gold, silver, tin, copper, copper containers, linen, garments with multicoloured trimmings, large and small monkeys, ebony, boxwood and ivory.

Assurnasirpal moved his capital from the ancient city of Assur on the river Tigris north to Kalkhu (the biblical Calah, modern Tell Nimrud) at the junction of the Tigris and the Greater Zab. Fifteen years of building works transformed Kalkhu from a small provincial administrative capital into an imperial city. The palace was decorated with glazed brick and stone relief sculpture of great refinement and opulence. The entrances to the state

A view of the city of Assur as reconstructed by Walter Andrae. (Fig. 57)

rooms were flanked by massive winged bulls with human heads, to ward off evil from the royal person. The excavation of the remains of this and later palaces has recovered many pieces of the booty and tribute from the Syrian and Phoenician cities of the west. Amongst these were thousands of pieces from the solid ivory thrones of the defeated kings. Assurnasirpal II campaigned annually to maintain his frontiers and sphere of influence. This policy was continued by his son, Shalmaneser III (858-824 BC) who, soon after his accession, received the tribute of Sidon and Tyre.

The turning point came in 853, when Shalmaneser marched his armies westward into north Syria where he received the submission of Karkamish, Melid, Gurgum and Aleppo. Then the king turned south to bring Hamath under Assyrian suzerainty. This was the first Assyrian attempt to gain direct influence over the states of central Syria. The Assyrians captured three cities belonging to Irkhuleni, king of Hamath, before moving on to the royal city of Qarqar on the Orontes river. Qarqar was sacked and destroyed. The Assyrian forces then confronted the army of a coalition led by Hadad-idri, king of Damascus. Altogether, twelve kings joined to oppose Assyria. The massed armies of the coalition included 2,000 chariots and 10,000 foot soldiers sent by Ahab, king of Israel, and 1,000 camel-borne soldiers from an Arab ruler. From Damascus, the 10,000 foot soldiers were supported by 700 chariots and an equal number of cavalry. These years of Assyrian expansion were to see the increasing use of cavalry.[11] There was also a small contingent of 1,000 Egyptian soldiers. Shalmaneser's victory inscription claims that 14,000 soldiers were slain. Nevertheless, the coalition continued to oppose Shalamaneser in the following years, when the king returned to the west in 849, 848 and 845. On this fourth occasion, the Assyrian annals record that 12 kings of the "Hittites" and the Sea Coast joined Damascus.

For some time the coalition was powerful enough to prevent the Assyrian armies from pushing farther south, but, following the death of Hadad-idri, it broke up. With the accession of a new king in Damascus, Hazael, who was apparently an usurper, relations with Israel deteriorated rapidly.[12] Conflict ensued, and, in a coup, Jehu seized power in Israel. Both kings now pursued a nationalist policy, attempting to expand their own frontiers. Further north, Hamath made peace with Assyria, and, when Shalmaneser marched to the west in 841, Damascus stood alone. Hazael's army was defeated, and he retreated into his city. Shalmaneser besieged the city which did not capitulate. In revenge, the Assyrian king ordered that the orchards surrounding it be cut down. He then devastated cities in the Hauran before turning towards the coast. Here Jehu brought tribute, along with the kings of Tyre and Sidon. The events are recorded on a remarkable monument, the so-called Black Obelisk. Jehu is depicted grovelling before

Camel-borne Arab warriors from an Assyrian relief. (Fig. 58)

the Assyrian king. Amongst the other tributaries was "Musri" – Egypt, which sent camels "with two humps", a "river ox" (hippopotamus), a *sakea*-animal (rhinoceros), and two types of monkeys. An elephant is also shown, although it more closely resembles the Indian than the African type.[13] The power of Assyria was now acknowledged across the whole of the west.

Despite its success, the campaign was not followed up. Towards the end of Shalmaneser's reign, a revolt by his eldest son brought chaos to Assyria, and for half a century Assyrian expansion was halted. Despite these problems, the territories which had been acquired were retained, and Assyria was still acknowledged as the leading power by the neighbouring states of north Syria.

Assyria's problems allowed Damascus to become, albeit briefly, the dominant power in south Syria. Hazael began to expand his kingdom and now entered into alliance with Tyre. He conquered territory to the west of the Jordan, and pushed into Philistia where he captured Gath. The effect was to reduce the power of Israel so much that it became almost a vassal of Damascus. From this conflict, Damascus not only enlarged its territory, but must have gained control of the trade-routes. Hazael next fixed his attention on Judah, and the capture of the capital city, Jerusalem. Its king responded rapidly, gathering up the treasures of the temple and his palace and sending them to Hazael. Judah, too, became virtually a vassal. Damascus was pre-eminent in the west.

Damascus must now have dominated the north-south trade routes which eventually ran to the Phoenician coast, but her supremacy lasted for one generation only; Hazael's son, Bir-Hadad III, was forced to yield once again to the Assyrians.

Hamath in north Syria seems to have become a major pro-Assyrian power in the region. Its ruler, Irkhuleni (who had been defeated by Shalmaneser III at the battle of Qarqar), had been succeeded by a new king, Zakkur, possibly an usurper. Zakkur added the neighbouring territory of Lu'ash to Hamath, and, with the threat of an expanding power in central Syria, a new coalition was formed to oppose him. Headed by Bir-Hadad of Damascus, along with Atar-Shumki of Bit-Agusi (Arpad) and the kings of Que, Umq, Gurgum, Sam'al and Meliz – in total 16 or 17 kings – the coalition besieged Zakkur in Hazrak, the capital city of Lu'ash.

To deliver his vassal, Adad-nerari III (810-783 BC) led the Assyrian armies westwards. The king took the opportunity to march against Damascus which was once again besieged. The defeat of Damascus allowed Israel to recover some of its territories. Israel once again allied itself with the Phoenician states – either in opposition to Assyria or in support of her former enemy Damascus against Judah. The conflicts were probably connected with the control of the trade-routes. Judah too began to expand and regain control of the north-south trade. The Red Sea port of Ezion-geber was rebuilt, and the caravan routes protected with forts.

There is little evidence of direct political or economic contacts between Egypt and Assyria in these years, but Egyptian goods, raw materials and manufactures continued to pass eastwards through the levantine ports. Some of the ebony, ivory and exotic animals received by the Assyrians as tribute of the coastal cities surely came from Egypt. Fine-quality linen was a renowned Egyptian product, dyed and made into garments in cities such as Tyre. Another of the Egyptian exports which seems to have increased enormously at this time is papyrus. In later periods the manufacture of papyrus was a royal monopoly, and this was quite probably the case at this period. The Aramaic language, which was written in ink on paper, was replacing Akkadian, written with a stylus on clay tablets, as the main diplomatic and administrative language, hence the need for paper. Throughout the late Assyrian empire, the vast increase in trade and political contacts with the states of the west necessitated scribes with facility in foreign languages, and, as early as the reign of Adad-nerari III, there were Egyptian scribes at the Assyrian court in Kalkhu.[14]

Assyria's resurgence was due largely to the dynamic figure of Tiglath-pileser III who ascended the throne in 745 BC. Tiglath-pileser was the

A reconstruction of the citadel of Hamath. (Fig. 59)

victor of another revolt in Kalkhu (Nimrud).[15] Reigning for 18 years (745-727), Tiglath-pileser III campaigned in all but one year, including the years of his accession and his death. He totally reorganised the Assyrian army, making it a formidable military machine with mercenary foot soldiers and largely Assyrian chariotry and cavalry divisions. In their later conflict with the Kushite pharaohs in Egypt, it may have been the Assyrian advantage of iron weapons which was the deciding factor.

Tiglath-pileser brought order to Assyria in three major campaigns directed against the borders. He resettled the Aramaean tribes in a newly constructed city, Kar-Assur. This policy of moving "difficult" populations was to become a feature of Assyrian foreign policy in the years of the westward expansion. These transported peoples were settled in Assyria in an attempt to forestall future rebellion, and to work on land and building projects. Texts from the reign claim that as many as 155,000 Chaldaeans were resettled.

The campaigns of Tiglath-pileser III brought the Assyrian armies much closer to Egypt's borders, but there is no evidence that the king yet contemplated an invasion of the country. These military successes began the process by which much of Western Asia was turned from tributary state into empire. Following the campaigns against Urartu, the Assyrians marched into north Syria (738 BC). This, Tiglath-pileser's first appearance in the west, saw the defeat of Azriyau of Yaudi (once identified by biblical scholars with Ahaz of Judah), and the submission of the major southern kingdoms, Hamath, Damascus and Israel, whose rulers, along with the coastal cities of Byblos and Tyre, paid tribute. The kingdoms of Arpad and Pattina/Unqi, along with Hamath's province of Hadrik, were annexed and transformed into provinces.

Now, for the first time since the battle of Qarqar in 853 BC, Egypt figures prominently in the record of events. Although there is little surviving evidence, it has to be assumed that Egypt had maintained her interests in western Asia. Even if the power of the states of Israel, Judah and Damascus would have prevented any recreation of the old Egyptian empire, the Libyan pharaohs doubtless did what they could to support anti-Assyrian policies, whenever possible.

From Egypt, the "Ways of Horus" led along the coast, through the desert of north Sinai, almost waterless and notoriously difficult to cross.[16] The main frontier fortress was at Tjel (Sile, modern Tel Abu Sefeh, near Qantara). The fortress was built on both sides of a canal which must have connected Lake Manzaleh with Lake Ballah. From here the road was marked by small stations at oases or wells. The road then approached the coast, passing along the southern edge of Lake Serbonis which was separated from the sea by a narrow spit, achieving the coast itself some 91 miles fom Tjel, at *Rhinocorura* (el-Arish) where the Wadi el-Arish also reaches the sea. After el-Arish the desert disappears, giving way to arable and meadows. Nearly thirty miles beyond el-Arish lay Repeh, the Assyrian Raphikhu, (Greek, Raphia), the location of several significant ancient battles. Another 20 miles brought the road to Gaza. The rulers of Gaza were usually Egyptian vassals, and the city itself served as an Egyptian garrison.

In 734 Tiglath-pileser again marched to the west. He first thrust down the coast, taking Byblos, Simirra and Arqa. Tyre surrendered, and Hiram, its king, brought tribute. The Assyrians pushed on to Gaza where Tiglath-pileser set up a stela at the *Nakhal-Musur*, the "Brook of Egypt". His army captured Gaza; the city was plundered and its king, Khanunu (Hanno), fled to Egypt. An Assyrian divine image with a golden statue of Tiglath-pileser was erected in the city, and an Assyrian trading centre was established. This might have been an attempt to control the south Arabian trade which passed through Gaza.

Any further attempt by the Assyrians to establish a presence on the Egyptian border were prevented by the rebellion which now broke out in Syria and Philistia. The leader of the rebellion was the king of Damascus,

Radyan (a name also read as "Rakhiunu" – the "Rezin" of the bible). Radyan was supported by Tyre, Israel and some of the Arab rulers, all of whom had paid tribute to the Assyrians four years earlier.

Damascus and Israel formed an alliance and jointly attacked Judah. No reason for the attack is given in the ancient records, but it may have been because of Judah's pro-Assyrian policy: its king, Ahaz, had made himself a vassal of Tiglath-pileser. Radyan and Peqah, king of Israel, besieged Jerusalem, sometime in 735-734, but were unable to capture the city. Ahaz sent messengers to his liege, affirming his loyalty and seeking help. The Assyrian force, accompanied by the rulers and contingents of their north Syrian allies, besieged Damascus. The city did not fall, and in revenge Tiglath-pileser ordered that its orchards should be cut down. He then attacked Bit-Khadara, Radyan's ancestral home, and deported its people. Damascus did not withstand the Assyrians for long. It was probably in 732 that Damascus fell, Radyan was put to death, and his kingdom turned into Assyrian provinces.[17]

The Assyrians now sought to bring the other rebels back under their control. An attack on Hiram, king of Tyre, followed. Hiram yielded and paid tribute. In Israel, Peqah was defeated and subsequently murdered, possibly in a conspiracy led by Hoshea who now seized the throne. Hoshea immediately pledged his loyalty to Tiglath-pileser, who confirmed the new king in his position. In the Assyrian royal Annals, it is claimed that Tiglath-pileser actually appointed Hoshea as king. Despite Hoshea's willingness to become an Assyrian vassal, the northern part of his kingdom was taken from him and turned into three Assyrian provinces. Hoshea was left with little more than the capital city of Samaria and the area immediately surrounding it.

Order restored, Tiglath-pileser was free to return to his original purpose: the control of Sinai and the road to Egypt.

Tiglath-pileser III faced rebellion not only in the west but also much closer to his centre of power, in Babylonia. He defeated the king of Babylon and, in a change of Assyrian policy towards the country, ascended the throne himself. In 728 BC, and again in 727, at the New Year festival, Tiglath-pileser performed the role of a Babylonian king. The festival lasted for the first 12 days of the month of *Nisan*, the first month of the year (March-April) and focused upon Esagila, the vast sanctuary of Marduk in Babylon.[18] The festival involved a boat procession to the ancient city of Borsippa nearby to convey the statue of Nabu to Babylon. On the eighth day the king "took the hand of Bel (Marduk)" which marked his reinvestiture as ruler of Babylon and the god's approval of him. Great processions, in which the king could display the fruits of military successes, and banquets ended the festival.

During his campaigns Tiglath-pileser had received the submission of one of the kings of the Sea Land, the far southern marshes of Babylonia. This ruler, Marduk-apli-idinna, better-known by the biblical form of his name, Merodach-baladan, was a Chaldaean and was to be a constant challenge to Assyrian authority in Babylonia for the next thirty years.[19] The Chaldaeans comprised three tribal groups, the Bit-Dakkuri, the Bit-Amukani and the Bit-Yakin. Marduk-apli-idinna was the king of Bit-Yakin. The Bit-Yakin had towns in the marshland and, judging from the Assyrian booty texts, were wealthy. They may have played an important role in trade. Although the Chaldaeans and Aramaeans were separate from, and at times in conflict with, the urban population of Babylon, they had wielded political power. Marduk-apli-idinna was the grandson (or perhaps son) of an earlier Chaldaean king, Eriba-marduk, who had also been king of Babylon.

On the death of Tiglath-pileser III and the accession of his son, Shalmaneser V, Hoshea king of Israel withheld his tribute and sent envoys to Egypt for help. The biblical text records Hoshea's appeal to "So, king of Egypt", whose identity has been a cause of much dispute. Flinders Petrie identified "So" with the Kushite king Shabaqo and thought that he was in Egypt acting as regent for Kashta or Piye. More recently, a number of Egyptologists has argued that the reading is actually for a place-name – *Sau* (Sais) – and that the ruler was Tefnakht.[20] Most writers, however, prefer to see in the biblical record a reference to a ruler of the eastern Delta, probably from Djanet, called Osorkon. Whoever "So" was, no assistance was forthcoming, and Shalmaneser V invaded Israel in 724. Only Samaria was able to resist and was besieged for two years. The city finally fell to the Assyrians in early autumn 722. Some of its population was later deported to Assyria. The fall of Samaria was followed closely by the death of Shalmaneser V in 721, perhaps in another palace coup. The news of Shalmaneser's death and the accession of a new king provoked another series of rebellions in both Mesopotamia and the western provinces.

Assyria's formidable southern enemy, Marduk-apli-idinna, King of the Sea Land and King of Babylon. (Fig. 60)

The new king's accession is shrouded in mystery, and it is uncertain whether he had any legitimate claim to the throne. His name, *Sharrukin*, means "the true ruler" and is usually interpreted to mean the exact opposite, that he was an usurper. Sharrukin, better known in literature as Sargon II,[21] consolidated the imperial expansion of Tiglath-pileser III. He maintained his seat at Kalkhu where Assurnasirpal II and Tiglath-pileser III had built palaces, but he also founded a new city some fifteen miles to the north-east of Nineveh. Called *Dur-Sharrukin*, the Fortress of Sargon, this great palace and city was completed in ten years of extensive building. Its ruins, known as Khorsabad, were well-preserved, and their excavation has supplied some of the most splendid examples of Late Assyrian art.

In 721 BC, taking advantage of the crisis surrounding Sargon's accession, the Chaldaean king of the Sea Land, Marduk-apli-idinna, made himself king of Babylon. He was supported by Humbanigash, king of Elam. The Assyrians, for unknown reasons, did not attempt to regain control of Babylon and did not involve themselves in the south for ten years. Marduk-apli-idinna, a skilful leader and politician, was a model Babylonian king. Under his rule, Babylon enjoyed a stable economy and the administration ran efficiently, without crisis. The king performed the royal duties, maintaining the canals and irrigation systems essential to the agriculture, and repairing and endowing temples. As a result, the disparate elements of Babylonian society – urban Babylonians and tribes of Chaldaeans and Aramaeans – became united and would prove a formidable opponent to Assyrian aggression in the future.

In the west, the revolt was led by Yau-bi'di (Ilu-bi'di), king of Hamath, who incited a number of states to join. It all sounds remarkably like the events of 853 BC. In 720 Sargon marched into Syria, defeating Yau-bi'di at Qarqar. He recaptured Arpad, Simirra, Damascus and Samaria which had all allied themselves with Hamath. Sargon then marched southwards, towards Gaza where the Egyptians had restored Khanunu. At Repeh (Assyrian: *Rapikhu*) he joined battle with an Egyptian force under the command of Re'e.

> Khanunu, king of Gaza, with Re'e, the *turtan* of Egypt, who had come out against me at Rapikhu to offer battle and fight, I defeated. Re'e became frightened at the clangour of my weapons and fled, to be seen no more. Khanunu, king of Gaza, I seized with my own hand.[22]

The name Re'e was read by earlier Assyriologists as "Sib'e", and it was suggested that he could be identified with "So, King of Egypt".[23] It is, however, equivalent to the Egyptian name Raia. In any case, Re'e is described as an army commander (Assyrian: *turtan*), not a ruler. Re'e's army was defeated, Khanunu captured and taken to Assyria, whilst Repeh was looted and destroyed.

Following this incident, the Assyrians made some attempt to exercise greater control over the eastern frontiers of Egypt. In 716, Sargon put the "sheikh of (the city of) Laban", leader of one of the nomad groups of southern Palestine and northern Sinai, in charge of the people brought to the region of "the City of the Brook-of-Egypt". Sargon also opened the "sealed-off harbour of Egypt", perhaps located at el-Arish. This move by the Assyrians gave them some control of the road which ran from Gaza through Repeh, el-Arish and Migdol to Pelusium and Tjel.

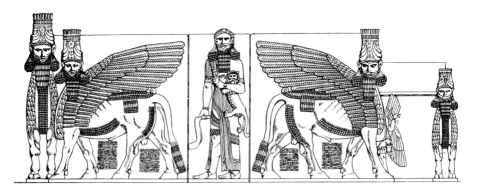

Part of the spectacular entrance to the throne room in the new palace at Dur-Sharrukin (Khorsabad). (Fig. 61)

Immediately after the activities of 716, the Assyrian texts record the tribute of an Egyptian ruler whose name is written "Shilkanni", along with that of Samsi, queen of Arabia, and It'amra the Sabaean. "Shilkanni" is certainly an Assyrian version of the name Osorkon.[24] This king's tribute included "12 great horses of Egypt, their like not to be found in (Assyria)". A letter from Nimrud, perhaps to be dated a little later, after 712 BC, reports that "the chieftains of the Egyptians, of Gaza, of Judah, the Moabites and Ammonites arrived in Kalkhu with their tribute" which included 45 horses from Egypt and 23 from Gaza.[25]

The records of the Assyrian expansion towards the Egyptian border throw little light on the internal events of late Libyan Egypt, and none on the Kushite conquest. All that can be said with certainty is that one of the Delta rulers – probably named Osorkon – was aiding Hoshea's anti-Assyrian rebellion in 725. By 715 a king Osorkon, perhaps the same, was forced to send tribute to Sargon. Yet, by 715, the whole of Upper Egypt from Aswan to Khemenu (*Hermopolis*) was under Kushite rule, and the Libyan rulers of the Middle Egypt and the Delta had sworn fealty to them.

X The Holy Mountain

Most archaeologists have considered the end of the Viceregal domain and the rise of the indigenous Kushite kingdom as completely separate and unrelated phenomena. The reason for this lies, to a very large extent, in our understanding of Egyptian chronology. All of the evidence from Nubia is dated by its relation to Egyptian artefacts, monuments and, of course, royal names.

The dates for the period of Kushite rule in Egypt, as the 25th Egyptian Dynasty, are tied to the dates for the succeeding 26th Dynasty, which are well-established and also themselves tied to the firm chronologies of Persia, Babylonia and Greece. The absolute dates for the Egyptian New Kingdom, and hence the period of Viceregal rule, are estimated in a different way. They were first calculated by European Egyptologists in the 19th century on the basis of the so-called "Sothic Cycle", a rather complex astronomical device, and "refined" by references in Egyptian texts to lunar dates.[1] A loose consensus was eventually achieved, with Egyptologists generally adhering to the "high", "middle" or "low" chronologies (based upon 1304, 1290 or 1279 BC for the accession of Ramesses II) referred to in an earlier chapter. Currently, most Egyptologists prefer the "low" chronology.

The origins of the Kushite kingdom were thought to be represented in archaeology by the cemetery of el Kurru, excavated by George Reisner.[2] Reisner's interpretation of this important site, which we must consider in some detail later, placed its earliest graves – and hence the beginnings of the kingdom – in the mid-9th century BC.

The result was a period between the end of the Egyptian New Kingdom and the beginning of the Kushite state for which there was no archaeological material from Lower Nubia and very little from Upper Nubia. This period has been characterised as, and recently labelled, a "Dark Age".[3]

Even those archaeologists who consider themselves "Nubiocentric" have had little to say about this phase. W.Y. Adams, a leading Nubiocentric archaeologist, summed up views on the period in characteristically colourful vein:[4]

Nubia vanished entirely from history. Its erstwhile Egyptian conquerors had returned to their native soil, and the indigenous population had retreated somewhere into the wilderness of Upper Nubia, whence they were to emerge with a vengeance three centuries later.

Despite the relatively small amount of archaeological work in Upper Nubia, compared with the intensive surveying of Lower Nubia, there has been little found, which can be ascribed to this period. As a result, the whole of Upper Nubia is said to have "regressed" to a "tribal level".[5] Because of the emphasis on archaeological evidence and the importance of the artefact, few scholars have really asked how the Kushite state developed. What were its economic, political and social bases? This approach led Adams, who accepted both Reisner's interpretation of the Kurru cemetery's development and the conventional dates for the Egyptian New Kingdom, to make the bizarre comment that:

it took some time for the lesson of the pharaohs to sink in.[6]

Egyptologists did not question the interpretation of the Nubian evidence. The usual portrayal of Egypt under Libyan rule emphasised the division within the country, and especially the declining importance of Thebes under a line of quasi-royal High Priests. With the focus of Egypt now presumed to be in the Delta, Lower Nubia depopulated, and the new power which eventually emerged in Nubia being situated far to the south, historians have assumed that polarisation occurred, that all major contact between Egypt and Nubia was sundered, and that only the backwater of Thebes maintained some sporadic contact with its "daughter shrine" at Gebel Barkal.[7]

This interpretation is essentially mid-20th century; it derives from the reassessment following the Archaeological Surveys of Nubia throughout this century and from some other archaeological material. The Egyptologists of the later 19th and early 20th century approached the problem in a very different way. Their assumptions were radically different from those of this century and their reconstructions were based largely on textual rather than archaeological evidence. In any case, "archaeology" as we understand it, was not yet practised, and there was, consequently, considerably less concern about the "lack" of material. They were also fully aware of the lacunae in the available evidence, and they had fewer chronological presumptions.

Egyptologists such as Heinrich Brugsch, author of one of the most influential of Egyptian histories, did see a connection between the late New

Kingdom and the 25th Dynasty. The name of the pharaoh "Piankhy" (now usually read as "Piye") was noted to be very similar to that of the High Priest of Amun, Paiankh, documented in the later years of the reign of Ramesses XI. To explain how an African people could achieve supremacy over Egypt, even an Egypt in decline, Brugsch suggested that the Kushite ruling house was, in fact, descended from the Egyptian High Priests:[8]

> where the minds of an imperfectly developed people must needs, under skilful guidance, soon show themselves pliable and submissive to the dominant priestly caste.

This theory was very widely adopted, and, with constant repetition, almost achieved the status of a fact. Indeed, with various modifications, it has retained its allure for some writers.[9] We shall return to these ideas when considering the portrayal of Piye in literature, but first we must consider the archaeological evidence.

Let us go back to the beginning of the problem, and try to unravel the various strands which have led to the view of Dark Age Nubia. Did everybody leave Lower Nubia? Where did they go if they did?

The idea, first mooted by Reisner and Firth, that there was a severe agricultural decline during the New Kingdom, actually has little to support it.[10] It has already been remarked that the decline in the numbers of indigenous types of grave, those of the C-Group, is actually due to their absorbtion into the Egyptian system. As the more recent UNESCO archaeological survey discovered, C-Group burial customs continued until the end of the 18th Dynasty, but the contents of the graves were entirely Egyptian in type. The change in the economic system in Nubia probably meant that the majority of goods available were of Egyptian type, including pottery, the artefact most used by archaeologists to identify "people".

This means that there was not necessarily a decline in the indigenous population at all, but that they came increasingly under the influence of Egypt in their material culture. This is not at all surprising. Nor is it surprising that the burial customs of the ordinary people remained largely unchanged; burial customs rarely change quickly. By the end of the 18th Dynasty, Lower Nubia had been occupied by the Egyptians for five hundred years. The persistence of traditional types of burial, rather than mummification, simply shows that although the material culture (pottery, jewellery, etc.) was predominantly Egyptian, the people retained many of their customs. There is evidence for mummification in the elite cemeteries.

Although recent interpretations of Nubian archaeology have recognised this "Egyptianisation" or "acculturation" as an explanation of the "disappearance" of the indigenous population, there has still been a feeling that there was some form of population decline.

Only one archaeologist, Helen Jacquet Gordon, challenged the *theory* (for such it was) that there had been a series of low Niles.[11] As she argued, the Nile flood behaved differently in Nubia than it did in Egypt. In Nubia the valley is narrow, constrained by the sandstone hills, through which the river easily cut its path. In time of low Nile, the water is still present, but the fields are lower; indeed, there may even be more space for fields. We have probably misinterpreted the archaeological record. The population of Lower Nubia, even under the Viceregal administration, was probably quite small. Its increased reorganisation and economic dependency on the Egyptian system had a massive cutural impact on the people, causing their "disappearance". We should also remember that the Libyan and Kushite periods in Egypt were notable for their high Niles, and, although the highest recorded levels come from the reigns of Shabaqo and Taharqo, already in the reign of Nesubanebdjed a high Nile flooded the temple of Luxor.

Nevertheless, many Nubian archaeologists have accepted that with the end of the Viceregal administration and the crisis in the reign of Ramesses XI, much of the population *did* abandon Lower Nubia. Some archaeologists have attributed the depopulation to the political and military hostility of Egypt and Nubia in the later years of Ramesses XI, others have sought an explanation in economic decline.[12] While it seems likely that the Theban administration wished to suppress Panehesy and his "rebellious" domain, which probably formed a threat to the security of Upper Egypt, the campaigning of Paiankh is hardly likely to have effected the movement of the entire population. Indeed, Panehesy was buried at Aniba, which suggests that he retained control of that town, and that it was safe from the army of Paiankh. If the Theban High Priests, who also claimed the Viceregal title, intended to reassert their authority over Lower Nubia, there would be little point in driving out its population. The campaign of Paiankh may have caused some local disruption between Aswan and Kubban (which Paiankh seems to have occupied), but the effect is still unlikely to have been severe enough to depopulate the country. In any case Paiankh's campaign is hardly likely to have been as forceful as those of the 12th or 18th Dynasty pharaohs, neither of which drove out the population.

If, indeed, Nubia was depopulated, where did the people go? It has been generally assumed that the "Egyptian settlers" (a group for which there is actually very little evidence) and administrators, Egyptianised Nubians, local princes and some of their retainers went to Egypt, and the rest of the population retreated to Upper Nubia or the Eastern Desert. One of the most

Favoured theories suggest that the Nubian population once again took up a nomadic lifestyle, as they had when the pharaohs of the 1st Dynasty attacked them. The Eastern deserts were capable of supporting nomadic groups, and appear to have done so throughout the New Kingdom and continued to do so into modern times. However, this theory overlooks the fact that the Nubians, particularly the elite, had been dominated by the Egyptians for five hundred years. The administration of Nubia seems to have been in the hands of the local elite themselves, and they enjoyed all the same privileges of power as the officials in Egypt itself. It seems unlikely that such power holders would readily give up their land and privileges for a nomadic lifestyle, for which they were probably ill-equipped. It is also rather unlikely that they would have been easily absorbed into the Egyptian bureaucracy.

It is more likely that changes in Nubia, and any disappearance of the population, are to be attributed to internal political factors. The local elites and former officials of the administration, probably a small and closely intermarried group of families, now carved out their own small fiefdoms. Any groups which did move from the Nile valley would undoubtedly have come into conflict with those already there over the limited grazing and water supplies.

After the death of Ramesses XI, the Viceregal titles continued to be held by members of the new royal family, or by high officials, throughout the Libyan period.[13] Until recently, Egyptologists were unanimous that the persistence of the office did not indicate any control of Nubia. The title, they thought, was purely honorary, without actual jurisdiction. The excavations of the German Archaeological Institute on Elephantine have recently recovered more monuments of the Viceroys of the Libyan period. Most of the Viceroys now known carry a similar set of titles relating their office to the temple of Khnum at Elephantine, and suggesting that the Viceroy (who usually combined the office with a number of other important functions in Upper Egypt) was responsible for the protection of the frontier region and for any Egyptian territories immediately to the south.

Whilst we might reject the theory that there was a decline in population throughout the New Kingdom due to low Nile floods, this does not mean that there were not problems which affected Nubia. These had already begun much earlier. The Papyrus Harris, one of the most important documents to survive from the reign of Ramesses III, records the yearly donations of gold made by the king to important sanctuaries. Much of this gold still came from Nubia. Altogether the temples received 2557.3 *deben* of gold (232.7 kg); this is far less than the donations of Thutmose III and Amenhotep III, and suggests a sharp decline in the gold production of Nubia by the early 20th Dynasty.

A decline in the output of the gold-mining regions of Wawat could be caused by a number of very different factors: firstly, there may have been increasing problems caused by the desert dwellers: these are well-known as a threat from the late 18th Dynasty onwards. There may have been increasing difficulties in mounting expeditions to the mining regions. Or, quite simply, the mines may have been worked out. They were reopened in the Ptolemaic period, but the indications are that different methods were used to extract the gold, and it is possible that the easily acquired gold was exhausted by the 20th Dynasty. The sites of Ptolemaic mining are actually very much more remote than those of the New Kingdom.

If this were indeed the case, then the economic importance of Wawat would have changed. Rather than the producer of one of the most important commodities of the imperial machine, it would have once again become the route by which the produce of the far south entered Egypt.

It is certain that the Viceroys controlled Wawat until the crisis of the later years of Ramesses XI. But what about the south? There are reasons for thinking that the southern frontier of Egyptian control was already retreating much earlier in the 20th Dynasty. There are no monuments of Viceroys in the southern part of the domain, which can be dated later than the reign of Ramesses IX. The evidence from the important viceregal centre of Amara suggested to one of its excavators, Peter Shinnie, that the site had been systematically closed down. There are also indications of renewed activity in the forts of the 2nd Cataract, as if the territory to the south had been abandoned and the frontier redrawn. Altogether, these, albeit scanty, data suggest that political turmoil within Nubia may have begun during the reign of Ramesses IX.

The campaigns of the Viceroy Panehesy in Middle and Upper Egypt during the reign of Ramesses XI would have taken troops from the south and presented ample opportunity for new powers to establish themselves in Upper Nubia. Even if Panehesy was not resident in Thebes, he was still involved with the city as late as year 17 of Ramesses XI, and the political situation in Egypt may well have distracted him from events in more southerly parts of Nubia. The military activities of Paiankh in Lower Nubia must have forced a further withdrawal of troops from the southern garrisons.

The reign of Ramesses XI must have been a time of considerable military and political disturbance throughout Egypt and Nubia. Panehesy seems to have continued to acknowledge Ramesses XI as his sovereign, and he was buried at Miam with Viceregal titles. Unlike Herihor, he never enclosed his name within a cartouche, or adopted royal titles. He was, apparently, loyal to the end.

The death of the last Ramesside may have been the turning point in the political situation in Nubia. With a new dynasty in the Delta, and the High Priests of Amun at Thebes arrogating the royal style, the successor to Panehesy, and perhaps other Kushite rulers, may likewise have assumed the symbols of a power they already actually possessed.

It has already been suggested that the Viceroys had abandoned Upper Nubia and redrawn the southern frontier at the 2nd Cataract, perhaps in the reign of Ramesses IX or X. Certainly, the main threat to Egyptian power in Nubia came from the far south, but whether it was from the Dongola-Napata Reach or the central Sudanese savanna is much more difficult to determine

Sety I and Ramesses II ordered campaigns against Irem which seems to have been particularly troublesome to the Egyptians in those first decades of the 19th Dynasty, perhaps under the rule of an aggressive and powerful ruler. There are no records of major campaigns in southern Nubia after this phase, and Egyptologists have assumed that the south remained quiet. A battle scene of the reign of Ramesses III is often dismissed as a copy of earlier such scenes and without historical significance, but there are details which suggest that it could be the record of a military action. There are also allusions to Irem and another Kushite country, Tirawa, in the king's inscriptions. Although we must enter into the realms of speculation, it would be surprising if the Kushite kingdoms did not take advantage of the problems of the reign of Ramesses XI. The Viceroy's absence and the withdrawal of troops must have exposed the remaining Egyptian territories to aggression from Kushite rulers and the expansion of power by local magnates.

We have already seen that, throughout the New Kingdom, Upper Nubia had local rulers. The Dongola Reach of the river was the most productive south of Thebes. Recent archaeological survey has shown that, during the Kerma kingdom, the Nile ran through two or three river channels. This would have allowed extensive arable production. By the New Kingdom, there may have been only one river channel, but the region was certainly still prosperous as a cattle-pasturing region.

In trying to explain the rise of the Kushite, or Napatan, state, it is important to consider how this region between the 3rd and 4th Cataracts functioned under Egyptian rule. Egyptologists have generally supposed that the Egyptians controlled the whole region in much the same way as they did Lower Nubia. They argue that the "lack" of Egyptian temples between Kawa and Gebel Barkal simply reflects the lack of archaeological work in the region, and that the evidence will, one day, be found. But even Egyptian temples do not necessarily indicate a widespread imposition of Egyptian culture.

A different model has been argued here. If, during the 500 years of Egyptian control, the region was left in the hands of local rulers who owed an allegiance to the pharaoh, then the degree of Egyptianisation of the ordinary people would have been considerably less than it was in Lower Nubia.

Altogether, it seems more likely that the whole of the Dongola-Napata reach of the river retained much of its own culture. The idea that this region "regressed" to a tribal level is based on the assumption that it was Egyptianised. If Egyptian culture had not been imposed, then there was no "regression". In any case, this idea of "regression" retains the vestiges of earlier, racist, attitudes. As we have seen, the Kerma kingdom was socially complex and highly sophisticated. The years of Viceregal rule would have seen a degree of Egyptianisation amongst the elite, but, for the mass of the people, there would not have been the acculturation found in Lower Nubia, but probably a more complex mixture of Egyptian and Kushite features.

Let us look more closely at the archaeological sites. The major Egyptian temples and administrative centres south of the 2nd Cataract were at Amara, Sai, Sedeinga, Soleb and Sesebi, all of which lie north of the 3rd Cataract and Dongola Reach. South of the 3rd Cataract, Egyptian monuments have been found, but they are not on the same scale. Many fragments of New Kingdom sculpture were excavated at Tabo, but the temple here was almost certainly built by Taharqo, and these blocks were reused, possibly brought from further north. At Kerma, there is, increasingly, evidence of New Kingdom and Napatan date.[14] Far from being destroyed by the campaigns of Thutmose I, as was once thought, Kerma continued to flourish throughout the Viceregal period, and was doubtless the seat of Kushite rulers.

South of Kerma lies Kawa. This vast site may hold the answer to many of the questions about the origins and history of the Kushite state. Only a small part has, so far, been excavated. But the evidence from those excavations shows that it was a city of great religious importance from the Napatan period until its destruction in the later years of the Meroitic kingdom. The city's origins may well go back to the Kerma kingdom. Of particular importance, it has New Kingdom monuments as well as important Napatan buildings. Yet, in discussions of the transition from the New Kingdom to Napatan periods, Kawa has scarcely figured. All attention has been focused on the sites to the south, around Napata itself.

From its confluence with the river Atbara, the Nile cuts a great S-bend before winding its way northward through the fertile lands of the Dongola Reach and the deserts of Wawat. Turning from the northeast to southwest towards the 4th Cataract, the river is full of islands, and the cataract is made virtually unnavigable by crosswinds and currents. Its banks are barren through much of its length. There is little evidence of ancient presence in this arid stretch of the river between Abu Hamed and Napata, apart from the inscriptions of Thutmose I and Thutmose III on the rock at Kurgus. Although the roads from Lower Nubia along the Wadi Allaqi and Wadi Cabgaba regained the river here, and were doubtless used by the Egyptian armies and desert patrols, the cataract formed a natural frontier. With desert to the south and east, and a virtually unnavigable river, it also served as an ideal political frontier. The main desert roads to the savanna lands of the south left the river downstream from the cataract, crossed the Bayuda desert, striking the river again close to the 6th Cataract, in the middle of the Shendi Reach, near Meroe.

Thutmose III was the first pharaoh to lead his troops through the fertile plains of Dongola to the 4th Cataract. Here he built a fortress, called *Semakhasetiu* "Hacking up the Foreign Lands", which contained a chapel dedicated to the god Amun. Remains of neither fortress nor chapel have been discovered, and they may have been situated on an island, like so many other forts in Nubia. Soon the fortress became known as Napata, perhaps its local name, and, from its walls, Amenhotep II had the body of one of the Asiatic princes captured in his first campaign hung as a warning to the rulers of Upper Nubia and the lands beyond of the pharaoh's response to rebellion.

Gebel Barkal stands at the foot of the cataract, an isolated flat-topped mountain some 300 feet high, dominating the landscape. Thutmose III

Gebel Barkal as illustrated by George Hoskins in 1835. (Fig. 62)

noted the mountain's resemblance to the hieroglyph for a throne, and called it the "Throne of the Two Lands" which was the dwelling place of Amun. Like many such hills in Nubia, Barkal was a "Holy Mountain", Abu Simbel was another. Here by the end of the 18th Dynasty, there was a small temple which was completed and enlarged by Sety I and Ramesses II. This temple was similar in size to the many other temples built by these pharaohs throughout Nubia.

Almost opposite Barkal is Nuri, the end of one of the desert roads to Meroe, and the site of the royal cemetery founded by Taharqo and used for the burial of the Kushite kings until the end of the 4th century BC. A few miles downstream from Barkal, on the southern side of the river, lies the modern village of Sanam Abu Dom. Standing at the end of another of the roads to Meroe, Sanam – its ancient name is unknown – was also a major Kushite centre in the 8th and 7th centuries BC, with a temple built by Taharqo and a large cemetery. Its position suggests that it was already important much earlier, and it may have been the seat of an indigenous princedom in the New Kingdom. Such a chiefdom would have controlled the desert road to the Shendi Reach and have been instrumental in the southern trade.

The site of Sanam was excavated by F.Ll. Griffith on behalf of Oxford University in 1912 and 1913.[15] The temple built by Taharqo and another building, dubbed the "Treasury", showed the town's importance during the Kushite period. The cemetery was partly buried beneath the modern town, and had been badly plundered in ancient times. Nothing remained of the superstructures which had originally covered the graves, and it was impossible to tell whether they had been simple tumuli, mastabas or pyramids: all traces had been completely destroyed. This was unfortunate, because it might have allowed some idea of the dating of the tombs. Altogether 1550 graves were excavated, many with more than one burial, and Griffith estimated that there had originally been at least 1700 separate graves and 3000 burials. Griffith thought that the earliest graves belonged to the reign of Piye, the Kushite conqueror of Egypt, but it is likely that some of them date much earlier, perhaps even to the Viceregal period.

Directly opposite Sanam lies the cemetery of el Arab, currently being excavated by a joint Italian-Sudanese team under the direction of Irene Liverani Vincentelli.[16] As with most cemeteries, the graves here have been robbed, but the evidence emerging can certainly be ascribed to these formative years of the Kushite state and is consequently very important.

A little further downstream still is the cemetery of el Kurru. This site was excavated by George Reisner, who was surprised by the importance of his discoveries.[17] Here he found the tombs of the Kushite pharaohs who had ruled Egypt (the "25th Dynasty") and who were known from

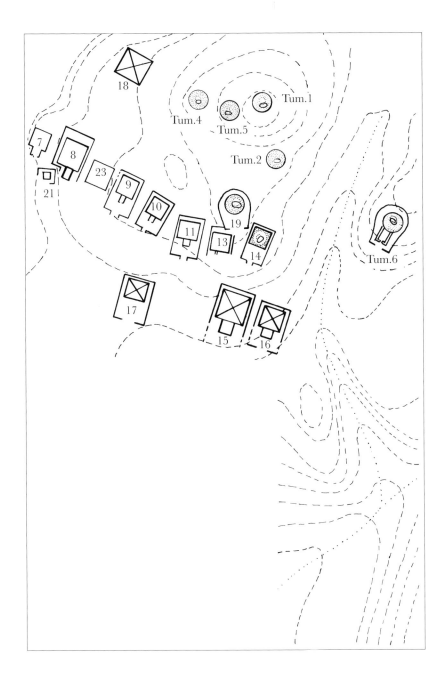

The main part of the cemetery at el-Kurru. The plan omits the large later pyramid "Kurru 1" and the separate group of burials belonging to the queens. The contours indicate the gently rising ground with the presumed earliest burials (Tum. 1-6) on the highest point and the latest, possibly pyramid burials, of Piye (17), Shabaqo (15), and Tanwetamani (16) in a row in front, with that of Shebitqo (18) tucked in at the back. (Fig.63)

Egyptian monuments: Kashta, Piye, Shabaqo, Shebitqo and Tanwetamani. Reisner had already found the tomb of Taharqo at Nuri. Alongside the burials of these kings were those of their consorts and their horses. There was also a series of graves which clearly predated those of the Kushite kings, and so Reisner assumed that he was excavating their ancestral necropolis.

These fourteen "ancestral" tombs, Reisner divided amongst six generations, assuming that a chief and his consort were buried in each generation. The last generation he ascribed to Kashta whose death he placed in 740 BC. Reisner estimated, at 20 years per generation, that the cemetery was begun around 860 BC. The tombs of the earlier generations seemed to develop from a simple tumulus burial, through a tumulus covered with stones, to a flat-topped mastaba structure, followed, Reisner assumed, by pyramid burials from the reign of Piye onwards. Reisner also assumed that the prime site in the cemetery, on the highest point, was taken by the earliest of the graves, and that the others spread out from it. This interpretation of the development had parallels at Nuri and Meroe.

Reisner's scheme, which was modified slightly by Dows Dunham who published the excavations,[18] was logical and became generally accepted. The conclusion was that the earliest graves at el Kurru belong to a period some two hundred years after the conventional date given for the end of the 20th Dynasty, 1070 BC. From this was developed the idea that Viceregal Nubia and its successor state were separated from each other by a 'Dark Age'.

The past decade has seen a renewed interest in the origins of the Napatan state. Since the Kurru cemetery was the only excavated site which was accepted as stretching back into the void, its analysis has assumed primary importance, and it has become a focus of violent controversy.

In 1982, Timothy Kendall re-examined some of the objects from the earliest graves and noted that they were of types familiar from the Ramesside period.[19] He therefore suggested that Reisner's chronology of the cemetery might be wrong. He cautiously proposed a radical revision of the cemetery's chronology, arguing that the earlier graves should be spread out over the whole of the period from about 1100 BC to the mid 8th century. The earliest graves would thus have belonged to the late New Kingdom. The Sudanese archaeologist, Ali Hakem, also proposed a "long" chronology of the cemetery, attributing the burials to males only, rather than to a ruler and his wife.[20] More recently, the Hungarian Meroitic scholar, Laszlo Török, has argued a similar scheme.[21] Both of these archaeologists would date the beginning of the Kurru cemetery to the period immediately following the end of the 20th Dynasty, sometime between 1070 and 1000 BC. They attribute the graves to rulers alone,

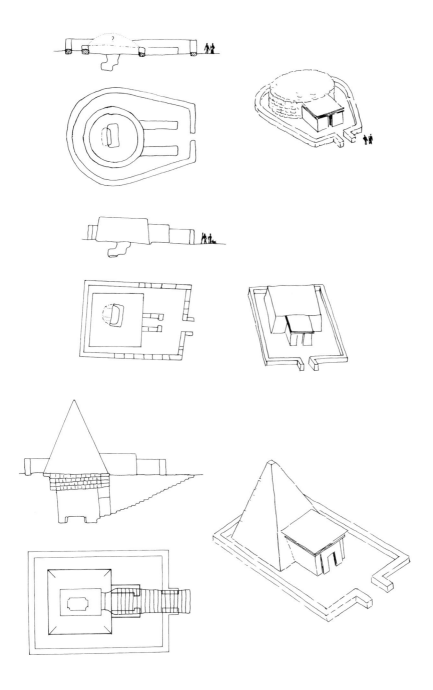

The cemetery at el-Kurru: Reisner's proposed scheme for the development of grave types began with a simple tumulus; this was followed by the flat-topped, stone-encased tumulus similar to C-Group burials; then a simple mastaba and finally a steep-sided pyramid. (Fig. 64)

assuming that their consorts were buried elsewhere. This would give about 16 generations, and far less rapid change of burial types.

In the meantime, Kendall has abandoned his earlier proposal and reverted to a model much closer to Reisner's original. How could this confusion arise? Surely it is possible to date objects quite closely, and should scientific techniques such as radiocarbon dating not resolve the problems?

A fragmentary, decorated faience bowl from el-Kurru. The style of decoration is typical of the late New Kingdom. (Fig. 65)

The problematic objects which he had earlier identified as Ramesside, Kendall now describes as either "heirloom", pillage from earlier graves, or made in Egyptian workshops that were producing antique-style objects specifically for a Kushite market. But the solution of a "long chronology" did not resolve the dating problems either. Even if the earliest graves belonged to the period around 1020/1000 BC, the alabaster and faience vessels must still be around three centuries old, since they *appear* to be of late 18th/early 19th Dynasty types. Of course, valuable objects could survive as "heirloom" over long periods, and there is ample evidence for reuse of objects looted from earlier graves. But the problem is really more fundamental.

Most archaeological sites are dated by the objects that they contain. This did not happen at el Kurru. The interpretation of the evidence from el Kurru was dictated by the date of the latest graves and by Reisner's assumption that the graves belonged to a ruler and his wife.

This current dissent over the dating of the graves at el Kurru is a fine example of an academic dispute, with various scholars arguing furiously over details which seem not to matter. An onlooker might be forgiven for thinking that the only thing that really did matter was personal vanity about which scholar is ultimately proven to be "right" (and therefore cited)!

Unfortunately (in the sense that we cannot simply ignore it), the chronology of el Kurru does matter. The evidence is certainly confused, and very confusing, but a number of solutions is possible. It must be remembered that all of these solutions are *hypotheses*. There are still many problems associated with dating the individual objects and their Egyptian parallels. The imported pottery, the presence of which has only recently been noticed, is equally difficult to date.

The few radiocarbon tests carried out on material from el Kurru have done little to rescue the situation.

Let us consider the various possible solutions. The first would assume that the conventional Egyptian absolute dates are correct, as is Reisner's internal chronology, and that there is simply a dearth of evidence for the intervening Dark Age *presently available*. This is the scheme found in most literature, and, with some modifications, once again proposed by Timothy Kendall.

The second model assumes that the conventional Egyptian dates are correct, and that Reisner's internal chronology is wrong: this is the solution offered by Török and Ali Hakem. This would place the graves in a single line over about 16 generations, with the earliest graves around 1050 to 1020 BC, shortly after the end of the 20th Dynasty.

Another option is that the cemetery actually comprised two groups of graves, which had no familial or dynastic connection.[22] This also assumes that the conventional Egyptian dates are correct. The earlier group would then be dated to the period of Viceregal control, sometime between the late 18th and 20th Dynasties. This cemetery would represent the chiefdom in this region. As such, it would be analogous to the Lower Nubian princely cemeteries of Toshka and Debeira. This scheme would make the graves and their contents contemporary. The second group of graves, including those of the Kushite kings, would then be the reuse of an older site, chosen to establish the new dynasty's continuity with the past, an important ideological factor.

Finally, the most radical solution to the Kurru material challenges the currently accepted dates for the Egyptian New Kingdom. Within this framework, there are two possibilities. Either a shorter internal development, along the lines of Reisner's, or a longer one. The "short chronology" would bring the earliest graves back to the 20th Dynasty, but would place that around 860 BC. The long chronology would take it back to about 1050 BC, which would place the graves in the early 19th Dynasty.

Most Egyptologists are violently opposed to such a radical reduction of the dates for the New Kingdom, and Nubian archaeologists have tended to follow them. The result is that the old problem remains: the Kurru graves contain luxury objects which are much earlier in date than the burials. Even on the long chronology of Hakem and Török, the alabaster and faience vessels would have had to be three hundred years old. As Peter James and his collaborators repeatedly emphasised, "heirloom" is the preferred description of objects found in contexts which their excavators think are wrong.[23] Without a complete re-examination of *all* of the available material excavated at Kurru, the problem will remain.

The "chieftains" buried at el Kurru were presumably the rulers of the region between Korti and the 4th Cataract, before expanding their power northwards. As such they would have been able to command the desert road to Meroe, and hence the transport of the luxury raw materials of the Sudanese savannah. This itself would account for the quantity of Egyptian manufactures found in their burials. Control of these commodities may itself have led to military expansion to protect their monopoly.

The foundations of one of the 'mastabas' at el Kurru. (Fig. 66)

The evidence from el Kurru with all of its chronological problems shows that there were significant powers in Upper Nubia during the Libyan period. Because of a lack of survey and excavation in the Dongola Reach, Kurru has perhaps dominated the discussion of the rise of the Kushite state. This is not to underestimate its enormous significance but there are other important ancient towns and cemeteries scattered throughout the region. There may also be material already excavated, which has not been considered because it was incorrectly dated by earlier excavators.

144

XI   Rivers of Ivory

Archaeologists are frequently presented with historical problems when they excavate sites, especially when they are recovering material from periods or cultures about which little is known. This happened in Nubia at many sites, but notably with the excavations of F.Ll. Griffith at Kawa on behalf of the University of Oxford.

Kawa is a vast site at the southern end of the fertile Kerma basin. Griffith began excavations there in 1929 and uncovered the central area of the city, with a large temple built by the kushite pharaoh Taharqo in the 680s BC. The two mounds concealing the ruins of the town, to the north and south of the temples, remain unexcavated. The inscriptions of the temple give the town's ancient name as "Gem-Aten", assumed to reflect its foundation in the late 18th Dynasty. This was apparently confirmed when the processional way leading from the river to the entrance of Taharqo's temple was excavated. On the southern side of the avenue stood two smaller temples. One of these was built in the reign of Tutankhamun, and the king was worshipped here as the "Lion over the south country".[1]

The second temple was labelled "B" by the excavators.[2] It comprised a small stone shrine with relief decoration and a brick court with stone columns. A stela of king Ary (or Aryamani) and some other stela fragments were excavated in the court.[3] The whole structure was dated by the excavators to the 4th-3rd centuries BC from the names of king Harsiyotef which appear on the columns. Because of the style of his stela and the titulary which he adopted, king Ary was placed with several other kings in a group which has come to be termed "Neo-Ramesside", because of their emulation of the titles and artistic style of the 19th and 20th Dynasties.

The term "Neo-Ramesside" was coined by M.F.L. Macadam in his publication of Griffith's excavations at Kawa. Five kings have been placed in this category and dated to the period between 320 and 275 BC. There were two main reasons for dating them to this time. Firstly, the stelae and reliefs which were attributed to them were written in "poor Egyptian" and their artistic style was "debased". These features were used to characterise the Late Napatan period in the 5th and 4th centuries BC:

much of the Egyptian veneer disappeared even from the court, and the last pyramids and hieroglyphic texts are almost a mockery of Egyptian culture. The final episodes of this process of cultural disintegration are lost in obscurity.[4]

The second reason was the premise that all these kings had been buried in a group of pyramids near Gebel Barkal. These pyramids, although carrying no royal names, had, on stylistic grounds, been dated to the period 320-275 BC.[5] The dating of the kings was thus based on circular arguments: the attribution of the uninscribed Barkal pyramids to otherwise undated kings who were themselves linked together as a group only through their supposed "Neo-Ramesside" titularies. A closer look at all of the monuments relating to these kings suggests that they have been lumped together as a scholastic convenience.

Two of the kings are named in one inscription, added to the doorway of the hypostyle hall in Taharqo's temple at Kawa.[6] It is obvious from the location of the inscription that these kings are successors of Taharqo, but only one of them has a title which could be considered "Neo-Ramesside". Nothing more about them is known and they do not concern us here. The name of a third king is preserved only on a piece of gold foil, and even there it is incomplete.[7] There is a possibility that it is actually the name of king Kashta, the father of Shabaqo and the God's Wife, Amenirdis I. The two remaining kings are the only ones to have names and titles which may properly be said to be modelled on "Ramesside" forms.

These two kings, Menmaetre-setepen-Amun and Usermaetre-setepen-Re, are each attested by several monuments, but scholars are, inevitably, divided as to their interpretation.

King Menmaetre is known from a door-jamb from Gebel Barkal,[8] a broken slab with relief decoration found in the temple of Amun at Gebel Barkal,[9] and a text copied by the Lepsius expedition at Nuri (now lost).[10] The monuments give the king's throne name as Menmaetre which had been used by both Sety I and by Ramesses XI. The Nuri inscription originally recorded a full five-fold titulary, several elements of which suggested Ramesside parallels.

Two of the monuments preserve a personal name, but the signs are very difficult to read. The German Egyptologist, Karl-Heinz Priese read the name as *Ktsn* and suggested that he was to be identified with "Aktisanes", the name given to a Meroitic king in the writings of Diodoros of Sicily.[11] The historical episode recounted by Diodoros is thought to be derived from an Hellenistic author writing in the early Ptolemaic period. Whilst scholars are agreed that there is no historical foundation to this

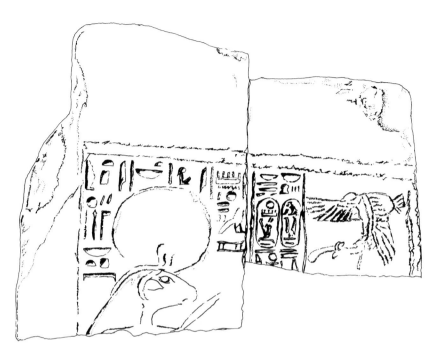

Fragmentary relief slabs from Gebel Barkal with the cartouches of king Menmaetre. (Fig. 67)

episode, they claim that the Hellenistic writer took the name of a contemporary Meroitic king, which was then given the Greek form "Aktisanes". The early-Ptolemaic date thus seemed to confirm the date already attributed to the Neo-Ramessides. There appears to be a circular argument here! In any case, the reading of the name is actually very uncertain, and Priese chose *Ktsn* in preference to other alternatives. Macadam, who published the Barkal door-jamb, actually refused to give a reading, although he commented on all of the hieroglyphs. Other possible readings of the name that have been suggested are Pa-tjener, Gatiaqo or Patiaqo, none of which remotely resemble "Aktisanes"!

The broken slab from the temple of Amun at Barkal depicted the ruler in front of a ram-headed deity whose name is given as Amun-Re-Harakhty-Atum. Hans Goedicke, an Egyptologist renowned for his controversial ideas, commented that altogether the style of the relief, the royal and divine names and epithets suggested a date closer to the 21st Dynasty than the early Ptolemaic period.[12] One cannot help but agree with him.

The second of the "Neo-Ramesside" rulers, Usermaetre-setepen-Re, is recorded on stelae from Kawa.[13] He also used the full five-fold titulary. The stelae were excavated in Kawa temple B. One of them depicts a king,

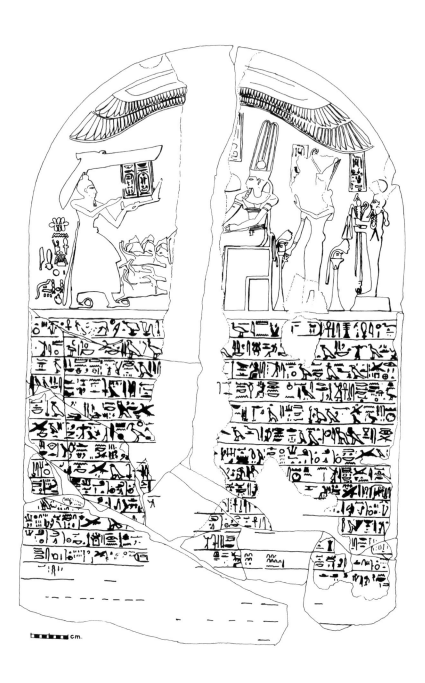

The broken stela of king Usermaetre Ary from Kawa. Protected by the flying vulture goddess, the king makes offerings to Amun, Mut and Khonsu. (Fig. 68)

with vulture hovering overhead, offering incense to Amun, Mut and Khonsu. He is called the Lord of the Two Lands, Usermaetre-setepen-Re, Lord of Might, Ary-mery-Amun. The title, Lord of Might is actually very rare after the Libyan period. Many Libyan pharaohs used the prenomen Usermaetre with additional epithets, so altogether the evidence for Ary being a contemporary of the Libyans is as good if not better than that for his being early Ptolemaic. Griffith, himself, thought that Ary was contemporary with the Ramessides, but Macadam rather dismissively commented that "Had he lived to consider the matter further he would probably have altered his decision". Macadam preferred to read the personal name as "Aryamani", which is closer to Meroitic names. The writing, however, is more typical of the New Kingdom epithet "mery Amun".

Macadam preferred a late date for this king, because of his association with the Kawa temple B. He identified Ary with the builder of the sanctuary of temple B, based upon the strong similarities between the figures on the stelae and the reliefs of the sanctuary.[14] Unfortunately, the upper parts of the sanctuary were destroyed and the names of the ruler lost. However, this interpretation presented him with problems in his reconstruction of the building history of the temple.

The small temple B is adjacent to the temple of Tutankhamun and faces the processional way. It was mostly built of mud-brick, with a stone sanctuary, gates and columns. Two of the stone columns carried inscriptions of king Harsiyotef and one was completely uninscribed. The fourth was made up of re-used column drums with the names of king Shabaqo. The sanctuary itself is a small chamber with a pylon-entrance. The conventional dating of king Harsiyotef, around 380 BC, led Macadam to a rather eccentric reconstruction of the temple's building history. Macadam argued that Ary had inserted the stone sanctuary into an already existing structure, built by Harsiyotef some 80 to 100 years before.

The sanctuary is very similar to small chapels built at Karnak throughout the Libyan and Kushite periods (notably that of Osiris Heqa-Djet built by Osorkon III at Karnak), in which a small stone chamber with a pylon entrance stands at the back of an open, or colonnaded, court. There are certain features of the decoration which suggest that the shrine is post-New Kingdom, but earlier than the 25th Dynasty. If this really is the case, then Harsiyotef simply enlarged the temple. In doing so, he may have believed that he was rebuilding a temple of king Alara, the earliest documented Kushite ruler.

The writing of the name "Ary" and that of "Alara" is very similar. Alara himself was regarded as founder of the Kushite state and is mentioned in inscriptions of several later kings. The inscriptions of Ary are

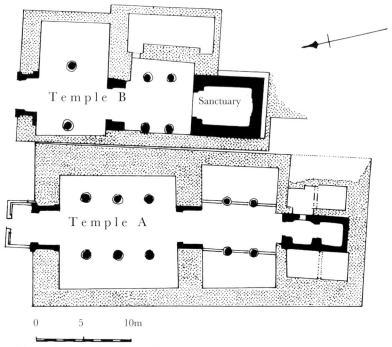

Plan of the temples A and B at Kawa. (Fig. 69)

dated, the highest year being 29. Alara is said to have had a long reign. It is tempting to equate these two kings.

The emulation of Ramesside art and titles *could* be a feature of the Late Napatan period, but it could also, as in Egypt, belong to the phase following on the rule of the Ramessides. In many ways the evidence fits better in the period following the New Kingdom than it does in the Late Napatan period. The art of Libyan Egypt continues and develops from that of the Ramessides. Even more strikingly, nearly every ruler until the very late Libyans adopted a throne-name and other titles which had a precursor in that of one of the Ramessides. The throne-name of Ramesses II, Usermaetre, was the commonest, being used by ten pharaohs. That the name should also have been adopted in Nubia, where Ramesses II built so many temples, is not surprising. Indeed, Piye himself assumed it.

King Menmaetre is documented from the region of Napata itself, whereas Usermaetre Ary is associated with Kawa. The attribution of these two kings to the Nubian Dark Age is still not widely accepted, but there is one monument which has long been acknowleged as belonging to this period, the inscription of queenKarimala (or Kadimalo) at Semna. The problems posed by this monument have ensured that it has been almost completely ignored in the literature.

150

The temple in the 2nd Cataract fortress of Semna. The relief of queen Karimala is to the left of the doorway. (Fig. 70)

The inscription is carved on the facade of the temple built by Thutmose III within the fortress of Semna, at the 2nd Cataract.[15] The original reliefs were carefully cut away to create a smooth panel on which the later relief was carved. The scene shows the queen, followed by a second much smaller figure, standing before the goddess Isis. Between queen and goddess are altar-stands with bread, vessels and bunches of flowers. Behind the goddess is a text of thirteen columns of hieroglyphs.

The queen wears a long full garment with loose sleeves, her body clearly visible through the fine linen. She wears a broad collar around her neck and carries a flail. On her head, a close fitting cap, or short wig, is decorated with the wings of a vulture, and surmounted by the typical crown of an Egyptian queen, the disk and falcon-feathers. Above the queen hovers the figure of the vulture-goddess Nekhbet, wearing her characteristic White crown.

The inscription above the queen calls her "King of Upper and Lower Egypt, King's Great Wife, King's Daughter". It is possible that instead of designating her King of Upper and Lower Egypt, the title should be read as "Wife of the King of Upper and Lower Egypt".

The hieroglyphic inscription itself is very difficult to read, and neither of the authors of the two major publications of the text, Hermann Grapow

151

and Ricardo Caminos, both accomplished philologists, were prepared to offer a complete translation. The text is dated to year 14 of an unnamed king, and appears to record some sort of rebellion against the king.

Despite the problems of understanding this text, a little historical information can be gleaned from it. The speech refers several times to an unexplained but clearly highly significant "matter". It is apparent that the cult of the god Amun had been abandoned, and that this is, to some extent, an explanantion of the problems. Opposition to the sovereign appears to

The scene of queen Karimala at Semna. (Fig. 71)

have been led by an individual named Makaresh, although he (or she), perhaps with difficulty, retained control. A particular incident (the "matter") caused the sovereign to "bow to Amun" and reinstate his cult. Following this, the enemies were defeated and the stability of the state restored. So the new Kushite state owed its defence to Amun, although whether this was the deity of Gebel Barkal or Kawa is not specified. Kawa seems, perhaps, the more likely.

Even the reading of the queen's name is controversial. There seems to be no very good reason, despite a superficial similarity, to read the name, as has recently been suggested, as a variant of the Libyan names Karoma(t) and Karomama and hence an indication of control of Lower Nubia by one of the Libyan pharaohs. It was originally read as "Katimala" which might correspond to the Meroitic *kdiml(ye)*, "Kadimalo", a personal name meaning "beautiful woman". After close inspection of the original text, Ricardo Caminos suggested that the name should be read as "Karimala".

The queen's figure is similar in style to those of Ramesside royal women and to the figures of the family of Herihor in the temple of Khonsu at Karnak. Karimala lacks the characteristic steatopygy of the Meroitic period, or even the 25th Dynasty.

The language of the inscription also has its closest parallels in the Libyan period and it seems certain that queenKarimala lived sometime during the 9th or 8th centuries BC. Who was she? She might have been the wife of one of the kings, Usermaetre Ary or Menmaetre, or perhaps the wife of one of the Kurru rulers; she may have ruled in her own right. The choice of the Semna temple for the carving of such a large and obviously important relief must remain a mystery. The remoteness of the site from the traditional centres of power in Nubia makes it more likely that Semna marked the northern (or perhaps, although less likely, southern) frontier of the domain which she ruled.

It is generally assumed that, before the first invasion of Egypt, Kush had become united under one king. It is also assumed that power in the Dongola-Napata Reach expanded southwards, and absorbed the central Sudan. In order to achieve that, there must have been either political alliance or extensive military activities. The question is, what were the benefits of southern expansion?

Some archaeologists have argued that the conquest of the Berber-Shendi Reach gave the Kurru rulers access to the agricultural and pastoral wealth of the Butana. It certainly did. But was it *only* the pastoral and agricultural wealth that was important? Surely it was the access to the "luxuries" which had for so long formed the basis of Nubia's importance to Egypt – ebony, ivory, skins and incense – which provided the motive. The new ruling elite must soon have sought to gain control of foreign trade.

For the unification of Kush under the one ruler, two possibilities present themselves. First, that a power based in the Dongola-Napata Reach controlled the flow of commodities northwards, but eventually, in order to gain direct access to the source, directed military activities to the south. Alternatively, a central Sudanese state, with control of the supply, expanded northwards.

Egyptologists have generally assumed that, with the end of the 20th Dynasty, Kushite exports more or less ceased, or that, if they did continue, were infrequent. This is most unlikely. The Assyrian economic and tribute texts refer to commodities of Kushite origin, and some of these certainly came via Egypt through Djanet or Per-Bastet. We should seriously consider whether the Kushite powers – in this case, those of the Berber-Shendi, Meroe, Butana region – were able to benefit from the changing trade axis, and take advantage of the Israelite, Phoenician or Arabian activity along the Red Sea and Arabian routes.

The records of Assyrian expansion into western Asia document the commodities presented by the cities of the Sea Coast. Amongst these can be found monkeys and other exotica, but more important were the ebony, ivory and elephant skins. Assurnasirpal II, for example, records ebony and ivory.[16] The Black Obelisk of Shalmaneser III (853-824) depicts an elephant ("Indian") as part of the tribute of Musri (Egypt). Tiglath-pileser III (744-727) received ivory and elephant hides.[17] An Assyrian document from the early Kushite period (reign of Sargon II), records the receipt of elephant hides, rolls of papyrus, and garments made of byssos (the finest linen) from Ashdod and another nearby city-state, probably Gaza or Ashkelon, by the palace at Nineveh.[18] These elephant hides must surely be of central Sudanese origin, and, if elephant hides were being exported, then it is reasonable to assume that ivory was as well.

The 10th-8th centuries saw the flourishing of ivory-working in western Asia, in both the Phoenician cities of the coast and the cities of north Syria. It is universally accepted that the indigenous Syrian elephant was extinct by this time. In which case we must ask, where was this ivory being brought from? Some of the ivory worked in Assyria probably came from India via Babylonia, but the size of some of the surviving pieces excavated at Tell Nimrud (Kalkhu) and Samaria makes it more likely that tusks of African Bush elephant were being worked.

The origin of many worked pieces in the Phoenician cities again suggests that the ivory was imported from Africa. Kush must be the most likely source of this ivory. Although elephants were hunted in north-west Africa, they were of the forest type with smaller tusks, and it is unlikely that the Phoenician expansion into the western Mediterranaean actually brought large quantities of ivory, at least early enough to coincide with the major periods of Phoenician and Syrian ivory carving.

The contacts between the pharaohs Sheshonq I, Osorkon I and II and the city of Byblos are attested,[19] and later Egyptian trade with that city is well-known, as is trade with Ashdod, Sidon and Tyre. Whether ivory and elephant hides were being brought by the Nile route, or whether they were going along a Red Sea route, the source must surely have been the central Sudanese savanna.

The iconography of the western Asiatic ivories shows strong Egyptian influence, some of which is certainly contemporary, rather than being a residue of New Kingdom influences. It seems likely that faience amulets and vessels may have served as the model for many of the designs.

The importance of the ivory trade to the economy of Kush has been rather ignored in relation to the obvious value of its gold production. Certainly, gold had been the most important Kushite product of the New Kingdom, but the gold mines were principally in Lower Nubia. They may already have been worked out by the end of the New Kingdom. Gold can, in any case, be recycled.[20]

Looking back further into the past, there is good reason to see ivory as one of the most important exports of Nubia in the A-Group phase (see Chapter 4). Looking forward in time, in the Persian period, the Nile was called *Pirava*, meaning "the tusks" or perhaps "the ivory river". Egypt itself was certainly not an ivory producer so late, and the foundation texts from Susa tell us that ivory was brought from India and Kush.[21] It is also worth recalling that the great chryselephantine statues of classical Greece – such as the Athena Parthenos and the Zeus of Olympia – must have required huge quantities of the material, even if it was thinly veneered. The Greek writer, Pausanias (*fl.*150 AD) states that the Greeks brought ivory from India and Aithiopia for these statues. The principal source of the ivory in this trade would have been the central Sudanese savanna.

All of the earlier historical reconstructions of this period, from Brugsch to Adams, have assumed that only one major family was involved: following Reisner's excavations, it was identified as that buried at el-Kurru.

The chiefdom based on the region of Sanam and el-Kurru was probably the master of the desert road to the Shendi Reach, and important in the transport of the raw materials to Egypt, but it does not seem to have been the major power throughout Nubia until the reigns of Alara, Kashta, Piye and Shabaqo. It is proposed here that other rulers, such as Usermaetre and Menmaetre, were initially the most powerful Kushite rulers and perhaps had Kawa as their base. The evidence from the south, which is still relatively unexplored archaeologically, indicates that Meroe was a major centre by the reign of Piye at the latest.

We have no surviving inscriptions which narrate the expansion of power into the south, but this must have required extensive economic and military resources. The Kushite kings who conquered Egypt must have pursued constant and extensive activities in the south, even if their attempts at military domination of the region were a comparatively late aspect. Such activities would not have been necessary, or so extensive, if the dynasty had its origins in that region – as has been suggested. It is most likely that there was more than one family group involved in the development of the Kushite state, and that the process was one of mixed military and diplomatic actions cemented by marriage alliances.[22]

So we turn to el-Kurru which, ever since Reisner's excavations, has been regarded as the ancestral cemetery of the dynasty. The earliest grave in the Kurru cemetery, which contained the name of a king, was that of Kashta who is well-attested as the father of the God's Wife of Amun, Amenirdis I. However, inscriptions of Taharqo and some of the other, later, Kushite kings refer to an earlier ruler, named Alara. This man was apparently regarded as the founder of Kushite power.

The inscription of king Nastaseñ,[23] who ruled around the middle of the 4th century BC, says that on his way from Meroe to his coronation at Barkal, he stopped at the "Great Lion House" where king Alara grew up. Since Nastaseñ crossed the desert road from Meroe and had already camped at Ast-reset (perhaps the Fura wells),[24] this place is perhaps to be located somewhere in the vicinity of Nuri. Taharqo was particularly proud of his relationship with Alara, his mother Abar being the daughter of Alara's sister. Taharqo built a new temple for the god Amun at Kawa, "on account of the wonder which [Amun] wrought for his mother in the womb before she gave birth".[25]

> For the mother of my mother was committed to [Amun] by her brother, the Chieftain, the son of Re, Alara, with the words "O excellent god, swift of step, who comes to him that calls you, look for me upon my sister, a woman born together with me in one womb. Act for her even as you acted for me, ... for you thwarted him that plotted evil against me and you set me up as king. Do for my sister likewise. Distinguish her children in the land, and cause them to attain prosperity and the appearance as king, even as you have done for me."

Unless it is a complete fabrication of Taharqo's reign, this text may have been copied from a dedicatory inscription set up by Alara at Kawa. It tells us that Alara was the first member of Taharqo's family to assume the kingship, and that there was some opposition to him. This recalls the opposition of Makaresh to the ruler recorded in the Karimala inscription, although there is no evidence to link Karimala with Alara. It does, however, emphasise that the process of state-formation in Kush was violent. M.F.L. Macadam, who first published the inscription, thought that the phrase "a woman born together with me in one womb" indicated that Alara and his sister were twins. It seems more likely that the phrase is simply meant to indicate that they were the children of the same mother, rather than, as so often in the royal family, the same father by different wives.

A further memory of Alara is preserved in the inscription of king Irike-Amanote who reigned some 250 years later. Recording his coronation voyage to Kawa and the three day festival he gave for Amun there, he beseeched the god:[26]

> Grant me a long life upon earth, and act for me as you acted for king Alara.

Alara's devotion to the Amun of Kawa might suggest that he had his power base in that region. Although it was assumed by George Reisner and all succeeding Nubian scholars that Alara was buried at el Kurru, no objects carrying his name were found there. Indeed, no contemporary objects carrying his name have been found, unless (a remote possibility) he should be identified with the king Ary of the Kawa stelae and temple. The writing of the names is very similar, and the stelae show that he reigned for at least 29 years – a long reign such as Irike-Amanote requested. Against the equation of Ary and Alara, it can be objected that Taharqo refers to his predecessor as the "Chieftain" and "Son of Re" in such a way that suggests that Alara, although a Kushite king, may not have adopted the style of a pharaoh.

It is possible that, in his rebuilding of the temple at Kawa, Harsiyotef believed he was restoring a monument of the founder of the Kushite state.

A daughter of Alara, queen Tabiry, was buried at el Kurru where her funerary stela was discovered.[27] She gives her mother's name as Kasaqa, so far the only known wife of Alara. Like her cousin, Abar, Tabiry was married to Piye.

In their reconstruction of the royal genealogy, Dows Dunham and Laming Macadam assumed that Alara was the elder brother of the next Kushite king, Kashta, and that they had both married their own sisters. There is actually no clear evidence to support this assumption, and the reconstruction was influenced by the theory that the royal succession passed from brother to brother.[28]

Kashta is little better known than Alara. His reign is presumed to have followed that of Alara. He certainly assumed the style of an Egyptian pharaoh during his lifetime, since his name is enclosed in a cartouche on a fragmentary offering table from his tomb,[29] on a stela fragment in Cairo and on a bronze aegis.

The stela fragment was discovered on the island of Elephantine,[30] and depicts Kashta in front of the Cataract deity, Khnum. It is good evidence that Kashta had attained the frontier of Egypt and made dedications to the gods using the Egyptian royal style.

A bronze aegis also carries the king's name and shows him being suckled by a goddess, probably Mut.[31] Such scenes are associated with coronation or jubilee festival rituals, but are also frequently used in a symbolic way: this piece cannot be used as *evidence* that Kashta was acknowledged and crowned as king at Thebes. A badly preserved cartouche in the Priestly Annals of Karnak temple has also been accredited to Kashta.[32] The cartouche carries a regnal year-date: one. Again, this cannot be used as proof that Kashta invaded Egypt, or that he began to date his reign from his coronation at Thebes.

These few monuments alone belong to Kashta's reign; all other inscriptions and building works carrying his name are demonstrably posthumous, and associated with his daughter, Amenirdis I. An earlier generation of Egyptologists thought that Kashta had forced the God's Wife of Amun, Shepenwepet I, to adopt his daughter as her eventual successor in that most important Theban office.[33] In more recent years, it has been suggested that it was actually Piye who ensured that Amenirdis was adopted.[34] The theory that brother succeeded brother as Kushite king was so widely accepted by historians that they proposed that kings installed their sisters (rather than their daughters) in the religious benefice. For this, there is no evidence. More importantly, every other God's Wife was installed by her father.[35] There is no direct evidence that Amenirdis was the sister of Piye, as has been rather too generally assumed. Amenirdis is only referred to on her monuments as the sister of Shabaqo. Although the inscriptional proof is lacking, it is most probable Kashta did indeed install his daughter as the heiress to the Libyan princess.

The members of Kashta's family are much better known than those of Alara's. The princess Amenirdis I who was installed as Adorer of the God (heiress to the God's Wife of Amun) at Thebes is explicitly designated "daughter of Kashta" on many of her monuments, on others she is also said to be sister of Shabaqo.[36] No monuments, however, associate her with Piye. It is unlikely that Amenirdis was the princess's birth-name. The name is purely Egyptian, and was probably assumed by her at the time of her adoption. Part of a statue of Amenirdis calls her daughter of Kashta and of queenPebatjma. It has generally been assumed that Pebatjma was a sister-wife of Kashta's.[37] Amenirdis was probably Kashta's eldest daughter.

Another daughter of Kashta and Pebatjma was queen Peksater (or Pekareslo), who married Piye. She was buried at Abdju (Abydos) and may have died during Piye's campaign in Egypt.

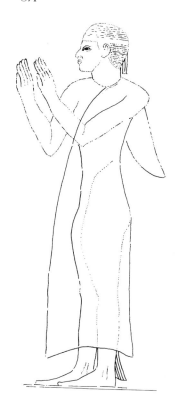

Figure of the king's daughter, Meritamun, from her stela found at Abydos. She wears the loose, ankle-length robe typical of Kushite women, and her hair is very close cut.
(Fig. 72)

Pebatjma is the only wife of Kashta so far known. Two stelae from the cemetery at Abdju have been ascribed to her burial.[38] The stelae, quite clearly a pair carved by the same sculptor, were set up by the general Paqattereru (Pekatror). They record the Chantress of Amun-Re, King's Sister, King's Daughter, Mother of the Adorer of the God, Pa-abt-ta-mer, whose "beautiful name" was Meres-Nip ("Beloved in Napata" or "She loves Napata").

One of the stelae states that Pekatror had just come from Nubia, aged 20, when his mother's burial was requested from Osiris. It is unclear whether the royal lady was resident in Egypt, or whether both she and her son had accompanied a larger Kushite royal progress (such as, for example, that of Piye). It is possible that Pa-abt-ta-mer is simply an Egyptianisation of the name Pebatjma although, as Egyptologist Anthony Leahy has pointed out, the titles given to the queen differ from those on other monuments, and Pekatror is not called "King's Son".

If we accept that Pebatjma and Pa-abt-ta-mer are indeed the same, then she was a King's Wife (of Kashta), but also a King's Sister and King's Daughter. This last title is particularly intriguing, since there were (in the conventional interpretations of Kushite history) no kings earlier than Kashta. Some scholars have therefore assumed that the title was granted retrospectively.[39] The problem is resolved if it is assumed that the names Pebatjma and Pa-abt-ta-mer are not the same, and that Pa-abt-ta-mer was

The stela of Pekatror discovered at Abydos. (Fig. 73)

160

the mother of either Shepenwepet II (and hence wife of Piye) or Amenirdis II (as wife of Taharqo).

The stela depicting Pekatror gives him the titles Generalissimo and Army Leader. The German Meroitic scholar, Steffen Wenig, argues that the name Pekatror is the same as the Meroitic military title *peqar(-tor)*.[40] The general also had a "beautiful name" Ir-pa-ankh-qenqenef. The stelae from Abdju do not give Pekatror the title "King's Son" and it has been proposed that he was the son of queen Pa-abt-ta-mer by a second, non-royal husband. The Abdju stelae highlight the problems of the ancient sources when attempting to reconstruct genealogies. We are often working from very limited sources, and we cannot understand the evidence as those for whom the monuments were set up understood it.

Kashta is thought to have been the father of a number of other princes and princesses. Most notably, he is assumed to have been the father of his successor, Piye. In this case, the evidence is circumstantial rather than direct, and Nubian scholars are divided on the subject. As well as Peksater, two of Piye's other wives are thought to have been daughters of Kashta, Khensa and Nefrukekashta.

The reconstruction of the royal genealogy by M.F.L. Macadam and Dows Dunham was undoubtedly influenced by the theory of succession to the kingship passing from brother to brother in each generation. Unfortunately, this tidied up the genealogy and obscured many of the problems associated with the material. As a result, the idea that only one royal family was involved in the creation of the Kushite state has become firmly rooted in Nubian studies.

The reality was certainly more complex, and more turbulent. The Kushite state was welded together by civil wars and dynastic alliances. Hints of opposition to rulers appear in the Karimala inscription and the prayer of Alara, and the erasure of the names and images of Piye suggest it may have continued. The assumption of the kingship by Alara does not mean that he adopted the style of a pharaoh.

Kashta's reign must have seen the consolidation of the kingdom. But more than this he invaded Egypt. The fragment of a stela from Elephantine confirms his activities on the frontier, and there can be little doubt that his army seized Thebes. The Kushite king then ensured that the God's Wife Shepenwepet I adopted his daughter as her eventual heiress, with the name Amenirdis.

To achieve this expansion of Kushite power northwards, Kashta must have had considerable military strength backed up by economic and political control. The Assyrian evidence – which is not generally cited in discussions of the early Kushite period – offers an insight into this military power. The Assyriologist, Stephanie Dalley has presented the evidence relating to foreign chariotry and cavalry in the Assyrian army, amongst which she noted some texts which refer to "Kushite" horses. This term had already been discussed by a number of Assyriologists, and they were unanimous that the reference was indeed to African Kush, rather than any Asiatic country with a similar name. They were generally less certain that it meant that all of the horses actually came from Kush.

According to the texts, all horses of this type were chariot horses. In later texts they are specified as "large". Such horses appear amongst the Assyrian booty after the campaigns of Esarhaddon and Assurbanipal against the Kushite kings, but they also appear as "tribute" from Egypt to Assyria in the reign of Sargon II. In this instance they were being sent to Assyria by the Delta ruler *Shilkanni* (Osorkon).

In addition to Kushite horses, a specific form of Assyrian harnessing is also called "Kushite". It may, in some way, be connected with these horses.

Even though the evidence for direct diplomatic contact between the rising power of Kush and the Assyrians belongs to the years around 712 BC, some Assyrian texts state that Kushites were at the Assyrian court as early as the reign of Tiglath-pileser III (*c.*732 BC). Stephanie Dalley suggested that they were perhaps horse experts. All of this Assyrian evidence is tantalising, but may actually make sense of some of the Kushite evidence which has been recognised for a long time. Many Egyptologists were struck by the numerous references to horses in the Victory Stela of Piye. Most, however, drew rather banal conclusions: that the king simply liked horses and was displeased by the mistreatment he found in Egypt. Also striking were the burials of horses in the cemetery at el Kurru. Altogether, four groups were found there, two of four horses and two of eight. Inscribed amulets named Shabaqo and Shebitqo, and it was assumed that the other two burials were for horses of Piye and Tanwetamani. These horses were probably chariot teams. At this time it was usual for a chariot to be drawn by two horses. There were plume-holders and other trappings in the burials.

The combination of Assyrian and Kushite evidence suggests the *possibility* that the Kushites were breeding and exporting horses.[41] The Dongola Reach would have been well-suited to horse breeding. In early modern times, Dongola was indeed a renowned centre of horse breeding, and the *mek* of Dongola paid his tribute to the Funj sultanate of Sennar in horses.

Kashta undoubtedly controlled the Dongola-Napata Reach of the river. The evidence from el Kurru suggests that it was the burial place of Kashta's ancestors and that they were influential in the control of the desert road to the south and the passage of its wealth to Egypt. At some point in the reigns of Alara or Kashta, as yet undocumented, there must have been military actions across the desert to the savanna. Our knowledge of the history and archaeology of that region at this date is so poor that we can only speculate on how that was achieved. If this region was indeed the kingdom of Irem, then we might assume that it had a power base around Meroe, one of the best positions for controlling the collection and transit of the southern trade. The desert roads connecting Meroe with Napata ensured its increasing importance. It was also well-placed to control the agricultural production of the savanna.

If our current knowledge of the expansion southward is negligible, we know only a little more of the expansion towards the Egyptian frontier.

How far the Libyan pharaohs had any control of Lower Nubia has long been uncertain. An inscription at Karnak, attributed to Sheshonq I, was taken by many Egyptologists to indicate that that pharaoh had campaigned in Nubia.[42] It has now been recognised that the inscription in question belongs to the reign of Taharqo, but, nevertheless, the accession of Sheshonq as pharaoh must have witnessed consolidation of his southern frontier. Following the death of Herihor, Paiankh and Panehesy it was assumed that the office of Viceroy of Nubia ceased to have any practical control of the country. Only one holder of the office was known in the Libyan period. This was Nesikhons, the wife of the High Priest of Amun, Pinudjem II.[43] Nesikhons has never been credited with any actual jurisdiction, and, at best, it was assumed that she may have derived some revenues from the region immediately south of Aswan. Reisner went so far as to say that the titles were bestowed on her "to satisfy the vanity of a woman"! Nesikhons held a number of other offices in the Cataract region, mostly priestly benefices, including that of Prophet of Khnum, Lord of the Cataract. In the light of new evidence from the excavations of the German Archaeological Institute on the island of Elephantine, this is extremely significant. A stela of Osorkon II carries a broken text which refers to a King's Son of Kush and Overseer of the Southern Foreign Lands who also appears to carry the title Prophet of Khnum.[44] A second stela, of the reign of Osorkon's successor, Takeloth II, names a King's Son of Kush and Overseer of the Southern Foreign Lands, Hat-nakht.[45] A little later, around the time of Osorkon III and Takeloth III, the Vizier Pamiu is also called Viceroy,[46] and another Vizier, Ankh-Osorkon, holds the titles Overseer of Southern Foreign Lands and Priest of Khnum.[47] This combination of titles suggests that the office of Viceroy was closely tied with the region immediately south of Aswan, what was later to be called the *Dodekaschoinos*.[48] Egyptian control may not have reached farther south than Kubban, but the Viceroys were presumably responsible for the conduct of trade through the region.

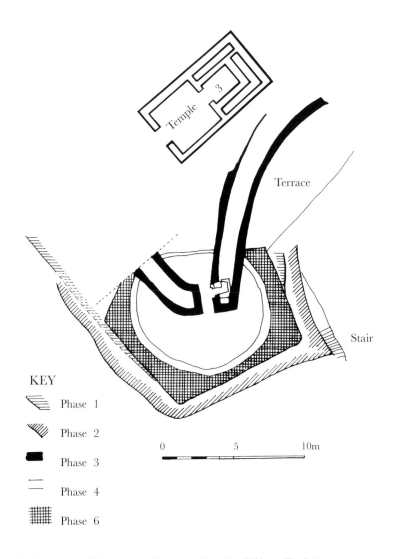

Temple 3

Terrace

Stair

KEY

Phase 1

Phase 2

Phase 3

Phase 4

Phase 6

0   5   10m

Qasr Ibrim: plan of the eastern bastion, gate and temple of Taharqo(Fig. 74)

New archaeological evidence for this period has also been found in the flooded region of Lower Nubia itself. In recent years, excavations at Qasr Ibrim have uncovered fortifications which pre-date the structures built in the reign of Taharqo.[49] These walls must belong to defences built in these years of Kushite expansion. Radiocarbon evidence from samples of camel dung have yielded dates between 1000 and 800 for the earliest walls,[50] and there were several rebuildings in mud-brick and dressed stone before the firmly datable works of Taharqo. Further excavations may clarify the development of this important site. It seems likely that the hill was defended as a staging-post and garrison by the Kushites to protect their northward trade and, eventually, military expansion.

It is impossible to place Kashta's reign precisely, and, over the past hundred years, a wide range of dates has been suggested. Recently, Egyptologists and Meroitic scholars have favoured the dates 760-747. Higher dates from 772-753 or from 760-751 for his reign have also been proposed, but earlier archaeologists made it somewhat later; George Reisner suggested 750-744; the biblical archaeologist W.F. Albright placed Kashta's death in 740, then 735; Sir Flinders Petrie suggested the lowest dates of all, 725-715. This uncertainty exposes the fragility of our historical reconstructions. It is equally difficult to place the Egyptian rulers exactly. Consequently, the historical context of the Kushite invasions of Egypt is presently unknown.

In this reconstruction of Kushite history, the reign of Kashta would have ended around 735 BC. The length of the king's reign is unknown, but it would probably have spanned the preceding one or two decades. The expansion of Kushite power into Upper Egypt and Thebes would thus have taken place in the middle of the 8th century.

Is it possible that this is one of the catastrophes alluded to in the record of the High Priest Osorkon? Most Egyptologists would think not. Many objections can be raised, and there are, admittedly, numerous problems resulting from this rearrangement of the data, but given that the reigns of Takeloth II and his successors must be lowered, and that Osorkon III was certainly a contemporary of Kashta and Piye, the possibility is worth considering.[51]

One of the principal groups of material for the dating of the Egyptian kings is the genealogical evidence derived from statuary, coffins and other funerary material. Recently, a number of detailed studies has shown that earlier dating attributions were too high. One study by David Aston and John Taylor came to the rather startling conclusion that at least seven of the children of Takeloth III "outlived him by two generations instead of one".[52]

This conclusion is probably unnecessary. As son of Osorkon III, Takeloth III was appointed co-regent in his father's twenty-third year. Doubtless the senior king was elderly and there is no need to doubt that the seven years documented for Takeloth III represent most of his actual reign. Rather than Takeloth's children outliving him by two generations, it was Takeloth's father who was granted a very long life. The effect of this would be that the dates ascribed to Takeloth III's reign could be reduced by a further generation (about 20-25 years). David Aston had already argued for a twenty-five year lowering of the dates of Takeloth II.[53] Altogether, it seems that the dates given to late Libyan kings can be reduced by at least half a century. This brings the troubled pontificate of the High Priest Osorkon, during the reigns of Takeloth II and Sheshonq III, quite close to the reigns of Alara and Kashta and the Kushite expansion into Upper Egypt.

Our understanding of the Libyan period in Egypt is growing with reassessments of the material in museums and with the recovery of new material from excavations at important Libyan centres such as Nen-nesut (*Herakleopolis*). However, more evidence is needed before we can fully understand the years of the Kushite expansion.

XII   The Mighty Bull, Arising in Napata

The lunette scene of the Victory Stela of Piye showing Amun, seated, with the goddess Mut standing behind and five grovelling Libyan chieftains: . (Fig. 75)

Piye remains the most enigmatic of the conquerors of the ancient world. The king's "Victory Stela" narrates his defeat of the Egyptian dynasts in a lively style and, at the Holy Mountain of Gebel Barkal, Piye greatly enlarged the temple of Amun, decorating its halls and courts with scenes of his victories; yet there is very little other information about this reign which lasted for about 24 years.

The "Victory Stela" of Piye was discovered in 1862, along with four other stelae, in the temple of Amun at Gebel Barkal.[1] In his excavations of 1916, George Reisner found the socle for the stela's emplacement in the first courtyard.

The "Victory Stela", a massive slab of dark-grey granite, is nearly 6 feet high and 4 feet $7^{1}/_{2}$ inches wide and about 1 foot 5 inches in thickness, weighing some two and a quarter tons. It is covered on both faces and on its sides with 159 lines of text. The stela has survived almost intact, except for one piece broken from the right-hand side of the reverse, causing the loss of parts of the lines 35-50. The scene which fills the top part of the stela shows Piye with his back to the god Amun receiving the supplication of Nimlot, ruler of Khemenu (Hermopolis), the obeisance of the three other Libyan kings and several princes. The inscription is dated to the first month of Akhet, day 1 – New Year's Day - of the king's 21st regnal year. This date is immediately followed by the king's command to publish the

The lunette scene of the Victory Stela: in front of the erased figure of Piye, Nimlot of Khemenu leads a horse, his wife preceding him, and the three other pharaohs kiss the ground.(Fig. 76)

record of his deeds, and then by the narrative of the campaign to Egypt. Although the text does not give any relation between the date of the stela and the narrative of the events which follow, it has been generally assumed that the stela was set up immediately on the return of Piye to Napata and, therefore, that the campaign took place in the king's 19th and 20th years. The king, we are told, left Napata after the celebration of a New Year Festival which is assumed to have been that of year 20. The army, therefore, must have been sent to Egypt in year 19. This date for the campaign has been generally accepted by Egyptologists. The few documents from Egypt, which are dated to the reign, belong to years 21, 22 and 24. This has been taken as confirming the assumed date for the campaign. However, it is clear from the text of the stela that the Kushites already had alliances with various of the Libyan rulers, and also had an army in Upper Egypt. Other factors, considered above, indicate that

Kashta must have established a Kushite presence in Upper Egypt. Scholarship has, therefore, been forced to assume that any evidence from the 18 years preceding the events recorded by the Victory Stela has simply been lost.

Earlier scholars read the king's name as "Piankhy", but in recent years it has been recognised that it should probably be read as "Py" or "Piye", the *ankh*-sign being introduced to give it an Egyptian quality (similar to the name of Paiankh, the High Priest of Amun in the reign of Ramesses XI).[2] A number of monuments which carried this name was noted by Egyptologists, but the throne-name which accompanied it varied. For some time, this caused considerable confusion. Sir Flinders Petrie, in his history of Egypt, attributed the monuments to five different rulers, whereas the French Egyptologist, Henri Gauthier, thought that there were as many as seven.

The problem was not resolved until George Reisner excavated in the temple of Amun at Gebel Barkal in 1916. Among the many important monuments brought to light was a sandstone stela, as well as a number of fragments of grey granite, some of which fitted the broken section of the Victory Stela. The sandstone stela is certainly from the early years of the reign, and the full titulary used by the king on it is certainly modelled upon the titulary of the pharaoh Thutmose III, as it is written on a stela from the Barkal temple.[3] In his publication of the sandstone stela, Reisner drew together the variant royal names used by Piye and was able to suggest that there was only one king called "Piankhy" and that he had adopted new throne-names at different points in his reign.[4] This is now generally acknowledged as the correct interpretation.

The earliest titulary is that of the sandstone stela and is modelled upon that of Thutmose III. The titulary comprised five names, of which the personal name and throne-name were both written inside cartouches. Piye's earliest throne-name was Menkheperre. This is also found on a stela, now in the Louvre,[5] which records the dedication of the king's daughter as Chief Prophet of the goddesses Mut and Hathor at Thebes. This stela, however, uses different "Horus", "Golden Horus" and "Two Ladies" names. These, indeed, have a distinctly militaristic style and suggest that the stela follows a victory in Egypt. The king is called "The one who makes warriors numerous" and "Uniter of the Two Lands". In the columned hall of his enlarged temple at Barkal, Piye adopted a new throne-name, Usermaetre, which had been the throne-name of Ramesses II, and is found in the older rooms of the Barkal temple.[6] Finally, in the outer court of the temple and in another building at Barkal, Piye again changed his throne-name, to Sneferre.[7] Unfortunately, it is difficult to date the changes in name precisely, and the Victory Stela, remarkably for such an important monument, carries only the king's personal name. Earlier pharaohs had varied their Horus, Golden Horus and Two Ladies names, but a change of throne-name is rarely found. Nevertheless, there is little reason to doubt that there was only one ruler named Piye, and that the changes in titulary reflect the expansion of Kushite power in Egypt.

The usual interpretation of the evidence places the campaign against Tefnakht in the 18th and 19th years of Piye's reign. Following the victory, it is assumed that the king returned to Napata where he inaugurated the vast building programme at Gebel Barkal. He apparently did not involve himself further in affairs in Egypt, although he continued to be recognised as pharaoh in Upper Egypt. The latest year attested, 24, is on a stela from the Oasis of Dakhla in the Western Desert.[8] Some Egyptologists, however, argue that the evidence implies that Piye's reign must have been as long as 30, or even 40 years.[9] Some of the rituals connected with a "jubilee" festival are depicted in the courtyard of the Barkal temple.[10] This festival was usually celebrated in the 30th year of a reign, but occasionally earlier: the Libyan king Osorkon II had staged a lavish celebration in his 22nd year.

An even more significant factor in favour of a longer reign is the scale of the building works at Barkal. These were certainly carried out in phases, and could not all have been achieved in three years.

Having established Kushite power in Upper Egypt, Piye began to enlarge the temple of Amun at the Holy Mountain of Gebel Barkal. He did this in three stages: the first enclosed the original temple built by Sety I and Ramesses II (rooms B 503-519) with a wall which also created a new hall with altar or dais (B 520-21); the second phase extended the temple by adding a vast columned hall and entrance pylon (Pylon II and B 502); and the last phase added a colonnaded forecourt and entrance pylon (Pylon I and B 501).

In recent years an epigraphic survey of the temple, carried out by Timothy Kendall of the Museum of Fine Arts, Boston, has added considerably to our knowledge of the decoration of the court 501, and the 2nd pylon, and has demonstrated their close relationship with the account of the invasion of Egypt narrated on the Victory Stela of Piye.[11] One scene shows the obeisance of the princes before Piye, and was an expanded version of the scene on the stela itself. The accompanying texts were almost identical, even to spelling mistakes. The decoration of the pylon's internal faces (B 502) seems to have shown the capture of Khemenu and a battle. The outer court must, therefore, have been built and decorated after the campaign, which, following the usual interpretation, means after year 21. The fragment of a scene showing Piye running alongside the Apis bull is indicative of Sed-festival scenes, but whether it is the record of a

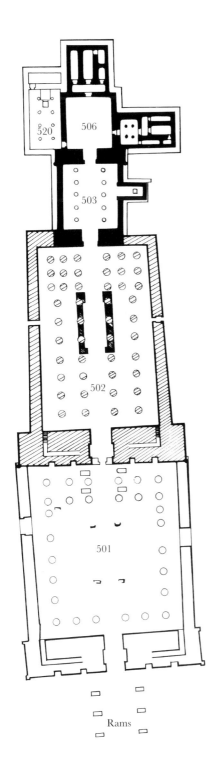

506

520

503

502

501

Rams

The Great Temple of Amun at Gebel Barkal. The original temple of Sety I and Ramesses II comprising rooms 503-519 (in solid black) was enclosed in a wall by Piye with the addition of a new hall (520), perhaps for his coronation. The second phase saw the construction of the pylon and court 502 with the hypostyle of 18 columns at its back, the court itself being filled with four rows of columns at a later date. The final phase was the construction of the new entrance pylon and colonnaded court, 501. In front of the first and second pylon were granite rams brought from the temple of Soleb. Other statuary from Soleb stood in 501 and before the entrance to 503. Also in 501 Reisner found the socles for the Victory Stela, the Dream Stela of Tanwetamani and those of later kings. Tanwetamani enclosed columns in the central aisle of 502 to create a processional shrine. (Fig. 77)

171

Aerial view of the temple of Amun at Gebel Barkal. (Fig. 78)

celebration, or simply prospective, is as yet uncertain. So, it might appear that there are good reasons for the belief that Piye actually continued to reign until after his 30th year.

However, an alternative interpretation can be proposed, which would not require such a long reign. In this scheme, the extensive building works at Barkal would have begun much earlier in the reign, which is easily explained if the campaign against Tefnakht took place before the years 19 and 20, perhaps in years 3 and 4, or a little later around year 12. It is possible that the whole temple was completed in year 21 when the Victory Stela was set up in the first courtyard. Perhaps it was also at this time that the king celebrated his "jubilee" and adopted the new throne-name, Sneferre. To place the campaign in Egypt earlier in the reign than years 19 and 20 would resolve many of the problems which otherwise occur. There is other evidence which also suggests that this alternative to the conventional reconstruction of this important reign is to be preferred.

A stela fragment in the Egyptian collection in Berlin has long been recognised as an account of a Kushite invasion of Egypt, but has usually been assumed to belong to the period following the 25th Dynasty, perhaps to the reign of Aspelta (c.590 BC) or even as late as that of Nastaseñ (c.330 BC). The fragment was apparently found at Gebel Barkal by the expedition led by Richard Lepsius. Nearly 70 years ago, a Russian scholar, Gregory Loukianoff, pointed out that the form and size of the hieroglyphs of the Berlin fragment were almost identical to those on another fragment in the Cairo Museum (JE 47085), which carries the cartouche of Piye.[12] This piece with the cartouche is one of several fragments recovered by Reisner in his excavations at Barkal, but, unlike them, does not fit the year 21 Victory Stela.

This fragment also carries a reference to the celebration of the Opet festival in year 4. We know from the Victory Stela that Piye celebrated the Opet festival on his arrival at Thebes, before continuing northwards to the siege of Khemenu. These fragments make it very likely that a second historical stela once existed, which was smashed into small pieces.

Some scholars are reluctant to attribute the fragments to a stela of Piye, since, on the Cairo fragment, the king's cartouche is not preceded by a royal title. Others have argued that the style of the hieroglyphs of the Berlin fragment is much later than that of Piye's Victory Stela.

A further fragment, recovered by Reisner from one of the inner rooms of the Amun temple, preserves the end of a line, with the name [Kheme]nu followed by the cartouche of Nimlot. This could not be fitted to the Victory Stela by Loukianoff, although its subject is certainly that of the broken section in lines 35-50. If this fragment also belongs to the "second historical stela", then it would be a strong indication that a campaign took place in years 3 and 4.

The German Egyptologist, Karl-Heinz Priese, has proposed that the sandstone stela, also from Gebel Barkal, should be dated to year 3.[13] The text of this stela certainly implies military activities, which Priese associates with the events of year 4 recorded by the fragments of the "second historical stela". Priese concluded that Piye established his authority in Upper Egypt early in his reign.

Whilst there is nothing in the surviving fragments of the "second historical stela" to prove that it recorded the same campaign as the year 21 stela, that possibility does exist. Placing the campaign in years 3 and 4 allows a whole new chronology for the reign, into which the extensive building works at Barkal and the changes in titulary may be more easily fitted.

If this is the correct interpretation, then the Victory Stela might be a second record of the campaign, which Piye chose to set in a prominent position in the first court of the Amun temple at Barkal, at the temple's completion around year 21. The phases of work on the temple would thus belong to the period between year 4 or 5 and year 21, a more realistic time-scale than the short period between years 21 and 24, and avoiding the necessity for extending the reign to over 30 years, with all of the problems that that introduces.

There is also the possibility that the campaign against Tefnakht occurred later than that of year 4, but still much earlier than year 21, perhaps around year 12.

In this reconstruction of the events of Piye's reign, it has been accepted that the fragments of the Berlin stela belong to a monument of Piye. The references to the celebration of the Opet Festival at Thebes make this likely. It is also accepted that the stela in the Louvre recording the installation of the princess Mutirdis should also be attributed to Piye. This stela which entered the collection of the Louvre Museum in 1826 was originally thought to be of 18th Dynasty date (because of the throne-name, Menkheperre). It was attributed to the Kushite period by de Rougé, and Mariette more specifically ascribed it to Piye. Recently, the French Egyptologist, Jean Yoyotte, a specialist on Libyan Egypt, has proposed that the stela belongs to an otherwise obscure Theban king, "Iny", known from one other inscription, now lost.[14] The titulary is certainly that of a conquering king, and, since Piye is already known to have used the throne-name Menkheperre, the evidence at least accords with what is known of his activities. Therefore, it is taken here as an early monument of the Kushite king.

The Victory stela launches directly into the narrative and it is difficult to fully reconstruct the events which led up to the crisis. The interpretation offered here differs from most conventional reconstructions, and must be recognised as speculative. The evidence available is detailed in parts, but overall very fragmentary. Nevertheless, there is enough to suggest the broad sequence of events which led to the Kushite control of Egypt.

Piye himself is elusive. There is no surviving relief or statue of him, which is undamaged. Many of the monuments on which he was shown were, at some point, effaced and later restored, whilst the others have suffered the ravages of time.

Whilst the king's physical appearance cannot be described beyond the broadest generalisations of Kushite royal imagery, there have been attempts to sketch the king's character. Drawing from the text of the Victory Stela, these judgements have been coloured by the prejudices of scholarship. Combined with various assumptions about the culture of

Kush, the conventional imagery of a just ruler which the inscription uses has been distorted. So we find Piye described as a "backwater puritan" or "humourless traditionalist" whose temperament combined "fanatical piety and a real generosity".[15] Religious fanaticism, even proselytising zeal, are deemed central to his character. This portrayal of Piye is not far removed from the idea of the "noble savage" and is contrasted with that of the "effete and sophisticated" Egyptians.[16] The "vigour and individuality" of the pharaoh and his successors is attributed to "fresh blood".[17] These, truly, are the "frontier barbarians" who rise up and overwhelm the luxurious and decadent descendants of their former overlords.[18] We become witnesses to "the spectacle of an ancient civilization delivered into the hands of a barbarian upstart".[19]

Such portrayals of the Kushite pharaohs and their conquest of Egypt, all written in the last forty years, owe their origin to a residue of late 19th century history writing. Throughout the century, there had been an increasingly methodical and rationalising approach to the past, notably in German Universities. At the same time, there was a considerable influence from the literary and artistic movements beginning with Romanticism. One important development in the later decades of the century was an attempt to create a "scientific" theory of cultural decadence.[20]

One result of this was the racial ideas adopted by influential anatomists such as Grafton Elliot Smith, and quickly introduced into the archaeology of Nubia by George Reisner. In the writing of ancient history, these theories became much more generalised: civilizations became decadent and fell to the newer, more vigorous states which had developed on their frontiers. Within Egyptology, these ideas were adopted, but somewhat diluted: Libyan Egypt never received the treatment that was given to the "great" decadent empires, Rome and Babylon. Egypt's decline under the Libyans was an altogether more prosaic affair. After all, the Libyans were already foreigners whose rise to power had been during the Ramesside decadence.

The most recent criticisms of the Victory Stela adopt a very different approach. They have focussed upon the language of the stela and its literary models. The stela is written in the classical language, rather than the contemporary idiom, "Late Egyptian", and draws extensively on earlier models. Whilst the narrative of events places the text at a precise historical moment, it is equally a document about the ideal role of a king. The inscription always asserts Piye's justice, and his actions are those of a true pharaoh. Any attempt to use the text to assess Piye's character must, therefore, be doomed.

If we have no images of Piye and reject the interpretations of his character, what can we know of this king?

The parentage of Piye is uncertain, although it has generally been assumed that he was the eldest son of Kashta. This assumption was contested by Karl-Heinz Priese,[21] and it has to be conceded that there is no direct evidence to support it. Piye married a daughter of king Alara and queen Kasaqa, Tabiry. A funerary stela of this lady was found by Reisner at el-Kurru and calls her the "First Great Wife of his majesty".[22]

As well as a daughter, Piye also married a niece of Alara, Abar. This lady was the mother of the future king Taharqo. Taharqo's inscriptions record with pride his relationship to Alara, and tell us that Abar was the daughter of Alara's sister who had been dedicated as a sistrum-player in the temple at Kawa. Abar lived to see her son crowned as king "as Isis beheld Horus".[23]

Another King's Wife, Peksater, was the daughter of Kashta and Pebatjma. The writing of the name varies and might reflect a Meroitic form, Pekareslo (or Pekasari).[24] Peksater appears in a relief at the rear of the columned hall (B 502) of the Amun temple at Barkal, where she accompanies Piye who, dressed in the robes of a High Priest, officiates in front of the barque of Amun. Timothy Kendall, who is preparing the publication of these reliefs, suggests that the decoration of the rear wall of this hall might belong to the early years of the reign, before the campaign against Tefnakht.[25]

Peksater was buried in Egypt, at Abdju (Abydos). Parts of the lintels and door jambs, and a stela, were excavated in the remains of the tomb.[26] As the daughter of Kashta and Pebatjma, Peksater was the full sister of the God's Wife of Amun, Amenirdis I. It is tempting to speculate that she was Piye's Great Wife at the time of the campaign against Tefnakht, and that she died in Egypt during the progress of the campaign and was buried at Abdju. If, as is possible, her mother Pebatjma is the same as the queen Pe-abt-mer, the two royal ladies died during the expedition, both being interred in the hallowed necropolis of Abdju.

The King's Wife, Khensa, was also a King's Daughter and King's Sister. These titles have suggested that she was a sister-wife of Piye, and therefore that they were both children of Kashta. She was also accorded the titles Mistress of the Two Lands, Mistress of all Women, Great one of the *hetes*-sceptre, Great of Praise. Some small monuments with her name were dedicated in the temple of Karnak.[27]

Reisner excavated the tomb of Khensa at el-Kurru.[28] It still contained fragments of the rich burial equipment, including some fine calcite vessels inscribed with the queen's name and titles, an agate bowl and many fragments of ivory and gilded silver. Canopic jars, shabti figures and the inlaid eyes from a coffin indicate that the queen was buried in the Egyptian fashion. The most impressive objects were found at the entrance to the tomb. A large bronze offering tray, with handles in the form of lions, held a silver bowl with spouts and another silver vessel inscribed with large cartouches. The spouted vessel is of a type associated with milk offerings, and its shape symbolises the breast. Suckling the divine milk brought about rebirth and was appropriate in the funerary context. Among the more extraordinary objects found in the tomb were fossil sea-urchins and sea shells, flint pebbles wrapped in gold wire and some stones which had clearly been shaped to imitate the flints.[29] One of these was carved with a human face and had originally had a wig or headdress attached. The stones presumably had some sort of religious or amuletic function: similar types have been noted at Deir el-Medina and the temple of Hathor at Serabit el-Khadim, as well as at other Napatan sites.

Another lady buried at el-Kurru has also been assumed to have been a wife of Piye. Her funerary goods carry no titles, nor is any relationship to a king stated. Her name, Nefrukekashta, suggests that she might have been a daughter of Kashta.[30] The burial contained a large collection of extraordinary faience amulets which strikingly combine Egyptian and Kushite elements. Plaques with winged scarabs have their closest parallels in the Phoenician ivories found at Nimrud and gold amulets from Carthage, but a silver amulet of the goddess Mut is purely Egyptian. Another amulet of silver depicts a Kushite royal lady being suckled by the goddess Hathor (or, perhaps, Mut). Such images are usual for the coronation and jubilees of kings, but are not known for earlier queens. The royal lady is not identified by any cartouche, and could perhaps be a God's Wife of Amun. The God's Wife Shepenwepet I is the first to be shown being suckled in this way in the chapel of Osiris-Ruler-of-Eternity at Karnak.[31]

With the exception of Taharqo, it is uncertain which of Piye's wives mothered the children who are documented. Piye had several daughters of whom the most important was undoubtedly the princess Shepenwepet, installed as heiress to the God's Wife of Amun at Thebes. Another daughter, the princess Mutirdis, was also given a benefice at Thebes, that of Chief Prophet of Hathor and Mut. The king's daughter Qalhata married king Shabaqo and was mother of Tanwetamani, whereas her sister Arty married king Shebitqo. A granddaughter of Piye, Wedjarenes, the daughter of prince Har, married the immensely powerful Egyptian official, Monthuemhat, who combined the offices of 4th Prophet of Amun, Mayor of Thebes and Governor of Upper Egypt.

Another son of Piye, prince Khaliut, is documented by a much later stela.[32] Set up in the reign of Aspelta (c.590 BC), the stela records donations for the mortuary cult of Khaliut who had been the Governor of the Nubian province of Kanad. The stela was set up by Aspelta in a prominent position at the entrance to the great temple of Amun at Gebel Barkal. Inevitably, the stela has provoked conflicting interpretations, some seeing it as homage by Aspelta to an ancestor, others as an attempt to placate descendants of Khaliut, who may have had a better claim to the throne than Aspelta's line. But these conflicts lay in the future. Piye's reign was to ensure that Kushite rule over Upper Egypt was recognised by the four pharaohs and all of the other Libyan princes.

XIII   Uniter of the Two Lands

Piye ascended the throne of Kush and was crowned in the temple of Amun at Gebel Barkal as Horus, the mighty bull, arising in Napata; the one of the Two Ladies, enduring in kingship like Re in heaven; the Horus-falcon of gold, holy of epiphanies, powerful of might. All of these names were taken directly from a stela of king Thutmose III, which stood in the temple at Barkal, even to the unusual inverse order of some of the elements.[1] The only small change was to the Horus name: the earlier pharaoh had been "the mighty bull, arising in Waset (Thebes)". But Piye himself was soon to appear as pharaoh in that most revered of Upper Egyptian cities. Piye's name as King of Upper and Lower Egypt is erased on the stela, but was surely that of Thutmose III, Menkheperre.[2]

Kushite garrisons, and perhaps some officials, had been established in Thebes and Upper Egypt by Kashta. Following Piye's coronation, he must have gone to Egypt to renew the oaths of allegiance.

The broken sandstone stela discovered by Reisner at Barkal is the earliest known monument of Piye (fig. 19).[3] There is no year-date, which usually appears at the beginning of the main text, but K.-H. Priese proposed to read a date, year 3, in the fragmentary line 29.[4] The surviving parts of the text strongly imply that the inscription followed military activities by the king in Egypt.

The god Amun addresses Piye as "Ruler of Egypt" [$hq3$ n Kmt], and in his own speech Piye says that "Amun in Thebes [Imn m $W3st$] has made him king of Egypt and that "Amun of Napata has caused me to be ruler of all lands". Piye is also given the power to establish rulers, or not:

He to whom I say "You are a Chief", he shall be a Chief.
He to whom I say "You are not a Chief", he shall not be a Chief.
He to whom I say "Make an appearance (as king)", he shall make an appearance.
He to whom I say "Do not make an appearance (as king)", he shall not make an appearance.

The text thus provides us with a hint of the situation after the establishment of Kushite power in Egypt. Piye must have confirmed some rulers in their office, perhaps removing others and replacing them with his

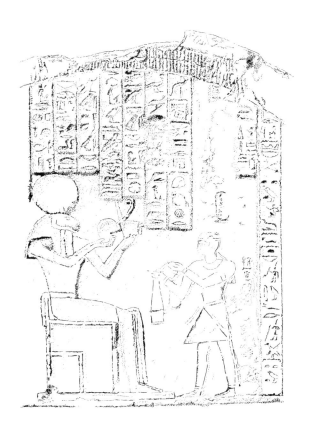

Amun presents Piye with the red crown and the cap crown on the 'Sandstone stela'. (Fig.79)

own vassals, just as the Assyrians did later. The text clearly distinguishes between the *wer*-chiefs – the Chiefs of the Ma – and the uraeus-wearing kings. It is certain from the Victory Stela that Nimlot of Khemenu (*Hermopolis*: modern el-Ashmunein) and Peftjauawybast of Nen-nesut (*Herakleopolis*: modern Ehnasya) had been closely allied with the Kushites. It is possible that these two may have actually owed their elevation to kingly office to Piye. Their kingdoms lay immediately to north of the Kushite domain of Upper Egypt, Khemenu sharing a border (probably in the region of Tjeny). These two rulers were to find themselves trapped between the Kushites in the south and the expanding power of Tefnakht, prince of the western Delta.

So Piye must have gone to Thebes to be acknowledged there and doubtless to be crowned in the temple of Amun. Having consolidated his position as ruler of Upper Egypt, Piye returned to Napata. He probably now commenced the vast building works in the temple of Amun at Gebel Barkal, which were to occupy the whole of his reign. The first phase enclosed the temple of Sety I and Ramesses II with a new wall, restored the pylon and columned hall and added a throne room on the west side. Recent work at Barkal has suggested that the structure of the great hall (B 502) was completed, and decoration perhaps already begun, when the campaign was launched against Tefnakht.

Immediately to the west of the great temple of Amun was another temple (B 800), apparently a small shrine built by Alara and extended by Kashta. This too was enlarged by Piye. Further still to the west, and probably standing outside the precinct wall, was the palace of Piye. Both the temple and palace were excavated by Reisner, and have again been investigated by Kendall.[5]

While Piye was in Kush, political events in Egypt moved apace. Piye's future opponent, Tefnakht, was the ruler of the western Delta. There were still great tracts of marshland in this region, and its history is far less well-known than that of the eastern Delta.[6] Tefnakht's capital, Sau (*Sais*), was an ancient city, the chief deity of which, the goddess Neit, was one of the patrons of the kingship. There were other cities near Sau of equal antiquity; the twin town: Pe and Dep (*Buto*) had been of great importance in the earliest periods of Egyptian history, and was the cult centre of the serpent goddess Wadjet, the uraeus which protected pharaoh's forehead.

The rise of the West as an independent Libyan princedom may have begun with a prince named Osorkon.[7] He carries many of the titles later used by Tefnakht, and was perhaps his immediate predecessor, even his father. Osorkon was a Great Chief of the Ma and Army Leader, Prophet of Neit, Prophet of Wadjet and of the Lady of Imau. This combination of princely, military and priestly offices is typical of the leading Libyan chiefs of this period. His name, Osorkon, and his rank as a Great Chief of the Ma suggest the possibility that this ruler of Sau was a scion of the Tanite royal house. The territory ruled by Osorkon probably covered much of the Delta west of the Rosetta branch of the river.

The increase of Tefnakht's power is documented by two stelae from the city of Pe. The earlier is dated to year 36 of a pharaoh whose cartouches have been left blank.[8] Such a high regnal year, however, can only belong to one of two Libyan pharaohs, Sheshonq III or Sheshonq V. Most Egyptologists have assumed the latter ruler. The stela gives Tefnakht the titles Great Chief of the Ma and Great Chief of the Libu. The second stela is dated two years later, year 38, the cartouches again blank.[9] Tefnakht is given more extensive titles, Great Chief [of the Ma], Army Leader, Great Chief of the Libu, Prophet of Neit, Prophet of Wadjet and of the Lady of Imau, *Mek*-prince of Pahut, *Mek*-prince of Kehten, the Ruler of the nomes of the West. Rather curiously, the text stops abruptly after the carving of the first two letters of Tefnakht's name, but, since these titles accord so closely with those given by the stela of Piye, there can be no doubt of the identity. The stela of Piye calls Tefnakht Chief the Ma, Chief of the West, Count and Grandee in Netjer, Prophet of Neit, mistress of Sau and *sem*-priest of Ptah. It is clear that between years 36 and 38 of the pharaoh Sheshonq, Tefnakht had been actively expanding his control over the whole of the western Delta and as far as Memphis itself. The events narrated by the Victory Stela probably followed closely on this year.[10]

There can be little doubt that the crucial event was the death of the pharaoh Sheshonq. No ruler of Tanis is named in the list of the uraeus-wearing kings at the time of Piye's campaign, and, whilst Sheshonq may not have been the last of his line, there may have been a disputed succession. Tefnakht seized the moment.

In Napata, Piye received the news of the events in the far north. One came to his majesty and said:

> The Chief of the West, the count and grandee in Netjer, Tefnakht ... has seized the entire West from the coastal marshes to Itjet-tawy, sailing south with a numerous army, the Two Lands united behind him, and the counts and rulers of domains as dogs at his heels.
>
> No fortress has closed its gates in the nomes of Upper Egypt: Mer-Atum, Per-Sekhemkheperre, Hut-Sobek, Per-medjed, Tjeknesh, all towns of the West have opened their gates for fear of him. When he turned around to the nomes of the East they opened to him also: Hut-benu, Teudjoi, Hut-nesut, Per-nebt-tep-ihu. Now he is besieging Nen-nesut. He has circled it completely, not letting goers go, not letting entrants enter, and fighting everyday.

Piye was acknowledged as overlord of Upper Egypt by the two kings, Nimlot of Khemenu and Peftjauawybast of Nen-nesut. This had probably been formalised by treaties. Tefnakht had captured all the cities to the south of Memphis, and was now besieging Peftjauawybast in his own city. Tefnakht's forces had moved well south of Nen-nesut and were approaching Nimlot's territory. In the face of Tefnakht's advance, Nimlot had defected. Letters arrived in Napata from the desperate rulers of Upper Egypt (probably Thebes), requesting help.

> Have you been silent in order to forget the Southland, the nomes of Upper Egypt, while Tefnakht conquers all before him and finds no resistance? Nimlot, [king of Khemenu], count of Hut-weret, has demolished the wall of Nefrusy. He has torn down his own town out of fear of him who would seize it for himself ... Now he has gone to be at Tefnakht's feet, he has spurned the water of his majesty.

182

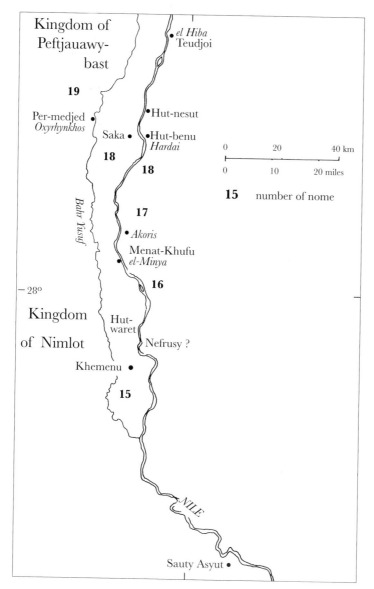

Map of the campaign in Upper Egypt. (Fig. 80)

The news of Nimlot's defection angered Piye who now wrote to his generals, Lemersekny and Purem, and ordered them to attack the Hare nome. The names are illuminating: Purem was certainly a Libyan,[11] and Lemersekny is a Kushite name.[12] Piye despatched his army northward, ordering them to wash themselves in the river and make obeisance to Amun, when they arrived at Thebes.

Having performed the rites required by their sovereign, the army proceeded north by river. They encountered another force coming south from the Delta, which they engaged, apparently in a naval battle:

> A great bloodbath was made among them, the number of their dead is unknown. Their troops and ships were captured, and taken as prisoners to where his majesty was [ie. Napata].

The army continued northwards to relieve the siege of Nen-nesut. Piye's forces engaged the coalition in another battle. The text of the stela implies that this battle saw the presence of all of the princes of the north led by two kings, Nimlot of Khemenu and Iuput of Tjent-remu. King Osorkon of Per-Bastet was also present. The massed armies of the northern coalition may have seen this as the crucial battle for them to retain their independence, but they were defeated. The Kushite army:

> went forth against them; they made a great slaughter of them, exceedingly great. Their ships on the river were captured. What remained crossed over and landed on the west side in the vicinity of Perpeg. At dawn of the next day the army of his majesty crossed over against them ... they slew many of their men and countless horses. Terror befell the remnant and they fled to Lower Egypt.

Amongst the dead seem to have been the Chief of the Ma, Sheshonq of Per-Usir-nebdjedu (Busiris: modern Abu Sir Bana), who was succeeded by his son, Pamai. The ruler of Hut-hery-ib (Athribis: modern Benha), Prince Bakennefi, was also slain. With the Kushite victory, the surviving princes fled back to their own towns. King Nimlot sped to Khemenu and entered his city to defend it while the army of Piye was ranging throughout the Hare nome. Khemenu was besieged.

Piye was furious that part of the enemy army had escaped to Lower Egypt to regroup, and resolved to go in person to Egypt:

> I shall let Lower Egypt taste the taste of my fingers.

But he did not hurry. He waited until after the celebration of the New Year Festival[13] before he set out, apparently in a leisurely fashion, accompanied by his wives and other members of his family. It has generally been assumed by Egyptologists that the New Year was that of Piye's 20th regnal, but a date far earlier in the reign seems more likely, perhaps year 4 or year 12.

Whilst Piye made preparations, the army in Egypt "heard of the anger his majesty held against them", and began to attack other cities. Permedjed of the nome of the Two Sceptres (*Oxyrhynchos*; Bahnasa) they captured "like a cloudburst"; but Piye was not appeased. They invested "the-Crag-Great-of-Victories", and set up siege towers against it. Its walls were thrown down, and the garrison slaughtered, including a son of Tefnakht; but Piye was not appeased. Then they stormed Hut-benu: still Piye was not appeased.

Piye and his entourage left Napata in the 1st month of akhet, day 9. Altogether the journey must have taken about five weeks.

On his arrival at Thebes, Piye celebrated the Opet Festival. This was the greatest of all the Theban festivals, beginning in the middle of the second month of akhet (the Inundation season). Originally, this had been when the flood was at its height, but the gradual shift in the Egyptian calendar meant that these events no longer coincided.[14] A number of pharaohs had lengthened the festival, and, by the end of the reign of Ramesses III, it lasted for 27 days.

The golden statues of the god Amun-Re, his wife, Mut, and their son, the moon-god, Khonsu, were brought from the sanctuaries of their temples at Karnak, placed inside veiled shrines on the decks of the sacred barques. The barque of Amun, made of cedar wood and having massive images of the god's ram head at prow and stern, needed ten carrying poles. The barques were carried in great procession to the quays of the temple and placed on the great river barges. Under the pharaohs of the New Kingdom, the barge of Amun was towed by the barge of the king, itself towed by barges carrying the highest officials of the realm. The procession was accompanied along the bank by the army and musicians, and the wives of the officials who acted as musicians and singers. The flotilla sailed from the temple of Ipet-sut (Karnak) two miles (3 km) southwards to the temple of Ipet-resyt (Luxor), where the god took up residence in the "Southern Opet". The exact nature of the rites which were then performed is obscure, but a prominent role was allotted to the God's Wife of Amun. There was certainly a fertility aspect to this festival, and it has been assumed that it, in some sense, celebrated the god's marriage.[15] The Egyptian religious festivals were local rather than national, but those associated with the chief deities were often celebrated by the pharaoh in person. So, in the past, the Opet had been a time when the king visited Thebes to reward and install officials, and to view the building works carried out in his name.

It may have been now that Piye installed his daughters, the princesses Mutirdis and Shepenwepet II, in religious offices at Thebes.[16] Shepenwepet was adopted by Amenirdis I, the daughter of Kashta, as a future God's Wife of Amun. Shepenwepet I was certainly still reigning as

God's Wife, with Amenirdis in the position of her heiress, the Adorer of the God. Shepenwepet II lived for half a century after her installation, and was probably little more than a child at this time. She witnessed the full flowering and the end of Kushite power in Egypt, and was reigning when, with the triumph of Psamtik I of Sau, that king sent his own daughter, Neitiqert, to Thebes.

Two statues of the god Osiris, dedicated by officials who served these votaresses, prove that the three princesses were alive and in office at the same time.[17] They refer to the God's Wife Shepenwepet, daughter of king Osorkon; her daughter, the Hand of the God, Amenirdis daughter of king Kashta; and her daughter, the Adorer of the God, Shepenwepet, daughter of Piye. Such Osiris statues were usually dedicated in the funerary chapels of these priestesses, perhaps at the time of the burial. It is still uncertain when Shepenwepet I died and Amenirdis I ascended the throne as God's Wife of Amun, but probably in the reign of Shabaqo.[18]

A stela, now in the Louvre,[19] records the installation of the princess, Mutirdis, as Prophet of the goddesses Hathor and Mut. The name, Mutirdis, is Egyptian and was doubtless assumed by the princess at this time, replacing her Kushite name.

On this stela Piye uses the throne name of Thutmose III, Menkheperre. The other names differ from those of Thutmose III used on the Barkal stela; the Horus-name "Sema-tawy", "Uniter of the Two Lands" and the Golden Horus "Who makes warriors numerous" are those of a conqueror.

The stela is carved in fine low relief. Beneath the spreading wings of the sun, the king wearing a diadem approaches the goddess Mut; behind him, his daughter, wearing a long tight dress, extends her arm, shaking a sistrum. The accompanying text sings a hymn of praise to the beauty of the newly appointed princess:[20]

> Sweet, sweet of love,
> The prophet of Hathor, Mutirdis,
> Sweet, sweet of love,
> says the King of Upper and Lower Egypt, Menkheperre,
>   given life,
> Sweet, sweet say all men,
> Mistress of love, say all women,
> She is a king's daughter, sweet of love, the most beautiful
>   of women,
> A virgin [whose like] was never seen before,
> Her hair is blacker than the blackness of the night, than
>   grapes and figs,

Her teeth are [whiter] than flour,
Her breasts are like [garlands].

At which point the stela is broken. No other major monuments of this royal priestess are known, although a carnelian amulet in the St.Petersburg collection carries the same name written within a cartouche, and might have been hers. An alabaster vase fragment carrying the cartouches Menkheperre and (erased) Piye might also be associated with the princess's installation.[21]

The Victory Stela specifically expresses Piye's wish to celebrate the "Night of Opet", "the conveyance of Amun to Ipet-resyt", the festivals of "Abiding in Waset" and of "Making the god enter". This last, perhaps marking the end of the celebrations and the god's return to Ipet-Sut, took place on the 2nd day of the 3rd month. The festival completed, Piye sailed north from Thebes to the nome of the Hare, where king Nimlot had prepared its capital, Khemenu, for a siege. Piye was still accompanied by members of his family, and was now joined by Theban dignitaries, such as the Chief Lector Priest Pediamen-neb-nesut-tawy.[22] The army established a camp and enclosed the town with embankments and siege towers.

> Days passed, and Khemenu was a stench to the nose, for lack of air to breathe. Then Hare-town threw itself on its belly, to plead before the king. Envoys came and went with all kinds of things beautiful to behold: gold, precious stones, clothes in a chest, the diadem from his (Nimlot's) head, the uraeus that inspired awe of him...

But Nimlot's messengers and gifts, even the king's diadem, had no effect on Piye.

> Then they sent his (Nimlot's) wife, the king's wife and king's daughter, Nestjent, to implore the king's wives, the king's concubines, the king's daughters, and the king's sisters. She threw herself on her belly in the house of the king's wives before the royal women...
> Only then did Piye accept the submission of Nimlot.
> Nimlot threw himself on his belly before his majesty... then he presented silver, gold, lapis lazuli, turquoise, copper and all kinds of precious stones. The treasury was filled with his tribute. He brought a horse with his right hand, and in his left hand a sistrum of gold and lapis lazuli.

Nimlot and his wife are depicted on the stela of Piye, approaching the king, Nimlot shaking the sistrum and leading a horse. His wife precedes him, her role to supplicate the king. A small silver lid inscribed with the name of Nimlot was discovered at Sanam in Nubia, probably part of this booty which Piye sent back to Nubia.[23]

> His Majesty arose in splendour from his palace and proceeded to the
>   temple of Thoth, Lord of Khemenu ... where he made a great
>   sacrifice...
> The army then sang a paean in honour of the triumphant king:
> How beautiful is Horus who rests in his city, the Son of Re, Piye.
> May you make for us a *sed*-festival as the protector of the Hare nome.

Then Piye went to the palace of king Nimlot. He went through all the rooms, the treasury and the storehouse. Nimlot presented the royal wives and royal daughters to Piye as befitted a conqueror, but Piye "did not turn his gaze upon them". Throughout the text, Piye is portrayed as a just ruler who does not abuse his power. He therefore forgoes the conqueror's rights of taking his opponent's women into his harem.

> Then his majesty went to the stable of the horses, and the quarters of
>   the foals. When he saw that they had been left to hunger he said:
> As Re loves me ... that my horses were made to hunger pains me
>   more than any other crime you committed in your recklessness...
> Then his goods were assigned to the treasury, and his granary to the
>   endowment of Amun in Thebes.

Although rather difficult to translate, Piye's speech to the rebel is bitter in tone, revealing the king's disappointment at Nimlot's disloyalty. At some point during these events in the Hare nome, the siege of Nen-nesut had been lifted. Now king Peftjauawybast, its ruler, came to pay fealty. He brought precious gifts, and his finest horses. His relief and joy at his sovereign's arrival overflowed in praise:

> Hail to you, Horus, mighty king, Bull attacking bulls!
> The underworld seized me, and I was submerged in darkness, but
>   now the light shines upon me!
> I could find no friend on the day of distress, none to stand by me on
>   the day of battle; but you O mighty king, you have driven the
>   darkness from me.
> I shall serve you with my property, Nen-nesut shall be supplier of your hall.
> For you are Harakhty, above the imperishable stars!
> As long as he is, you are king.
> As he is immortal, so you are immortal, O King of Upper and Lower
>   Egypt, Piye, living for ever!

The fleet again sailed north to the canal at the entrance to the Faiyum, controlled by the great fortress of Per-Sekhemkheperre. Piye found the city defended with earthworks and strongly garrisoned. Piye exhorted the garrison to surrender:

> Do not close the gates of your life, so that you are brought to the chopping block this day! Do not love death, so as to hate life!

The city capitulated and its defenders yielded up another son of Tefnakht. The gates were opened to the army, but none of its occupants slain. Again the treasury was taken by the king, and the granaries assigned to the temple of Amun.

Mer-Atum (Meidum), however, had decided to fight, and its gates were closed fast against the conqueror. Piye gave them the choice:

> Look, two ways are before you: choose as you wish. Open, you live; stay closed, you die! For my majesty will not pass by a closed town!

They immediately surrendered, and Piye entered the city to make offerings to its deity, Menhy. The treasuries and granaries were given to the temple of Amun. Next was Itjet-tawy (near Lisht), once the residence of the 12th Dynasty kings; it yielded. The king offered up a great oblation to the gods of the city, claimed the treasury and gave the granaries to the temple of Amun.

Piye now sent messengers ahead to Memphis, offering peace if the gates were opened to him, and assuring the people that there would be no slaughter of innocents. They closed the gates and sent out an army against him. Tefnakht himself arrived in the city at night to take charge of his troops, 8,000 men, the best of his army. Tefnakht harangued his force: the city, he told them, was well-equipped for siege; its storehouses were full, its granaries overflowing, its cattle sheds were stocked with animals; the ramparts were strong and there were weapons of all kinds. Tefnakht told his troops he would go and take presents to the rulers of Lower Egypt to regain their support, then he would return.

The Kushite record imputes less soldierly motives for Tefnakht's exit from the city.

> He mounted a horse for he did not trust a chariot, and he went north in fear of his majesty.

At dawn the next day Piye arrived with his fleet at the walls of Memphis.

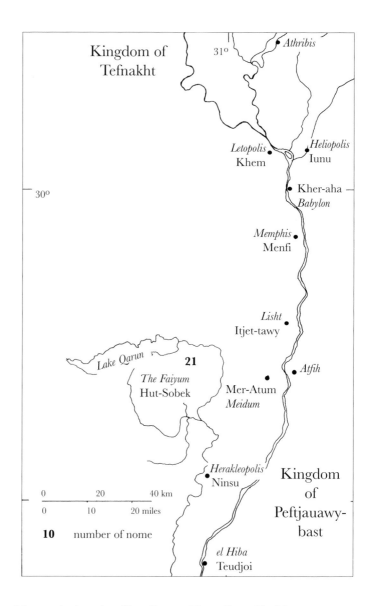

Map of the campaign in northern Upper Egypt and Lower Egypt. (Fig. 81)

His majesty saw that it was strong, the walls were high with new construction and the battlements manned in strength. No way of attacking it was found.

Piye held a council of war, and his generals suggested ways of taking the city. Some wanted to besiege it, others to build earth ramps up to its battlements; some proposed to construct siege towers, using the ships masts. None of these proposals appealed to the king who flew into a rage.

> I shall seize it like a cloudburst, as my father Amun has commanded me!

Piye then took control and ordered an attack on the harbour of Memphis. All of the ships found there were brought and lined up against the ramparts. In a day's fierce battle, the city belonged to the Kushite army and its allies, many of its residents were slain, or taken as captives. The stela always portrays Piye as conscious of acting justly; he refused the conqueror's rights over the women of Nimlot's family, now he sent his troops to protect the temples, so that there was no desecration or pillage. Then, in the wake of the bloody attack, he began the restoration of order culminating in his appearance as pharaoh in the most august of the Memphite fanes, the House of Ptah-South-of-his-Wall.

> Now when it dawned the next day ... Memphis was cleansed with natron and incense. His majesty proceeded to the House of Ptah, his purification was performed in the House-of-the-Morning ... and a great offering made to Ptah-South-of-his Wall.

All of the surrounding towns and villages yielded immediately, the remainder of Tefnakht's troops fleeing. The Delta dynasts now recognised that there was little hope for further resistance.

> Then came king Iuput, and Akanosh, Chief of the Ma, and Prince Pediese, and all the counts of Lower Egypt, bearing their tribute, to see the beauty of his majesty.

Iuput, the ruler of Tjent-remu (*Leontopolis*: perhaps Tell Muqdam) and Taan, had been one of the leaders of the coalition army. Iuput is known from some other monuments. At Per-Banebdjed, the induction of a Great Chief of the Ma and Army Leader was recorded in his 21st regnal year. Two handsome faience panels, originally inlays, perhaps from a shrine, depict Iuput. One of these shows the king wearing the close-fitting cap crown typical of this period (Fig.82). This monument alone gives the king's throne name, Usermaetre-setepenamun.[24]

Akanosh was the ruler of a large territory in the northern Delta: Tjeb-netjer (*Sebennytos*: modern Samanud), Per-heby (*Isidopolis*: modern Behbeit el-Hagar) and Sema-behdet (modern Tell el-Balamun). It seems probable that a marriage alliance was arranged between Akanosh and the

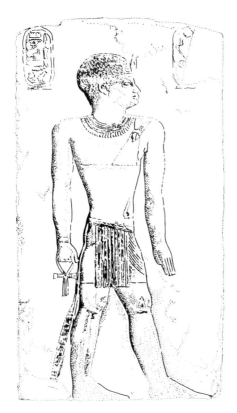

A faience plaque depicting Iuput of Tjent-remu and Taan, one of the four "uraeus-wearers". The proportions are typical of the 'archaising' style of the Saite and Kushite periods. (Fig. 82)

Kushite king, perhaps at this time. A large bronze statue, now in the Athens Museum, depicts Akanosh's daughter, Takushit ("The Kushite"). Another daughter, Nes-Bastet-rud, carried the title, King's Wife, but it is uncertain whether she married a Kushite or a Libyan pharaoh.[25]

The third prince to pay homage, Pediese, was a son of Prince Bakennefi who had been killed at the battle of Nen-nesut. Piye is now called Pediese's "protector", which may disguise a family dispute. During the southward advance of the coalition army, Bakennefi had been accompanied by his eldest son, the Count and Chief of the Ma, Nesnaisu of Hesbu. It is possible that, in the confusion following the battle and Bakennefi's death, Pediese had siezed the territory of Kemwer, and now sought Piye's help to retain it. A statuette can plausibly be ascribed to this king, depicting him wearing the close-fitting cap crown favoured by the Libyan and Kushite rulers.[26]

From Memphis, Piye set out for Iunu (*Heliopolis*), pausing to make offerings to Atum in the temple of Kher-aha, later the site of the fortress of Babylon, now Old Cairo. From here, he passed over the mountain to Iunu, and one of Egypt's most hallowed sanctuaries, the temple of Re-Harakhty. The king rested overnight, and at dawn the next day underwent the purification rituals, in order to make offerings to the rising sun-god.

He was cleansed in the pool of Kebeh; his face was bathed in the River-of-Nun, in which Re bathes his face. He proceeded to the High Sand, which is in Iunu and a great oblation was made before the face of Re at his rising.

He mounted the stairs to the great window to view Re in the House of the Pyramidion. The king stood by himself alone ... He entered the temple of Atum and worshipped the image of his father Atum-Khepri, the Great One of Iunu.

Then came king Osorkon to see the beauty of his majesty.

Osorkon was the last of the four pharaohs to pay fealty. He was the ruler of Per-Bastet (*Bubastis*: modern Zagazig) and Ranofer. His identity has been much disputed, and, in recent years, Egyptologists have assumed him to be the fourth ruler of that name, an otherwise utterly obscure pharaoh. An earlier generation recognised in him the formidable Osorkon III (Fig.84), erstwhile High Priest of Amun and father of the reigning God's Wife of Amun, Shepenwepet.[27] This king Osorkon is certainly the same king who, in 725 BC, as "So, king of Egypt", aided Hoshea, king of Israel, against the armies of Shalmaneser V; and the *Shilkanni* of the Assyrian texts who sent large horses as tribute to Assyria, after Sargon had established control of Gaza in 716 BC.

Piye rejoined his fleet and sailed to the nome of the Black Bull, Kemwer, at the entrance to the Delta. Here Piye established his camp, and received the capitulation of the Delta.

Then came those kings and counts of Lower Egypt, all the plume-wearing chiefs, all viziers, chiefs, king's friends from the west, the east, and the isles in the midst, to see the beauty of his majesty.

The ruler of the nome, prince Pediese, threw himself on his belly and insisted that the king go to his capital of Hut-hery-ib where his treasury would be opened to him and the choicest horses of the stable made over. Piye agreed, took up residence in the palace of Pediese and made offerings to the local deity, Horus-Khenty-khety. All of the delta rulers followed Pediese's example and brought the choicest gifts from their treasuries and the finest horses from their stables.

At this point the stela gives a list of all the rulers of the north. Precedence, of course, was given to the two uraeus-wearing kings, Osorkon of Per-Bastet and Ra-nofer, and Iuput of Tjent-remu and Taan.

The list of other rulers is headed by two princes who had figured prominently in the disastrous battle at Nen-nesut: the Great Chief of the Ma, Djedamenefankh of Per-Banebdjed and Granary-of-Re, with his

Osorkon III kneels and presents a sacred barque. The style of the statue owes much to Thutmoside sculpture of the mid-18th Dynasty. (Fig. 83)

eldest son, the General Ankh-Hor, commander of Per-Djehuty-wep-Rehwy. The Chief of the Ma, Akanosh of Tjeb-netjer, Per-Heby and Sema-Behdet, had already paid his homage to Piye in Memphis.

The Chief of the Ma and Count, Patjenfy of Per-Soped and Granary of Inbu-hedj, was to be amongst the most loyal of the Libyan princes, dedicating stelae under Piye's successors, Shabaqo and Shebitqo. He too may have contracted a marriage alliance with the Kushite royal house.[28] His son, Peqrur, was later to be prominent as the leader of the Delta dynasts.

The Count and Chief of the Ma, Pamai of Per-Usir-neb-Djedu, was the son of Sheshonq who had been killed at the battle of Nen-nesut. The heir of another of that battle's victims was the Count and Chief of the Ma, Nesnaisu, the son of Prince Bakennefi. Apparently the elder brother of Piye's host, Pediese, Nesnaisu may have been ousted from the nome of Kemwer, but retained his old principality of Hesbu, to its north-west.

Little is known of the remaining rulers who are named; the Count and Chief of the Ma, Nakhthorneshu of Per-gerer; the Chiefs of the Ma, Pentaweret and Pentibekhenet; the Prophet of Horus, Lord of Khem, Pedi-

Hor-sema-tawy; the Count Horbes of Per-Sekhmet-nebet-Sau and Per-Sekhmet-nebet-Rehes-sawy; the Count Djedkhiyu of Khent-nefer and Count Pabasa of Kher-aha and Per-Hapy.

News was now brought of Tefankht who had taken Mesed (Mosdai) on the border of Pediese's realm. This may have been an attempt by the Saite prince to cause disaffection, since Mesed lay in the territory of prince Nesnaisu. Piye, as the "protector" of Pediese, dispatched an army which captured Mesed, the town being presented to Pediese as a gift.

With this defeat, Tefnakht finally yielded. But he did not go in person to Piye. Instead, a messenger was sent to supplicate the king:

Be appeased! I cannot look on your face in my days of shame; I cannot stand before your flame!

I dread your awesomeness.

You are Nubti (Seth), foremost of the Southland! You are Monthu, the mighty bull!

Whatever town you turn your face to, you will not be able to find your servant there, until I have reached the islands of the Sea. ...

Is your majesty's heart not cooled by the things you have done to me? Although you did not smite me according to my crime. Weigh with the balance, judge by weight, then multiply it against me threefold. But leave the seed, that you may gather it in its season! Do not cut down the grove to its roots!

Have mercy! Terror of you is in my belly, fear of you in my bones.

I do not sit in the beer hall, they do not bring the harp for me. Ever since the day that you heard my name I have eaten the bread of the hungry and drunk the water of the thirsty. Illness is in my bones, my head is bald, my clothes are rags, until Neit is appeased toward me...

Let my property be received into the Treasury; gold, precious stones, the best of the horses...

Send me a messenger quickly, to drive fear from my heart! Let me go to the temple in his presence, and cleanse myself by a divine oath.

So Piye sent the Chief Lector-priest, Pediamen-neb-nesut-tawy, with the commander of the army, Purem, to receive the prince's submission in Sau. The Chief Lector-Priest, Pediamen-neb-nesut-tawy, is almost certainly the same who was also Third Prophet of Amun at Thebes and married to a daughter of Takeloth III. His descendants held the same offices throughout the Kushite rule of Egypt, and continued to serve the succeeding dynasty. The

Chief Lector-Priest was doubtless only one of the many important Theban officials who had accompanied Piye on his progress northwards. Tefnakht presented gifts, then, in the temple, he took the oath:

> I will not disobey the Royal Decree. I will not thrust aside his majesty's words. I will not do wrong to any prince without your knowledge, and I will do only what the king says. I will not disobey what he has commanded.

With the submission of Tefnakht, the last of the nomes to resist now yielded to Piye; these were Hut-Sobek (the Faiyum) and Meten (*Aphroditopolis*: modern Atfih).

At dawn the next day, all of the rulers came again to pay their fealty to Piye, before he began his triumphant journey southwards.

> There came the two rulers of Upper Egypt and the two rulers of Lower Egypt, the uraeus-wearers, to kiss the ground to the might of his majesty. Now the kings and counts of Lower Egypt who came to see his majesty's beauty, their legs were the legs of women. They could not enter the palace because they were uncircumcised and were eaters of fish, which is an abomination to the palace. But king Nimlot entered the palace, because he was clean and did not eat fish. The three stood there while the one entered the palace.

This brief passage reveals an enormous amount: that the Libyan rulers, although related, had differing customs, or degrees of adherence to ritual; also that Piye observed the ritual purity which is supposed to have accorded to Pharaoh, although badly documented.

Piye journeyed home in glory, his ships laden with the booty of the north, with the produce of Syria and the finest timber.

> O mighty ruler, O mighty ruler,
> Piye, mighty ruler!
> You return as ruler of the North Land.
> You made bulls into women!
> Joyful is the mother who bore you,
> The man who begot you
> The valley dwellers worship her,
> The cow that bore the bull!
> You are eternal,
> Your might abides,
> O ruler, beloved of Thebes!

XIV   The Bull, Ruler of Egypt

Piye's triumphant return south is not recorded, although it might be assumed that he spent some time in Thebes. It is possible that the princesses Shepenwepet and Mutirdis were dedicated to the service of the Theban deities at this time, rather than on the northward journey.

A statuette of the lioness-headed goddess Bastet-Wadjet from Karnak was dedicated in the name of Piye and queen Khensa.[1] Although it cannot be associated with the return voyage, it marks a different phase in the reign, since the Chief Wife is now queen Khensa, and the king's throne name is no longer Menkheperre, but Usermaetre. It is this throne name that is found in the extensive building works at Barkal, recording the campaign against Tefnakht. Other monuments of this period, although carrying no throne name, call the king "Horus who pacifies the Two Lands".

Piye had doubtless brought architects and sculptors from Egypt. The timber and treasures he had received from the defeated rulers went towards the aggrandisement of the Kushite sanctuary which was now adorned with statuary brought from the older temples of Nubia. The most spectacular sculptures came from the temple of Amenhotep III at Soleb, some 200 miles north of Napata. Ten grey granite rams were shipped south to line the avenue leading to the temple pylon, massive black granite falcons, images of the gods Sopd and Horus of Nekhen, black granite serpents and a vulture were placed in the temple forecourt. Most impressive of all, two red granite lions, with their eyes inlaid, which had represented the divine Amenhotep III as the "Lord of Nubia", were also brought to Barkal. Later they were inscribed with the name of the Meroitic king Amanislo, and in 1835 were removed by Lord Prudhoe (later 4th Duke of Northumberland) and given by him to the British Museum. When Prudhoe had them removed, they stood outside the entrance to a building to the side of the Amun temple, now thought to be the palace of Piye. In addition to these massive animal sculptures, statues of earlier pharaohs, Thutmose III and Amenhotep III, and of officials of the Egyptian viceregal administration added prestige to the new halls and courts of the temple.[2]

Most Egyptologists, assuming that the campaign against Tefnakht was in years 19 and 20, would date these building works to the last few years of the reign, but it is more likely that the campaign was much earlier. If so, it seems likely that the construction of the temple was completed in year 21, when the great Victory Stela was set up in the first court.[3] In that year the king may also have celebrated a *sed*-festival and once again changed his titulary.[4] In this outer court, there are scenes which relate to the *sed*-festival, and, although it was traditionally celebrated after 30 years of rule, there are instances when it took place before then: most notably, the jubilee of Osorkon II, which was lavishly enacted in his 22nd year. Perhaps to be associated with this *sed*-festival is the section of an obelisk discovered at Kadakol in the Letti Basin.[5] On this monument Piye finally becomes "[Horus] the Mighty Bull Arising in Waset, the King of Upper and Lower Egypt, the One of the Two Ladies, the Ruler of Egypt". He is also "Bull of his two lands" and "the Bull". The last throne-name, found only in building 800 at Barkal, is Sneferre, "He whom Re perfects".

Following his victorious return to Napata, it has been rather generally assumed that Piye never went to Egypt again. This is based on a number of presumptions, and on the lack of inscribed monuments attributable to him from the Theban region.[6]

Exactly what happened in Egypt following the campaign is very difficult to elucidate. Monuments attributable to the named rulers are few, and even fewer are dated. Any changes in the political landscape resulting from the campaign are almost impossible to discern. Only in Sau itself is there an indication of change.

A stela in the Athens Museum depicts a king Tefnakht and is dated to his 8th regnal year.[7] Some Egyptologists have attributed this stela to Piye's opponent. They argue that Tefnakht assumed the style of a pharaoh directly after Piye's campaign, since the Victory Stela refers to him as Chief of the West. This, however, creates a problem. It is likely, as we will see, that Piye's successor, Shabaqo, himself invaded Egypt, in the 6th year of the Saite ruler Bakenranef. Therefore, if Piye's campaign was in his 21st year, and Tefnakht ruled for 8 years after that, with his successor Bakenranef reigning for a further 6 years, then Piye's reign *must* have been over 30 years.

To resolve this problem various theories have been proposed. Some scholars suggest that the Athens stela actually belongs to a Tefnakht "II", who was a ruler of Sau in the later years of the Kushites (perhaps early in the reign of Taharqo).[8] In support of this, the Ptolemaic historian, Manetho, is invoked.[9] He lists the rulers of Sau as "Bochchoris" in the 24th Dynasty, then Ammeris the Aithiopian governor, Stephinates (= "Tefnakht II"), Nechepsos (= Nekauba) and Necho (= Nekau I). Others, notably Donald Redford, have argued that Piye simply ignored the kingship of Tefnakht. Kenneth Kitchen thought that Tefnakht assumed the kingship following the campaign because he was the only Libyan who had not submitted to Piye in person, and was hence "ritually pure".[10]

If the campaign against Tefnakht is actually placed earlier in the reign than years 19-20, then most of these problems disappear, and the complex explanations, such as the creation of a "Tefnakht II", become unnecessary.

If Piye's campaign was, as has been proposed above, earlier than years 19 and 20, either in years 3 and 4, or around year 12, then the reigns of Tefnakht and Bakenranef would fit comfortably within the 24 years attested by the monuments for Piye.

The scene on the "Bocchoris Vase" from Tarquinia in Etruria. The lower panel shows captive Kushites (Fig. 84)

It has usually been supposed that Tefnakht's assumption of the pharaonic style was an act of antagonism towards the Kushites. This need not have been the case. Piye's earlier declaration of his power to make and unmake kings may have been tempered with political expediency. Despite his successes, Piye had failed to crush Tefnakht completely and may have felt that Tefnakht's power had been sufficiently limited by the war for him to be unable to rapidly recover. Following the oath of fealty taken by Tefnakht in Sau, Piye may have allowed, or even encouraged, the Saite to assume the royal style as a vassal. Our knowledge of Tefnakht's capital city is sadly limited, although there are some indications that it may have been increasingly important in the trade with Phoenicia.

Tefnakht himself must have been a man of mature years, as his sons had been placed in charge of garrisons during the war. Six years of, presumably peaceful, reign would have allowed Sau to recover from the defeat inflicted by Piye.

It is assumed that the next Saite ruler, Bakenranef, was the direct successor, perhaps a son, of Tefnakht. In the tradition preserved by Manethon, he is the only pharaoh of the 24th Dynasty. The first four years of his reign would have been the last years of Piye's.

Most remarkably for the king who conquered Egypt, Piye's names and figure were erased from his monuments, and later restored. Some scholars see this as an indicator of an insurrection between year 21 and the completion of the Barkal temple where the king's names are intact; others suggest that there was a later conflict within the royal family, perhaps in the reign of Shabaqo or Shebitqo, between Prince Khaliut, a son of Piye, and Taharqo.[11] A stela was set up to honour Khaliut in the reign of king Aspelta, a full century after Taharqo's accession.

There are no known dated monuments from Egypt until year 21. In the eyes of some Egyptologists this confirmed that the campaign against Tefnakht was in years 19 and 20. However, as argued earlier, the evidence of the Victory Stela itself quite clearly shows that the Kushites controlled Thebes at the beginning of the campaign. They had undoubtedly maintained their authority in the southern city following Kashta's appearance there, and the lack of earlier dated monuments is probably accidental. Two papyri from the Theban region are apparently dated to the king's 21st and 22nd years, and the latest date of all, year 24, comes from the Oasis of Dakhla.[12]

As already noted, placing the reign of Piye precisely is very difficult. Most scholars agreed that the accession of Shabaqo to the Kushite throne should be dated around 715 BC. Consequently, Piye's accession was generally dated somewhere around 747 BC with the campaign against Tefnakht (assumed to have taken place in regnal years 19-20) in 728. Donald Redford placed these events a little later, with the accession in 735 and the campaign in 716.[13]

The date of 715 BC for Shabaqo's accession was, however, based upon the misreading of an Assyrian text.[14] Many Egyptologists – although there are still some dissenting voices – would now accept that Shabaqo led his army to Egypt, not in 715 BC, but sometime after 712 BC. His invasion can probably be dated to the period 711-709.[15]

The Assyrian evidence is preserved in a number of sources: the Annals of 711, a Prism fragment from Nineveh, and the Display Inscription at Khorsabad.[16] The events narrated in these texts must therefore belong to the very last years of Piye's rule. Kush, for the first time, appears prominently on the international stage, and these events doubtless influenced the Kushite strategy of the following reign.

The trouble started in the coastal city of Ashdod, in Philistia. Ashdod had, so far, remained outside the Assyrian sphere of influence. Sargon now claimed that its king, Aziru, had conspired with the kings of the surrounding areas and planned not to pay his tribute. In 713 BC Aziru was deposed and the Assyrians replaced him with "his full brother", Akhimetu. The people disliked Akhimetu and he was soon ousted. A new ruler, apparently unrelated, was installed. His name, Yamani, means "the Greek", and he may have been a Cypriot.[17] The Assyrian records say that Yamani was "without claim to the throne" and that he was installed by the "Hittites", that is the rulers of the small kingdoms of north Syria.

Yamani promptly began to organise an anti-Assyrian coalition and also sent to Egypt for help.

> [He sent] ... to the [kings] of Piliste (Philistia), Iaudi (Judah), [Edom], Moab, who dwell by the sea, payers of tribute [and] tax to Assur my lord, [they sent] numberless inflammatory and disdainful (messages) to set them at enmity with me. To Pi'ru, king of Egypt, a prince who could not save them, they sent their presents and attempted to gain him as an ally.

The identity of this "Pi'ru" – pharaoh – has been extensively disputed, but it is almost impossible to identify him with certainty.[18] He was not a Kushite, but certainly a Delta ruler. The later Assyrian texts *always* call the Kushite rulers *sharru Kusu Musri* or *sharru Kusu*, and never *sharru Musri* alone, nor Pi'ru. Some Egyptologists have argued that Pi'ru was Bakenranef, which is possible, but there is no supporting evidence, beyond the certainty that he was reigning as a pharaoh at this time.[19]

The Assyrian Annals give the impression that Sargon led the campaign in person, but another source, the "Eponym Chronicle",[20] states that Sargon was "in the land", that is, in Assyria. The army was under the command of the *turtanu*, the military officer ranking next below the king. The biblical text of the prophet Isaiah [20.1] also states that "Sargon king of Assyria sent his *turtanu* to Ashdod and he took it by storm". This is followed by Isaiah's prophecy:

> a sign and warning to Egypt and Kush:
>   All men shall be dismayed, their hopes in Kush and their pride in Egypt humbled.
>   On that day those who dwell along this coast will say "So much for our hopes on which we relied for help and deliverance from the king of Assyria; what escape have we now?"

The prophecies of Isaiah, along with the other biblical books which cover the events of this period, were written down much later. They were compiled from a number of different sources and were extensively abridged and modified. There are some striking conflations of events (as with the siege of Jerusalem and the death of Sennacherib) and the text cannot be used as evidence that the Kushites were seen as a potential defender against Assyria in 712 BC. Nevertheless, the Kushite kings must have been fully aware of the events, and may have sent contingents to aid the Delta rulers in any potential threat to Egypt's eastern frontier. Egypt was certainly seen as a refuge for rebellious rulers fleeing the Assyrian advance. Although the *turtanu* led the army, Sargon claimed the credit.

> I, Sargon, the rightful ruler, who fears the curse of Shamash and Marduk, who observes the command of Assur, [crossed] the Tigris and Euphrates, at the high[est] flood, the high water of the spring of the year [in boats and] made my way on the dry land. And that Yamani, their king, who had trusted in his own strength and had not [submitted] to my rule, heard of the progress of my march [from afar], and the terror of [Assur, my lord] overwhelmed him ...
>
> ...Yamani of Ashdod feared my weapons, left his wife, his sons and daughters (behind), fled over the border of Egypt which is on the frontier of Meluhha and lived there like a thief.

The incorrect reading of this part of the text as Meluhha "which now belongs to Egypt" was seen as evidence that Shabaqo's invasion had already happened. In Assyrian texts of this date, Meluhha is another name for Kush, although it might possibly have reference to a specific part of it.[21] Exactly where Yamani fled to is unclear, since Upper Egypt was still under Kushite control (unless there had been some sort of rebellion).

> Ashdod, Gath, Asdudimmu, I besieged, I captured; his gods, his wife, his sons, his daughters, the property, goods (and) treasures of his palace, together with the people of his land, I counted as spoil.

The third city captured, Asdudimmu, is Ashdod-Yam, some 3 miles (5 kms) northwest of Ashdod, where excavations revealed the remains of the defences hastily constructed by Yamani. The city wall of sun-dried mud-brick, three metres thick, was protected by glacis on the inner and outer sides. The outer glacis was an attempt to resist the attacks by siege engines, towers and battering rams, that on the inside to counteract the pressure. These defences failed.

In Ashdod itself, level VIII was probably the city of Yamani and his predecessors. Here, excavations uncovered the remains of 3,000 individuals, many with traces of wounds, who might be the people who died during Sargon's assault. A fragment of a basalt stela of Sargon recording his victory was also found.

The reliefs from the palace of Khorsabad, which apparently relate to this campaign, show cities labelled as Ekron and Gibbethon; another, unnamed, might be Ashdod itself. Some of the defenders of Gibbethon have been identified as "negroes", suggesting that there were Kushite contingents, even if the Kushite king was not directly involved.[22]

> Over the whole of his wide land and his prosperous people I set my officials as governors. I extended the borders of Assur, king of the gods.

Ashdod and its surrounds were made an Assyrian province.

The fate of Yamani is recorded in the texts, but in broken sections. Here, for the first time, the Kushite kings enter the Assyrian record. Couched in the traditional phraseology of such texts, Sargon claims that the Kushites had never before had contact with Assyria. This *might* have been so, but we know from other records that the phrase was used in cases where there had been long-standing diplomatic contacts: it simply heightened the drama and emphasised the extensive power of the king.

> The king of Meluhha, who is in the midst of ..., an inapproachable region, a ... road ... (dwelt), whose fathers since far-off days of the moon-god's time, had not sent greetings – (that Kushite king) heard from afar of the might of Assur, Nabu and Marduk and the terrifying splendour of my royalty overpowered him and fright overcame him. In fetters, shackles and bonds of iron, he cast him [Yamani] and they brought him before me into Assyria (after) a most difficult journey.

So, the Kushite king returned Yamani to the Assyrians, and in so-doing apparently entered into an amicable relationship. As yet, the realm of the Kushites did not extend into Western Asia, and hence there was no clash of interests.

A newly published inscription of Sargon II at Tang-i Var in Iran now reveals that the Kushite king who extradited Yamani to Assyria was, in fact, the *sar Meluhha Sa-pa-ta-ku-u*, who can only be Shebitqo. This text raises a number of important questions, but it may be safe to conclude that the other records of the Yamani incident actually conflate the time scale, and that Yamani's flight from Ashdod to Kush was followed by a period of residence there lasting, perhaps, three or four years, during which time Shabaqo ascended the throne, crushed the "rebellion" of Bakenranef and established himself as ruler in Memphis. He must then have appointed

Shebitqo as his representative in Kush, necessitated by the vast size of the realm. Friendly relations with Assyria at this time are suggested by other sources, and doubtless led to the deportation of the Yamani to Nineveh.[23]

Piye died in his 24th or 25th year, and was buried at el-Kurru. His tomb was assumed by George Reisner to have been surmounted by a pyramid, but only the foundation courses survived, and Reisner's reconstruction has often been doubted. The tomb consisted of a subterranean burial chamber, approached by a staircase cut in the rock. The pyramid, or mastaba, was raised over the burial chamber, with a chapel attached, and the whole surrounded by an enclosure. There was no decoration surviving in the burial chamber. Although it was badly plundered there were still fragments of the furniture, including a fine bronze libation stand, shabti figures and amulets with the king's name and fragments of gold foil and lapis lazuli.

These last years of the king's reign may have seen crisis in Kush: on some of his monuments the king's figure was destroyed and later restored. It is difficult to date either the destructions or restorations, and the problem is further confused by the inconsistent way in which they were carried out. The rise and expansion of the Kushite state had been rapid: that the new dynasty may have faced opposition from some regions, tribal groups or factions is to be expected. But, at present, we can only speculate. So far, very little is known of the southern regions around Meroe in these early years of the Kushite kingdom. There must have been military activities there, and perhaps also against the peoples of the surrounding deserts. Certainly the earliest graves in the elite cemeteries at Meroe date from the reign of Piye, but, until further information is forthcoming, the role of the savannah lands in the expansion of the Kushite state cannot be assessed. For all its conventions, the Victory Stela throws one period of Piye's reign into brilliant light, but it also emphasises how little we know of the remainder.

XV   The Broken Reed

The new ruler of Kush and Upper Egypt was the son of Kashta and brother of the God's Wife of Amun elect, Amenirdis I. It has long been assumed that he was a younger brother of Piye, although there is no direct evidence to support the idea. A number of inscriptions states his relationship to Amenirdis, and hence his parentage.

A number of Shabaqo's wives and children is known. Queen Tabakenamun was a king's daughter, king's sister and king's wife.[1] In addition, she held the religious offices, Priestess of Hathor, Mistress of Tepihu (*Aphroditopolis*), Priestess of Hathor of Iunyt (*Dendera*), and Priestess of Neit. The royal titles suggest that she was a sister-wife of the king, but the priestly offices raise the possibility that she was the daughter of one of the Libyan kings. Another wife, Mesbat, was named on the sarcophagus of the High Priest of Amun Haremakhet, and was presumably his mother.[2] A third wife, queen Qalhata, was the mother of Tanwetamani.[3] As such she is depicted on the "Dream Stela" and in her tomb at el-Kurru. Following the Assyrian evidence, Qalhata was a sister of Taharqo, and hence a daughter of Piye. Tanwetamani was thus one of Shabaqo's youngest sons. Besides Tanwetamani and the High Priest Haremakhet, Shabaqo was probably the father of his immediate successor, Shebitqo. Of the king's daughters, Istemkheb, who was also Chief Wife of a king, was buried at Abdju (Abydos).[4]

Shabaqo figures prominently in the Graeco-Roman sources. In them, he represents the whole of the Kushite dynasty and is a semi-legendary figure. This prominence in later tradition is not balanced in the Egyptian and Nubian record, and, although a large number of buildings survives from his reign, there is no known historical document comparable to the inscription of Piye.

The Greek writers recognised Shabaqo as the founder of the 25th Dynasty, and thought that it was he, rather than Kashta or Piye, who had brought Egypt under Kushite rule. The reason for this is undoubtedly his choice of Memphis as his major residence city.

Herodotos portrays Shabaqo – Sabacos – as a just ruler who, instead of punishing criminals with death, made them raise the level of the soil around their native towns. This clearly alludes to the dykes which

Portrait of Shabaqo from the naos he erected in the temple at Esna. (Fig. 85)

protected the towns from the Nile flood. The Aithiopian oracle had predicted a reign of fifty years for Sabacos and, when that time had elapsed, Herodotos writes, Sabacos dreamt that he would commit sacrilege. Rather than do this, Sabacos left Egypt.

The other ancient traditions record a renewed conflict between Kush and the Saites. The surviving versions of Manetho state quite baldly that:

> Sabacos ... taking Bochchoris captive, burned him alive.

Bochchoris (or Bocchoris) is the Greek form of the Egyptian name, Bakenranef. The reign of Bocchoris figured prominently in later traditions, and the pharaoh was revered as a law giver.[5] It is claimed in Manetho's history that during his reign a lamb spoke. A bizarre episode in Plutarch's life of the Hellenistic king Demetrios recounts the Solomonic judgement of Bocchoris in dealing with a dispute between a young man and a courtesan.

Two versions of Manetho's history ascribe to Bocchoris a reign of 44 years, and one a reign of 6 years. The highest date so far attested on a monument of the reign is 6 years.

The only rather slender support for the classical tradition comes from the Serapeum at Saqqara. The Serapeum was the burial place of Apis, the sacred bull which was regarded as a manifestation of the god Ptah. The bull lived in a splendid stall near the temple of Ptah in the heart of the ancient city, and after its death it was mummified and then taken along the great processional way to the underground catacomb in the desert necropolis. The catacomb, commenced in the reign of Ramesses II, comprised an underground corridor with vaults on either side. A new catacomb was begun by Psamtik I and here the bulls were laid in massive granite or basalt sarcophagi. Unfortunately, the excavations of the earlier vault were not well-conducted or published, and there remains much confusion regarding the burials. It seems that these earlier bulls were mummified and laid in the chambers without the large sarcophagi, but it is now unclear whether there was only one bull buried in each chamber (as happened later) or whether two or more burials were made in a single chamber.

The Serapeum was cleared by the French Egyptologist, Auguste Mariette, between 1850 and 1854. Huge numbers of funerary stelae were discovered, which record the burials and the officiating priests.[6] A number of stelae was found, which were dated to year 6 of Bakenranef, and Mariette claimed that in the same chamber there was a graffito of Shabaqo, dated to his second year. The evidence is, alas, very confused, other sources claiming that it was not a graffito, but a stela of Shabaqo. Nevertheless, this evidence has been interpreted as support for the ancient sources: that Shabaqo invaded Egypt in his second year, Bakenranef's sixth, captured Memphis, and immediately paid his respects to the Apis which had only recently been buried.

Despite the problems associated with the Serapeum evidence, it is certain that Shabaqo was in Egypt in his second year – an inscription on the quay at Karnak is dated to it, as is a stela from Horbeit (*Pharbaithos*).[7] The Horbeit stela was dedicated by the Great Chief of the Ma, Patjenfy, who had submitted to Piye at the great durbar in Hut-hery-ib. It is thus clear that, even if Sau opposed the new Kushite pharaoh, some of the Libyan dynasts remained loyal.

As in the reign of Piye, the Saites were the main opposition. Bakenranef had certainly been acknowledged in Memphis, and had expanded his control right across the Delta to Djanet (*Tanis*). In the ruins of that city, an architectural fragment carries his name.[8] No pharaoh was recorded in the city on the stela of Piye, and the Saites must have taken this opportunity to bring it under their own control.

The details of Shabaqo's campaign are unknown. The Kushites doubtless still held Thebes, and it must be assumed that, having ensured his position in Kush was accepted, Shabaqo marched northwards. Perhaps Bakenranef, as Tefnakht before him, was marching south to absorb Middle and Upper Egypt into his kingdom. Unless an equivalent of Piye's Victory stela is discovered, the events are unlikely ever to be known.

Not only has the detail of the events surrounding Shabaqo's military action in Egypt been a source of controversy, but so has the exact date of his accession. Most scholars agreed that the accession of Shabaqo to the Kushite throne should be dated around 715 BC. This, however, was based upon the misreading of the Assyrian text relating to the rebellion of Yamani of Ashdod. It now seems that the invasion, and the accession of Shabaqo to the throne in Memphis, was *after* 712 BC.

If any credence is to be given to the surviving excerpts of Manetho's history, the defeat of Bakenranef saw the installation of a Kushite governor in Sau, the temporary eclipse of Saite influence and the acknowledgement of Shabaqo and his successors as overlords of the Delta. Within Saite territory, a stela of Shabaqo's 4th year from Sau and another of his 6th year from the twin towns of Pe and Dep (*Buto*) depicts the king before the city's patron deities, Horus of Pe and Wadjyt.[9]

From about 710 or 709 BC, the Kushites controlled all of Egypt but, unlike Piye, Shabaqo set about establishing himself as a pharaoh in Egypt, with his residence at Memphis. Shabaqo, as Piye before him, doubtless confirmed the Delta rulers in their positions, or replaced them with others more amenable. He probably contracted marriage alliances with the Libyan dynasts and other elite families.[10] He followed the tradition of the Libyan pharaohs in placing a son as High Priest of Amun, although he did not install any daughter as future God's Wife of Amun.

Unlike Piye who changed his titulary a number of times during his reign, Shabaqo modelled himself upon the Old Kingdom pharaohs. His throne-name, Neferkare, had been used by Pepy II and many of his successors. Also in Old Kingdom style, his Horus, Two Ladies and Golden Horus names were the same, Sebaq-tawy, probably meaning "He who blesses the Two Lands".[11]

Whether the new pharaoh immediately courted the alliance of the rulers of western Asia is uncertain, but doubtless it was to his advantage to do so. The timber of the Lebanon and the products of the Phoenician cities were now traded for the commodities of Kush. In these early years, the Kushites seem to have maintained friendly relations with Assyria, and seals from Kuyunjik suggest that Sargon and Shabaqo exchanged diplomatic correspondence.[12]

A letter to Sargon from the Crown Prince Sennacherib lists gifts sent by Azuri, king of Ashdod, and the ruler of another Philistian city (Gaza or Ashkelon) to Nineveh. These included rolls of papyrus and garments of the finest Egyptian linen, as well as elephant hides.[13] The Kushite pharaohs were doubtless able to benefit from both the Egyptian royal monopolies and the produce of Kush itself.

A large scarab, reputedly from Jerusalem, and now in the Toronto Museum *might* indicate military activities in north Sinai to regain control of the coastal road, but its conventional language negates its value as an historical document.[14]

For some years, there was little direct intervention by the Assyrians in the west, and this must have allowed Shabaqo to gain a foothold there. Following the "rebellion" of Yamani and the campaign against the west, Sargon was increasingly distracted by events to the north and east of Assyria, and then by events in Babylonia. Sargon led two campaigns into Babylonia against Marduk-apli-idinna. In these southern campaigns the Assyrians were at a disadvantage. When confronted by an Assyrian advance, the Chaldaeans and Elamites could withdraw into the marshes or mountains where the Assyrians were unwilling to follow. This is exactly what happened. The Assyrians intimidated the Elamite king, received the submission of some of the northern towns of Babylonia, and the Chaldaean king was forced to retreat into the marshlands. Babylon submitted, and, at the New Year festival of 709, Sargon "took the hand of Bel" as Tiglath-pileser III had done, re-establishing the dual monarchy. In 707 Marduk-apli-idinna's capital city of Dur-Yakin was captured, although the king escaped. Assyrian governors were appointed in the south, and Sargon claims to have removed some 108,000 Aramaeans and Chaldaeans to western Asia.

In 705, Sargon was killed on campaign in Tabalu (in Cappadocia). His body could not be recovered for burial, and this was taken as a sign that he had sinned against the gods. So fearful was Sargon's successor of associating himself with his ill-fated parent, that he never mentioned him in his inscriptions, and he immediately transferred the capital from the recently completed city of Dur-Sharrukin to Nineveh.

The great city of Nineveh, standing close to the river Tigris in the rich farm lands of central Assyria, was already an ancient and important town. Now it was to remain the capital of Assyria until the empire's fall to the Medes and Babylonians in 612 BC. Here the new Assyrian king *Sin-ahhe-riba*, Sennacherib, began the building of a new royal residence – the "Palace Without a Rival". The facade had a portico with columns of bronze resting on bases cast in the form of lions and bulls; its public halls were decorated with stone slabs covered in painted bas-relief; fresco and glazed tiles enriched the halls. The palace had extensive parks and gardens, the water for these and the rest of the city was brought along canals and aqueducts for 40-50 miles (64-80 km). New walls, about seven and a half miles (12 km) in length, with fifteen entrance gates and a moat, encircled the city.

Sennacherib's reign (704-681 BC) was dominated by events in Babylonia.[15] At Sargon's death, Assyria's persistent rival, the Chaldaean king, Marduk-apli-idinna, had again seized the Babylonian throne: he was still able to muster strong support.

Whenever the Assyrians were preoccupied with other borders of their empire, the West took the opportunity to reassert its independence. The death of Sargon and the confusion that followed, with the renewed independence of Babylon, allowed the states of Philistia, Judah and Phoenicia to contemplate rebellion. Egypt, in the person of Shabaqo, became involved.

Shortly after his restoration to the throne of Babylon, Marduk-apli-idinna sent an embassy to Hezekiah of Judah.[16] Whether the fulminations of the prophet Isaiah are to be treated as an useful historical source is debatable. He refers to envoys seeking the assistance of the chariotry of Zoan (Djanet) and Nen-nesut.

Sennacherib was concerned first of all with Babylon. An Assyrian force confronted an alliance of Babylonians, Chaldaeans, Aramaeans, Elamites and Arabs – all of Assyria's southern enemies. Nevertheless, Babylon was recaptured, along with members of Marduk-apli-idinna's family. The king himself escaped and fled into the marshland where he later died. The death of Assyria's adversary was not the end of Babylonian opposition which was to continue, led by the Chaldaean king's sons. In Babylon, Sennacherib now installed his own nominee, only to replace him shortly afterwards (in 700 BC) with his own son, Assur-nadin-shumi.

Having reasserted Assyrian authority in Babylonia, Sennacherib turned to the West. This episode has, for long, been a cause of considerable dissent amongst Egyptologists, Assyriologists and biblical scholars. The events are narrated in the biblical books of *Kings* and *Isaiah* and in the Annals of Sennacherib. In addition, there are reliefs from Sennacherib's palace at Nineveh, which can be associated with certain incidents. There is no Egyptian evidence from these years, but incidents mentioned in the inscriptions of Taharqo from the temple at Kawa have been associated with them.

The focus of the controversy is the biblical reference to Taharqo's presence at the battle of Eltekeh. In the biblical narrative which was written many years after the events, it is clear that there has been a conflation of events. The retreat of Sennacherib's army is followed immediately by the account of the king's death which did not happen until 681 BC. For that reason, a number of scholars has preferred to understand the reference to Taharqo (and all of the succeeding events) as belonging to a second campaign by Sennacherib. This would have taken place sometime after Taharqo's succession in 690 BC, and after 689 BC when Sennacherib was still involved in events in Babylonia.

Egyptologist Kenneth Kitchen has argued strongly and cogently against two Assyrian campaigns.[17] He regards the reference to Taharqo as king (*melek Kush*) as a "gloss" of the time when the text was written (sometime after 680 BC). However, since Kitchen prefers a "high" chronology for the 25th Dynasty, he places the events of 701 immediately following the death of Shabaqo and the accession of Shebitqo. The inscription of Taharqo (discussed more fully in Chapter 16) tells us that the prince was summoned to Egypt by Shebitqo, along with other princes and an army. Taharqo was aged twenty at the time. Kitchen proposes that, following the death of Shabaqo (702 BC), the new ruler decided to adopt a more aggressive foreign policy and, having received an appeal for help from Ekron, he summoned an army from Kush, which Taharqo accompanied.

The biblical and Assyrian narratives of events agree, reasonably well (in so far as ancient sources ever agree) and the reference to Taharqo's presence apart, do not necessitate two campaigns.

The "low" chronology for the dynasty is preferred here, in which case the events narrated by Taharqo's inscriptions must have taken place around 695 BC. It also presents a problem for Kitchen's arguments, since Taharqo would have been too young in 701 to have taken any role in the action (and the Kawa text explicitly states that he left Nubia, aged 20, in the reign of Shebitqo).

The biblical reference to Taharqo's presence at the battle of Eltekeh is either an interpolation using the name of a known, and contemporary, ruler, when the biblical narrative was written, sometime after 680 BC, or it *could* indicate events in the 680s. Whilst there is no *direct* evidence that Sennacherib led a second expedition to Palestine, some biblical scholars and some Assyriologists, such as Kirk Grayson, still prefer that interpretation of the record.[18] Such interdisciplinary disputes bedevil attempts to reconstruct ancient history.

As interpreted by Kirk Grayson, the campaign of 701 would include all of the events up to the battle of Eltekeh, the siege of Jerusalem and Hezekiah's agreement to pay tribute. The second campaign, sometime after 689 BC, saw the siege and sack of Lachish, the second siege of Jerusalem and the approach of an Egyptian-Kushite army led by Taharqo. Hostilities were suddenly terminated when Sennacherib's army suffered a plague.

Although the *possibility* of a second campaign which was confronted by the army of Taharqo cannot be totally discounted, the evidence seems to favour only one action, that of 701. In this case, the reference to

Taharqo is simply an interpolation when the narrative was being drawn up, sometime after 680 BC.

In Judah, Hezekiah made a bid for independence and began to expand his kingdom into Philistia. First, he took Gaza in the south-west and then Gath in the north-west. In Philistia itself, some rulers, notably those of Gaza and Ashdod, remained loyal to Assyria, but others, such as the kings of Ashkelon and Ekron, sided with Hezekiah.

In Ashkelon there was a coup. The city had had pro-Assyrian kings for three decades. In 733 BC, following the defeat of Radyan of Damascus by Tiglath-pileser III, Ashkelon's king, Mitinti, who had also rebelled, was overthrown in an attempt to forestall retaliatory action by the Assyrians. In response, Tiglath-pileser installed the leader of the rebellion, Rukibti I, as king. His successors had maintained the pro-Assyrian position and not joined any of the insurrections. Now, Rukibti II was deposed, and his brother, Sidqa, ascended the throne. Sidqa wished to throw off the Assyrian yoke and joined the coalition headed by Hezekiah.

In Ekron, the ruler, Padi, was dethroned by his officials and the populace:

> the officials, nobles and people of Ekron, who had thrown Padi, their king, bound by (treaty to) Assyria, into fetters of iron and had given him over to Hezekiah, the Jew – he kept him in confinement like an enemy, they became afraid and called upon the Egyptian kings, the bowmen, the chariots and horses of the king of Meluhha, a countless host, and these came to their aid.

In Phoenicia, Luli, king of Sidon, joined the rebels.

Hezekiah prepared for the inevitable Assyrian assault. He rebuilt or repaired the walls of Jerusalem, raising towers or bastions along its length. Of great importance was the digging of the Siloam tunnel which brought water into the city. In 1880 part an inscription recording the quarrying of this tunnel was found.[19] The city's defenders were equipped with shields and hand weapons. Martial law was introduced, and the king harangued the assembled populace.

Sennacherib's army arrived in the West, marching first to the coast. Luli, the king of Sidon, fled to Cyprus, and a new king, Ittobaal II, was installed. Ittobaal now ruled over Great Sidon, Little Sidon, Bit-Zitti, Zaribtu, Mahalliba, Ushu, Akzib and Akku. At a durbar near Tyre, Sennacherib received the submission of the Phoenician and Transjordanian rulers – Menahem of Shamshimurun, Ittobaal of Sidon, Abdiliti of Arvad, Urumilki of Gubla (Byblos), Pudu-ilu of Beth-Ammon, Kammusu-Labdi of Moab and Aiarammu of Edom. From Philistia, only

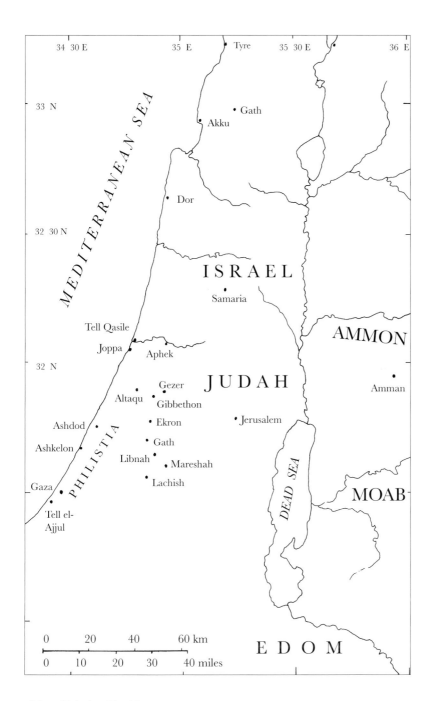

Map of Palestine. (Fig. 86)

213

Mitinti of Ashdod submitted: Sidqa was in open revolt; Gath was under Judaean control. In Gaza, Sillibel, the city's ruler, had remained loyal when Hezekiah rebelled, but does not now appear. In the face of the Assyrian advance, the Egyptian army had probably already marched and established its headquarters at Gaza. Sillibel may have left the city and sought the protection of Sennacherib.

The Assyrian army marched southwards. Joppa, a dependency of Ashkelon, along with its hinterland of Beth-Dagon, Beni-Baraq and Azor, were captured. This seems to have resulted in another coup in Ashkelon itself. The rebellious Sidqa was deposed, and his nephew, the son of the former king Rukibti, was installed, with the Assyrian name Sharruludari ("May the ruler live!"). Sennacherib received the submission of the new king, but annexed some of his territory.

The Assyrians now moved on towards Ekron, but their path was barred at Eltekeh (Assyrian: Altaqu) by the arrival of an Egyptian and Kushite force. Eltekeh, is probably Tell esh-Shallaf some 15 km south of Joppa.

> In the plain of Altaqu, their ranks were drawn up before me, they sharpened their weapons. Upon a trust(-inspiring) oracle (given) by Assur, my lord, I fought with them and brought about their defeat. The Egyptian charioteers and princes, together with the charioteers of the Kushite king, my hands took alive in the midst of the battle.

Sennacherib claims to have taken prisoners from the chariotry, but not to have defeated any Kushite king or prince. The army was routed, and the Assyrians continued their march southwards unhindered. After this first defeat at Eltekeh, the Egyptian-Kushite army retreated and prepared for a second attack. The Assyrians captured Eltekeh, Timna and Ekron.

> Altaqu and Timna I besieged, I captured and took away their spoil. I drew near to Ekron and slew the governors and nobles who had committed sin and hung their bodies on stakes around the city.

The Assyrian advance trapped Hezekiah in Jerusalem "like a bird in a cage".

The Assyrian army now broke into four divisions. One advanced on Lachish, one on Libnah, one was raiding Mareshah and the fourth besieged Jerusalem. Sennacherib himself was with the division of the army which now invested Lachish. From Lachish, the king sent the Turtan, and two other officals, the *rab-saris* and the *rab-shaqeh*, as envoys to Jerusalem. Hezekiah sent a deputation to meet them. The people of Jerusalem

214

gathered on the city walls to watch and listen. The *rab-shaqeh* addressed the deputation *in Hebrew*.

> On whom then do you rely for support in your rebellion against me? On Egypt? Egypt is a splintered cane that will run into a man's hand and pierce it if he leans on it. That is what Pharaoh king of Egypt proves to all who rely on him.

This characterisation of the Kushite pharaoh as a "broken reed" has dominated European perception of the Kushite pharaohs for a very long time. The chamberlain, Eliakim, asked him to use Aramaic, so that the discussions would be confidential, but the Assyrian continued to use Hebrew.

> Is it to your master and to you that my master has sent me to say this? Is it not the people sitting on the wall who, like you, will have to eat their own dung and drink their own urine?

Then the *rab-shaqeh* shouted to the besieged inhabitants in Hebrew:

> Hear the message of the Great King, the king of Assyria. These are the king's words:
> Do not be taken in by Hezekiah. He cannot save you from me. Do not let him persuade you to rely on the Lord, and tell you that the Lord will save you and that this city will never be surrendered to the king of Assyria ... Make peace with me ... Do not listen to Hezekiah; he will only mislead you by telling you that the Lord will save you. Did the god of any of these nations save his land from the king of Assyria? Where are the gods of Hamath and Arpad? ... Where are the gods of Samaria? Did they save Samaria from me? Among all the gods of the nations is there one who saved his land from me? And how is the Lord to save Jerusalem?

According to Sennacherib's record, forty-six towns, forts and villages were captured. Altogether, 200,150 people were captured and transported. Lachish is not specifically mentioned in the Annals, but is the subject of impressive reliefs from Nineveh.[20] Here the full might of the Assyrian military machine is displayed. The pitched battles, such as that at Eltekeh, were still dominated by the chariotry divisions, but they were of no use in sieges. Ramps of stamped earth were pushed up against the city walls, whilst sappers set to work to breach the defences. Battering rams and wheeled siege-engines, with archers, are shown being pushed up the ramps to the city walls. Archers and slingers provide covering fire. From the battlements and towers the defenders throw down stones and lighted torches and shoot arrows. After the fall of the city, Sennacherib turned on Libnah.

> But when the king learnt that Taharqo king of Kush was on the way to make war on him, he sent messengers again to Hezekiah, king of Judah, to say to him, "How can you be deluded by your god on whom you rely when he promises that Jerusalem shall not fall into the hands of the king of Assyria? Surely you have heard what the kings of Assyria have done to all countries ... can you hope then to escape?"

There is no further mention of the Egyptian-Kushite army, and Kenneth Kitchen has suggested that, unable to oppose the massed Assyrian forces, it probably made a tactical withdrawal. The biblical narrative concludes with Hezekiah's prayer and the divine promise of Jerusalem's deliverance.

> That night the angel of the lord went out and struck down a hundred and eighty-five thousand men in the Assyrian camp; when morning dawned, they all lay dead. So Sennacherib, king of Assyria, broke camp, went back to Assyria and stayed there.

The Greek historian Herodotos (II.141) includes a similar episode. Sennacherib's army is camped at Pelusion, when, during the night, the quivers, bowstrings and leather handles of shields are eaten by field-mice. According to Herodotos, this happened in the reign of "Sethos" who is usually equated with Shebitqo.[21]

It is generally assumed that both texts recall an outbreak of plague in the Assyrian army. Understandably, nothing of this is to be found in the royal annals.

Hezekiah sent his tribute to Nineveh. It included 30 talents of gold and 800 talents of silver, couches and chairs inlaid with ivory, elephant hides, boxwood and ebony. The ivory, elephant hides and ebony suggest strong trading contacts with the Kushites. The king also sent his own daughters and concubines, with male and female musicians. Padi of Ekron was released to the Assyrians and restored as king. Some of Hezekiah's cities were given to him, probably including Lachish. Others of Hezekiah's cities were given to Mitinti king of Ashdod and to Sillibel of Gaza. So the rebellious Hezekiah was now surrounded by Assyrian client kings. Some others of Judah's neighbours may have taken advantage of Judah's weakened state: Edom moved to sieze Beersheba and Arad. Hezekiah continued to rule his much reduced kingdom until 687/686, when he was succeeded by his 12-year old son, Manasseh.

The confrontation had not been an outright success, and the military action had ended in stalemate. As Kenneth Kitchen pointed out, if Sennacherib had been successful, he would have speeded up the reduction of the kingdom of Judah by a hundred years; if the Kushite army had been successful, they may have been able to make a bid for supremacy in Western Asia, which was not again attempted by a pharaoh until the reign of Nekau II in 605 BC.[22]

Following the campaign, Sennacherib became preoccupied with events in other parts of his empire. Although there were Assyrian vassals and governors throughout the west, Sennacherib and his army did not return. For a further twenty years, the Kushite pharaohs were free to involve themselves in the affairs of the region. The lack of evidence for military action by the Kushites might simply be due to accident of survival, but perhaps they were more intent on trade.

In Egypt, Shabaqo's last years saw Kushite supremacy at Thebes. At some point in the reign, Shepenwepet I died, and the king's sister, Amenirdis I, at last assumed the office of God's Wife of Amun.[23] The king's son, Haremakhet, was appointed as High Priest of Amun, bringing the control of the domain of Amun firmly into Kushite hands. There is also some indication that other offices may have been taken from old Theban families and reallocated.

Shabaqo's reign saw the first major building works of the Kushites in Egypt. These have survived best in the Theban region where the Saite pharaoh Psamtik II was content to have their names altered, but, in recent years, excavations at Memphis have yielded increasing numbers of blocks from the Kushite constructions there. The most significant building so far identified is the embalming house of the Apis bull.[24] Following the death of the Apis bull in year 6 of Bakenranef (Shabaqo's second year), a new bull must have been installed. Since the cartouches were later recut for Psamtik II, it can be assumed the embalming house continued in use for nearly a full century and does not indicate that a bull died during Shabaqo's reign.[25]

One of the most important Memphite survivals from the reign is the so-called "Memphite theology" or "Shabaqo Stone".[26] This block of basalt carries a text which purports to be copied from an ancient worm-eaten document written on papyrus or leather. The lines therefore contain many gaps, increased by the surface damage caused by the stone's use in more recent times as a millstone. The original text, written in a form of language similar to the Pyramid Texts, has long been thought to date from the Old Kingdom, but some Egyptologists think that it is a much later

The High Priest of Amun, Haremakhet, son of Shabaqo. A red quartzite statue found at Karnak. It is dated by its inscriptions to the reign of Tanwetamani. Haremakhet may have been appointed to his office by Shabaqo or by Taharqo. (Fig. 87)

creation, perhaps of Ramesside date. Whatever the date of the original text, the copy is an important document demonstrating the enormous interest in the ancient traditions during the Kushite and Saite periods. This phenomenon, usually described rather dismissively as "archaism", was a primary stimulus to the renaissance in the arts.[27] The text of the Memphite theology concerns the role of the creator god Ptah, and the importance of the city of Memphis as the balance of the two lands.

Also from Memphis, a superb relief block depicted the pharaoh before the Theban goddess Mut who, like her consort Amun, had shrines in the northern city. The surviving fragment carries only the king's double crown and parts of his Horus name and the goddess's titles. Nevertheless, it is of excellent work and shows the influence of earlier models. It probably belongs with other, stylistically very similar, blocks carrying the king's names, which are in the Berlin and Cairo Museums.[28] There is a strong similarity between these blocks and those of an obscure Tanite pharaoh, Gemenefkhonsubak.[29] All of them look back to Middle or Old Kingdom models, notably the scenes in the underground chambers of the Step Pyramid of Djoser at Saqqara.

Subsequent historical events make it unlikely that much Kushite royal statuary from Memphis will have survived undamaged. A head of Shabaqo crowned by a sun-disk, believed to have come from the city, is now in the Munich collection.[30] Two other statues carry invocations to the Memphite deity Ptah-south-of-his-wall, but Shabaqo enlarged the temple of that god at Thebes, and the statues may well have originated there. One of them, was taken to Rome in the Julio-Claudian or Hadrianic period, and, in the 18th century, came into the collection of Cardinal Albani.

A stela from Dendera, which depicts the king before the goddess Hathor and her son Hor-sema-tawy, records the construction of enclosure walls undertaken by the king's builder, Pedienhor, and is evidence that Shabaqo's concern was for temples throughout Egypt, not just the shrine of Amun at Thebes.[31] But it is at Thebes where the king's works are best-preserved.

At Thebes, Shabaqo added a new porch to the temple of Ipet-resyt (Luxor). The main entrance was the pylon covered with scenes of Ramesses II's victory over the Hittites at the battle of Kadesh. The doorway was flanked by obelisks and colossal black granite seated statues of the same king, with four other standing colossi in red granite. Between the two wings of this pylon, Shabaqo built a new main gate, with huge images of himself with various deities, carved in high relief.[32]

Even more striking was the colonnaded entrance which was built in front of the great gateway. This portico seems to have consisted of a long colonnade leading up to the gateway, its own gateway decorated with lists of conquered enemies, copied from the lists of Thutmose III.[33]

Within the precincts of Ipet-sut, the temple of Amun at Karnak, a structure of Shabaqo's was later dismantled and its blocks re-used in the building of Taharqo's temple by the Sacred Lake. Amongst the re-used blocks is one carrying a particularly fine relief head of the pharaoh (Fig.88).[34]

Within the great temple of Amun, surviving Kushite additions are few. Undoubtedly there were statues of the pharaohs, but many of these

Shabaqo wearing the white crown and double uraeus on a reused relief block from a building by the Sacred Lake at Karnak. (Fig. 88)

would have been later destroyed. Throughout the centuries the main entrance had been brought further and further to the west. Behind the great pylon of Horemheb, "Illuminating Waset", lay the hypostyle hall completed by Ramesses II, and another pylon, Amenhotep III's entrance to the temple. Behind this massive pylon, stood the obelisks and old entrance to the temple, the pylon of Thutmose I. The space between the two pylons was one of the axial points of the temple, and still open to the sky. On the southern side, the wide doorway of Ramesses IX opened onto the courts and processional routes to the Sacred Lake and south gate. At the northern entrance to this space, Shabaqo erected a portico of twenty columns, arranged in five rows of four.[35] In front of Thutmose I's pylon stood that king's two obelisks, their tips plated in gold, with those of his grandson, Thutmose III, in front of them, and perhaps another pair erected by Amenhotep II. Between the towers of the pylon stood the great gate of electrum called "Amun-Re is Awesome". The porch, which is depicted in a number of reliefs, had been added to the gateway by Thutmose IV. This gate was now restored by Shabaqo (it was later rebuilt in the Ptolemaic period, when both the Thutmoside and Kushite inscriptions were replicated). The inscription of Shabaqo states that its decoration was renewed. The step on which it stood was plated with gold, the two columns with electrum and the column bases with silver.[36]

To the north of the Amun temple, Shabaqo built a new treasury or "Hall of Gold".[37] He also added a new gateway to the small Thutmoside temple of Ptah, which stood on the roadway running from the great temple of Amun towards the palace quarter.[38] It may have been from this temple (if not from Memphis) that the seated statue of Shabaqo was removed in Roman times. This statue, excavated either in Rome itself, or Hadrian's villa at Tivoli, entered the Albani collection, and was one of the earliest monuments of a Kushite pharaoh known to European scholars.

On a road to the north of the Ptah temple, Shabaqo, jointly with Amenirdis I, constructed one in a series of chapels, which was devoted to the cults of the God's Wives.[39] From this chapel came the celebrated alabaster statue of Amenirdis. Inscriptions in the Wadi Hammamat are dated to year 12 of Shabaqo, and some also name Amenirdis. They record quarrying of stone for some of these monuments.[40]

South of Thebes, a splendid granite shrine was erected at Esna, carrying one of the most striking images of the pharaoh. At Edfu, blocks from a chapel of Shabaqo or Shebitqo have recently been found re-used in the Ptolemaic temple. Although the names and figures were altered in the reign of Psamtik II, the work is typically Kushite, and of high quality.[41]

Very little from Shabaqo's reign has, so far, been discovered in the Kushite cities of the south. At Kawa, some column drums from a temple were re-used in the enlarging of Temple B by king Harsiyotef. The name of the king was accompanied by the epithet "beloved of Anuket", and it is assumed that the blocks were parts of pillars from a chapel dedicated to that goddess.[42] At Amentego in the Dongola Reach, a seal-stamp in the form of a cartouche with the name Shabaqo-mery-Amun was found. Otherwise the objects naming the king are restricted to scarabs and beads.[43] There are no surviving monuments from the temples at Gebel Barkal.

Although he adopted the style of a pharaoh and chose Memphis as his royal residence, Shabaqo was buried in the ancestral cemetery at el-Kurru. Reisner thought that the tomb, like that of Piye, was surmounted by a pyramid.[44] It had a rock-cut staircase descending to the burial chamber where traces of painted decoration survived. Although badly plundered, the fragments of rich funerary furniture were recovered, including vessels of alabaster and porphyry, many pieces of finely worked ivory and gold amulets and inscribed foil. Most splendid was the bronze mirror with a gilded silver handle decorated with the figures of four goddesses. The king's horses were also buried at el-Kurru, standing and facing north-east. The horses had been draped in bead nets, amulets and bronze ball-beads, with silver collars and plume-holders.

The reign of Shabaqo had seen the consolidation of Kushite rule in Egypt and the crushing of Saite opposition. The Kushite pharaoh had also established himself as the opponent of Assyrian interference in the politics of western Asia. This new stance was to have repercussions for decades to come.

XVI "Enduring of Epiphanies"

Shebitqo, depicted on the façade of the chapel of Osiris Heqa-Djet at Karnak. (Fig. 89)

Shebitqo is the least-known of the Kushite pharaohs; even his family relationships have been the subject of debate. The preserved epitomes of Manetho's history call *Sebichos* (Shebitqo) the son of *Sabakon* (Shabaqo). Whilst Manetho is a far from trustworthy authority, this is the only surviving ancient tradition. In his publication of the inscriptions from the temple of Kawa, Laming Macadam discussed the evidence for reconstructing the royal genealogies, and, based upon his idea of brother succession, he argued that Shebitqo was the elder brother of Taharqo, and hence son of Piye.[1] Macadam's arguments were generally accepted within Egyptology and Nubian studies.

Macadam had based his idea on parts of two inscriptions of Taharqo, which state that the prince was summoned from Nubia when Shebitqo was in Thebes:[2]

> I came from Nubia in the company of the Royal Brethren whom his majesty had summoned, that I might be there with him, since he loved me more than all his brothers and all his children, and I was preferred to them by his majesty ...

223

Macadam noted that there were ambiguities in both texts, but felt that they indicated that Taharqo was one of Shebitqo's brothers, probably the youngest. The inscriptions of Taharqo certainly belong to the genre of royal justification. More problematic, the term "royal brethren" (*snw nsw*) was probably extremely wide, embracing cousins and perhaps more remote lineages of the royal house.[3] Macadam used the text to support his theory of brother succession.

As with so much ancient genealogical evidence, we are dealing with probabilities, rather than facts.

The German Egyptologist, Karl-Heinz Priese, pointed out that an inscription of Shebitqo's wife, queen Arty, names her as a daughter of Piye, but does *not* give her the title, King's Sister, which would be expected if she was the sister-wife of Shebitqo.[4]

Another piece of evidence which suggests that Shebitqo was the son of Shabaqo comes from a royal burial at Abydos. Amongst the remains of the funerary equipment were over 300 shabti figures, some inscribed, broken alabaster canopic jars, and some coffin fragments. All of these belonged to Istemkheb who is named on the coffin fragments as a daughter of Shabaqo.[5] This royal lady is also given the titles King's Chief Wife and King's Sister. It is possible that the king alluded to is Tanwetamani, but it is equally possible, and perhaps more likely, that the burial is earlier than that troubled reign, and that Istemkheb was sister, and Chief Wife, of Shebitqo.

The recently published inscription of Sargon II at Tang-i Var indicates that Shebitqo was ruling Kush before 706 BC, while Shabaqo was in Egypt. He may have become co-regent in the last years of Shabaqo's reign, although there is no clear evidence to support the idea.[6] The preserved versions of Manetho's history grant Shebitqo 8 or 12 years, but the highest date so far known from the monuments is year 3.[7] Some confusion was caused in the academic literature when a stela in the Metropolitan Museum in New York was quoted as dated to the king's year 10: it actually has no date surviving.[8]

On the quay at Karnak, an inscription records a high Nile in Shebitqo's third year, one of many exceptionally high floods in the late Libyan, Kushite and early Saite periods.[9] The text might also, in a typically ambiguous way, suggest that the king had now appeared as sole ruler.

Year 3 [x] month of shomu, day 5, under the majesty of Horus, the Mighty Bull Arising in Thebes, the King of Upper and Lower Egypt, the One Beloved of Two Ladies, Djed-kau, the Golden Horus, Djedkaure, the Son of Re, his beloved, Shebitqo, beloved of Amun-Re Lord of the Thrones of the Two Lands. Now his majesty appeared in the Temple of Amun (when) he granted that he should appear with the two serpent goddesses like Horus on the throne of Re. His father Amun has accorded him an exceedingly great inundation. Great is the inundation in his time, 20 cubits 2 palms.

The number of the month was omitted from the text, and it is tempting to associate the date with the Feast of the Valley which happened in the 2nd month of shomu.[10]

Following the death of Shabaqo in Memphis, Shebitqo had probably been crowned there, then returned to Kush to bury his father's body at el-Kurru. Following this, he would have needed to establish his authority in the southland, and doubtless be crowned at Napata, before returning to Egypt.

Shebitqo's throne-name, Djedkaure, is modelled on Old Kingdom types, but his other titles follow New Kingdom precedents. He was the "Horus, Enduring of Epiphanies"(*Djedkau*), or "Horus, the Mighty Bull, Arising in Thebes". As the One of the Two Ladies, he was "Great of awe in all lands" or "Manifesting Maet, beloved of the Two Lands". He assumed the Golden Horus names "Great of strength, smiting the Nine Bows" and "Satisfied with victory". The apparently "militaristic" nature of these titles has led some Egyptologists, notably Kenneth Kitchen, to argue that the king adopted a more aggressive foreign policy than his predecessor.[11] Kitchen proposed that Shebitqo was the reigning pharaoh at the time of the battle of Eltekeh in 701 BC. The historical evidence, however, must mean that it was Shabaqo, not Shebitqo, who was the ruler in 701 BC. The change of policy at that time must be due to factors other than a new king, such as the lack of Assyrian intervention in the west in the years immediately preceding. The apparently militaristic nature of Shebitqo's titulary cannot be used as evidence for historical events, it tells only about the ideological programme of the reign.

Shebitqo was identified by early Egyptologists with the king "Sethos" of Herodotos (II.141) because of the connection with Sennacherib's campaign.[12]

Very little can be said about the events of Shebitqo's reign. Sennacherib was still preoccupied with events in Babylonia and the eastern borders of the empire, which would have allowed the pharaoh to establish good political and trading relations with the Phoenician cities and the Syrian states. The internal history of Egypt and Kush is also badly documented.

In an inscription from the temple of Kawa, Shebitqo's successor, Taharqo, records that:

Now his majesty [Taharqo] had been in Nubia as a goodly youth, a royal brother, pleasant of love, and he came north to Thebes in the company of the goodly youths whom his majesty king Shebitqo had sent to fetch from Nubia, in order that he might be there with him, since he loved me more than his brethren ...

This text has caused much confusion. Following the biblical reference to Taharqo being at the battle of Eltekeh in 701, and the assumption that Shebitqo was king at that time, many scholars thought that, upon Shabaqo's death, Shebitqo ascended the throne and immediately became involved in the rebellion of Hezekiah; that he sent to Nubia for his brothers and an army which was despatched to aid the anti-Assyrian coalition under the command of the young prince Taharqo. This interpretation became widely accepted, but is certainly wrong.

The events recorded by Taharqo's inscription must be dated to the mid or late 690s, perhaps 695 or 694. Shebitqo summoned an army from Kush, and his call to his brothers must be seen in a different light. The army *might* have been sent into western Asia, but, if so, there is no Assyrian record of any conflict.

Rather few buildings can be attributed to Shebitqo. Those which survive are at Thebes, but it is possible that any in Memphis were later dismantled by the Saite kings.

A stela in the Metropolitan Museum in New York from Horbeit depicts Shebitqo making offerings to local deities, Hor-merty and his consort Hathor.[13] The king is accompanied by the smaller figure of a Great Chief of the Ma who, the inscriptions inform us, is none other than Patjenfy who had offered fealty to Piye and dedicated a similar stela in the reign of Shabaqo. Patjenfy's domain was Per-Soped and Granary of Inbu-hedj which controlled the Wadi Tumilat and one of the main routes to the east.

A black granite statue of Shebitqo was found at Memphis, and a colossal red granite head can probably also be attributed to him (Fig.92).[14]

The most notable of the king's monuments are at Thebes. To the east of the main temple of Amun, Shebitqo and Amenirdis I added to the chapel of Osiris Heqa-Djet "Ruler of Eternity".[15] This had been constructed during the co-regency of Osorkon III and Takeloth III. The decoration of the inner shrine, in bas-relief, depicts the coronation of the two kings. It also shows Osorkon III's daughter, the God's Wife Shepenwepet I, being suckled by a goddess and being crowned. The stone chapel stood at the back of a court, surrounded by a mud-brick enclosure. The temple was now enlarged. A single-pylon entrance and small court were added to the original building by Shebitqo and Amenirdis I. The façade has striking images of the Kushite king, in superb bas-relief. One scene is almost completely preserved, and shows Amun presenting the king

The chapel of Osiris Heqa-Djet at Karnak. (Fig. 90)

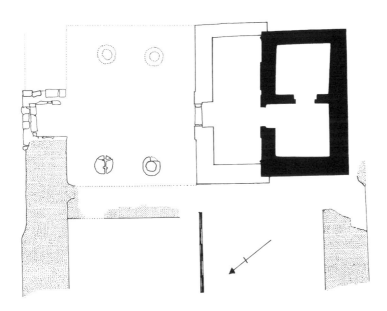

Plan of the chapel of Osiris Ruler of Eternity (Heqa-Djet) at Karnak. The two-room shrine was built by Osorkon III and Takeloth III, the outer room added by Shebitqo and Amenirdis I. (Fig. 91)

Colossal red granite head, probably of Shebitqo, found at Memphis. (Fig. 92)

with a scimitar. The king's features are quite distinctive, with his broad shoulders and long columnar neck. He wears the close-fitting cap with the double serpent twisting over his head. The scenes in the court, carved in high relief, show Shebitqo and Amenirdis I making offerings to Amun. On the south side of the Sacred Lake, Shebitqo raised another, similar chapel. Parts of this shrine were removed to the Berlin Museum by the Lepsius expedition [16]

No monuments of Shebitqo, other than his tomb, are known from Nubia.[17] The burial chamber itself had a stone bench on which the coffin was to be laid. In the sides of the bench recesses for bed legs were cut. Even though the Kushite pharaohs were now mummified and buried in anthropoid coffins, they retained the tradition of the Kushite bed-burial. Numerous fragments of beautifully carved ivory, shabti figures, canopic jars and broken pottery were all that remained of the burial furniture.

XVII   The City of Amun

Taharqo was the son of Queen Abar, herself the niece of Alara, and Taharqo makes much of this relationship in his inscriptions. Although not explicitly stated, Taharqo's father was certainly Piye. The relationship is confirmed by the text of the Neitiqert Adoption Stela, where it is said that Taharqo gave his daughter, Amenirdis II, to his sister, Shepenwepet II, to be adopted as her heiress;[1] numerous inscriptions call Shepenwepet the daughter of Piye.

Black granite head from a colossal statue of Taharqo from Thebes. (Fig. 93)

The Kawa inscriptions which tell how Taharqo was summoned to Egypt by Shebitqo also state that the prince was aged twenty when he left Nubia. If those events occurred in 695 BC, or thereabouts, Taharqo would have been born in about 715 BC.[2] He was thus about 25 years old at his own accession and, reigning for 26 years, would have been in his early fifties when he died. He must have been one of Piye's youngest children.

> I received the crown in Memphis after the Falcon soared to heaven, and my father Amun commanded me to place every land and country beneath my feet, southward to Retehu-Qabet, northward to the wells-of-Horus, eastward to the rising of the sun, and westward to its setting.[3]

It has been suggested that Taharqo seized the throne.[4] Certainly, on our present evidence, it is difficult to understand exactly how the Kushite succession worked.

The new king assumed a throne name which associated him with Memphis, Khu-Nefertem-Re, "whom Nefertem and Re protect". His Golden Horus name, Khu-tawy, "Protector of the Two Lands", was also associated with Nefertem. Taharqo used Qa-khau, "Exalted of Epiphanies", as both Horus and Nebty names.

The early years of the reign seem to have been peaceful and prosperous, and there is no recorded conflict with Assyria for fifteen years. Admittedly, there is no direct evidence regarding the relationship between Assyria and Egypt during the years of Sennacherib's reign following the incidents of 701, but the stalemate of that campaign, and Assyrian problems on the other borders of their empire, may have resulted in a wary peace.

Although not precisely dated, there is evidence for Egyptians in Nineveh at this time. One document records the sale of a house at Nineveh by a group of people to Silli-Assur who, despite his Assyrian name, is called "the Egyptian scribe". He was presumably involved in diplomatic correspondence.[5]

The Kushites were now firmly established in Egypt, and their royal residence was at Memphis. A number of monuments has been identified there, but they were all dismantled, or their stone reused, in the reign of the Saite king Psamtik II. Some fragments of statues of Taharqo excavated in Assyria probably came originally from Memphis.[6] On the evidence of stelae from the Serapeum with texts naming Taharqo, it has been proposed that the king buried an Apis bull early in his reign.[7] A bull died in the king's 24th year, and since the life expectancy of a bull was between 18 and 26 years, it seems likely that one was buried either by Shebitqo, or early in Taharqo's reign. This would have been the bull which was installed as successor to that which died in year 6 of Bakenranef and 2 of Shabaqo.

Smaller monuments are known from all over the remainder of the country, and it should be remembered that many of the cities which were particularly important during this period of Egyptian history have had very little excavation. The time of Kushite rule was one of great building activity throughout Egypt and Kush.

The sixth year of Taharqo's reign saw an exceptionally high Nile.[8] There had already been high floods in the reigns of Osorkon III, Shabaqo and Shebitqo. On the quay at Karnak two inscriptions document this flood. It seems that the first records what was thought to be its highest point, but that the flood's waters then rose even more. These inscriptions are the highest of the Nile level texts. The succeeding years, 7, 8 and 9, brought inundations almost equally high.[9] The most remarkable benefit of the year 6 inundation was that it came without any of the ill-consequences which could attend it. Egypt needed ample floods to ensure good crops – but when too high, the flood could be worse than a low Nile, causing destruction of towns and villages and other catastrophes. Taharqo recorded the events of year 6 on stelae which were set up at Djanet (*Tanis*), Matanah, Gubtu (*Koptos*) and Gem-Aten (Kawa).

The high Nile was accompanied by four "marvels": splendid cultivation, the extermination of rats and snakes, prevention of damage by locusts, and the failure of any damaging south wind (which could often accompany the flood).[10]

These early years may have seen the king active in the politics of western Asia. There is no direct evidence that the king actually campaigned in western Asia, as some scholars have suggested,[11] but an image of the king "smiting the foreign lands" was given to the Kawa temple in year 8.[12] Even if there were no military activities, Taharqo established close diplomatic and trade contacts with the Phoenician cities. The donations to the king's new temple at Kawa, in Kush, include timber – cedar and juniper – which certainly came from Lebanon, as well as "Asiatic" bronze. The renewal of the temple of the goddess Mut at Thebes also used cedar from Lebanon. Gubla (Byblos) was doubtless one of the main suppliers of this cedar, and, when they once again reasserted their control over the Phoenician cities, the Assyrian kings were to ban the rulers of Byblos from sending timber to Egypt.

Taharqo was acknowledged throughout the Delta. It was at least thirty years since Piye had first received the submission of the dynasts, and they doubtless found it to their advantage to accept the Kushite pharaohs. The use of Memphis as one of their principal residence cities enabled the Kushite pharaohs to maintain control of the Delta.

In the western Delta, some small objects with Taharqo's name have been found at Sau.[13] It is uncertain whether the city was ruled directly by the Kushites, perhaps through a governor, or whether the princely family had been restored. As the reign advanced, Sau was to emerge once again as the major seat of opposition.

The tradition preserved by the epitomators of Manetho's *Aigyptiaka* begin the 26th Dynasty with "Ammeris" a Kushite governor. Some Egyptologists regard this name as the corruption of the throne name of one of the earlier Kushite rulers, either "Nemaetre" (Kashta) or "Usermaetre" (Piye).[14] Ammeris is followed by a "Stephinates", a form of the name Tefnakht.[15] This figure has been identified as Tefnakht "II", and the royal inscriptions have been attributed to him. After Tefnakht comes the short reign of "Nechepsos" equated with Nekauba whose cartouche is preserved on a broken amulet.[16] It is only with "Necho" that a certain identification can be made with a monumentally attested ruler.[17] This is Nekau I, the ruler of Sau and Memphis in the Assyrian record. The regnal years attributed to these rulers in Manetho's king-list barely covers the reign of Taharqo and certainly does not amount to the length of time since Shabaqo's defeat of Bakenranef.

For the present, the years of Kushite rule over Sau must remain obscure. It has generally been assumed that the family of Nekau and Psamtik I was somehow related to that of Tefnakht and Bakenranef. Whether the family was originally reinstated as Kushite vassals or whether they regained control of Sau in opposition to the Kushites is unknown.

Since Nekau is documented as ruler of Sais in the later years of Taharqo's reign, the family may have regained control of the city during the first conflict with Assyria.

There is a little more evidence from the eastern Delta. Kushite involvement, both trading and military, with western Asia ensured that the cities of the eastern Delta remained important. Doubtless much of the timber imported and goods exported went throught the port of Djanet. Taharqo commemorated the great flood of his sixth year by setting up a stela in the city. A granite statue of the king is also noted from there, and there may have been other building works.[18] There was no ruler in Djanet to pay fealty to Piye, and it was Osorkon of Per-Bastet who reigned over the eastern Delta, but, by the end of Taharqo's reign, the situation was reversed. Blocks from monuments of a king Pedubast were found by French Egyptologist Pierre Montet in his excavations of the Sacred Lake at Djanet.[19] This king can certainly be identified with the *Putubishti* of the Assyrian record. Monuments of another Tanite king, Gemenefkhonsubak, were also found by Montet.[20] The style of relief on these blocks is very similar to that of reliefs of Shabaqo from Memphis, and it is possible that Gemenefkhonsubak was installed as king in his reign. No ruler of Per-Bastet is recorded by the Assyrians later in Taharqo's reign, and the line of the Pharaoh Osorkon who had submitted to Piye must have come to an end.[21]

Piye had been the "protector" of Pediese, the ruler of Hut-hery-ib (*Athribis*) at the apex of the Delta, and the city remained loyal to the Kushites. Taharqo rebuilt the sanctuary of the local deity, Horus Khenty-khety, although little beyond the foundations remains.[22] As with so many Kushite temples, there seems to have been a colonnaded portico at the entrance. An avenue of sphinxes led up to it. On the surviving architectural elements, the names of Taharqo have been replaced by those of Psamtik II (whose wife was buried here), as happened at many sites when Kushite monuments were not pulled down. The counterpoise from a necklace also associates Taharqo with Horus Khenty-khety.[23]

In Middle Egypt, where there has been far-less excavation of sites of this period, a stela of Taharqo's year 7 comes from Hermopolis and a splendid painted limestone head from Akhmim. A granite lion from Koptos can also be attributed to him.[24] The city of Tjeny (*Thinis*) may already have been the seat of the Upper Egyptian Vizier. The only Kushite work known from the city is a fragment of a large stone vessel dedicated in the name of Shebitqo.[25] At Abdju, some members of the Kushite court were buried, following the precedent established by Queen Pebatjma and Peksater.

By far the most extensive remains of Kushite rule in Egypt are to be found in the Southern City, *Waset* (Thebes). Great emphasis has always been placed on this, and the impression is that the main devotion of the Kushite pharaohs was to Amun, and that their great interest in Egypt was the Theban region. The main residence of the Kushite pharaohs in Egypt was Memphis, but even if we wish to place greater emphasis on the Kushite activities in the northern part of Egypt, it cannot be denied that Thebes figured very prominently in their building activities, and that Kushite monuments have survived there more completely than anywhere else in Egypt.

Thebes was one of the major cities of Taharqo's vast realm. The Kushite pharaohs certainly adopted Memphis as their major residence city, but they undoubtedly travelled around their domains. They must have visited the main cities, such as Thebes, for the celebration of the great religious rites – in Thebes, the Opet and Valley Festivals – and now must have occasionally returned to Kush to inaugurate new building works, perhaps also on military expeditions. There must also have been constant shipments of timber from Syria and Lebanon for the building of the temples in the Kushite homeland, and vessels bringing trade goods from the south.

The city of Waset had risen to importance during the period of local independence of the First Intermediate Period (*c*.2181-2040) and one of its rulers, Menthuhotep I, had reunited Egypt. Again, during the Second

One of a series of statues of the Fourth Prophet of Amun and Mayor of Thebes, Monthuemhat, which combine individuality, stylisation and archaising references. Monthuemhat, who married Wedjarenes, grand-daughter of Piye, played a
significant role in the reign of Taharqo, witnessing the Assyrian sack of Thebes and the transition to Saite rule. (Fig. 94)

Intermediate Period, Waset and parts of Upper Egypt formed a separate kingdom and the local rulers, Kamose and Ahmose, brought about the reunification of the country. Their successors – the pharaohs of the New Kingdom – set about the glorification of the city and of its chief deity, Amun. Amun was assimilated with the solar god Re of Iunu (*Heliopolis*), and his city became the "Southern Iunu". It was also known quite simply as *Niw*, "the City", or *Niw n Imn* – the biblical No-Ammon – "the City of Amun". The Greeks called it Thebes, by which name it is now generally known. For five hundred years Thebes, although not a capital in the modern sense, was one of the principal residence cities and it was the burial place of the kings. By the time of Kushite rule, the city must have presented – as must the other major cities of Egypt – what, to us, would be a strange combination of splendour and decay.

A number of hymns and poems celebrates the beauty of the great city:

> Waset is the pattern for every city,
> Both the flood and the earth were in her from the
>   beginning of time,
> The sand came to delimit her soil,
> to create her soil upon the Primal Mound when earth
>   came into being.
> Then mankind came into being within her,
> to found every city after her true name,
> since they are all called "City"
> after the example of Waset, the Eye of Re.[26]

Thebes lies on a bend in the broad river, and is dominated by the magnificent cliffs and the natural pyramid of the peak on the west bank. The cliffs make a spectacular backdrop to the temples and to the foothills which formed the cemetery, everywhere dotted with small brick pyramids. Along the edge of the cultivation the pharaohs of the New Kingdom had built their "Houses of Millions of Years". Most of these vast temples had long before lapsed into desuetude. Their fixtures and fittings were gone, and some of them stood as empty shells, others had been partly plundered for stone. The main residential districts of the city lay on the east bank around the great sanctuaries. The processional ways divided the city into quarters. These must have been densely built with houses of two or three storeys, narrow winding streets and blind alleys. Towering over the whole city were the pylon gates, colossal statues and obelisks of the main temples. In the north, surrounded by smaller temples and chapels lay Ipet-Sut (Karnak) "the most select of places", the abode of the city's heavenly architect, Amun. To the south of Ipet-sut was Asheru, the residence of Amun's consort, the goddess Mut. Further south still lay the focus of the Opet Festival, the temple of Ipet-resyt (Luxor).

Despite its religious importance, and its role as a royal residence city, Thebes was far away from the centres of population and agriculture. These were the broad, rich lands of Middle Egypt and the Delta. Yet Thebes had been the ancestral home – and burial place – of many of the "greatest" pharaohs. Consequently, it had been richly endowed with monuments, and its patron deity, Amun, had risen to become one of the national gods. We perhaps forget that the preservation of the monuments of Thebes is largely due to the remoteness of the city from the later centres of power, and that the centres of power in ancient times were not very different from those later ones. The great shrines in Memphis and Heliopolis were *at least* as magnificent as those of Amun in the Southern City.

During the years of Libyan rule, Upper Egypt had shown the inclination to become independent – something that was to be repeated frequently in the later phases of Egyptian history. More than ever before, the focus of activity was in the Delta and northern part of Egypt. The loss of the Nubian domain must also have led to a decline in importance of parts of Upper Egypt, and it must also have been of some significance that Thebes was no longer the royal burial place.

After the transfer of the kingship from the double line of Tanite pharaohs and High Priests to the Libyan kings, Theban importance declined further. There was little major building work carried out in the name of the Libyan kings. A new development was the building of small chapels dedicated to forms of the god Osiris, the first dating to the reign of Osorkon II.[27]

The resources of the Delta rulers had been expended on the glorification of the residence cities of the north, Djanet (*Tanis*) and Per-Bastet (*Bubastis*) in the eastern Delta, Sau (*Sais*) in the west, and the ancient city of Memphis. More significantly, perhaps, for many years after the reign of Osorkon II, the Delta rulers could hardly be said to have controlled Upper Egypt, Thebes was in rebellion and civil war had broken out.

The Libyan period had seen the domination of many of the offices of Upper Egypt by small and closely inter-related groups of elite families.[28] The extensive genealogies recorded on their monuments enable us to see far more closely than ever before the ways in which offices were inherited and the connections established between these powerful families. These offices were technically royal appointments, but claims could be made through both the father's and mother's families.

The kings needed to keep control of this powerful nobility, especially when they were mostly resident far to the north, in Tanis or Memphis, and the practice of appointing one of the king's sons as High Priest of Amun and a daughter as God's Wife ensured royal representatives in the city. Marriage alliances were soon established between the Libyan royal house and the leading families of Thebes, and, by the time of the Kushite conquest, a large number of them could claim royal blood.

The Kushites, perhaps Shabaqo, seem to have broken the hereditary hold of some families on certain key offices.[29] The appointment of a Kushite, Kelbasken,[30] as 4th Prophet of Amun and Mayor of Thebes, removed those offices from the family of Nakhtefmut, which had held them for generations. After Kelbasken, sometime in the reign of Taharqo, both offices were granted to Monthuemhat who allied himself by marriage to the Kushite royal house. Although he was appointed to these two influential positions (and made Governor of Upper Egypt), Monthuemhat's family lost their control of the Vizierate of Upper Egypt, which now passed to that of Nesipeqashuty. Such a shuffling of positions would have emphasised that rank came from the pharaoh.

The appointment of Kushites to some other offices, and to the key Theban benefices, ensured a strong presence in the city. Shabaqo followed Libyan custom and installed his own son, Haremakhet, as High Priest of Amun. Prince Haremakhet may have followed the precedent of earlier High Priests and concluded marriage alliances with the Theban nobility. A fine and well-preserved statue of the prince, in red quartzite, was recovered from the Karnak Cache, and other statues of his have recently been excavated in the temple of the goddess Mut, extensively rebuilt during his pontificate.[31] He continued in office during the reign of Taharqo and into that of Tanwetamani, before being succeeded by his own son, Harkhebi. Although the sarcophagi of both High Priests are preserved, we have little other information on this branch of the royal family.[32] Harkhebi was still officiating after the transfer of power to the Saites, being depicted on the "Saite Oracle Papyrus" of year 14 of Psamtik I.

Taharqo too appointed one of his sons, Nesishutefnut, to serve the King of the Gods as 2nd Prophet.[33] The immensely powerful 4th Prophet of Amun, Monthuemhat, who was to become a leading player in the political crisis to come, married, as his third wife, the pharaoh's niece, Wedjarenes. This lady was the daughter of Prince Har, one of Piye's other sons.

At the time of Taharqo's accession, the Kushite presence in Thebes must have been large and long-established. It was now nearly half-a-century since Kashta had installed the Kushite princess, Amenirdis I, as prospective God's Wife of Amun. Piye and Shabaqo had made further appointments. Amenirdis now reigned with Taharqo's sister, Shepenwepet II, as her adopted daughter and designated successor, the Adorer of the God. Taharqo gave his own daughter, Amenirdis II, to his sister, to be *her* daughter, so, for a time, there were three Kushite princesses in the Inner Abode of Amun. Amenirdis the elder died sometime during Taharqo's reign.[34]

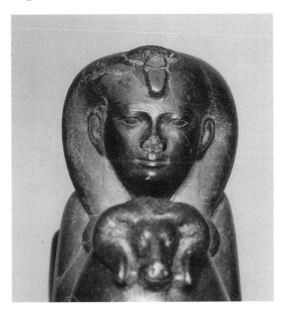

The God's Wife of Amun, Shepenwepet II in the form of a sphinx offering a ram-headed vase. Her features are very similar to those of her brother, Taharqo. From Karnak. (Fig. 95)

The God's Wife presided over the college of priestesses, the Inner Abode of Amun, which comprised royal daughters and the daughters of various of the Libyan chiefs and other important families. So, in his tenth year of reign, King Peftjauawybast had sent his daughter, Iruatj, to join the temple. Another chantress, a contemporary of Amenirdis I, was Nebet-imau-emhat, a daughter of a Chief of the Libu, Ankh-Hor.

The increasing importance of the God's Wife was reflected in the growing number and power of her attendant officials. The office of Chief Steward of the God's Wife now became one of the most prestigious in Thebes, and, to judge by the scale of their tombs, one of the wealthiest. It may have taken over the importance of the office of Chief Steward of Amun, whose holders had been so influential in the 18th and 19th Dynasties. Many officials who served these women are documented, from the Stewards, scribes and Chamberlains, to the door-keepers and priests responsible for their cults. One Chamberlain of the God's Wife Amenirdis I, also carried the title "Ambassador to Ta-Seti", testifying to close contacts with the Kushite centres.[35]

Many of the new chapels and shrines erected in Thebes under Kushite rule were jointly in the names of the pharaoh and the God's Wife. In the quarries of the Wadi Hammamat, their names can be found alongside those of the kings, or sometimes standing alone.

Although their economic power must have ensured them temporal power, the main function of the God's Wife of Amun and the Adorer of the God was the worship of Amun. Dominating the city, physically and spiritually, was the great temple of Amun, Ipet-Sut, "the Most Select of Places". The massive walls which enclose it today were constructed three hundred years after Taharqo's reign, by Nekhtnebef. In Kushite times, the temple was somewhat different.

There were four entrances to Ipet-Sut, three of them adorned by the Kushite pharaohs. For six hundred years the main river gate to the temple had been the pylon (now the second) completed by Horemheb, called "Illuminating Waset". In front of it the processional way, flanked by ram-headed sphinxes, led through gardens to the quay and canal. During the Libyan period, the front of the quay was used as a Nilometer, the high point of the floods being marked and the date. The highest of all floods was that of Taharqo's 6th year, but there were others from the time of Osorkon III to that of Psamtik I which nearly equalled it. Adjacent to the quay, a series of ramps led down to the canal. These were used for the collection of water for rituals, but they must also have served for the unloading of the produce brought to the temple stores, and perhaps also for the stone and timber used in the many constructions. Inscriptions along its balustrade, indicate that one of these ramps was constructed in Taharqo's reign. This entrance to the temple played an important role in the two great Theban festivals, Opet and the Feast of the Valley.

The avenue of sphinxes, with trees behind them, led from the quay through gardens to the precinct wall and the open court in front of the great entrance pylon of Horemheb. Sety II and Ramesses III had built small temples as resting-places for the sacred barque in its processions, and the Libyan king Sheshonq I had enclosed the area with colonnades on the north and south sides. The construction of the colonnades may also have seen the building of a brick pylon. Now the court was to be transformed. Taharqo built a new way-station in the middle of the court, consisting of ten open papyrus columns equal in height (69 feet, 21.5 m.) to the central aisle of the great hypostyle hall. The sphinxes were moved to the side of the court. The vast entrance pylon, 370 feet (113 m.) long, was probably also begun at this time. The southern tower rises 100 feet (30.5 m.), three-quarters of its intended height. Behind it are the remains of the mud-brick ramps used in its construction. The work was abandoned, perhaps at the time of the Assyrian sack of the city, and never completed.[36]

The gateway of Horemheb's pylon was flanked by colossal statues of Ramesses II. Its great cedar wood doors, plated with bronze and figured in gold and silver, opened onto the vast hypostyle hall. Only the central nave was lit through a clerestory. The pylon of Amenhotep III formed the back of the hall, its doors opening onto a narrow court. To the south, the gate of Ramesses IX gave onto the southern courts and the processional way to the Sacred Lake and Ipet-resyt. To the north stood the colonnaded portico of Shabaqo. Ahead lay the pylon of the temple of Thutmose I. Flanked by the gilded obelisks of Thutmose I and Thutmose III, its entrance was the great gate of electrum, rebuilt most recently by Shabaqo. The Kushite pharaohs left the sanctuary rooms which lay beyond unchanged, although their own gilded images doubtless adorned the sacred barque of the King of the Gods.

The Sacred Lake, which played an important role in rituals, lay to the south of the sanctuary rooms, and the main access was through the southern courts. It was probably enlarged during the Kushite period. On the north side of the Lake, Taharqo ordered a new temple, perhaps to replace an earlier structure of Shabaqo's. The main part of the shrine stood on a high podium and was approached by a broad ramp and staircase from a courtyard which had direct access to the Sacred Lake. This elevated temple was a solar court. Staircases led down into crypts in the mass of the podium. The reliefs which decorate the walls of the crypts depict the events which happened during Amun's visit to the temple of Djeme on the west bank. Essentially, these are acts of creation. Much about the rituals enacted here remains obscure, but, in the crypts, the statue of the god journeyed through the underworld, then, in the solar court above, was united with the sun disk. The proximity to the Sacred Lake, which represented the waters of the primeval flood, Nun, was an essential element.[37]

On the southern side of the Sacred Lake were the temple storerooms and administrative buildings and the fowl pens. The goose was one creature sacred to Amun who, in one of his manifestations, was the "Great Cackler" who had laid the primordial egg. Also on this side of the lake were some cultic structures: a tiny chapel of Thoth, built by Osorkon III, and the chapel of Shebitqo, part of which was removed by the Lepsius expedition to Berlin.[38]

On the eastern side of the Sacred Lake, between it and the enclosure wall, were the streets of houses for the priests when they were on duty in the temple.[39]

In the area north of the priests' houses, immediately to the rear wall of the main temple, lay the Eastern Temple.[40] The first chapel here had been erected by Hatshepsut. Altered by Thutmose III, its central shrine was a single block of alabaster, hollowed out to show two over-lifesize

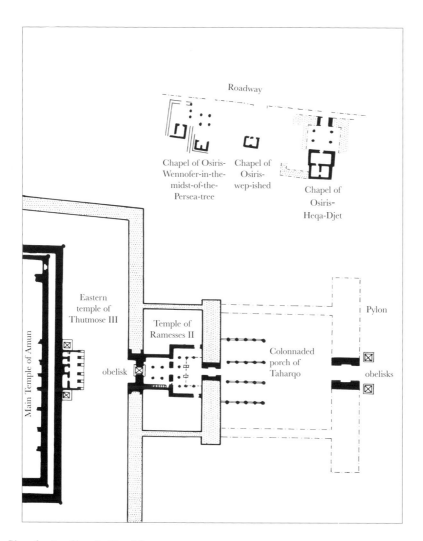

Plan of eastern Karnak. (Fig. 96)

seated figures. The chapel was flanked by two obelisks. This shrine, within its own enclosure, became the focus of the "Upper Court of Ipet-sut". At the centre of the courtyard, Thutmose IV set up the enormous single obelisk which had lain unfinished in the workshops of the temple since his grandfather's time. The single obelisk designated this a solar-court, and on the pyramidion were carved images of Amun and Atum – the morning and evening sun. This obelisk, the largest surviving, now stands in front of the Church of St John Lateran in Rome. Ramesses II sealed off the court by building a small temple of his own in front of it. The temple, known as the "House of Ramesses, beloved of Amun, who hears prayer", had gardens,

241

great doors of cedar plated with electrum, and an entrance gateway, flanked by obelisks and statues, which opened onto the streets of the city. Within, a seated black granite statue of the king was the vehicle through which the people's prayers were channelled. Here the king merged with the god Amun. There is evidence for the continuing identification of the ruling pharaoh with the god into Ptolemaic times. Taharqo built a colonnaded portico of twenty columns with low screen walls in front of the doorway.[41] This was very similar to the portico of Shabaqo at the north of the hall behind the 3rd Pylon. It may have been within this temple that the colossal black granite statue of Taharqo stood, of which only the head has survived.[42] Its crown, originally covered with gold foil, was surmounted by tall falcon plumes. These are too badly damaged to be certain whether, as in a very similar statue of the king from Napata, they were the four plumes of the god Inheret, or whether they were the two plumes of Amun.

The God's Wife of Amun, Shepenwepet II, shooting arrows. Behind her is the Mound of Djeme. From a relief in the building of Taharqo by the Sacred Lake at Karnak. (Fig. 97)

The enclosure wall on the northern side of the precinct ran much closer to the temple than on the south and east. Outside the precinct there were administrative buildings, some of which dated back to the 18th Dynasty. There were also more recent additions, such as the treasury of Shabaqo. Flanking the roads was a number of chapels dedicated to Osiris. The largest was that of Osiris Ruler-of-Eternity (Heqa-Djet), built by Osorkon III, Takeloth III and Shepenwepet I and enlarged by Amenirdis I and Shebitqo. Close by was the tiny chapel of Osiris Wep-ished from the later years of Osorkon II. Next to it, the chapel of Osiris-Wennefer-who-is-in-the-midst-of-the-persea-tree was built by Taharqo's sister, Shepenwepet II.[43] The door jambs show the God's Wives Amenirdis I and Shepenwepet II, each in a close embrace with Amun. Inside, Shepenwepet is accompanied by one of the chantresses of the Inner Abode of Amun, Diesehebsed, a relative of the 4th Prophet Monthuemhat.

A road ran northwards from the portico of Shabaqo to the palace quarter of the city. This too became lined with chapels, dedicated by the pharaohs and God's Wives of Amun. That of Osiris-Neb-Ankh was constructed by Taharqo and Shepenwepet II. The road then passed the more substantial precinct of the Memphite god Ptah. This small temple, built by Thutmose III, was given a new gateway by Shabaqo. A road ran in from the east, lined with more chapels of the God's Wives. The oldest was that built by Takeloth II and the God's Wife, Karomama. In the chapel of Osiris-Neb-ankh, dedicated in the reign of Shabaqo, one of the most splendid of the statues of the God's Wife Amenirdis I was found. Another chapel was dedicated in the names of Shepenwepet II and Taharqo.[45] Taharqo's reign also saw the rebuilding of the chapel of Osiris-Pedeankh/Nebdjet. The decoration depicts Taharqo and Shepenwepet II making offerings to various deities, including the deceased Amenirdis I. A number of statues was found in the chapel, including two of Taharqo, sadly headless.[46]

Adjacent to these chapels was the temple of the goddess Maet, and, on the same axis, but facing north, the temple of Monthu. Built by Amenhotep III, Monthu, the original patron god of Thebes, was a solar deity, depicted with a falcon's head and wearing the double uraeus. The cult of Monthu was of great local importance during the Libyan period, and the burials of many priests of the god are known. At the entrance to the temple, Taharqo erected another colonnade.[47] An avenue led northwards to a canal which connected with the temple of Madu (Medamud) a few miles north-east of Thebes. The temple of Madu was rebuilt in the Ptolemaic period, and, although numerous blocks from earlier shrines were recovered (many of Middle Kingdom date), it is certain that a lot of building material was brought from the Karnak area. Reliefs from a chapel of the God's Wife Shepenwepet II were probably brought from Karnak rather than from a building of hers at Madu itself.[48]

Many of the important Theban families held land and priesthoods in Madu. The region north of Thebes towards Madu was a rich agricultural region, and many of the great estates attached to the Theban benefices must have lain there.

The great palace complexes probably lay between the river and the temple of Monthu, although the area has not been excavated.

The processional way to Asheru and Ipet-resyt left the main east-west axis of the temple through the gateway of Ramesses XI and passed through a series of large courts and other pylons, the gateways flanked by colossal statues and obelisks, the axis gradually changing, until it passed through the gateway of the massive southernmost pylon. This gate was dominated by a colossus of Amenhotep III, the largest free-standing statue erected by the Egyptians, which must have been visible from a considerable distance.

West of the southern gateway, towards the river, stood the temple of Khonsu, a moon-god, and son of Amun and Mut. The temple, begun by Ramesses III, using stone from the ruined "mortuary" temple of Amenhotep III on the west bank, was completed and decorated by the later Ramessides and the High Priests Herihor and Pinudjem I. In front of its pylon entrance, Taharqo erected yet another colonnade of twenty columns, using blocks of a structure built by Osorkon III and his son, the High Priest Takeloth.[49] An avenue of ram-headed sphinxes connected this temple with a quay and harbour.

The main avenue, running from the south gate directly towards the temple of the goddess Mut, was a wide, paved roadway, lined with sphinxes. Behind the sphinxes, trees were planted. Today, shattered and eroded fragments of the ram-headed sphinxes mark the avenue's route through a dusty, almost lunar landscape to the eerie temple of the goddess. On higher ground close to the avenue, Taharqo raised a tiny chapel which was completed by Tanwetamani.[50] The relief decoration of the interior is of the best quality.

The southern complex of temples is surrounded by a wall of the 30th Dynasty, although each originally had its own precinct. The main temple, of the goddess Mut, is now overgrown with reeds from which emerge hundreds of statues of the goddess with the head of a lioness. Surrounded by a crescent lake, this was "Asheru", where Amun's wife was worshipped as the Eye of the Sun, a ferocious lioness goddess.

The temple of Mut was only one of several related sanctuaries which stood close together.[51] At rightangles to its entrance stood a small temple built by Ramesses II. Taharqo enlarged it, and its function (if it still functioned) changed. The temple now became a "Birth House" (*mammisi*), in which the divine birth of the king as son of Amun and Mut (in the form of the queen) was celebrated. Two colossal statues of Ramesses II were left standing at the pylon entrance to the temple, and a processional way was created, passing through the wall which surrounded the whole precinct, and joining with the road to Ipet-resyt. In an early excavation on the site, the base of an over-lifesize statue of a queen was discovered. The names had been erased, which, allied with the choice of titles, suggests that the statue represented a Kushite queen, almost certainly Taharqo's mother, Abar.

Taharqo also added to the temple of Mut. A statue of Monthuemhat at Berlin records the role played by that great official in the work.

I have renewed the temple of Mut-the-great, the mistress of Asheru, so that it was more beautiful than before. I adorned her barque with electrum, all its images with precious stones.

I renewed the barque of Khonsu-the-child, and the barque of Bastet-residing-in-Thebes, so as to satisfy her majesty [Mut] with what she wishes.[52]

Monthuemhat says that he built a colonnade and the sacred lake, all in sandstone. Recent excavations by a team from the Brooklyn Museum have identified works which might be those of Monthuemhat. The temple was altered further in the Ptolemaic period, and this has obscured exactly how it looked in Kushite times. A number of statues of the Kushite period has been recovered from the site, but it is not certain whether this was where they originally stood, although it is likely. They include a sphinx dedicated by Monthuemhat; a statue of a God's Wife; and one of the High Priest Haremakhet.

Adjacent to the temple of Mut, within its own enclosure, stood the remains of a temple built by Ramesses III. No longer in use, the temple was used as a quarry by Taharqo's builders. The processional way passed in front of this temple and ran to a quay and canal connecting with the river, where the sacred boats of Mut and Khonsu could join the river procession to Ipet-resyt (Luxor). Another branch of the avenue took an abrupt turn which aligned it with the temple of Ipet-resyt.

The broad processional way, lined with sphinxes and trees terminated in a court preceding the pylon built by Ramesses II. At the point where the avenue entered this court, Taharqo built a small chapel with Hathor-headed capitals.[53] The main entrance, the pylon of Ramesses II, was adorned with obelisks and colossal statues, two seated, four standing. The main gateway had been renewed by Shabaqo and preceding it the same king had built a columned portico.

It was from Ipet-resyt that, every ten days, the image of Amun sailed to Djeme on the west bank. The town of Djeme had grown up around the "mortuary" temple of Ramesses III (Medinet Habu). A canal connected it to the river. As we have already seen, this temple had suffered looting during the disturbances of the reign of Ramesses XI. Parts of its great enclosure wall had been destroyed, and the massive fortified entrance gateways had been damaged and never repaired. The temple and the small palace attached to it had been looted, the metal stripped from the leaves of the doorways. It had offered some protection to the villagers who had taken up residence there, but, during the Libyan period its fortunes increased and it became an important town. The regular streets of the Ramesside village were gradually rebuilt, becoming a complex of winding lanes and blind alleys surrounding the great stone temple which now stood disused.[54]

A small temple dedicated to Amun and the eight creator gods had stood here long before Ramesses III chose the site for his own cult centre. This temple, a typically elegant structure of the joint-reign of Hatshepsut and Thutmose III, comprised a barque shrine which was surrounded by square piers with a suite of six rooms behind. The whole edifice stood on a platform, within a walled enclosure. When Ramesses III constructed his temple close by, this wall was pulled down and the older building was incorporated into the complex. The destruction of the main temple at the end of the 20th Dynasty was the end of its cult, but that of the small temple continued, indeed it received ever greater attention during the Libyan and Kushite periods. A building text records a restoration by Pinudjem I, and its importance must have increased significantly by the reign of Osorkon II, when the king's cousin, the High Priest of Amun, Harsiese, chose to be buried in a tomb on the southern side of the temple.

In this shrine, a rather complex theology associated Amun with the Kematef serpent which was believed to be buried here. Every ten days, the image of the ithyphallic Amun sailed from the temple of Ipet-resyt to present offerings to the Kematef serpent. More detail about the complex theology and the rituals associated with the journey is to be found in the shrine which Taharqo built by the Sacred Lake at Ipet-Sut. There is also a scene depicting the Sacred Mound of Djeme in the chapel of Osiris Ruler-of-Eternity. Amun had to repeat his act of creation, and was then united with the souls of the sun-god Re, in whom he was reborn. The reliefs show that the God's Wife of Amun played a significant role in the rites, and, since the pharaoh was frequently absent from Thebes, she may have been the main celebrant of the mysteries.

At the beginning of Kushite rule, the temple was essentially that of Hatshepsut and Thutmose III. Apart from some restoration, there had been no additions. The temple was now enlarged, and, although some of this Kushite building was dismantled in the reign of one of the later Ptolemies, many of the Kushite blocks were used in the foundations and have recently come to light during conservation work. They are executed in sunk relief, and are painted. In style, they are very similar to blocks excavated at Edfu. They should probably be ascribed to the reign of Shabaqo.[55]

The temple was now entered through a small pylon which was built on the solid foundations of the girdle wall of Ramesses III, which had here been destroyed. The pylon had emplacements for four flagstaffs set into its facade. On the back side of the pylon, in the hall, reliefs showed the king smiting his enemies. The temple later acquired a colonnaded porch. Elsewhere at Thebes, this feature is typically Kushite, but it has been assumed that here, at Medinet Habu, it was added in the 26th Dynasty.

Until recently it was thought that the pylon opened onto a narrow, dark hall, but the recent excavations by Jean Jacquet and Helen Jacquet Gordon have shown that the area between the pylon and Thutmoside temple was occupied by a colonnade of the type found in the first court at Karnak, albeit on a much smaller scale. This would have created a rather striking, and perhaps unique, architectural ensemble.[56]

The whole temple was enclosed with a brick wall, separating it from the town site. This wall was renewed by Taharqo who added stone gateways on the north and south sides, and a small chapel for Osiris behind the main sanctuary.

Two stelae of Taharqo's third year record the rebuilding of the walls.[57] The temple must have had access to the quay and canal, by which the image of Amun arrived from Ipet-Resyt.

It may have been the importance of Djeme in the cult of Amun, and the role of the God's Wife, which led these princesses to choose the court between the temple of Ramesses III and the ruined fortified gate for their tombs.[58] The God's Wife Shepenwepet I was the first to be buried here. Over her tomb, a mud-brick chapel in the form of a small temple was raised.

Next to the chapel of Shepenwepet I, Amenirdis I was buried in a vault, with a chapel of mud-brick above. Later, probably during the reign of Taharqo, this chapel was dismantled and rebuilt in stone by Shepenwepet II. A small pylon entrance with columned porch opens onto a court, with a cloister supported by four columns. Two doorways lead from the court, one to the chapel of Shepenwepet I and the other to that of Shepenwepet II. In the centre of the court stands a massive black granite offering table. The shrine itself stands above the vault of the God's Wife and is surrounded by a corridor. The decoration of the pylon and court, in elegant sunk relief, is some of the best of surviving Kushite work in Thebes. Throughout, Shepenwepet makes offerings to her adopted mother. Inside the dark shrine the sculpture is impressive. That of the corridor is in quite deep sunk relief with fine detailing. On the walls of the shrine itself, the figures and texts are cut in strong raised relief. Throughout, the features of Amenirdis and Shepenwepet are quite distinctive.

The decoration of the outer wall of the chapel was never completed, probably because work was soon begun on the chapel which Shepenwepet II built for herself. This was to have followed the same plan as that of Amenirdis, a pylon entrance with a columned porch opening onto a small court with chapel at the rear, but was later altered to include burial places for the Saite God's Wife, Neitiqert, and her mother, Queen Mehyt-en-weskhet. These additions covered some of the reliefs which had been carved on the outer wall of the Amenirdis chapel. This scene showed large figures of Shepenwepet and Amenirdis making offerings to two registers of seated figures. One row of these figures emerges from behind the chapel wall of Neitiqert, but they are, alas, unnamed. A Kushite king, perhaps Piye or Kashta, is accompanied by two women.

The entrance gate to Medinet Habu with the chapels of the God's Wives on the right and the New Kingdom temple of Amun of Djeme, with its Ptolemaic pylon entrance, on the left. (Fig. 98)

The burial places of the God's Wives are remarkably small for women of such enormous power and wealth, and form a striking contrast to the vast scale of the tombs of the officials of this period, particularly the Stewards of the votaresses. These tombs mark a change in burial practice. Throughout the Libyan period, temples such as the Ramesseum had been used as burial places. Sometimes older tombs were re-used, but often the coffins and funerary goods were placed in collective graves. Royal burials, notably those at Tanis, had also been made within the temple precincts. At Tanis, the kings were buried in underground tombs with chapels above, in an enclosure lying off the first courtyard of the temple. This was also, if we are to believe Herodotos, the practice at Sais. The burials of the God's Wives follow this custom. The great officials of the later Kushite and the Saite periods constructed tombs for themselves, which rivalled those of earlier kings.

Along the edge of the cultivation to the north of Djeme were the ruins of other temples. The temple of Merneptah had long since been used as a quarry. Next to it lay the wreck of the vast temple of Amenhotep III, its entrance flanked by the seated images of the king – the "Colossi of Memnon". The temple had already suffered damage, and much of its stone had been used by Merneptah to build his own temple, and its statues taken to adorn firstly the Ramesseum, then Medinet Habu. The cult of Ramesses II had been transferred from the Ramesseum, still further north, to Medinet Habu, an act which must have signalled the closure of the older shrine. During the Libyan period it was used as a burial place by the noble families, and the God's Wives of Amun. These "Houses of millions of years" had been visited by the image of Amun during the "beautiful feast of the valley" which took place in the second month of summer, at the time of the new moon.[59]

On the morning of the festival, Amun left Ipet-sut and sailed in great procession across the river accompanied by the barges of Mut, Khonsu, and Monthu. In former times he had visited any of the royal cult temples which were still functioning, and the cult statues of the deceased kings joined his procession. Then the royal and divine images proceeded to the temple of Hathor, built by Hatshepsut in a bay in the cliffs opposite Ipet-sut, towards the northern end of the necropolis. Here the barque of Amun resided overnight in the candle-lit sanctuary.

The festival was a time of renewal when families visited the tombs of their ancestors and celebrated overnight in them. At dawn, as the image of Amun emerged from the sanctuary to greet the rising sun, the people came out of the chapels and extinguished their torches in bowls of milk.

There was a resurgence in the festival's importance under the Kushite and Saite kings, with Deir el-Bahari still the centre of the rites. A canal ran from the river to the landing stage, and a broad processional way led from there to the terraces of the temple which rose against the sheer cliffs. Here, on the flat plain, in the great bay of the cliffs, the magnates of Kushite and Saite Thebes constructed their massive tombs, some of them with entrances facing onto the processional way.[60] Above ground the tombs were marked by brick pylons. Long staircases led down to the subterranean chambers. But in these tombs, unlike those of the New Kingdom, there were also open courtyards.

Amongst those who had their tombs here were the Chief Steward of Amenirdis I, Harwa;[61] Kelbasken the Mayor of Thebes; and Ramose, who served Taharqo as Royal Scribe, Chancellor, Sole Companion, Eyes and Ears of the King and Overseer of the Treasury.[62] A smaller tomb contained the fine coffins of the lady Kheriru.[63] The names of her parents, Pewen and Ritjemdi, show that she was a Kushite, and, although the face of the coffin is conventionally Egyptian, the scenes on its body which show the judgement of the deceased, depict her with the figure and close-cut hair typical of Kushite women. In a neighbouring chamber was the burial of another Kushite (perhaps Kheriru's husband) whose name, Il, is written very similarly to that of Alara. Amongst other close associates of the palace, was the lady Tjesreperet who was nurse to a daughter of Taharqo. Her intact burial, now in Florence, was discovered in 1829, by Rosellini and Champollion. The most splendid tomb of all is that of Monthuemhat, 4th Prophet of Amun, Mayor of Thebes and Governor of Upper Egypt.[64]

After decades of decline and civil war, the reigns of the Kushites had brought a renewed prosperity to Thebes. The shrines of Amun had once again been lavishly endowed, his festivals renewed. With the constant traffic between Egypt and Kush, Thebes once again took her place as a major royal and religious city. But the resurgence of Thebes was to be halted by a catastrophe from which she would never completely recover.

XVIII   The Throne of the Two Lands

The two decades following the battle of Eltekeh were apparently prosperous and peaceful. The endowment of the Egyptian temples was now extended to the Kushite homeland.

There must have been constant movement between the main centres of Kushite power in Egypt and those in Nubia. The timber imported from the Phoenician cities had to be transported south for the new constructions and the products of the savanna shipped north. Artisans and sculptors were sent from Egypt to work on the new temples; specialists in vine growing were brought from the Oases of the western desert. There must have been great difficulties in controlling an empire so vast and made up of regions separated by deserts, so troops, royal envoys and officials of the administration would constantly have been travelling on state business. At present, we have no evidence of any problems encountered by the Kushite pharaohs in the south. There may have been rebellions and opposition from different tribal groups, or even members of the royal family seeking power for themselves. The new wealth now diverted to the Kushite towns may have attracted raids by desert-dwelling groups; these certainly became a problem in later years. There were probably garrisons in each town to offer some protection, and the reoccupation of some of the fortresses of Lower Nubia provided safe staging-posts for the vessels travelling between Kush and Egypt.

In Egypt south of Thebes, little Kushite work has, so far, been identified. Shabaqo dedicated a shrine in the temple of Esna, and, at Edfu, recent restoration has uncovered many blocks from a Kushite building buried beneath the pavement of the Ptolemaic temple.[1] The relief decoration is very similar to the sculptured blocks from Medinet Habu and perhaps also belongs to the reign of Shabaqo, although there are also strong similarities with reliefs of Shebitqo from Karnak.[2] The royal figures were later altered: one uraeus removed from the forehead, the ram-headed earrings and cord erased, the cartouches recarved, as so frequently at Thebes, for Psamtik II. Although no work of the Kushite kings survives at Elephantine which must have been a major centre at this time, there is some evidence from the frontier region. An altar carrying the names of Taharqo still stands in the temple of Isis on the island of Philae.[3] It is dedicated to a form of Amun. The earliest surviving building on Philae dates from the 26th Dynasty, and the island's association with the goddess Isis may date only from then. Fragments of Ramesside and Kushite buildings were uncovered in the foundations of the Ptolemaic temple when it was dismantled to remove it to Agilkia during the UNESCO campaign. All of the other temples built by the Kushites in Lower Nubia were dedicated to forms of Amun, and it is probable that another shrine of the god was located on Philae island.

To protect the navigation and to provide supplies, some of the New Kingdom fortresses were garrisoned and their temples restored. On the rock of Qasr Ibrim, the fortifications were elaborated and a temple built, decorated with painted scenes.[4] Opposite Ibrim, some of the New Kingdom tombs in the old viceregal centre of Miam were reused. At the foot of the 2nd Cataract, the great fortress of Buhen was reoccupied. The temple was renewed, and a pillared portico with screen walls added.[5] Some New Kingdom tombs were reused, probably by the garrison. Other Kushite burials were found at Mirgissa, with objects strongly paralleling those from the cemetery of Sanam, near Napata.[6] At the southernmost point of the cataract, the fortress of Semna was reoccupied and a new temple constructed.[7] This again was the work of Taharqo. Of mud-brick, with lintels and door jambs in stone, the decoration was probably painted plaster as at Ibrim. An altar shows that this temple was dedicated to Senusret III, a pharaoh worshipped in the forts of Semna and Kumma as the conqueror of Nubia.

There is some limited evidence for Kushite settlement between the 2nd and 3rd Cataracts. Blocks carrying the names of Taharqo were found in a pyramid tomb at Sedeinga, leading to the fanciful suggestion that the king had been deposed and buried in a remote part of the country. These blocks were actually reused (the pyramid itself being of later, Meroitic date) and had come from a chapel, presumably built by the pharaoh somewhere in the region of Sedeinga.[8] Excavation has been limited in the Dal-Abri stretch of the river, and, although there are indications of Napatan period remains, the great New Kingdom sites of Soleb and Amara have not yet been completely cleared. The major surviving monuments lie in the region of Gebel Barkal and the rich pasturelands between the 3rd and 4th Cataracts.

The desert road from Meroe joined the Nile again at Sanam, opposite the royal cemetery of el-Kurru and a few miles downstream from Gebel Barkal. Taharqo dedicated a new temple here, and the remains of other buildings of this period show that it must have been an important town site. The other two large temples were also built in important sites, at Kawa and at Tabo, both near the ancient Kushite centre of Kerma. The best-preserved of Taharqo's temples was that excavated at Kawa by the Oxford University expedition led by F.Ll.Griffith, the work completed by L.P. Kirwan and M.F.L. Macadam.[9] The archaeological site of Kawa marks the ancient city of Gem-Aten. The name of the town suggests that it was founded in the reign of Amenhotep III or Akhenaten. Tutankhamun built a small temple dedicated to Amun in his manifestation as a ram-headed sphinx. Adjacent to Tutankhamun's temple was that built by king Ary. The inscriptions of Taharqo state that Alara had dedicated his sister, Taharqo's grandmother, as a priestess of Amun in a temple at Gem-Aten, and Taharqo himself had seen the ruin into which the temple had fallen when he stopped there on his way north, having been summoned by Shebitqo.

Taharqo's new temple was dedicated to Amun of Gem-Aten, represented as human with the head of a ram. This god actually had the characteristics of the god of the Cataract town of Elephantine, Khnum, and, like that god, was accompanied by the goddesses Anuket and Satjet.

The temple, founded in Taharqo's fifth year, replaced an older mud-brick shrine. The dedication ceremonies took place in year 10, at the beginning of the inundation season. The temple was built according to the conventional Egyptian plan, with a processional way flanked by granite rams leading from the river to the pylon entrance. Kawa differs from the temples built by the Kushite kings in Egypt in not having a colonnaded portico in front of the main entrance. Such porticos are typical of this period in Egypt, yet here, in the Kushite heartland, are not found. The great double doors of the temple were of cedar wood from Lebanon, plated with bronze and elaborately decorated with images of the gods inlaid in gold, silver and copper. In front of its pylons soared the flagstaffs, single pine trees from the mountains of Lebanon. Beyond the pylon lay an open courtyard with date-palm columns forming a sheltered walkway around its edge. Here Taharqo set up the stelae recording the building work and his donations to the temple. A second pylon formed the entrance to the inner rooms of the temple, where the rituals were performed. A dark hall supported by sixteen date-palm columns preceded the sanctuary rooms. In this hall Taharqo later inserted a stone-built shrine between the columns, and, nearly a century later, one of his successors, Aspelta, constructed a second shrine by building a wall between two columns.

Although built according to the classical Egyptian plan of a temple, Kawa has one feature which is uniquely Kushite, a room to the south of the sanctuary with a dais. A room of this plan can also be found in the great temple of Amun at Barkal, in the Amun temple at Meroe and in the other temples built by Taharqo at Sanam and Tabo. This type of room always appears on the south side of the sanctuary, irrespective of the orientation of the temple. The Sudanese archaeologist, Ali Hakem, has argued that these rooms are to be identified with the hall, mentioned in a number of texts, in which the king took his place upon a golden throne.[10]

The temples of Egypt and Kush were long-ago stripped of their furnishings, but the stelae from Kawa record the donations made by the king to the new temple over a period of eight years. These texts give some idea of the richness of the furniture provided for the celebration of the cult.

The Hathor-headed columns of the rock-cut temple of Taharqo at Gebel Barkal which was described by Geotge Hoskins in 1835 as "not only the most curious of all the temples of Gibel el Birkel ... but ... also in every respect the most picturesque and interesting". (Fig. 99)

The new temple must have presented a splendid sight. In front of the temple and along its south side, remains of the temple garden have been excavated. The trees were planted in brick-lined pits to conserve moisture. The relief decoration was painted, and there is evidence that parts of the walls and columns here at Kawa, and in other Kushite temples, were covered with gold leaf which would have added to the rich effect. One notable feature of the decoration of Kawa is the conscious copying from the pyramid temples of the pharaohs of the Old Kingdom near Memphis. The date-palm columns of the courtyard and hall were modelled on those of the pyramid temple of the 5th Dynasty king Sahure (ca.2458-2446 BC) at Abusir, in the northern part of the Memphite necropolis. The decoration on the back of the pylon showed Taharqo as a sphinx trampling his enemies. The scene is adapted from one in the temple of Sahure with close parallels in those of Neussere and Pepy II. It is probable that it was Sahure's relief which served as the model, since the names of the wife and sons of the defeated Libyan chief are the same at Kawa as those in the relief of some 1770 years earlier.[11] The building inscriptions record that the king sent architects and builders from Memphis to work on the Kawa temple. This "archaising" is also shown in one of the smaller statues found in the temple of Taharqo as a lion, the king's face emerging from the lion's mane.

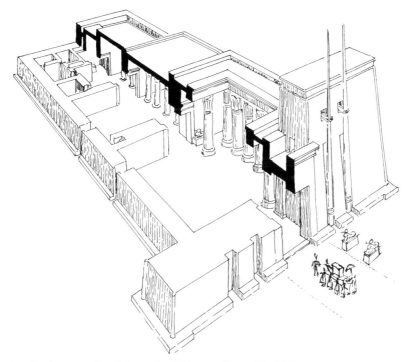

A sectional reconstruction of the temple of Taharqo at Kawa. (Fig. 100)

The inspiration for this statue may have been similar images – but on a much larger scale – of the 12th Dynasty pharaoh, Amenemhat III, which stood in the temple of Tanis.[12] The furniture listed in the temple records includes different types of vessels for offerings and use in the rituals. Of these, at least ten were of gold, over forty of silver and more than 220 of bronze. The king also gave gold and silver censers, altars and offering stands. The religious images too were made of gold and silver. Amongst those described, was a statue of the king, its face covered with gold, and another golden image of the king in the act of smiting the foreign lands. Musical instruments were provided to accompany the rituals, and a scene in the columned hall depicted the temple musicians, two harpists, and two men carrying what appear to be trumpets. Two male singers are shown, each with a hand cupped around his ear. One of the singers might be blind, since he is being guided by one of the two men playing double-ended drums. One of the figures carries what appears to be an elephant-tusk trumpet. Such trumpets were still used in Sudan in this century. They were covered with a skin membrane and blown from the side, creating a fearsome noise. Astronomical instruments to chart the course of the stars were an important item for calculating religious festivals. One of the most notable donations was a chapel made of silver which weighed 172 kg (about 3 cwt). This chapel may have stood in the sanctuary or on the sacred barque. Cedar wood, used for the temple doors and the flag poles, and juniper wood were imported from Lebanon and Syria.

The temple was staffed with priests and servants "even the children of the chieftains of Tjehenu (Libya)". Gardeners were appointed from the Delta and from Djesdjes – the Oasis of Bahariya, which was noted for its wines. Taharqo had vineyards planted on the temple estates.

The two other large temples built by Taharqo in Kush were also in important towns, but their remains were not as well preserved as that of Kawa. Both were almost identical to Kawa in plan and dimensions.

On the island of Argo, north of Kawa, and close to the ancient Kushite city of Kerma, Taharqo built a sanctuary for Amun Lord of Pnubs. This form of Amun was depicted as a ram-headed lion (a "criosphinx"), crowned with a solar-disk and seated upon a shrine beneath the nebes-tree. The temple was excavated by a Swiss team in the 1960s, and the foundations and many sculptured fragments were recovered from the site. These included blocks reused from temples of the New Kingdom pharaohs, probably brought from the region north of the 3rd Cataract. Pnubs continued throughout the Meroitic period to be one of the main towns in this part of Kush, and the focus of coronation voyages.[13]

Taharqo's other foundation was at Sanam, downstream from Gebel Barkal and opposite the cemetery of el-Kurru. Sanam stood at the end of the desert road to Meroe. Here F.Ll. Griffith excavated the temple of Amun-the-Bull, Lord of Nubia.[14] Built in soft, grainy-textured sandstone, the remains had not survived well. The stone had been difficult to carve delicately, so the reliefs were thus much more rudimentary than the fine work at Kawa. It is likely that the Sanam reliefs were originally covered with plaster which allowed better modelling of details. The long foundation text, sadly damaged, records that ships brought statues from the island of Shaat. This was Sai, the site of a New Kingdom fortress and temples. It seems that Taharqo was filling his temples with monuments from earlier, now disused, shrines, just as Piye had done at Barkal. Indeed, from Sanam came a piece of a seated statue, originally of Amenhotep III, which had been re-inscribed for Piye.

Once again the temples at Barkal were the focus of building work. Neither Shabaqo nor Shebitqo had added to the great temple built by Piye. Nor, it seems, had either of them built any other temples near the Holy Mountain. Although Taharqo made no architectural additions to the great temple of Amun, he did set up an altar in the hall preceding the sanctuary, and a colossal black granite statue was erected, probably in the first court. Some 13 feet (4.18 m) high, the king is shown wearing the tall, four-plumed crown of the god Inheret (Onuris). Originally, the cap-crown, plumes, jewellery and sandals were covered in thick gold foil. This image, found along with a number of other broken royal statues buried outside the great temple, served as the model for Kushite royal statues for the next hundred years.

Although no further enlargements were made to its structure, the great temple of Amun must have presented a splendid sight. The avenue of grey granite rams brought from the temple of Amenhotep III at Soleb led to the pylon gateway which gave onto a long colonnaded courtyard. The great Victory Stela of Piye probably stood here, later joined by the stelae of Tanwetamani, Aspelta, Harsiyotef and Nastasen. The red sandstone stela of Piye was also discovered here. Statues of Egyptian high officials were found in the court, and, brought from shrines further north, they added a lustre of antiquity to the new shrine. A black granite image of the goddess Serket, in the form of a rearing cobra, stood at the back of the court in front of the double colonnade. It was originally faced by another similar serpent figure. Like so many other sculptures at Barkal, both had been fashioned for Amenhotep III's temple at Soleb. Four more rams stood between the columns, preceding the entrance through the second pylon. Beyond the second pylon lay the forest of columns of the hypostle hall. The gateway of the third pylon was flanked with more sculptures from Soleb, the two black granite falcons representing Sopdu and Horus of Nekhen. Fragments of other sculptures originally designed for Soleb temple have been found in the region of Barkal and Sanam. These include black granite vipers and a colossal vulture.[15]

Taharqo undoubtedly added to the furnishings of the temple, and, if the donations to the new temple at Gem-Aten can be used as a model, they must have been spectacular. Only a very few fragments of the temple's furniture survived. One of the most important was part of a bronze figure of a king offering an image of the goddess Maet. It is of a type familiar from the period, which served as part of the sacred barque, or votive groups. But, unlike most other surviving examples, this figure retains its original gold leaf on the cap crown, necklaces, bracelets and kilt.[16]

Taharqo's most significant addition to the Barkal complex was two temples cut into the mountain. The larger, apparently on the site of an earlier shrine, has an outer hall with columns in the form of the dwarf-god Bes. The building inscriptions state that it was built by Taharqo as a residence for the goddess Mut of Napata and that it served a ritual function as a birth-house. It thus has parallels with the rebuilding of the temple of Mut at Thebes. Two large scenes show the king making offerings, once accompanied by his mother queen Abar, and once by his chief wife, queen Tekahatamani.[17]

The construction of new temples in the stretch of the river between Kerma and Gebel Barkal emphasises the importance of this region of Kush to the rulers. However, the southern sphere of their control, the savanna lands between the Nile and Atbara rivers, must also have been of great economic value. Very little is known of the archaeology of the savanna from this early period, and it is still uncertain at what point the region around Meroe was united with the kingdom of the Dongola Reach. Military activities of the earliest kings, Alara, Kashta and Piye, are, as yet, undocumented, but they must have taken place.

Taharqo and his predecessors undoubtedly built at Meroe, but, as yet, there are no monuments which can with certainty be attributed to them. The burials in the West cemetery contained many faience amulets of types found at el-Kurru. In one grave was a gold amuletic figure of the goddess Bastet, carrying a dedicatory text of the Great Chief Pamai who had submitted to Piye at Athribis. Another grave contained a gold ring with the cartouche of Taharqo. Clearly, important officials and, perhaps, members of the royal family were being buried in this important southern city.[18]

To the south of Meroe, the extent of Kushite control and influence is unknown. Excavations at Gebel Moya found scarabs with the names of Shabaqo and Taharqo, along with alabaster vessels and faience which have close parallels in contemporary burials at Sanam. These objects probably indicate that there were local rulers who supplied the kings with valuable commodities, probably ivory.[19]

XIX War

Now, after a quarter of a century, Assyria once again became active in the west. Following the campaign of 701, Sennacherib had been absorbed with events in other parts of his empire.[1] He campaigned east of the Tigris and in Cilicia (southern Anatolia), but most of the wars were in the south, against Babylonia and its neighbour and ally, Elam (south-west Iran). Sennacherib attacked Elam in 694 BC, using Phoenician-built boats to sail down the Tigris and Euphrates and then through the marshes into Elamite territory. The Elamites retaliated and captured the town of Sippar in northern Babylonia. Sennacherib's eldest son and designated heir, Assur-nadin-shumi, had been installed as king of Babylon (in 700 BC), but was now seized and taken to Elam where he died in captivity. Three years of military action followed. The conflict saw the accession to the Babylonian throne of Nabu-shuma-ishkun, the son of Assyria's old adversary, Marduk-apla-idinna. In the face of three decades of Assyrian aggression, the leadership of Marduk-apla-idinna had welded the apparently disparate Babylonian urban and tribal groups into a formidable nation. Despite a succession of internal crises – two kings were deposed within a year – Elam was able to withstand the Assyrian offensive. Sennacherib was unable to gain any ground and in 691, the southern coalition marched north to attack Assyria itself. The forces met at Halule (perhaps near Samarra). The Assyrians claimed a victory, but they still made no advance, and the *Babylonian Chronicle* (a history of the Babylonian kings[2]) recorded that the Assyrians had been forced to retreat. The following year the Assyrian army renewed the offensive and besieged Babylon which fell after fifteen months.

The vengeance of Sennacherib on the rebellious city astounded and horrified even his own people. Babylon was an ancient city; it and its gods had always been revered by the Assyrians. Sennacherib ordered that Babylon should be razed to the ground, its temples, city walls and ziggurats pulled down. Symbolically, debris from these sacred buildings was dumped into the Arakhu river. The surface soil was stripped off and hauled down to the Euphrates, to be washed down to the Gulf. So great was the amount that it was visible as far as Dilmun (Bahrain). Canals were dug into the ruins of the city to flood it and turn it into a swamp. Salt was ploughed into its fields to make them sterile. Babylon should be no more.

It was during these years of aggression against Babylon that Taharqo ascended the throne. The new king must have renewed the alliances with the cities of the levantine coast, indicated by the use of cedar wood and pine in the building works of these early years. The Assyrian preoccupation with its neighbours to the south, and the progress of the war, must have encouraged the rulers of the west to again enter into anti-Assyrian alliances.

The Assyriologist, Kirk Grayson, proposes that Sennacherib led a second expedition against Hezekiah of Judah, sometime after 689 BC.[3] This would explain some of the slight inconsistencies in the various sources relating to the campaign of 701 (see Chapter 15), most notably the biblical statement that Taharqo led his army to Hezekiah's aid. Although this intepretation of events has some support amongst biblical scholars, Egyptologists such as Kenneth Kitchen are opposed to it, as we have already seen.

Following the death of Sennacherib's eldest son, Assur-nadin-shumi, in captivity in Elam, a new Crown Prince was appointed. Under the influence of the formidable queen Naqia, Sennacherib overlooked his second eldest son, Ardi-Mulissi, and chose his, and Naqia's, youngest son, Assur-ahhe-iddina (Esarhaddon). Ardi-Mulissi, who was popular in some court circles, was resentful, and the sickly Crown Prince Esarhaddon became unpopular. Early in Sennacherib's 23rd year (about April 681 BC) Sennacherib sent the Crown Prince away from Nineveh, but did not revise the succession. Ardi-Mulissi, fearful that his brother might acquire prestige and support by gaining military victories, concluded a treaty of rebellion. On 20 Tebet 681, Sennacherib was murdered whilst worshipping in the temple. He may have been stabbed to death by Ardi-Mulissi himself, or, as some of the records imply, crushed beneath a winged-bull colossus at the temple entrance.[4] Both the biblical and Babylonian records regarded Sennacherib's murder as divine retribution, the one for his attack on Jerusalem, the other for the destruction of Babylon. Esarhaddon, far away from the capital, moved swiftly when the news reached him.

> I was not afraid of the snow and cold of the month Shabatu (in which) the winter is (at its) hard(est) – but I spread my wings like the (swift-) flying storm (bird) to overwhelm my enemies. ... I reached the embankment of the Tigris and upon the (oracle-)command of Sin and Shamash, the (two) lords of the celestial embankment, I had all my troops jump over the Tigris as if it be a small ditch.

The civil war lasted 42 days, from January until March, when Esarhaddon triumphed.

In the month of Addarru, a favourable month, on the 8th day, the day of the festival of Nebo, I entered joyfully into Nineveh ...[5]

The new king had his brothers and their male heirs executed. The reign of Esarhaddon in many ways reflected the fears instilled by the crisis surrounding his accession. These fears were manifested in the constant use of divination by dreams, omens and extispicy – the examination of the entrails of sacrificed rams. Esarhaddon's empire was vast, and his vassals always seemed to be trying to reassert their independence. Assyria was surrounded by powerful states which involved themselves in the unrest of its peripheral regions and fostered rebellion. The internal security of his empire must have been a continuous, if expected, cause of anxiety. More disturbing, the loyalty of his own officials – even less his own family – could not always be guaranteed. In his 11th year, the annals record, "the king put many of his magnates to the sword".

Esarhaddon's reign was characterised by an increasing use of oracles and divination.[6] Many tablets excavated at Nineveh are inscribed with questions to the sun-god Shamash about military activities: should the army be sent against such and such a town or state? Would there be battle? These questions were presented to the god, and the oracle was divined by examination of the entrails of a sacrificed ram. Astrology was also employed to predict events, although the astrologers did not always agree on their observations or interpretations.

These various types of omen text reveal the fears and concerns of an Assyrian king. But in addition to the military questions, and those enquiring about the loyalty of officials, there are many relating to medical

The Assyrian sun-god, Shamash, in his winged disk. (Fig. 101)

matters, and it seems that Esarhaddon frequently fell ill. To ward off evil from the royal person, the ancient practice of installing "surrogate kings" was revived, and used more and more frequently in the later years of the reign. When an omen predicted that misfortune would befall the king, a surrogate was appointed to rule for 100 days, then executed: the fatal blow thus avoided the king and fell on the surrogate.

In the south, Esarhaddon still faced opposition from Babylonia, and despite the detailed accounts of its destruction, parts of Babylon must have remained undespoiled. Soon after Esarhaddon's accession, another of Marduk-apla-idinna's sons, Nabu-zer-kitti-lishir, marched against the city of Ur which had an Assyrian governor. The prince failed to capture the city, and, when the Assyrian army once again marched south, Nabu-zer-kitti-lishir fled to Elam for safety. But Elam was no longer a safe haven for the Chaldaean princes, "the king of Elam took him prisoner and put him to the sword".[7] His brother, Na'id-Marduk, "fled from Elam to Nineveh, my lordly city, to do obeisance as my slave, kissing my feet". Na'id-Marduk was then installed as king of the Sea Land.

Esarhaddon now adopted a conciliatory policy towards Babylonia. He rebuilt Babylon and its great temple of Marduk, called Esagila, and the ziggurat, Etemenanki. The divine statues which had been carried off to Assyria were returned. Later, spoils from the king's Egyptian campaigns were used for the rebuilding programme at Babylon, and also at Borsippa, Nippur and Uruk.

In addition to the troubles in the south and east, the empire in the west was again asserting its independence, but now, after nearly 25 years of peace, Egypt was once again aiding Assyria's enemies. The extent of Taharqo's involvement in the affairs of western Asia is unclear, but it was undoubtedly the cause of Assyrian actions against Egypt. The main issue at stake was probably control of the Mediterranean trade and Phoenician timber.

During the earlier years of Assyrian expansion, the timber trade had been encouraged, subject to the payment of taxes by the coastal cities. The taxes were resented, and a letter (to be dated between 738-734) of an Assyrian official based in Tyre records that the Assyrian tax-collectors in Sidon and Tyre had been attacked. In consequence the decree was issued to the coastal cities: "do not sell timber to Egypt and to Philistia".[8] The fluctuating fortunes of Assyria and Egypt in the succeeding decades may have seen this decree rescinded and reinstated. By the 680s it was being ignored.

It is likely that Taharqo was actively supporting the local Phoenician rulers against the Assyrians. After the defeat of Taharqo, Esarhaddon carved an inscription at the Dog River,[9] in which Taharqo is associated with Ashkelon, Tyre and 22 kings, suggesting that the Kushite pharaoh had assumed the role of protector or leader of the West against Assyria.

In 679 BC Esarhaddon marched to the Brook of Egypt where Tiglath-pileser III had set up his statue. This had continued to mark the south-western limit of Assyrian power, although the campaign of 701 and events of the succeeding years had probably pushed Egyptian and Kushite control beyond it, into Philistia.[10]

Following the Assyrian victory, Asukhili, king of Arza (el Arish) was taken as captive and "put in fetters together with his councillors". He was taken to Nineveh, where he was "made to sit in fetters near the gateway to the inner city of Nineveh, together with a bear, a dog and a pig".[11]

The next crisis came when Abdi-milkutti, king of Sidon, renounced Assyrian vassalship. Was Sidon aided by Taharqo? It might be assumed so, even though the direct evidence is lacking. There were strong trading connections between Egypt and Sidon and cultural influence there had been strong for some time (and continued to be so). In Esarhaddon's 4th year, 677 BC, the city was captured and its walls torn down. Esarhaddon notes that amongst the booty he carried off were ivory, elephant hides and ebony, three items which suggest strong trading contacts with the Kushite rulers of Egypt.[12] Abdi-milkutti escaped by boat, but was captured "out of the open sea, like a fish". The Babylonian Chronicle adds that "in the month Tishri the head of the king of Sidon was cut off and conveyed to Assyria".[13] His family and some of the people were deported to Assyria. The next year, one of Abdi-milkutti's allies, Sanduarru, king of Kundu and Sisu (in Cilicia), was also captured – "like a bird in his mountains" – and decapitated (in the month Addaru). The fate of the two kings was made public in a grisly spectacle.

> I hung the heads of Sanduarru and Abdi-milkutti (around) the necks of their chief officials to demonstrate to the people the power of Assur, my lord, and paraded them through the wide main street of Nineveh accompanied by singers (playing their) harps[14].

Following the fall of Sidon, two dependent cities of Sidon were granted to Baal of Tyre. A new city, Kar-Esarhaddon – the Port of Esarhaddon – was built; in its construction the Assyrians were "aided" by the 22 kings of the Sea Coast and Syria. It was settled with peoples transported from the east of the empire.

The vassal treaty ensuring Baal's loyalty has survived.[15] A royal deputy was appointed, and Baal was allowed to open letters only in his presence: if the deputy was absent, Baal could not read his post.

This campaign reasserted Assyrian authority and in 676 Esarhaddon listed all of the coastal states of Syria-Palestine as having supplied materials for his building works at Nineveh. These included Baal of Tyre, Manasseh of Judah (the successor of Hezekiah), Qaushgabri of Edom, Musuru of Moab, Sillibel of Gaza, Metinti of Ashkelon, Ikausu of Ekron, Milkiashapa of Gubla (Byblos), Matanbaal of Arvad, Abibaal of Samsimuruna, Pudu-ilu of Beth-Ammon, Ahimilki of Ashdod. Some of these kings had played a role in the events surrounding the rebellion of Hezekiah in 701 BC. These rulers are followed by the 10 kings of Iadnana (Cyprus).

The kings organised the transport to Nineveh of precious materials for the building of the "Palace in which everything is gathered". Large beams and columns of cedar came from mount Sirara and mount Lebanon. There were slabs of alabaster for the thresholds. The door-leaves were of cypress wood "whose smell is sweet" and were coated with silver and copper. Massive protective winged bulls flanked the entrances.

The situation did not remain stable for long. The next incident in the conflict is certainly recorded by only one of the ancient sources, the *Babylonian Chronicle*.

> The seventh year: in the month Addaru, the 5th day, the army of Assyria was defeated in a bloody battle in Egypt.[16]

Addaru was the last month of the year (Feb/Mar 674 BC). The tablet known as the *Esarhaddon Chronicle*[17] has a conflicting report that the "on the 8th day of the month of Addaru the army of Assyria [marched] to Sha-amele" – Sha-amele has been identified as a city in southern Babylonia, but the Egyptologist Gerhard Fecht, in an attempt to reconcile the apparently contradictory chronicles, proposed that it should be read as an Assyrianised version of the name of the Egyptian frontier fortress of Tjel[18]. Therefore, Fecht suggested, there were two battles in close succession, one successful, one not. Fecht's interpretation is not generally accepted. It is assumed that the author of the *Esarhaddon Chronicle*, who was singularly biased in the king's favour, not mentioning any defeat or disgrace, probably chose to omit the Assyrian defeat in Egypt, preferring instead to record the less important action in Babylonia.

Although the texts are inadequate, it is likely that Esarhaddon had invaded Egypt and joined in battle with Taharqo. He had been defeated.

Three years later, Esarhaddon again prepared for war with Taharqo, and this time ensured he would be victorious. The campaign of Esarhaddon's 10th year is recorded in several sources, but the ideological concerns of the texts abbreviate the events of the war in preference to records of the tribute and booty and the absorbtion of Egypt into the Assyrian empire. Only a fragmentary text gives details of the march and the dates of the events.

The official records of the war against Egypt were the stelae that Esarhaddon had carved at the Nahr el Kelb and those which were set up at

Sam'al (Zenjirli) and Kar-Shalmaneser (Til Barsip).[19] The Nahr el Kelb, the Dog River, flows into the sea a little way north of Beirut. Here the mountains of the Lebanon range come down to the sea, forcing the road to follow a narrow path along the coast. The route was used by many passing armies, and inscriptions had been left here recording their triumphs by the Egyptian pharaohs Thutmose III and Ramesses II and by the Assyrian emperor Shalmaneser III. In later centuries the Babylonian, Nebuchadnezzar, and the Roman emperor, Caracalla, were to add their own monuments.

The other stelae, massive stone monoliths, were set up in the provincial cities of Zenjirli and Kar-Shalmaneser (Til Barsip). The decoration of these three monoliths is the same (Fig.102). A massive figure of Esarhaddon dominates the field, with small images of the Assyrian gods and their emblems hovering before his face. In his left hand he holds a cord to which are attached two small figures. One, standing, wears Phoenician costume, the other, kneeling, is shown with Kushite features. The identity of these two captives has been disputed ever since the discovery of the monuments, and there is still no consensus amongst Egyptologists or Assyriologists.[20] The standing figure might be Abdi-milkutti of Sidon, or Baal of Tyre. The Kushite has often been said to be Taharqo, because he is shown wearing a cap with the royal uraeus. But it is more likely (as many scholars have argued) that it is actually Ushanukhuru (as the Assyrian texts call him), Taharqo's son. Esarhaddon never captured Taharqo himself. The text runs across the relief in typical Assyrian fashion. The Zenjirli stela is well-preserved, those from Til Barsip having suffered some weathering. On the sides of the stelae are small figures of Esarhaddon's two appointed successors, the crown Prince Assur-bani-apli (Assurbanipal) and Shamash-shumu-ukin, designated to become king of Babylonia. These stelae narrate the swift defeat of Taharqo and capture of Memphis, but give no details of the events which led up to the battles. The *Esarhaddon Chronicle* is equally brief, but a little more detail may be culled from the *Babylonian Chronicle*.

None of these official sources gives details of the prelude to the war. Following his victory over Esarhaddon in 674 BC, Taharqo may have responded with an even more aggressive foreign policy. In the succeeding events it is clear that he was supporting the rebel cities with troops. Two oracle requests concerning Ashkelon survive.[21] They were addressed by Esarhaddon to the sun god Shamash. The first asks whether the king and his army should march against the city. The second, damaged, text also has references to the troops of Egypt, who may be defending the city. The texts are difficult to date precisely, but they are earlier than 669 BC.

The opposition may have begun with an embargo on Assyrian trade, effected by the closing of the Phoenician harbours to Assyrian merchant ships. Open revolt followed, when the tribute was not paid.

One of the two stelae of Esarhaddon from Til Barsip (Aleppo Museum) (Fig.102), with detail showing the kneeling Kushite figure, perhaps Taharqo's captured son, Ushanukhuru. (Fig. 103)

The letter of an Assyrian official complains about the hostile attitude of one of the local rulers, probably to be identified with Yakinlu (Assyrian: Ikkalu) of Arvad. An oracle request addressed to Shamash by the Crown Prince Assurbanipal asks whether he should send Nabu-Sharru-usur to Yakinlu, and, if he does send him, will Yakinlu listen to, and comply with, the message. The request, quite understandably, does not say what the message itself is.[22] Yakinlu was deposed some years later by a pro-Assyrian faction, so we might suspect he did not comply.

Another request by Assurbanipal, carrying the same date as the Arvad request, asks whether Nabu-Sharru-usur should be sent to Egypt.

The anti-Assyrian coalition was large. The very fragmentary inscription at the Dog River mentions Ashkelon and other cities which Taharqo had made as strongholds, and refers to the "22 kings" who had joined together. Some Assyriologists have dismissed this as too large a number. One of the most prominent rebels was Tyre.

Both the *Esarhaddon Chronicle* and the *Babylonian Chronicle* omit reference to the king's ninth year (672 BC), prompting the Assyriologist,

Kirk Grayson, to suggest that throughout this year preparations were being made for the major offensive against Egypt. This is almost certainly the case. Two oracle requests addressed by Esarhaddon to the Assyrian sun-god, Shamash, ask whether he should lead his army to Egypt to fight against Taharqo "as he wishes".[23] Two other texts are very similar and although they are fragmentary and any reference to Egypt is lost, they too probably belong to this year.

> [Shamash, great lord], give me a firm positive answer [to what] I am asking you!
> [Should Esarhaddon, king of] Assyria, strive and plan?
> [Should he take the road] with his army and camp, and go to the [dis]trict of Egypt, as [he wis]hes?
> [Should he wage] war [against Taharqo], king of Kush, [and the troops which] he has?
> [If he go]es, will he [engage in battle] with [Taharqo, k]ing of Kush and his army?
> In waging [this war, will the weapo]ns of Esa[rhad]don, ki[ng of Assyria, and his army, prevail ov]er the weapons of T[aharqo], king of Kush, and the troops w[hich he has]? Will (Esarhaddon's troops) ... defeat them ... and overrun them in victory, power, might and conquest? ...
> [Shamash, great lord? Will he who can see, se]e it? Will he who can hear, hear it? ...
> Be present in this ram, [place] (in it) a firm positive answer, [favourable designs], favourable propitious [omens] by the oracular command of your great divinity, and may I see (them).

One of the fragmentary texts refers to the beginning of the coming year (Nisan), until the month Du'uzu (the fourth) as the planned time of the campaign.

It was indeed at the beginning of the new year that the king and his army left Assyria.[24]

> Esarhaddon, the great king, the mighty king, king of the universe, king of Assyria, viceroy of Babylon, king of Sumer and Akkad, king of Karduniash, king of the kings of Lower Egypt, of Upper Egypt and of Kush.
> I am powerful, I am all powerful, I am without an equal among all kings.
> [I] called up the numerous army of Assur ... In the month Nisan, the first month (of the year), I departed from my city Assur. I crossed the Tigris and the Euphrates at (the time of) their flood; I advanced over

the difficult territory (of my route) (as quick-footed) as a wild ox. In the course of my campaign I threw up earthwork (for a siege) against Baal, king of Tyre, who had put his trust upon his friend Tarqu, king of Kush, and (therefore) had thrown off the yoke of Assur, my lord, answering (my admonitions with) insolence. I withheld from them [the inhabitants of besieged Tyre] food and (fresh) water which sustain life. I removed my camp from Musru and marched directly towards [Egypt] – a distance of 30 double-hours from the town of Apku which is in the region of Samaria as far as the town of Rapikhu in the region adjacent to the "Brook of Egypt" – and there is no river (all the way)!

Leaving Assur, the army had made straight for the coast. After the siege of Tyre it marched south, to the coast road from Gaza to Rapikhu (Raphia). The fragmentary text gives details of the route, the stones and strange animals encountered.[25] The route was certainly difficult, and water had to be brought from wells. Aid was given by the Arabian rulers who brought camels. The Assyrians confronted the Egyptian-Kushite army, and a fragmentary text records that: "I scattered their well arranged battle force ... his brother, his governors [... from] Ishkhupri as far as Memphis".[26]

Taharqo's army must have begun the advance to meet the Assyrian force, first engaging in battle at Ishkhupri. From Ishkhupri to Memphis was 15 days march, which would place it somewhere on the coast road between Tjel and el-Arish. The Zenjirli stela claims that the Assyrian army fought the Kushite forces "daily, without interruption". The *Babylonian Chronicle* is, typically, more realistic and states that there were three battles over the 15 days, on the 3rd, 16th and 18th of Du'uzu, between Ishkhupri and Memphis. The mighty Assyrian army gradually forced the massed Egyptian and Kushite forces back to Taharqo's capital. The pharaoh himself seems to have played a leading role in the battles outside the city.

> I fought ... very bloody battles against Tarqu, king of Egypt and Kush, the one accursed by all the great gods. Five times I hit him with the point of (my) arrows (inflicting) wounds (from which he should not) recover...[27]

Taharqo must have realised that the Assyrian capture of Memphis was inevitable. Wounded, he abandoned the city and withdrew, probably to Thebes.

> Mimpi (Memphis), his royal city, in half a day with mines, tunnels, assault ladders; I destroyed (it), tore down (its walls) and burnt it down.

Four days after the last pitched battle, on 22nd Du'uzu (July 11th 671 BC), Esarhaddon entered the city.[28] But resistance was strong and the battle raged within its streets, resulting in appalling carnage. A tablet from Tell Kuyunjik (Nineveh) records the events:[29]

> I defeated and killed them with my weapons ... In the city square their corpses were heaped upon each other, I erected piles of their heads...
> After I had prayed to Assur, to Marduk, to Shamash and the great gods of heaven and the underworld, as many as there are, and after they had granted my hearts desire ... I entered into his plundered palace. There I found his wives, his sons and daughters, who like him, had skins as dark as pitch ...

The texts detail the booty of Egypt – the Assyrians seem to have been so staggered by this that it received constant repetition in the texts. Amongst the treasure removed from the palace was 16 tiaras and 30 headgears for "queens". There were also descriptions of the military equipment and personnel captured. The Egyptian and Kushite army must have suffered enormous losses yet it was soon able to recoup and rearm.

Taharqo had escaped, but many members of the royal family were captured, including his eldest son, Ushanukhuru (probably the Assyrian writing of Nes-Inheret), and various of the king's wives and brothers.

> His queen, his harem, Ushanukhuru his heir, and the rest of his sons and daughters, his property and his goods, his horses, his cattle, his sheep, in countless numbers, I carried off to Assyria. The root of Kush I tore up out of Egypt and not one therein escaped to submit to me. Over all of Egypt I appointed anew kings, viceroys, governors, commandants, overseers and scribes.

The *Babylonian Chronicle* adds:[30]

> .. its king escaped (but) his son and [brother] were [cap]tured.

Another fragmentary text, a parallel to the Dog River Stela also emphasises the capture of the king's relatives:[31]

> The seed of the house of his father, the sons of the earlier kings (?)...

The fall of Memphis must have had a devastating effect on the Kushite royal house. It is clear from the records that the city's capture was, initially,

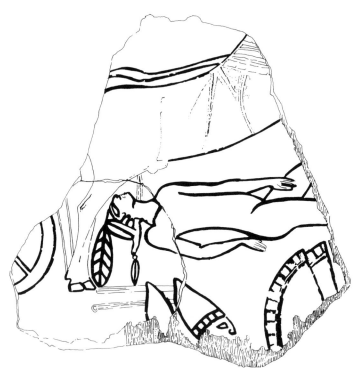

Esarhaddon's Egyptian campaigns were depicted in the palace at Nineveh in glazed tiles. Here, a dead Kushite is crushed beneath an Assyrian chariot. (Fig. 104)

unexpected. Other members of the royal family were probably resident in other cities such as Thebes, and in Kush itself, but it is clear that a significant number was in Memphis.

With the fall of Memphis, the Assyrians set about trying to remove the "root of Kush" from Egypt. The Kushite, but not apparently the Egyptian, officials were ousted. Some were deported, both Kushites and Egyptians are later found at Nineveh. The people who were deported to Assyria were, as was usual, mainly high-ranking members of the court or artisans, although some groups are mentioned who belong to neither. These included animal physicians, snake-charmers, singers, bakers, carpenters of ships and wagons, and possibly also iron workers.

The presence of Kushites at the Assyrian court, along with many other captives from the empire, is well-documented. Amongst the many thousands of tablets and fragments excavated at Tell Kuyunjik was a group relating to the administration and personnel of the palaces. The majority of records is undated, and although some belong to the reign of Sargon, most can safely be attributed the reign of Esarhaddon and the early years of Assurbanipal.

One tablet lists palace women, including musicians, and, rather less expected, scribes, smiths and stone borers, by country of origin.[32] The list is headed by a group including Aramaeans, Tyrians and Assyrians along with 15 (or 16) Kushite women. This group is totalled together with their maids, denoting their high rank.

Another tablet records the activities of two Kushite eunuchs, Dari-sharru and Shulmu-sharri.[33] Both were apparently in positions of authority, with the power to send royal bodyguards on business. There is no direct evidence for eunuchs, or the practice of castration, in Egypt. In Assyria it was thought that eunuchs, having no descendants, would be especially loyal.[34] The evidence from this text raises questions about one

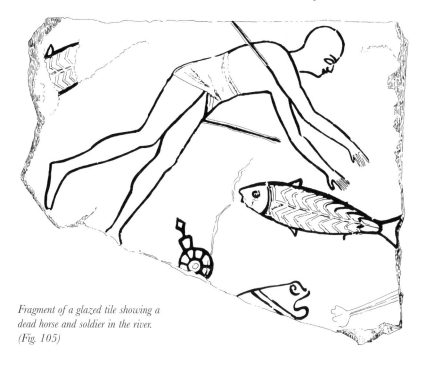

Fragment of a glazed tile showing a dead horse and soldier in the river.
(Fig. 105)

of the most striking of images to have survived from the Kushite period in Egypt, the statue of Irike-takana.[35] The inscription calls Irike-takana "hereditary prince and count" and "Royal friend". These titles place Irike-takana in a high social position, but indicate no specific office. The invocations are to the Theban deities, Monthu and Amun-Re, and the statue was itself excavated at Karnak. Most writers have assumed that Irike-takana was, quite straightforwardly, fat, and the comments on this statue have tended to focus on it as an example of the 'brutal realism' attributed to sculpture of this period. It is quite possible that the physical characteristics of Irike-takana indicate that he, too, was a eunuch. Although the inscription accords him no specific office, he was of very high rank and perhaps was attached in some way to the household of the God's Wife of Amun. Half-a-century later we find another reference to a Kushite eunuch, Ebed-melech, who was in the service of Zedekiah, king of Judah[36].

We can only speculate on the lives and feelings of these deportees. The lives of those women who entered the palace may not have been particularly different or worse than before, whereas some officials, such as Dari-sharru and Shulmu-sharri, continued to exercise, and perhaps abuse, their power.

A text from the reign of Assurbanipal casts more light on deported officials. The king is warned to be wary of Shuma-iddin, the governor of Nippur in Babylonia.

> Maybe they are saying nice things about Shuma-iddin. It should be known to the king my lord, however, that this very day a conspiracy is being made and planned in the king's presence, right before him, and Shuma-iddin has his hands in it.

> May the king, my lord, live forever! The Egyptian Sharru-lu-dari, a friend of Bel-etir, the governor of HAR, and a friend of Sasiya, may have been induced to join the conspiracy of Shuma-iddin. The king should be wary of them.

Bel-etir a commandant and governor of HAR is known from other letters which also refer to someone who for three years has been inciting Bel-etir. HAR is a city in Babylonia, the correct reading of the name and its exact location are unknown. The Egyptian Sharru-lu-dari has adopted an Assyrian name meaning, ironically under the circumstances, "May the king live". The fears revealed in the texts of Esarhaddon certainly had a basis in the realities of court intrigues.

Even if the deportees ultimately enjoyed rank and privilege in Assyria, this must have been preceded by terror and trauma, and, for many less-fortunate, death, wounding and loss of family. Taharqo himself did not escape the disaster of war. Perhaps badly wounded, the king, and what was left of his army, retreated, probably to Thebes. Many members of the royal family had been captured, and the Libyan dynasts of the Delta had submitted to the Assyrians – they had little choice. Assyria was triumphant, and Egypt was set to become the newest of her provinces.

XX Assyria in Egypt

Esarhaddon now moved to make Egypt part of the Assyrian empire. Later texts of the reign of Assurbanipal specify that it was Memphis and the Delta, rather than all Egypt, that was added to Assyria. The Assyrian control did not extend as far as Thebes, and presumably the border between north and south was once again in the region of Nen-nesut or Teudjoi, or perhaps near Tjeny.

Assyrian officials were installed, yearly tribute was imposed on the cities individually (rather than on the country as a whole), and regular offerings were to be made to the Assyrian gods in the Egyptian temples. The cities were given new Assyrian names, and their rulers replaced or reappointed as vassals. The main Egyptian opponent to Kushite rule, the city of Sau, became Kar-bel-matati, and its king, Nekau, was reinstated. No Assyrian monuments have been discovered in any of the Egyptian cities, but, even if a parallel to the Zenjirli and Til Barsip stelae was set up in, for example, Memphis, it would not long have survived the triumphant return of Taharqo.

Many of the new officials were probably Assyrians, but the cities were left under the rule of their dynasts. Remarkably, there is no evidence for the permanent presence of some of the highest-ranking Assyrians officials; the *turtanu*, the *rab-shaqeh* and others are noted to have been sent to Egypt, so could not have been resident. The cities appear to have been left independent in their local administration – the system reflecting Assyrian rule in Phoenicia - but it is uncertain whether the local rulers were obliged to open all letters in the presence of the Assyrian *qepu*, as Baal, king of Tyre, had to do.[1]

A record from early in the reign of Assurbanipal lists the rulers as they were installed by Esarhaddon.[2] All of them are referred to by the Assyrian term *sharru*, king, which does not distinguish their Egyptian titles.

Niku of Mimpi and Saa, Sharru-lu-dari of Si'nu, Pishanhuru of Nathu, Pakruru of (Pi-)Shaptu, Bukkunanni'pi of Khaat-khiribi, Nahke of Hininshi, Putubishti of Saanu, Unamunu of Nathu, Harsiaeshu of Sabnuti, Buiama of Pitinti [Bentiti or Pentiti], Shishak of Bushiru, Tabnahti of Punubu, Iptihardeshu of Pihattihurunpi(ki), Nahtihuruansini of Pishabdi'a, Bukurninip of Pahnuti, Siha of Siautu, Lamintu of Himunu, Ishpimatu of Taini, Mantimanhe of [Thebes].

The Egyptian equivalents of many of the names and towns can be understood, although a few remain uncertain.[3] A number of the individuals is also known from monuments and other Assyrian records. The list makes a fascinating comparison with the list of the opponents of Piye, and shows that the Kushites had, in most cases, let the Libyan dynasts retain their power.

Niku of Memphis and Sau is beyond doubt Nekau. He appears to have been installed as ruler of Memphis by Esarhaddon.

Sharruludari of Si'nu has often been assumed to have been an Assyrian. The name Sharruludari, meaning "May the king live!", was often assumed by loyalist vassals, such as the ruler of Ashkelon installed by Sennacherib. This Sharruludari was governor of the frontier fortress of Tjel (Si'nu), and may have been an Egyptian prince. He was to figure in the succeeding events.

The name Pishanhuru is certainly the Egyptian Pasenhor,[4] but the identification of Nathu remains uncertain.

Pakruru of (Pi-)Shaptu, is Pakrur of Per-Soped in the eastern delta. The son of Patjenfy, Chief of the Ma and ruler of Per-Soped, who had submitted to Piye at the Athribis durbar, Pakrur was to figure prominently in later events.

Bukkunanni'pi of Khaat-khiribi is well-documented. This city, the Egyptian Hut-hery-ib, better known by its Greek name *Athribis* (modern Benha) held a strategic position at the base of the Delta. Here Piye had been welcomed by its prince, Pediese, and had held his great durbar in which he received the submission of the delta rulers. It was the son of that prince Pediese, Bakennefi, who now ruled in the city.[5]

Putubishti of Sanu is the pharaoh Pedubast of Djanet. The Assyrian record has no mention of the kingdom of Bubastis and Ra-nefer which occurs in the Piye list, and we can probably safely assume that the dynasty of Osorkon III had ended. Piye recorded no ruler in Djanet, so Pedubast (or a predecessor such as Gemenefkhonsubak) may have been installed as king by the Kushites.

Shishak of Bushiru is Sheshonq of Djedu (Per-Usir). This Sheshonq was probably the son of Pimay, who became ruler of the city at the time of Piye's campaign against Tefnakht. The family continued to be rulers of the city under the Saites.[6]

The remainder of the Delta rulers are slightly more problematic. In many cases the Egyptian form of their names can be understood, but the seats of power remain uncertain. Tabnahti of Punubu seems to be Tefnakht, perhaps a relative of the Saite house.[7] Nahtihuruansini of Pishabdi'a is Nakht-hor-neshu; Unamunu of Nathu, Wenamun and Harsiaeshu of Sabnuti is Harsiese. The name Iptihardeshu has been suggested to represent the Egyptian "Nefertemirdis" although the first part 'Ipti' is probably more likely to be "Pedi", as in Pedi-Hor.[8]

Four rulers of Middle and Upper Egypt are named. Djedhor (Siha) of Sauty (Asyut) is otherwise unknown. Lamintu of Himunu is particularly intriguing. This name certainly is Nimlot and the town Khemenu (Hermopolis). Most Egyptologists have considered it highly unlikely that this is the same as the Nimlot who was ruler of Khemenu in the reign of Piye, preferring to see this dynast as a grandson.[9] Moving further south, the town of Taini was once equated with Aswan, but is undoubtedly Tjeny (Thinis), north of Abdju.[10] Its ruler, Ishpimatu, was Nespamedu, the Vizier of Upper Egypt. Nespamedu's family had strong connections with the Abdju-Akhmim region, and both he and his father were buried at Abdju.[11] Nespamedu was succeeded as Vizier by his son, Nesipakashuty. The last of the rulers, Mantimanhe, is the Fourth Prophet of Amun and Mayor of Thebes, Monthuemhat.[12]

It was not only Per-Bastet which had ceased to have a king by the time of the Assyrian list; Nen-nesut (Herakleopolis) too, is omitted. Peftjauawybast, ruler of the city at the time of Piye, must now have been dead, and there is no evidence that he had been succeeded by a son. At this time, the city was ruled by a prominent family which carried the title "master of the harbour". This title can be equated with an Assyrian title which is attested from the time of Esarhaddon and Assurbanipal, that of *rab kari*, "the master of the quay", whose duty was to collect taxes for the Assyrians.[13] The first holder of the title "master of the harbour" was called Pediese. He also carried a large number of important priestly titles, all of which associate him with the region of Nen-nesut and the Faiyum. His wife was a king's daughter, with the rather lengthy name Ta-khered-en-ta-ihet-weret ("the child of the great [white] cow"). It is usually assumed that this princess was related to the Saite royal house, but her name associates her with the local form of the goddess Hathor of Tep-ihu (Atfieh). She might, therefore, have been a daughter of king Peftjauawybast. Indeed, there is a likelihood of an even closer relationship between this most prominent family of Nen-nesut and its earlier king. Pediese himself was son of a priest named Ankh-Sheshonq who was the grandson of king Sheshonq III. Pediese's own mother, Taperet, was the daughter of the High Priest of Memphis, also called Pediese (descended from Osorkon II). If, indeed, the king Peftjauawybast is to be identified with the like-named High Priest of Memphis, then Pediese would have been his nephew, and probably his son-in- law as well. Pediese died in year 18 of Psamtik I, and was succeeded in his offices by his son, Sematawy-tefnakht, who was to play a significant role in the events which marked the transfer of power to the Saite kings.[14]

Assyrian control of Egypt was brief, and it seems that even Esarhaddon suspected treachery. An oracle request[15] made by the king to Shamash asks whether the the Chief Eunuch, Sa-Nabu-su, who had been sent to Egypt, will be safe. Sa-Nabu-su had been sent to Assyria's most loyal adherents, Nekau and Sharruludari.

Events moved quickly. Taharqo again established himself in Memphis. In Assyria there must have been a major rebellion against Esarhaddon, and the chronicles bluntly report that "the king put his numerous officers to the sword".[16] Having reasserted his authority, the Assyrian king launched a third campaign against Egypt (669 BC), but became ill during the journey, and died in Palestine on the 10th day of the month Arakhsamni (Marchesvan – November). Taharqo was spared.

Esarhaddon had tried to ensure an undisputed succession, nominating two of his sons to succeed him. Assurbanipal was to rule Assyria, and Shamash-shumu-ukin to take the throne of Babylon. In 672 the king had called representatives of the empire to Nineveh to swear to carry out his wishes – a number of the documents recording the oaths survives. After Esarhaddon's sudden death, his mother, the formidable queen Naqia, ensured that these oaths were resworn by the brothers of the two new kings, by the officials and by the people. It seems that, for once, the succession was without civil war.

The reign of Assurbanipal is the best documented in Assyrian history, but there are still problems of interpretation and chronology of events. The death of Esarhaddon granted a brief respite for Taharqo, but it was all too brief. Assurbanipal established his authority at home and within two years (667-666 BC) the vengeance of Assyria was unleashed. Like his father before him, Assurbanipal sought divine advice and consulted the omens. An astrological text[17] of March 29, 668 predicts that:

Assurbanipal (668-626 BC), the last of the great Assyrian emperors. From one of the magnificent reliefs in his palace at Nineveh which show the king hunting lions. (Fig. 106)

[If the moon] becomes visible in Nisan on the 1st day: the north [wind] will blow; ... Mercury [became vi]sible in the west in Aries; it is good for the king my lord, [bad for the Westland]. The king of the Westland will fall in battle. [The troops of the king] my lord who are in Egypt will conquer..."

Assurbanipal's first two campaigns were directed against Egypt. The events are recorded on the "Rassam Cylinder"[18] which was found in 1878 by Hormuzd Rassam, in the ruins of Tel Kuyunjik.

I am Assurbanipal the great king, the mighty king, king of the universe, king of Assyria, king of the four quarters; offspring of the loins of Esarhaddon, king of the universe, king of Assyria, viceroy of Babylon, king of Sumer and Akkad; grandson of Sennacherib, king of the universe, king of Assyria.

In my first campaign I marched against Magan and Meluhha.

Tarqu king of Egypt and Kush whom Esarhaddon, king of Assyria, my own father, had defeated, and in whose land he had ruled, - that Tarqu forgot the power of Assur, Ishtar, and the (other) great gods, my lords, and he trusted in his own strength. He marched against the kings and governors whom my father had appointed in Egypt. He entered and took up residence in Memphis... A swift courier came to Nineveh and reported to me. At these deeds my heart became enraged, my soul cried out. I raised my hands in prayer to Assur and Ishtar. Then I called up my mighty armed forces ... and took the shortest road to Egypt and Kush ...

Although Taharqo had regained control of Memphis, his earlier defeat in Egypt seems to have damaged his credibility amongst the rulers of western Asia. On his march, Assurbanipal received the submission of the 22 kings of the Sea Coast, the islands and the mainland. Clearly they wanted to demonstrate their loyalty to the new king whom they regarded as more powerful than their former champion. Assurbanipal made them join the expedition with their armies, or accompany the fleet. When the Assyrian army arrived in Egypt it defeated the forces of Taharqo at Karbaniti (an Assyrian name).

Tarqu, king of Egypt and Kush heard of the advance of my army, in Mimpi, and called up his warriors for a decisive battle against me. Upon a trust(-inspiring) oracle (given) by Assur, Bel and Nabu, the great gods, my lords, who always (march) at my side, I defeated the battle (-experienced) soldiers of his army in a great open battle. Tarqu heard of the defeat of his armies, while in Mimpi. The terrible splendour of Assur and Ishtar blinded him and he became like a madman. The glory of my majesty, with which the gods of heaven and earth have crowned me, dazzled him. He forsook Mimpi and fled to save his life, to No [Thebes]. Mimpi I seized. My troops occupied it.

Then follows the long list of the rulers of Egypt.

These kings, princes and governors, whom my father had appointed in Egypt and who had deserted their posts before the advance of Tarqu, and had scattered into the open country, I reinstated in their former offices. With many prisoners and heavy booty I returned safely to Nineveh.

Parts of a relief from the throne room of Assurbanipal's palace at Nineveh show the capture of an Egyptian city (Fig.107), but it is unknown whether it depicts Memphis or one of the Delta cities. The scene combines the attack on the city with the capture of soldiers and its inhabitants. Scaling ladders have been set up against its walls, archers shoot from behind protective screens, and a soldier attempts to set fire to its gates. Kushites killed in the action fall from the walls and towers, the heads of others are carried triumphantly by Assyrian soldiers. Defeated Kushites are bound and led away.

Although it is impossible to place it in relation to these events, Memphis witnessed another calamity, in the death of the sacred bull, Apis. Several stelae from the Serapeum record the bull's burial, in the season of Peret.[19] Perhaps because of the political upheavals, a successor was not installed immediately.

It seems that Taharqo prepared to defend himself at Thebes, probably on the west bank. The Assyrian army marched south, but news of the treachery of the Delta dynasts diverted them.

... all the kings whom I had appointed broke the oaths (sworn to) me, did not keep the agreements sworn by the great gods, forgot that I had treated them mildly and conceived an evil (plot). They talked about rebellion and came, among themselves to the unholy decision: "(Now when even) Tarqu has been driven out of Egypt, how can we, ourselves, (hope to) stay?" And they sent their mounted messengers to Tarqu king of Kush, to establish a sworn agreement; "Let there be peace between us and let us come to mutual understanding; we will divide the country between us, no foreigner shall be ruler among us!"

A detail from a large relief of the reign of Assurbanipal showing the capture of an Egyptian town next to a river. Four shackled Kushite prisoners are being led away. The feathers probably indicate that they are members of the elite. (Fig. 107)

Nekau, Sharruludari and Pekrur communicated secretly with Taharqo, seeking an alliance. It seems strange that Nekau, who usually opposed the Kushites, was, in this instance, intriguing with them against the Assyrians.

> ... my officials heard about these matters, seized their mounted messengers with their messages and learned about their rebellious doings. They arrested these kings and bound them hand and foot with bonds and fetters of iron. The (consequences of the broken) oaths (sworn) by Assur [king of the gods, overtook them, because they had sinned against the oath they had sworn. I required at their hands the good which I had done to them in kindness]. And (my officers) put to the sword the inhabitants, young and old, of the towns of Sau (Sais), Pindid and Sa'nu (Djanet, Tanis) and of all the other towns which had joined with them in plotting evil. They did not spare any among them. Their corpses they hung on stakes. They flayed their skins and covered the city walls with them.

A second record,[20] is written in the voice of the king:

> The hearts of the inhabitants of Sau, Bindidi, Sa'nu who had revolted and collaborated with Tarqu, I hung on poles; I flayed them and covered the walls of the towns with their skins.

Two Assyrian soldiers impaling enemies. This detail comes from the scene of the capture of the city of Lachish by Sennacherib. The practice of impaling enemies is known from Egypt and was the fate of some of the Libyans defeated by Merneptah.(Fig. 108)

Those kings who had planned evil against the armies of Assyria they brought before me alive, to Nineveh. I had mercy only upon Niku. I spared his life and laid an oath, more drastic than the former, upon him. I clothed him in splendid garments, laid upon his neck a golden chain, rings of gold upon his fingers, and an iron girdle dagger with a golden haft. I sent him back to his post in Kar-bel-matati, where my father had set him up as king, and Nabu-shezzi-banni, his son, I set over Limir-ishshak-Assur.

Nekau's loyalty is expressed by the Assyrian name which his son now adopted, Nabu-shezzi-banni, "Nabu deliver me". This prince was later to succeed his father as ruler of Sau, and re-assume his Egyptian name, Psamtik. Sau itself is referred to by its new Assyrian name, Kar-bel-matati, just as Hut-hery-ib was renamed Limir-ishshak-Assur. Bakennefi, the prince of Hut-hery-ib, was presumably one of those executed. In addition to his retribution on the rebellious cities, Assurbanipal may have deported people from Kirbit and settled them in Egypt.

As for Tarqu, in the place to which he fled, the terror of the sacred weapon of Assur my lord overwhelmed him and the night of death overtook him.

XXI   The Osiris, Taharqo

Taharqo was buried, not in the ancestral cemetery at el-Kurru, but at Nuri, almost opposite Gebel Barkal. Nuri was excavated by George Reisner between 1916 and 1918. Altogether, Reisner cleared pyramids belonging to some twenty kings and fifty-three queens from the time of Taharqo down to that of Nastasen whose great historical stela had been one of those found at Gebel Barkal in 1862. The evidence from the pyramids enabled Reisner to reconstruct a sequence of Kushite rulers from the 25th Dynasty kings to the reign of Nastasen (ca. 330 BC), and, with the evidence from the cemeteries at Meroe, continue it to the end of the Meroitic kingdom in the 4th century AD. Reisner based his reconstruction on the position of the pyramids within the cemetery and other criteria of their design. This chronology was refined by Dows Dunham in his publication of Reisner's excavations and, although some further modifications have been made, is still regarded as essentially sound.[1]

The pyramid burials of Taharqo's immediate successors, Anlamani, Senkamanisken and Aspelta in the royal cemetery at Nuri. (Fig. 109)

Taharqo chose the highest point of the ridge for his tomb. It was by far the largest of the Kushite royal tombs, although today it is badly denuded. When Waddington and Hanbury visited Nuri in 1821 they found that the pyramid rose to a height of 103 feet 7 inches (31.6 m). All of the earliest European visitors noted that there were signs of an inner structure and this appears clearly in the drawings of Waddington and Hanbury, and of Linant de Bellefonds. The inner structure is no longer visible due to the denudation, but it is clear that the original pyramid was encased within a considerably larger monument. Taharqo's first pyramid was about 28.50 metres square, covered with smooth sandstone masonry and rose with a slope of about 65°. The second pyramid was considerably larger, completely surrounding the earlier structure, although not centred upon it. It too was of sandstone masonry, but rose at an angle of 69° and, instead of smooth sides, each course was slightly stepped. This stepping is also found in many of the later Kushite pyramids at Nuri, Barkal and Meroe.

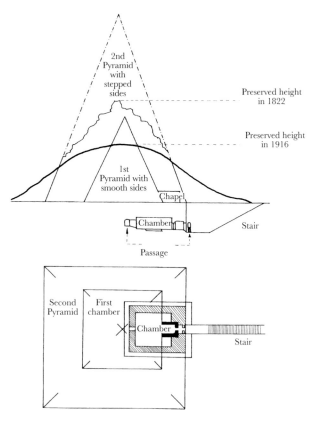

Plan and section of the pyramid of Taharqo at Nuri. (Fig. 110)

Some scholars have suggested that the enlargement of the pyramid was carried out by one of Taharqo's successors. It is significant that tomb 36 at Nuri, standing on the ridge to the east of Taharqo's, was also enlarged, although not on the same scale. This pyramid belonged to Atakhebasken, one of Taharqo's wives. Again a smooth-sided masonry pyramid was encased with a pyramid of stepped courses, enlarging it from 7.50 metres square to 11.10 metres square. Exactly when, and why, these pyramids were enlarged is unclear. It is most likely that the work belongs to Taharqo's own reign, but, if not, it may have been an act of reverence by a later king descended from him and queen Atakhebasken.

The enlargement of the superstructure was not the only unusual feature of Taharqo's tomb, the substructure too differs from those of his predecessors at el Kurru. A staircase of 51 steps leads down into a rock hewn vault. A small antechamber opens onto the burial chamber. This rectangular room has six square piers cut from the rock, the central aisle being covered with a barrel vault. A narrow corridor from the antechamber runs all around the outside of the burial chamber. Although the tomb had been looted in antiquity, there were still fragments of the king's burial equipment including his canopic jars. Around the walls of the burial chamber, originally arranged standing in rows, were at least 1,070 shabti figures, the finest collection to survive from any Kushite royal grave. Carved from granite, green ankerite and alabaster, the figures ranged in size from 18 cm to 60 cm in height. The body of the king had been laid in the centre of the barrel vaulted hall, but nothing remained of his coffins.

There is no reason to doubt that, despite the catastrophe at the end of his reign, Taharqo was buried in the pyramid at Nuri. In 1963 some blocks carrying Taharqo's name were found in a small pyramid at Sedeinga by the Michela Schiff Giorgini expedition from the University of Pisa. Schiff Giorgini suggested that this was either a burial-place or cenotaph for the king: perhaps, because of his ill-fate, Taharqo had been buried in this remote province – or even exiled there. It has since been realised that the blocks were simply reused and that the pyramid in fact dates from the late Meroitic period. The blocks come from a temple, or perhaps more likely a small chapel, erected by Taharqo in the region of Atiye (Sedeinga).[2]

Taharqo's reign marked the zenith of Kushite power in Egypt and western Asia. Undoubtedly the problems which afflicted Assyria's other borders enabled Taharqo to establish himself as defender of western Asia against Assyrian aggression in the first decade of his reign. In Egypt, Kushite rule was no longer new; Shabaqo and Shebitqo had ruled as pharaohs for some twenty years and before that Kashta and Piye had controlled Upper Egypt and been acknowledged as overlords by the Libyan dynasts. Most of those Libyan dynasts of the Delta had been confirmed in their hereditary fiefdoms, and marriage alliances had probably been established with the Kushite royal house. In Thebes, the noble families had, apparently, similarly accommodated the dynasty. Kushite authority was recognised from the Mediterranean to the confluence of the Niles (modern Khartoum), if not further south, and in Syria-Palestine.

Although the reign of Taharqo is quite well-documented, his personal influence on any of the developments of the reign remains largely a matter for speculation. However, his persistence in the face of the Assyrian invasions and Libyan changes of allegiance suggests that he was a dynamic leader, well-able to maintain his position despite severe setbacks. His policy of temple construction in the Kushite homeland is a sign of the king's piety, no doubt tempered with political astuteness: in Kawa he emphasises his relationship to Alara. This temple building programme must have been important in forging the identity of the relatively new Kushite state by providing splendid new foci for its settlements. The building work also brought artists and sculptors from Egypt, stimulating the production and style of the Kushite workshops. This artistic renewal also affected Egypt where building works were on a scale which had not been attempted for many decades.

One of the characteristics of the period, in both art and literature, is frequently termed, rather dismissively, as "archaism".[3] The influences and models of the past were a constant stimulus to Egyptian artists of all periods, and this is particularly true of the Libyan, Kushite and Saite dynasties. Whilst much of the art of the Libyan period, frequently and unfairly ignored in many studies, develops from the style of the later Ramesside period, some sculpture reflects earlier, Thutmoside, models. The style of the Kushite and Saite periods sought inspiration in the art of the Old, Middle and New Kingdoms. This process apparently began in Sais. The "Bocchoris vase" (Fig.84) and the stela of king Tefnakht in Athens both display the characteristic long torso and short legs which are seen even more clearly on the faience plaque of king Iuput (Fig.82).

One of the most remarkable "archaising" monuments is the series of sculptures found in the Sacred Lake at Tanis from a gateway of the obscure king Gemenefkhonsubak. Although it is difficult to date this king precisely he was certainly a contemporary of the Kushite or early Saite dynasties. The striking similarities between the depiction of the king himself, the style and detailing of the hieroglyphic texts suggest that the reliefs of the subterranean galleries of the Step Pyramid of Djoser at Saqqara formed the model. Some of these 3rd Dynasty reliefs still carry the grid-squares of a copyist. The proportions used in these squares conform to the 'Saite Canon', now known to have been in use already in the 25th Dynasty.[4]

The significance of the Kushite contribution to Egyptian art of the 'Late Period' has long been recognised. In a seminal study of the sculpture of Late Period Egypt, art historian Bernard Bothmer commented on treatment of faces. Whilst these cannot be considered as portraits, a certain degree of realism, but still firmly within the conventions of Egyptian depiction, indicates that they can be called a likeness. In his discussion, Bothmer commented that at "the close of Dynasty XXV and during the reign of Psamtik I ... there set in a trend of almost brutal realism". Alas, Bothmer's comment has become a cliché, frequently misused. Sculptures are said to display a "brutish realism" which is certainly different from what Bothmer intended. Worse, the term seems to have been dropped in reference to the sculptures of the 26th Dynasty and is now used only of the Kushite period, but perhaps some Egyptologists still regard "brutish" as an appropriate adjective for the Kushites? Those images singled out particularly are the statue of the offical Iriketakana (in the "more realistic and even brutal style of the dynasty" according to Cyril Aldred) and the lion figure of Taharqo from Kawa which, we are told, possesses an "almost grotesque brutality".[5]

A relief head of a king on a block discovered in the Sacred Lake at Djane (Tanis). It is part of a monument built by the obscure king, Gemenefkhonsubak. The style of the reliefs is modelled on those of the 3rd and 12th Dynasties. (Fig. 111)

Other than that representing the God's Wives of Amun, there is hardly any surviving statuary of Kushite royal women. From Egypt, there is only one example, from the temple of Mut at Karnak.[6] On the evidence of its titles and the fact that the name has been erased, this statue can be ascribed to Taharqo's mother, queen Abar. This lack of female images is perhaps due to accident of survival, rather than any cultural prejudice, since the royal women figured prominently in temple reliefs Indeed, in Kush itself, discoveries of large-scale royal sculpture have been confined to Gebel Barkal, and, even from there, the finds were limited in number and begin only with Taharqo. There are remarkably few monumental royal statues surviving from the succeeding eight hundred years of the Meroitic kingdom. This lack of royal statues may reflect a different cultural tradition in Kush: to date there is no known royal statuary from Kerma.

Some scholars have seen Assyrian influence on Kushite art, notably in the musculature of figures. Old Kingdom models seem a more likely source for this feature which is found on the Iuput plaques and the Bocchoris vase and which may be part of the Saite style.

One of the most original creations in relief decoration is the procession of horses at Gebel Barkal. The loss of early Kushite relief work and a general lack of contemporary Egyptian temple scenes prevents a comparison – and one must suppose that the artist was Egyptian. Most surviving temple reliefs of the Libyan period are rather traditional images of a king before a deity (many are from gateways). Occasionally, however, some unusual scenes survive. The chapel built for the sed-festival of Osorkon II at Per-Bastet has reliefs which are certainly modelled upon the scenes of the sed-festival of Amenhotep III, but probably derived from an archival source, rather than a standing monument. The chapel of Osiris Ruler of Eternity at Karnak has scenes of the God's Wife of Amun, Shepenwepet I, being suckled by Hathor, an adaptation of a conventional royal image; but in one example she wears two double crowns. This innovation (as it seems to be) must have been stimulated by the changing role and importance of the God's Wife at this time. The temples of the Kushite period display a wide repertoire of scenes, some of them conventional, some of them derived from earlier models (such as those on the pylon at Kawa) and some, such as the processions of royal women, clearly dictated by unique historical and cultural circumstances.

Under the Libyan pharaohs, monumental architecture was largely concentrated in the Delta cities and appears to have been fairly traditional. Whilst the larger Kushite temples, such as Barkal and Kawa, were also essentially conventional, innovation does seem to be found in the colonnades built in front of many of the temples at Thebes. In some cases, as at the Eastern temple of Karnak and the temple of Khonsu, these structures comprised four rows of columns with screen walls. Elsewhere, as in the first court of Karnak, at Luxor and at Medinet Habu, the colonnade is arranged in two rows of monumental columns. This type of kiosk or colonnade perhaps has its origins in wooden structures, such as the great gate of electrum before the fourth pylon at Karnak, but this is the first time they are constructed on such a massive scale in stone. Despite its splendour, Taharqo's great colonnade in the first court at Karnak was considered to be a failure by H.R. Hall. Hall, writing in 1925, assumed that Taharqo intended to erect a hypostyle hall and that the surviving avenue was simply what was left after the work was abandoned – "for want of money or want of skill". Hall's prejudice was typical of his time. Although Hall acknowledged the resurgence of building activity under the Kushites, he dismissed the architecture and decoration as "poor in comparison with those of old days" – another unfair criticism, reflecting the Egyptological attitude to anything post-New Kingdom. In comparison with the columns of the Ramesside hypostyle hall, Taharqo's are, if anything, more elegantly formed. The relief sculpture of Shebitqo's chapels, and those of the God's Wives of Amun, stand comparison with anything from earlier periods as do numerous surviving examples of royal and private statuary.[7]

A real Kushite originality seems to be found in small objects, notably amulets and jewellery, and these are artistically and technically equal to that of the New Kingdom. The Kushite royal tombs have yielded a number of superbly crafted and original items which have no close parallels from Egypt. A number of these comes from a tomb at el-Kurru (no. 55), suggested to be that of a wife of Piye. One amulet is formed from a ball of rock-crystal 2 cm high, surmounted by a beautifully modelled head of the goddess Hathor, her features similar to those of the God's Wife Shepenwepet II. A gold tube passes through the crystal to secure the base plate. The whole object is only 5.3 cm high. This piece has been compared with an alabaster amulet shaped into two nodes, one carved with a female head and prepared to receive a head-dress in a different material. This amulet was found in the tomb of queen Khensa along with natural double- and multiple-noded flints, fossils and shells from the Red Sea. Such stones have also been found in votive deposits, and their odd shape clearly had some amuletic significance. Also from tomb 55 at el-Kurru came other unusual amulets: one, a rod of rock crystal surmounted by a ram's head, another a ram-headed lion (crio-sphinx) with closed falcon wings incised on its back seated on top of a column inlaid with cloisonné in feather pattern.[8]

Faience funerary amulets also reveal great originality, notably the winged Hathorian figures from the tomb of Nefrukekaskta at el-Kurru. The iconography of a winged goddess with uraei and Hathorian head-dress is typically Egyptian, yet the full hips and thighs and pendulous breasts are purely Kushite, as is the close cut hair.[9]

The most distinctive types of Kushite regalia, apart from the diadem, are the ram-head ear-rings and pendants, symbols of Amun. Varying slightly in form, they comprise a ram's head with curling horns surmounted by double uraeus, sometimes also by a solar disk. Examples have been found in many materials: gold, semi-precious stones and faience. Three such ram-head pendants on the looped cord are first worn by Shabaqo and, as ear-rings, by Shebitqo. They may both have been used earlier, but we lack well-preserved depictions of Piye.[10]

Kushite Queens too had their special regalia. A number of reliefs from the Kawa temple and from Gebel Barkal shows queens and princesses wearing a head-dress with a type of plume which seems to denote their rank. At Kawa, in the sadly fragmentary scene showing the female relatives of Taharqo, one queen wears a diadem with three small images of goddesses on its rim. One goddess wears a sun-disk, another the cow's horns and sun-disk, the third is indistinct; two of the goddesses appear to have lioness heads. From each of these figures emerges a plume. In the same scene, a junior princess has only a single plume, emerging from a papyrus umbel holder. The princess Amenirdis, who married the Vizier Monthuhotep, is also depicted wearing a single plume. Elsewhere, the king's chief wives are shown with the tall double falcon-plume crown characteristic of their Egyptian predecessors.[11]

Bronze-working, which had achieved new heights under the Libyan pharaohs, continued to flourish throughout the Kushite and Saite periods. Many small kneeling figures of Kushite kings survive. They are the type which would have adorned the sacred barques or stood in the temple shrines. One of the more striking is a kneeling figure of Taharqo before the rather obscure deity, Hemen the Lord of Hefat. The superb bronze figure of Taharqo is rather crudely fitted into the base in front of the falcon figure of the god. The whole of the divine image and its base is covered, again rather clumsily, with gold and silver foil. The disparity between the workmanship of the royal image and the assembly of the whole suggests that an ancient image of the god has been updated.[12]

In Thebes, the stimulus to building, probably owing to the Kushite pharaohs' devotion to Amun and perhaps to the renewal of Thebes as a royal residence city, saw the return to monumental funerary architecture. These monuments, reflecting the vast wealth and power controlled by magnates such as the Stewards of the God's Wives of Amun, were on a scale rarely matched for private individuals in earlier periods. The earliest of these tombs belongs to the Steward of Amenirdis I, Harwa. From massive pylon entrances of brick, steep staircases lead down to subterranean chambers, with, as a focus to the complex, a large solar-court, open to the sky. Many of the tombs were oriented towards the processional way of the temple of Deir el-Bahari, others had a separate access directed to it. One feature of the decoration of these tombs, much of it in fine relief sculpture, is the direct copying of scenes in earlier tombs. A fragment of relief from the tomb of the Mayor of Thebes, Monthuemhat, renders in bas-relief a painted scene in the nearby 18th Dynasty tomb of Menna. The style of relief shows the influence of Middle Kingdom models. Slightly later, in the tomb of Ibi, Steward of the God's Wife of Amun, Neitiqert, are copies of scenes from a tomb at Deir el-

Gebrawi in Middle Egypt, which belonged to an official of the Old Kingdom, also named Ibi.[13]

Religious texts formed a major part of the decoration of these tombs and included a new form of The Book of the Dead, the so-called "Saite recension". In the Memphite necropolis, the large scale tombs (although not quite as large as their Theban contemporaries) of the 26th dynasty officials (the Kushite period necropolis awaits rediscovery) have copies of the Pyramid Texts from the nearby Old Kingdom royal tombs.[14]

By the reign of Taharqo, the Kushites were established throughout Egypt with a strong presence, and doubtless there were many second generation Kushites born in Egypt, as well as children of marriages between elite Egyptians and Kushites. In addition to the members of the royal family and others with powerful positions, such as Kelbasken the Mayor of Thebes and Iriketakana, there were many other Kushites in slightly lower official positions. Several Kushite royal ladies were buried at Abydos, and there is evidence for their entourage also. The lady Taniy was recorded by a stela which has parallels with works of the 12th Dynasty. Another stela from Abydos depicts two Kushite ladies accompanied by an Egyptian woman.[15]

A large number of papyri sheds light on economic matters in the Theban region during the 25th Dynasty and into the reign of Psamtik I. The majority of these documents records the sale of land in the region of Thebes and Medamud by members of the elite families, including women. A few papyri relate to the sale of slaves, some of them suggested to have been captives taken during the Kushite invasions. Most of the papyri are written in a script known to Egyptologists as 'abnormal hieratic', a rather difficult form of the classic scribal hand. In the north of Egypt at about the same time, we find the first instances of the 'demotic' script which was to become the bureaucratic writing of the Late Period.[16]

It was not only in art and writing that changes were apparent. The Iron Age brought changes in military technology and warfare too. Perhaps too much has been made of the Assyrian advantage of iron weapons. The chronicles of the Kushite conflict with the Assyrians do record a number of pitched battles. Such evidence as we have suggests that chariot warfare typical of the Bronze Age may still have been the norm within Egypt. There is little evidence that the Kushites, or Libyans, had taken to using cavalry on a large scale, and the Kushite horses taken to Assyria are specified as chariot horses. It is certain that by the 8th century the Assyrian army was using more cavalry than chariots, but perhaps their most effective military advantage was their siege apparatus – seen so graphically in the reliefs of the investing of Lachish. Taharqo's defeat at the hands of the Assyrians was not – as has sometimes been portrayed – inevitable. One Assyrian invasion appears to have met with disaster, and, although the subsequent invasion saw the sack of Memphis, Taharqo was able to re-establish himself. The intrigues of the Delta dynasts were doubtless a decisive factor in the Kushite successes and failures.[17]

Despite the numerous surviving monuments and other documents relating to this reign, we are still remarkably badly informed about many aspects of the period. Even our knowledge of the royal family itself is insubstantial. In part the destruction of the upper parts of the temples of Sanam and Kawa has been a contributory factor. At Kawa, a large scene depicted a procession of Taharqo's female relatives, but little survived other than their feet. Of his wives, queen Tekahatamani (read as Dukhatamun by earlier Egyptologists) appears with Taharqo in the rock-cut temple of Mut at Barkal. She has many titles and may have been the king's sister as well as his Chief Wife. Although a tomb at Nuri has been attributed to her, it contained no inscribed objects. As the king's Chief Wife, she may have been the mother of Ushanukhuru, captured at Memphis, and of Amenirdis II. Tekahatamani may have been one of the queens who was taken to Assyria following the capture of Memphis. Of Taharqo's other children, only Nesishutefnut, appointed to be Second Prophet of Amun at Thebes, has left any monuments. The inscription on a statue from Karnak states that Nesishutefnut was the son of the King's Chief Wife, but her name was erased in ancient times: he, too, may have been a son of Tekahatamani. On the evidence of a later royal genealogy, it has been assumed that king Atlanersa was also a son of Taharqo's. Atakhebasken, who carried the title King's Chief Wife, and was buried at Nuri, has been assumed to have been a wife of Taharqo, and the proximity of her pyramid to his makes this likely. Atakhebasken does not have the elaborate titulary used by most other Great Royal Wives and she may have been elevated to this rank following the deportation of other royal women to Assyria. This elevation in her rank may also explain the enlargement of her pyramid. Another queen, whose name is only partly preserved (... salka), was apparently the mother of Atlanersa, and hence a wife of Taharqo's. Naparaya, a king's wife, perhaps of Taharqo, was buried at el-Kurru. Queen Iret-irou carries the titles king's daughter, king's sister and king's wife. She was probably a wife of Atlanersa, and is known only from the pylon of temple B 700 copied by Orlando Felix in 1829. Although her titles suggested to Dows Dunham and Laming Macadam that she was a daughter of Taharqo and sister-wife of Atlanersa, the name Iret-irou is purely Egyptian, which is rare in the Kushite royal family; perhaps she was an Egyptian princess. She was buried in Nuri 53, with a painted burial chamber. Another princess depicted in the reliefs of B 700 is Peltasen, who is assumed to have been a daughter of Taharqo. Although the Assyrian texts record the capture of some of Taharqo's wives and children at

(left) The lady Kheriru as depicted on her coffin from Thebes. (right) Two Kushite and one Egyptian woman, their arms raised in adoration of Re-Harakhty, on a painted stela from Abydos. Apart from their colour, the Kushite women are distinguished by their enveloping fringed robes. (Fig. 112)

Memphis, some other wives and children may have been resident elsewhere. Evidence for this may be the burial of Tjesreperet, a nurse of one of Taharqo's daughters which was found intact at Thebes, by Ippolito Rosellini.[18]

There may have been a dynastic crisis on the king's death. The capture of many members of the king's immediate family in the Assyrian storming of Memphis may have left Taharqo without mature sons to succeed him. In recent years a controversy has arisen amongst specialists as to the laws of succession to the Kushite throne. Laming Macadam proposed that the succession passed from brother to brother and then to the sons of the eldest of the brothers, an idea followed by Kenneth Kitchen and many other writers on this period. Other scholars have argued in favour of a matrilineal system, that the throne passed to the son of the king's sister. The evidence is, however, far from clear, and does not appear to support either hypothesis; it does, however, appear to indicate that each king was a son of a former king – but not necessarily his immediate predecessor.[19] Later Kushite inscriptions indicate that kings were 'elected' from amongst the 'Royal Brethren'. These were presumably all of the princes whose lineages made them eligible. The 'election' took place in the temple of Amun at Gebel Barkal and was apparently pronounced by the oracle of the god and greeted with the acclamation of the army. The not altogether surprising combination of the priesthood and military leaders was thus influential in the choice. However, the choice may have been a foregone conclusion: the personal power of a prince undoubtedly being a significant factor. Apart from the Assyrian reference to Ushanukhuru as Taharqo's heir, there is no direct evidence for the office of Crown Prince, and the death of a king may have seen a struggle amongst the strongest of the eligible princes. Following the catastrophe of the Assyrian invasions, with the capture of many members of the royal family, Taharqo may have been left with sons too young to seize the reins of power at this critical time. Thus Taharqo was succeeded by the son of his sister, queen Qalhata, Tanwetamani.

XXII   The Triumph of Sau

Thereupon, Tandamane son of Shabaku seated himself upon his royal throne. Thebes and Heliopolis he made his strongholds. He gathered together his forces. To battle with my troops stationed at Memphis he mustered his battle array. Those people he shut up in the city and cut off their retreat. A swift messenger came to Nineveh and told me of it.[1]

The name of the new pharaoh, written Tanwetamani, is probably to be pronounced in a way similar to the Assyrian rendering, as "Tandamane" or "Tantamani".

Tanwetamani's accession is also recorded by a Kushite text, usually known as the "Dream Stela".[2] This monument, now in the Cairo Museum, was one of those stelae found with the Victory Stela of Piye, at Gebel Barkal in 1862. It is of grey granite, about 4ft 4ins (132 cm) high and 2ft 5ins (72 cm) wide. The scene in the semi-circular lunette is of the usual type. Divided centrally, beneath the spreading wings of the sun, Tanwetamani is shown twice making offerings to the two forms of Amun. He presents an image of the goddess Maet to the human-headed Amun-Re, "Lord of the Thrones of the Two Lands, who is in Ipet-Sut", and he offers necklaces to the ram-headed Amun-Re, "Lord of the Thrones of the Two Lands, upon the Holy Mountain". The king is accompanied in each scene by a female figure. Both wear a loose garment and the close cap of kushite queens, and they shake a sistrum with one hand while pouring libations with the other. One of these women is called "the royal sister, the Mistress of Egypt, Qalhata", the other is "the royal sister, the Mistress of Ta-Seti, Pi-(ankh)-Arty". By comparing this stela with others, we can recognise that queen Qalhata was Tanwetamani's mother, and queen Pi-(ankh)-Arty his wife.[3] Fortunately, the tomb of Qalhata was excavated at Nuri, and its fine paintings, depicting the queen, give her the title "King's Mother", while objects found in the foundations of the pyramid show that it was built during the reign of Tanwetamani. This is the closest to proof that we have, that Qalhata was mother of Tanwetamani.

The Assyrian text quoted above, calls Tanwetamani the son of Shabaqo. Other Assyrian texts call him son of Taharqo's sister. This has caused

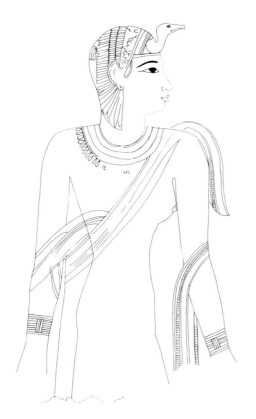

Figure of Queen Qalhata from a painted scene in her tomb at el-Kurru. Her white robe is edged in bands of blue and red. (Fig. 113)

problems to Egyptologists, many of whom preferred to emend the text to read "Tandamane, son of Shebitqo".[4] These scholars had assumed that Shebitqo was son of Piye, and that he had been succeeded by his brother Taharqo. Hence Taharqo was succeeded by his brother's son (and, following the other texts, the child of a brother-sister marriage). This explanation actually altered the ancient sources to fit the modern theory that the succession passed from brother to brother and then to the son of the eldest brother. However, it seems that Shebitqo was actually the son of Shabaqo, and hence Taharqo was not his brother. It also complicates the genealogy further, since there is evidence that both Shabaqo and Shebitqo married daughters of Piye!

The narrative of the stela opens with king's names and descriptions of him as "lord of valour like Monthu, great of strength like a fierce-eyed lion". In the first year of his reign, Tanwetamani had a dream of two serpents, one on his right hand and one on his left. On waking, the king's advisors interpreted the dream: "the southland is already thine, seize the northland".

This is, curiously, followed by a passage which says that Tanwetamani then "rose on the throne of Horus", which usually indicates the accession. Some scholars have seen in this evidence for a brief co-regency with Taharqo,[5] but the Assyrian texts make it quite clear that Tanwetamani ascended the throne after Taharqo's death. Tanwetamani is assumed to have been in Egypt at the time of his accession, since "he went from where he was to Napata, and there was none who stood up to oppose him". The king entered the temple of Amun and was acknowledged by the god. Then the god was brought out in a processional appearance.

Having swiftly established his authority in Kush, Tanwetamani sailed north, stopping at Elephantine, and bringing out the image of Khnum, Lord of the Cataract in a festival procession. Then he sailed on to "the City, Waset, of Amun" – Thebes. Here again he celebrated an appearance of the god's image. Then he sailed northwards to Memphis, where:

> the sons of revolt rushed forth to fight against his majesty. His majesty made a great slaughter amongst them, and it was not known how many of them were killed.

It is probable that amongst the dead was the leader of the Delta coalition, Nekau of Sau. His son, Nabu-shezzi-banni, still loyal to the Assyrians, fled to Asia.[6]

Tanwetamani captured Memphis and entered the temple of its patron god Ptah, as Piye had done. He presented great offerings to Ptah-Sokar, and to his wife Sakhmet. The king then issued instructions that a new chapel should be built for Amun of Napata. It was to be of stone overlaid with gold, with sections of cedar wood and the leaves of the door plated with electrum. This chapel is probably to be identified with the kiosk built around some of the columns of the central aisle of the hypostle hall of the great temple of Amun at Gebel Barkal. The king also had two statues of himself, similar to those of Taharqo, set up within the temple.

Having established himself in Memphis, and having ordered the construction of the processional chapel at Barkal, Tanwetamani prepared to attack the Delta.

> His majesty sailed down the river .. and he did battle with the princes of the Northland and they went into their huts as rats go into their holes. And his majesty passed many days by them, and not one of them came forth to do battle with his majesty; and his majesty made a sailing up the river to Memphis and he sat down in his palace to think out and plan how he could make his soldiers surround them with mounds. And one said to him: "These princes have come to where the sovereign is." And his majesty said, "Have they come to do battle? Or have they come to pay fealty to me? If they come to pay fealty, they live from this hour". They said before his majesty: "They have come to pay fealty to the sovereign, our lord."

Tanwetamani now understood the dream.

His majesty said, "Where are they at this moment?" They said "They wait standing in the court." Then his majesty went forth from his house and his appearance was like the shining of Re upon the horizon, and he found them prostrate upon their bellies, smelling the earth before him.

Then the ruler of Per-Sopd, Pakrur stood up to speak. With the death of Nekau, Pakrur was now the leader of the princes of the Delta. Pakrur himself may have been related to the Kushite royal house. His father, Patjenfy, has submitted to Piye and later dedicated stelae in association with Shabaqo and Shebitqo; it is quite likely that he had contracted a marriage alliance with the Kushite royal house. Pakrur tells Tanwetamani to kill whom he wishes and spare whom he wishes, then the princes beseech the king for clemency, which was granted, and they returned to their cities, sending gifts to Tanwetamani.

Tanwetamani was not to enjoy his success for long. Assurbanipal mustered his army and in 663 it marched on Egypt. Nabu-shezzi-banni, doubtless in the hope of being restored as an Assyrian vassal, accompanied it.

In my second campaign, I made straight for Egypt and Kush. Tandamani heard of my campaign and that I trod the soil of Egypt. He abandoned Memphis and fled to Thebes to save his life. The kings, princes and mayors whom I had set up in Egypt came and kissed my feet. I took the road after Tandamani and marched to Thebes, his stronghold. He saw the approach of my terrible battle array and he fled to Kipkip. Thebes in its entirety I captured with the help of Assur and Ishtar. Silver, gold, precious stones, all the possessions of his palace, many-coloured clothing, linen, great horses, two obelisks of electrum, the doorposts of the temple door I took from their bases and removed to Assyria. Great booty, beyond counting, I took away from Thebes. Against Egypt and Kush I let my weapons rage and I showed my might.[7]

The temple of Amun was looted of some of its greatest treasures. The "doorposts of the temple" referred to in the text may have been Thutmose IV's great gate of electrum, renewed by Shabaqo. The attack on the city was one of the great catastrophes of the ancient world, invoked half-a-century later by the jewish prophet Nahum:

Will you fare better than No-Amon? – She that lay by the streams of the Nile, surrounded by water, whose rampart was the Nile, waters her wall; Kush and Egypt were her strength, and it was boundless. Punt and the Libyans brought her help. Yet she too became an exile and went into captivity. Her infants too were dashed to the ground at every street corner. Her nobles were shared out by lot, and all her great men were thrown into chains.[8]

In his excavations near the temple of queen Tawosret on the west bank at Thebes, Flinders Petrie found a large group of iron tools, and some bronze objects. The iron tools were of an un-Egyptian type, and Petrie suggested that they were Assyrian and to be associated with the occupation of the city. There was also an Assyrian bronze helmet.[9]

Despite the destruction of Thebes, Tanwetamani was still acknowledged as pharaoh there until his eighth year. Inscriptions at Luxor date the installation of priests by his name and the Kushite regime still had a large official presence in the city.[10] Piye's daughter, Shepenwepet II reigned as God's Wife of Amun, with Taharqo's daughter, Amenirdis II, as her designated successor. In Ipet-Sut, the High Priest of Amun at the beginning of Tanwetamani's reign was his uncle, Haremakhet; by year 9 it was Haremakhet's son, Harkhebi. The administration of Upper Egypt was in the hands of the formidably powerful 4th Prophet of Amun, Monthuemhat, whose wife, Wedjarenes, was a granddaughter of Piye. The office of 2nd Prophet of Amun was, at some unknown point, also assumed by Monthuemhat. It is possible that Taharqo's son, Nesishutefnut, who had held the office, died, or was captured by the Assyrians during the storming of Thebes.

Continued Kushite rule in Upper Egypt was, as yet, unaffected by the changing politics of the Delta. The son of Nekau of Sau, who had been installed by the Assyrians as ruler of Limir-ishshak-Ashur (Hut-hery-ib), with the Assyrian name, Nabu-shezzi-banni, now assumed his father's throne in Sau, once more taking his Egyptian name, Psamtik. He counted his regnal years from the time of his father's death at Tanwetamani's hands. Psamtik soon sought to shake off the Assyrian yoke and expand his power across the Delta princedoms.[11]

It is possible that, following Assurbanipal's campaign, Tanwetamani once again attempted to regain control of Lower Egypt. There is nothing in the Egyptian or Assyrian sources to confirm this, but some later Greek sources suggest it. The principal evidence is a brief passage in the work of Polyaenus of the second century AD. He states that Psamtik, aided by Carian mercenary troops, defeated "Tementhes" (ie Tanwetamani) near the temple of Isis at Memphis. Although not accepted by all Egyptologists as a valid source, this episode was taken by Serge Sauneron and Jean Yoyotte to indicate that Tanwetamani had, indeed, regained control of Memphis. Their

Tanwetamani, wearing the characteristic regalia of double uraeus, cap-crown, ram pendant and earrings, as depicted in his tomb at el-Kurru. The king's robe has a border of alternating blue and red squares with rosette decoration. (Fig. 114)

interpretation has been supported by Stanley Burstein, using a hellenistic jewish source, which seems to refer to the same event. Without more reliable, contemporary, evidence, it is impossible to be certain, but it seems likely that Tanwetamani did attempt to regain control of all Egypt after the Assyrian invasion of 663 BC. Assurbanipal's narrative of that campaign records the flight of Tanwetamani, but no battle between their armies. With Assurbanipal's withdrawal, and the establishment of the new vassal ruler in Sais, Tanwetamani may have felt confident enough to return north.

The reference in Polyaenus's account to Psamtik being aided by Carian mercenaries certainly reflects the foreign policy of Psamtik, confirmed by the Assyrian records. Early in his reign, Psamtik had formed an alliance with an Anatolian ruler, Gyges king of Lydia. The cuneiform historical text known to Assyriologists as "Prism A" states that Gyges "sent his troops to the aid of Pishamilki (ie Psamtik), the king of Egypt, who had overthrown the yoke of my kingship".[12] The implication of the Assyrian texts is that Psamtik had broken off the treaty which must have been drawn up when he was installed as an Assyrian vassal.

Following the Egyptian campaign, Assurbanipal was called to the west again in 662 when Baal king of Tyre yet again rebelled. But this was the last time that Assyria was able to march westwards. Although he might complain about the behaviour of his vassals, Assurbanipal was powerless to intervene. Assyria, itself preoccupied with revolts, made no attempt to regain control of Egypt, and Psamtik was able to expand his power.

Whether or not he defeated Tanwetamani in battle at Memphis, Psamtik's kingdom was centred upon that city and his ancestral fiefdom of Sau. In these early years of his reign, Psamtik recognised the status quo in the south whilst he gradually extended his power over the other Delta princedoms. In Middle Egypt, the rule of Nen-nesut passed from Pediese to his son, Sematawytefnakht, in Psamtik's year 4. According to a later tradition, Sematawaytefnakht, was brought up at the Saite court: soon he was to play an important role in the event which marked the re-unification of Egypt.

In his ninth year, also the ninth year of Tanwetamani, Psamtik sent his daughter, Neitiqert, to Thebes, to enter the service of Amun. The events, as narrated by Psamtik, were recorded on a stela set up in Ipet-sut,[13] and by a series of reliefs in the temple of the goddess Mut.[14]

> I (Psamtik) have heard that a king's daughter is there, (a daughter of) the Horus Lofty-of-Diadems, the Perfect God [Taharqo], justified, whom he gave to his sister to be her eldest daughter and who is there as Adorer of the God. I will not do what in fact should not be done, and expel an heir from [her] seat...

> I will give her (Neitiqert) to her (Amenirdis) to be her eldest daughter, just as she (Amenirdis) was made over to the sister of her father.

Thus Psamtik recognised the inviolability of the office, as Kashta had done a century beforehand, and refused to dethrone either the God's Wife, or her heiress. He agreed that Neitiqert should eventually, as daughter of Amenirdis II, become God's Wife. The transfer of power seems to have been effected diplomatically, although there must have been a threat of force behind it.

Neitiqert left the palace of Psamtik, presumably in Memphis, in the king's 9th year, the first month of Akhet, on the 28th day, calculated to be March 2nd 656 BC. The age of the princess is unknown, but she was perhaps verging on puberty.

She arrived at the quay of Ipet-sut 16 days later, on the 14th day of the second month of Akhet, a few days before the beginning of the Opet festival. A series of blocks excavated by Margaret Benson and Janet Gourlay in the temple of the goddess Mut depicted this great event, and form a complement to the text of the stela. There may originally have been three registers depicting the fleet accompanying the princess. The prince of Nen-nesut, Sematawytefnakht, is given a very prominent position.

A flotilla was sent from Thebes to meet the princess and escort her southwards. This included several ships from the "harim" of Amun, and one called the "ship of Piye".

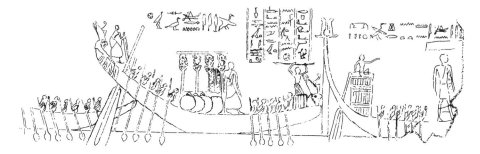

Part of the relief from the temple of Mut showing the procession of ships conveying the princess Neitiqert to Thebes. Here, the prince Sematawytefnakht stands on the central boat. (Fig. 115)

Now after she came to the God's Wife Shepenwepet, the latter saw her and was pleased with her; she loved her more than anything and made over to her the testament which her [Shepenwepet's] father [Piye] and mother [ie the God' Wife Amenirdis I] had executed for her; and her eldest daughter, Amenirdis, daughter of king Taharqo, justified, did likewise. Their wish was done in writing: "Herewith we give to you all our property in country and in town. You shall be established upon our throne firmly and enduringly until the end of eternity".[15]

The legal document was witnessed by the priesthood of Ipet-Sut. Neitiqert was richly endowed with land and daily foodstuffs, which are detailed in the text. Some leading members of the Theban clergy were to supply foodstuffs as well. The 4th Prophet of Amun and Mayor of Thebes, Monthuemhat, his wife, the Kushite princess Wedjarenes, and his eldest son Nesptah provided bread, beer, milk and cakes daily, with three oxen and five geese every month. The Kushite prince Harkhebi, High Priest of Amun, also provided bread, beer and milk daily. A similar requirement was placed upon Pedi-amen-neb-nesut-tawy, the 3rd Prophet of Amun, and grandson of the lector-priest who had received the oath of fealty from Tefnakht in Sau, some six decades before. The estates of Shepenwepet and Amenirdis had, technically, been made over to Neitiqert, but probably remained under their control during their lifetimes. We may assume that most of these estates lay in the Theban region. The Saite pharaoh endowed his daughter with estates in the nomes of Nen-nesut, Per-medjed (Oxyrhynkhos), Duen-anwy, Khemenu, Wadjet and Hut-Sekhem (all between the entrance to the Faiyum and Dendera), and further grants of land were made in the Delta. These totalled 2,230 acres (902.5 hectares). The king himself supplied his daughter with 6 bushels (200 litres) of grain per day. Neitiqert also received daily bread rations totalling 300 pounds (136.5 kg) from the temples in Sau, Per-Wadjyt (Buto), Per-Hathor-mefek (*Terenuthis*; Kom Abu Billo) and Per-neb-Imau (Kom el-Hisn), Iunu, Djanet, Per-Bastet, Per-Soped and Tjel. All of these lie in the Delta, and clearly the bread would not have been shipped to Thebes everyday!

Psamtik had concluded his treaty with Amun and his clergy, and, as with all treaties, there were two sides to the bargain. The god received a wife and priestess, Psamtik was now recognised as pharaoh in Thebes and expected the deity to defend his interests.

> I have given my daughter to him [Amun], to be God's Wife and I have endowed her more richly than those who were before her. Surely he will be gratified with her worship and protect the land of him who gave her to him.[16]

Certainly Neitiqert's estates were more extensive than those of earlier God's Wives, since they included vast tracts of lands in the Delta and Middle Egypt. Despite the protestations of Psamtik that Amenirdis would not be displaced, on the death of Shepenwepet II it was Neitiqert who ascended the throne in Ipet-sut. She lived for seventy years after her arrival at Thebes, dying in the 4th year of the reign of her great-nephew, Haaibre (Apries), in the 4th month of Shomu, day 4 (December 16th, 586 BC).[17]

What became of the God's Adorer, Amenirdis? There is a possibility that she may have predeceased her adopted mother, but neither tomb nor funerary artifacts are known from the Theban region. Egyptologist Labib Habachi suggested that she was to be identfied with a Kushite princess called Amenirdis who is known to have married the Vizier Monthuhotep.[18] That princess, however, was more probably a daughter of Shabaqo, and it is unlikely that the designated wife of a god would have been married off to an official, even one of the rank of Vizier. On her monuments, Neitiqert always names her mother as Shepenwepet II, not Amenirdis II and it seems most likely that Amenirdis did, in fact, return to Kush.

There is one later reference to her, in an inscription of the Kushite king, Aspelta, who reigned around 590 BC. The inscription, another of those found with the great Victory Stela of Piye, at Gebel Barkal, gives a list of the female ancestors of Aspelta's mother, queen Nasalsa. For some reason, all of the names were erased in ancient times, but their titles remain. Most were called, simply, "King's sister", but the mother of Nasalsa bears the title "King's sister, Adorer of the God in [Ipet-Sut]". This can only be Amenirdis II. Although it has been assumed by many Egyptologists that the list records a line of adopted descent, there is really no support for the idea. It is equally possible, and perhaps more likely, that the inscription records the actual descent of Nasalsa.[19] If this is so, then Amenirdis must have returned to Kush as the wife of the king. Indeed, this would have been the only appropriate husband for a princess formerly destined for marriage to a god.

How long Tanwetamani remained as ruler of Kush, we do not know. The records of year 9 are the last from Egypt, and there are no further dated monuments from Kush itself. Even the family relationship of Tanwetamani with his successor, Atlanersa, is unknown, although it has generally been assumed that Atlanersa was a son of Taharqo. There are no large inscriptions surviving from the reigns of Atlanersa and his successor, Senkamanisken. The loss of Egypt may have led to opposition to Tanwetamani's rule, although there is no evidence for the erasure of his name on surviving monuments. The monuments and sculptures of the reigns of Tanwetamani's successors continue the traditions established during the period of rule in Egypt, and there were probably still strong contacts with the north. It must have taken Psamtik some time to consolidate his position in Egypt, and he may not have supplanted all of the Libyan dynasts until the end of his reign. It would probably have suited Psamtik's ambitions to maintain a peaceful relationship with his powerful southern neighbour and the north-south trade would have been important to both kingdoms. The grave goods from the royal cemetery of Nuri contain many Egyptian imports, and local production, such as faience, is clearly influenced by contemporary developments in Egypt.

Psamtik seems to have effectively controlled the Libyan dynasts, depriving them of their fiefdoms or reducing them to the status of Mayors. Some priestly descendants of the Osorkons and Sheshonqs continued to hold offices and record their genealogies for several decades, but their political pretensions were abandoned. In Thebes, the Kushite prince, Harkhebi, was still officiating as High Priest of Amun in year 14 of Psamtik I (651 BC) and Shepenwepet II lived on well into the same reign. Conflict between Kush and Egypt does not seem to have broken out until some fifty years later, in the reigns of Psamtik II and Aspelta (593 BC). That conflict may have been due as much to aspirations of the later Saite kings to recreate the Egyptian empire, as much as any Kushite attempt to reconquer Egypt.

The distinctive profile of Psamtik I of Sau. Although he wears a cap crown similar to the Kushites, he has only one protective uraeus. (Fig. 116)

The conflict between Psamtik II and Aspelta has, indeed, served as the classic end for narrative of the history of the 25th Dynasty and its immediate successors. In his excavations at Gebel Barkal, George Reisner found a cache of broken colossal statues which had once adorned the first court of the great temple of Amun. Of black granite, most about twelve feet tall and originally gilded on their tall feather crowns, kilts and jewellery, the shattered statues had been buried in a large pit. The earliest of the statues was of Taharqo, identical to the image of the king from Thebes. All of his successors up to Aspelta were represented, many directly modelled on the statue of Taharqo himself. Reisner calculated that the reign of Aspelta coincided with the short reign of Psamtik II, and since that king's invasion of Kush was already known from the history of Herodotos and some Greek and Carian inscriptions carved on the colossi of Ramesses II at Abu Simbel, he attributed the destruction of the Barkal statues to that military action. As reconstructed by Reisner, the army of Psamtik II reached Napata, looting the temples and destroying the royal statues. As a result Kush's power was crushed. It was argued that now the Kushite kings had no real possibility of regaining control of Egypt, and that, although they still claimed the pharaonic titles, from this time on, Meroe in the southern savanna became their main residence city. The kings now only came north to Napata to be crowned and to bury their predecessor in the pyramid field of Nuri. Once again, it was claimed, all contact between Egypt and Kush was sundered. As a result, the 'Late Napatan' period is portrayed as a slow, lingering decline in which the 'veneer' of Egyptian culture is gradually peeled away. In earlier history writing the prejudices of scholarship were clearly exposed in the opinions expressed about this phase.

It makes a fine and classic end to a history of the Kushite kings if, like Babylon and Nineveh, Napata collapses in flames, its people are put to the sword and some sort of "Dark Age" descends. But the rather dull truth is, that our knowledge of the Late Napatan period is miserably scanty. There are a few historical texts written in hieroglyphic, and there are many objects from the cemeteries of Nuri and Meroe. The lack of material, and consequent lack of interest in this period is sadly paralleled in Egypt, where the 'Late Period' (as it is rather dismissively termed) is also a rather neglected area of historical (as opposed to philological) study. However, reassessments of earlier excavations are now showing that there is more happening than we previously realised. For example, Lisa Heidorn re-examined the material from the 2nd Cataract fortress of Dorginarti, thought by its excavators to be of Middle Kingdom date, and realised that it actually belongs to the Persian period (from 525 BC). With excavations at sites in the Dongola Reach of the Nile and in the regions around Meroe, we will doubtless learn much more about this phase. But rather than a sad aftermath to imperial glory, the Late Napatan period should perhaps be best seen as the prelude to the Meroitic period. During these three hundred years there must have been considerable changes within the area of the Kushite kingdom, but only very occasionally do historical texts shed any light on the events. But there was certainly continuity and the traditions of rulership established by the Piye, Shabaqo and their successors formed the model for the Kushite kingship for the next nine-hundred years.

NOTES

In the following notes the aim is to direct readers to the most recent works on the subject as well as standard texts. The references are not intended to be exhaustive, but the earlier literature is cited in the main works. For references given in 'Harvard' form (eg Adams 1977) see the Bibliography.

I Bow Land
There are still relatively few general accounts of the history and archaeology of Nubia and specifically for the "25th dynasty", or "Napatan" period, and much of the detailed argument and discussion has appeared as articles in academic journals or in the proceedings of the Nubian and Meroitic conferences. Most of the general accounts of Nubia (eg Adams 1977; Shinnie 1967, 1996; Welsby 1996), discuss the 25th Dynasty in the context of the monuments in Sudan and treat the Egyptian monuments, and to some extent the events/policies, as tangential. In consequence - and perhaps with some justification - the "25th Dynasty" is seen as a relatively brief phase within the continuum of Napatan-Meroitic history.

The two volumes of *Africa in Antiquity, the Arts of ancient Nubia and the Sudan*, published by the Brooklyn Museum in 1978 for the exhibition of the same name, contain some useful historical essays and discussion of the art of Nubia. The classic history written in the aftermath of the UNESCO campaign is that of Adams (1977). Whilst invaluable as an overview of Nubian archaeology, it suffers from an uncritical use of textual material. Trigger's (1976) study of Nubia under the pharaohs remains very useful. Shinnie's 1967 complementary volume on Meroe, presents the classic view of the period. The '25th Dynasty' makes an appearance in both volumes, but rather briefly. From the archaeological perspective, Shinnie (1967) has been superseded by Adams (1977) and Welsby (1996), although neither is strong on historical and textual material. The recent introduction to Nubia by Shinnie (1996) has good chapters on the earliest and latest phases, although those dealing with Egyptian domination and the '25th Dynasty' are very traditional in their approach. There are valuable sections on Nubia in Trigger et al. 1983. The *UNESCO General History of Africa II Ancient Civilizations of Africa*, unfortunately repeats, once again, the traditional views. The most recent edition of the *Cambridge Ancient History* which covers the 25th Dynasty (T.G.H. James 1991) is similarly conventional, lending weight to the characterisation of this series as the "accepted lies of our discipline". The recent volume by O'Connor (1993) is, however, a much more challenging study of Nubia from the earliest times to the Meroitic period. The best recent general history of the ancient Near East is Kuhrt 1995.

1. Generally, on place-names, the comprehensive work of Zibelius 1972 is fundamental. More specific – and controversial – are O'Connor 1986; 1987.
2. Edith Hall *Inventing the barbarian. Greek self-definition through tragedy* (Oxford,1989), 140-142; also see Snowden 1970.
3. Most writers have something to say on Nubian populations, but see particularly Trigger 1978 (one of the best discussions of Nubian ethnicity). On representations of Kushites see Vercoutter et al. 1976; Russmann 1974 (specifically 25th Dynasty Kings); on Greek and Roman evidence both literary and artistic see Snowden 1970; 1983.
4. The role of Nubia and Meroe in the rise of the Aksumite state is still unclear (see Abdalla 1989). The work of Rodolfo Fattovich and others in the region of the eastern Sudan is beginning to fill in some of the large gaps in our knowledge, although will doubtless raise many more questions. On Aksum see most recently S.C. Munro Hay *Aksum. An African civilisation of Late Antiquity.* Edinburgh 1991.

II Beyond the rivers of Kush
1. On Bruce see Moorehead 1972: 24-49.
2. Buckingham's career and dispute with Bankes is narrated in Lloyd 1980: 43-56, 60–65.
3. Linant's journal was edited and published by Margaret Shinnie (Linant/Shinnie 1958).

4. For Ismail Pasha's campaign, Waddington, Hanbury and Cailliaud, see Moorhead 1972: 175-190.
5. For Orlando Felix and his Barkal sketches see Griffith 1929.
6. On Botta and Layard see Lloyd 1980.
7. Brugsch's history first appeared in a French language edition in 1857; its substantial revision of 1877, in German, included the newly available texts. The preface to the English language edition of 1879 draws particular attention to the importance of the Assyrian material [p.ix]. The second English language translation was 1891.
8. A view held also by Jens Lieblein and others, and which continued into the 20th century (Petrie 1905: 277) although Erman 1897 had argued for adoptive relationships; see further in. n 33 to Chapter XI below.
9. Brugsch 1891: 3.
10. Brugsch 1891: 387.
11. Brugsch 1891: 2-3.
12. The development of Egyptology as an academic discipline, and the influences upon it, are discussed by Bernal 1987. His historiography, as so much else of his work, has been criticised, most comprehensively in Lefkowitz and Rogers 1996. For the debate, at times heated, see also n.14 to Chapter III, below.

III Rescuing Nubia's history
Accounts of the work of the archaeological surveys can be found in Emery (1965) and Säve-Söderbergh (1987). A useful table of excavators and sites can be found in Adams 1977: 78-80 and 83–86.

1. Adams 1977: 72.
2. For a re-assessment of Gebel Moya see Gerharz 1994.
3. Griffith 1922; 1923.
4. Published by Macadam 1949; 1955.
5. The discovery of the burials is told by Emery 1948; 1965.
6. Emery 1965; Emery Smith Millard 1979.
7. Säve-Söderbergh 1941.
8. Notably that of Nordström 1972.
9. Leclant 1954; 1961; 1965 and in numerous later articles on objects of 25th Dynasty date.
10. Horton 1991. Qasr Ibrim has now (1999) nearly vanished beneath the waters of the lake.
11. Pick 1989.
12. Adams 1977: 92.
13. Bernal 1987.
14. The principal Egyptological contributions to the debate are those of J.Baines and F. Yurco in Lefkowitz and Rogers 1996; see also 'The challenge of *Black Athena' Arethusa* (Special issue) 1989.
15. Breasted 1905. Breasted's work incorporates many of the more speculative ideas of Maspero (eg the Sea Peoples) and the idea of the priestly origin of the Napatan kings advocated by Brugsch and others.
16. Kitchen 1986; see Chapters VII-VIII and X-XI below and works cited there. Another view of the origin of the 25th Dynasty is Kendall 1999, with responses. The discussion of the same subject at the Nubian Conference Lille 1994 has been published see Török 1995; Morkot 1995; Yellin 1995.

IV The Elephant
1. Kendall 1982: 9.
2. Adams 1977: 244-45.
3. For this 'gap' and an alternative interpretation see Chapter X. This 'gap' has had an enormous - if subconscious - influence on our understanding of Kushite state formation.
4. For the classic interpretation of the A-Group see Adams 1977; Trigger 1976; and for reassessment Nordström 1972; O'Connor 1991; H.S. Smith 1991; 1994. For the radical theories of Williams 1980, 1986 see below nn 9 and 10.
5. Adams 1977: 152-154 argues against there being large herds of cattle in early Nubia regarding them as "an aspiration" rather than a reality (see also n.7 following).
6. With excavations at both Hierakonpolis and Abydos our understanding of the emergent pharaonic state is being radically altered.

7. Nordström 1972: 21, 26; Trigger 1976: 38. Piotrovsky identified the site at Khor Daoud as associated with dairy farming: rebutted by Adams (1977: 126).
8. On Seyala now see Smith, H.S. 1994.
9. Williams 1986.
10. Williams 1980.
11. Adams 1985, see also comments of Smith 1991, 1994 and O'Connor 1993.
12. See Chap. I n 3 above; S.O.Y. Keito '"Race", Bernal and Snowden' in *Arethusa* 26 no 3 (1993): 295-334; Celenko 1996.
13. Reisner's misinterpretation of the evidence relating to the B-Group was first discussed by Smith H.S. 1966; see also Smith 1991.
14. For the texts see Lichtheim 1973: 18-23 (Uni), 23-27 (Harkhuf).
15. For the locations see Zibelius 1972 and O'Connor 1986, 1991. For the location of Yam see O'Connor 1986 with discussion of earlier opinion.
16. The fullest account of the Nubian mercenary troops and material from Gebelein is Fischer 1961.
17. On the reliefs of Kemsit as examples of colour symbolism see J. Bourriau *Pharaohs and mortals*. Cambridge 1988: 15-16. Present location of the human remains found by Naville is uncertain.
18. Lichtheim 1973: 139-145.
19. These rulers have been discussed most recently by Zába 1974 and by Morkot 1999.
20. Simpson 1963.
21. Zába 1974: 39-3 inscription 10A.
22. Adams 1977. cf Trigger 1982 for a response and more acceptable interpretation. The evidence for the Middle Kingdom forts Dunham 1967; Dunham and Janssen 1960; Emery, Smith Millard 1979.

V The Kingdom of Kush

1. Posener 1940; for the place-names see Zibelius 1972.
2. Lacovara 1991.
3. Welsby SARS Newsletter no 8 June 1995: 2-7.
4. Smith 1976: Chapter VII.
5. The classic study of the C-Group cultural sequence is that of Bietak (1968), see also Bietak 1987; O'Connor 1993: 27-37.
6. For the original excavations at Kerma see Reisner 1923; for the recent Swiss-Sudanese excavations see Bonnet 1987, 1990; the reinterpretation of the sequence based upon the material from Sai, B. Gratien, *Les Cultures Kerma*, Lille, 1978; see also, more succinctly, Lacovara, 1987, 1991. See also Trigger 1976; Adams 1977; Kemp in Trigger *et al.* 1983. The most recent study of Kerma in English is Kendall 1997.

VI Gold is as Dust

1. Recent re-examination of the mummy shows that Seqenenre may have survived the first violent assault but have died later, also violently.
2. The translation of the Kamose stela follows Smith and Smith 1976; see also Lichtheim 1976.
3. Vandersleyen 1971; some new interpretations of family relationships make Ahmose a son of Kamose.
4. eg the inscriptions of Ahmose son of Abana (Lichtheim 1976: 12-15). For historical context see Kuhrt 1995: I, 185-194, 320-324.
5. See Arkell 1950.
6. Inscription of Ahmose son of Abana line 35 cf. Lichtheim 1976: 14.
7. Aswan inscription cf. BAR II 119-22.
8. For the campaigns of Hatshepsut see Säve-Söderbergh 1941: 207ff; Redford 1967, 60–62; Reineke 1977; Hintze and Reineke 1989, 172 no 562, Taf.239.
9. On the location of Miu see Zibelius 1972: 118-120; Kemp 1978: 290 n.68; O'Connor 1987: 122-124.
10. The Barkal stela, now Boston MFA EA 23.733: Reisner and Reisner 1933: 24-39.
11. Amada stela of Amenhotep II, lines 16-19: Mohamed Aly 1967: N7; Säve-Söderbergh 1941: 155-56; Gardiner 1961: 199-200.

12. For the campaigns of Amenhotep III Säve-Söderbergh 1941; Dehler 1984; Topozada 1988 cf. comments of Kozloff and Bryan 1992: 63 n.22.

13. The only full-scale study of the Viceroys which has been published (several unpublished doctoral dissertations detail the evidence) remains Reisner 1920. This is now completely out of date. The numerous works of Labib Habachi published many more inscriptions, monuments and prosopographical details: Habachi 1981 collects some of these, and gives references to others.

14. This view is not yet widely accepted. It was argued by Morkot 1991a, 1993 (chapter 3), 1995b. The archaeological evidence from the Dongola survey (Grzymski 1997) seems to lend some support to this interpretation. See also Habachi in *LdÄ III*, 630-40.

15. The economy of Nubia under the Viceregal administration is discussed in Morkot 1995a.

16. EA 16. Moran 1992: 38-41.

17. EA 35. Moran 1992: 107-108.

18. EA 14. Moran 1992: 27-34.

19. EA 32. Moran 1992: 104.

20. For the indigenous princes see Säve-Söderbergh and Troy 1991; Kemp 1978; Frandsen 1979; O'Connor in Trigger et al 1983: 265-267; Morkot 1991a., 1993.

21. Steindorff 1937.

22. Simpson 1963.

23. Säve-Söderbergh 1960; 1963; 1991; Säve-Söderbergh and Troy 1991.

24. Dewachter 1976.

25. For the burial see G. Daressy *Fouilles de la Vallée des Rois*. Cairo (1902). Steindorff thought that Maiherpri was a contemporary of Thutmose I, Daressy thought of Hatshepsut; Quibell of Thutmose III, whilst Maspero suggested he was the son of Thutmose III and "a negro princess", although later he ascribed paternity to Thutmose IV.

26. Kozloff and Bryan 1992: 23 discuss the theories of an Asiatic origin (advocated by Mariette, Petrie, Weigall) or Nubian origin (Theodore Davis) for Tiy and the suggestion (of v. Bissing) that she had white skin and blue eyes. On Nefertiti see Richardson 1990 and reponse of Yurco 1990.

27. Kozloff and Bryan (1992: 41-44) give a dispassionate assessment of the evidence.

28. O'Connor 1987.

VII *The Crisis Years*

1. Firth 1927.

2. Kitchen 1990 gives an historical survey of Libyan-Egyptian relations.

3. Mersa Matruh see Donald White "Provisional evidence for the seasonal occupation of the Mersa Matruh area by Late Bronze Age Libyans" in Leahy ed.1990: 1-14.

4. For discussion of the social organization of the Libyans see O'Connor 1990.

5. O'Connor in Trigger *et al.*, 1983: 273 fig 3.25. A plan in Habachi 1980. Excavations have recently been reopened under the direction of Steven Snape revealing that the fortress is far larger than the earlier excavations suggested.

6. See O'Connor 1990; also Kitchen 1990.

7. Cerny 1965.

8. eg Gardiner 1961, 294; R.O.Faulkner in *CAH* II, chap. 23; and in much popular literature.

9. O'Connor 1990.

10. For more recent considerations of the evidence see Trigger *et al.* 1983: 226-32; Kuhrt 1995: 209-210, 223-24.

11. Weinstein 1981: 22-28. There is evidence for the destruction of Egyptian buildings at eg Beth Shan, Aphek and Tell Mor in the late 19th Dynasty but reassertion of control under Ramesses III. The latest evidence of the reign of Ramesses VI at Megiddo, Serabit el Khadim and Deir el-Balah.

12. Steindorff 1937: 242-45; the most recent discussion of the text is Helck 1986.

13. For the upheaval in Thebes see Gardiner 1961: 299-314 to be modified in the light of later reassessments such as; Wente 1966; Aldred 1979 on the robbery in the tomb of Ramesses VI; Kitchen 1986; for the correspondence of Dhutmose-Tjuroy and Butehamun, see Wente 1967, 1990.

14. The classic study of the incident is Wente 1966; see also Kitchen 1986: 247; Bierbrier 1975: 10-13 (for his family).

15. On the 'Renaissance' see Kitchen 1986 especially Chapter 15 (pp 243-54). The radical reassessment by Jansen-Winkeln 1992 has not been followed here. It differs from the

conventional interpretation in reversing the order of the High Priests Herihor and Paiankh, so that Paiankh precedes Herihor.

16. Kitchen 1986: 16-23, 248-254, 569-71.
17. Kitchen 1986: 6, 16-17, 255-57, 531 (and index *sub* Smendes I).
18. Gardiner 1961: 306-313; Lichtheim 1976: 224-230.
19. The family relations of Paiankh, Nodjmet and Herihor have been subject of considerable debate following the new reconstruction of A. Niwinski: see Kitchen 1986: 40-45, 531-41; Jansen-Winkeln 1992.
20. This Osorkon might actually be the same as the future pharaoh Osorkon "the elder", uncle of Sheshonq I.
21. The alternative reconstruction of the genealogy by A. Niwinski, followed by Jansen-Winkeln 1992, makes Paiankh the father of Nodjmet and Pinudjem I (see n 19 above).
22. Wente 1990: 183-84, nos 301-04 with many others from the archive; two more letters (BM 10411,10440) from the archive were published by Jac J. Janssen *Late Ramesside letters and communications. Hieratic papyri in the British Museum, VI*, London, 1991: 11-14, 21-24.)
23. Spiegelberg 1921: 57 (no.714).
24. Kendall 1982: 9.

VIII   Interlude - Libya in Egypt

1. James *et al.* 1991. For the arguments against see most comprehensively (if not convincingly) the review article in *Cambridge Archaeological Journal* (James *et al.*1991a) with contributions by B.J. Kemp, K.A. Kitchen, J.N. Postgate, A. Snodgrass, A. and S. Sheratt. One of the most stimulating treatments of Libyan Egypt is Leahy 1985.
2. See James *et al.* 1991: 254-259, on p. 257.
3. See Kitchen (1986: 293-300) and Redford (1992: 312-315) accept the identification of Shishak with Sheshonq I; but see James *et al.* 1991: 229-231 for the problems.
4. For the classic interpretation of the evidence see Kitchen 1986. The genealogical evidence for some rulers has been recently reconsidered, see Aston 1989; Aston and Taylor 1990.
5. This statue, divided between Cairo and Philadelphia, was published by H. Jacquet-Gordon *JEA* 46 (1960): 12-13.
6. Nesitanebtasheru is not usually identified with the daughter of Pinudjem II (on chronological grounds) see eg Kitchen 1986, but her titles indicate a very close relationship with the High Priests of Amun, and would have given Harsiese an additional Theban lineage. Karl Jansen-Winkeln (1995) has recently disputed the equation of the King Harsiese and the High Priest.
7. David Aston (1989) argued that the reign of Osorkon II should be extended for another 20 years to total 40-45 years. The evidence for this is based solely on genealogies rather than dated monuments, and is not convincing. Aston, in overlapping the reigns of Takeloth II and Sheshonq III reduced the time allocated to them from 77 years (in Kitchen's chronology) to 52 years. A similar scheme was advocated by James *et al.* 1991: 255-56. Logically, the accession dates of Osorkon II and all other predecessors should then be lowered accordingly (as argued in James *et al.* 1991: 255-59), but this destroys the traditional equation of Shishak with Sheshonq I. Consequently, Aston preferred to defend the *status quo* by extending the reign of Osorkon II. Whilst Aston gives many insights into the period, the article, generally, displays some quite bizarre and irrational historical methodology.
8. The identification of Takeloth II with the HPA Takeloth 'F' was proposed in James *et al.* 1991 Table 10:2 on pp 240-241; proposed also by Jansen-Winkeln 1995: 138-39. Most writers (eg Kitchen 1986; Aston 1989; Aston and Taylor 1990) have assumed that Takeloth II was a younger son of Osorkon II.
9. Kitchen tentatively suggested that both Sheshonq III and Pedubast were sons of Takeloth II. There is no evidence to confirm or deny this.
10. Caminos 1958; Kitchen 1986: 330-33.
11. See A. Leahy 'Death by fire in ancient Egypt', *JESHO* 27 (1984) 199–206.
12. On the possible identification of the HPA Osorkon with Osorkon III the old and new literature is copious: vehemently against the identification Kitchen 1986: 106-107, 180-182, 199-200, 330-333, 546-549. The most recent advocates for the identification are Aston 1989, with literature; Leahy 1990; James *et al.* 1991.

IX The Hand of Assur

1. For the end of the Late Bronze Age see Liverani 1987; Drews 1993. The rise of the Late Assyrian empire and the history of the kingdoms of Judah and Israel have been most recently discussed in the new edition of *The Cambridge Ancient History*, Redford 1992 and Kuhrt 1995. A number of studies has examined the role of the Arabs (eg Eph'al 1982) and reassessed the evidence for the Neo-Hittite states (eg the fundamental study of David Hawkins 1982 in *CAH* III.1: 372-441).
2. The Sea Peoples problem, both archaeologically and historiographically, has been most recently, and most thoroughly, examined by Robert Drews (1993).
3. For the Arameans see Kuhrt 1995: 393-401; for the Arabs see Eph'al 1982.
4. Pitard 1987.
5. For the controversy around the date of the founding of Carthage see James *et al.* 1991: 51-55.
6. For the Omrides and Samaria see Mitchell 1982: 466-87.
7. Ophir has been identified with Oman, India and even Malaysia. The more likely equation with Punt or another Red Sea region is preferred by Mitchell 1982: 494-5 amongst others.
8. For a recent account of Urartu see Kuhrt 1995: 547-562.
9. For this translation of *Isaiah* 14, 5-6, 16-17 see Tadmor 1975: 36.
10. For the rise of Assyria see Kuhrt 1995: 473-478.
11. Dalley 1985.
12. Pitard 1987: 148.
13. Tadmor 1961: 145-148; Kitchen 1986: 327; Kuhrt 1995: 466-469.
14. J.V. Kinneir Wilson *The Nimrud Wine Lists*, London 1972: 91, 93 refer to 'Egyptians and Kushites' who he suggests may be 'captives'; see also Redford 1992: 340.
15. Kuhrt 1995.
16. A.H.Gardiner, 'The ancient military road between Egypt and Palestine', *JEA* 6 (1920): 99-116.
17. Pitard 1987.
18. For a stimulating account of the New Year Festival and its importance see Kuhrt 1987.
19. J.A.Brinkman "Merodach-baladan II" in *Studies presented to A.Leo Oppenheim*, Chicago 1964: 6-53.
20. On the identification of 'So' with Sais, the problem and the literature are discussed by Kitchen 1986: 372-375 (opting for an Osorkon 'IV'), 551 (a critique of So as Sais); Redford 1985; 1993: 346-47 (identifying with Tefnakht). Ramadan Sayed 1967: 116-118 also proposed Tefnakht but took 'So' as a transcription of the Horus-name Sia-ib. On the rebellion of Hoshea see J.Reade *Syro-Mesopotamian Studies* 4 (1981): 1-9.
21. Tadmor 1958 Sargon was probably another son of Tiglathpileser III see F. Thomas 'Sargon, der sohn Tiglat-pilesers III' in M.Dietrich and O.Loretz (eds) *Mesopotamica-Ugaritica-Biblica: Festschrift für Kurt Bergerhof ...* (AOAT) (Neukirchen-Vluyn) 1993: 465-70.
22. Khorsabad Display Inscriptions see Luckenbill 1927: II 26-27; Lie 1929: 9, ll 53-57; *ANET*: 285.
23. Tadmor 1958: 35-9; Borger 1960; Kitchen 1986: 372-73, 375-76, 551; Redford 1992: 342.
24. Khorsabad Annals, Luckenbill 1927: II, 7-8; Nineveh Prism Fragment, Weidner 1941-44; Tadmor 1958: 78; Kitchen 1986: 143-44, 376, 551-52; Redford 1993: 347.
25. Nimrud Letter 16 (ND 2765), Saggs 1955: 134-35, 152-53; Tadmor 1958: 39; Postgate 1974: 117-18; on horses also see below pp. 161-2 and Chapter XI n. 41.

X The Holy Mountain

1. See James *et al.* 1991: 222-229.
2. Reisner's excavations at el-Kurru were published in a series of preliminary reports, followed by the more comprehensive volume of Dunham 1950. This remained the standard publication and interpretation until re-assessment began with Kendall 1980 and 1992 and the subsequent controversy. Welsby 1996 follows Kendall. One of the most significant contributions to the el-Kurru debate is the pottery analysis of Lisa Heidorn (1994), although this acknowledges the numerous problems in precise dating of late New Kingdom-TIP pottery from Egypt.
3. It was characterised as a 'Dark Age' in Adams 1964, 1977; UNESCO 1981: 274; Kendall 1980; it was called one by Morkot (in James *et al* 1991); 1994.

4.   Adams 1964: 114-115.
5.   Trigger 1967: 140.
6.   Adams 1977: 244-45.
7.   Kendall particularly emphasises Gebel Barkal as a 'daughter-shrine' of the Karnak temple. Our knowledge of the temple during the New Kingdom is so incomplete that we are not in a position to assess its role. Török, too, is convinced that the continuation of cult at Gebel Barkal was an important factor.
8.   Brugsch 1891: 387.
9.   Found in many early histories. Petrie (1905: 267) was sceptical of a connection between the High Priest Paiankh and the later kings. Reisner elaborated a theory that the Kushite royal family was descended from Libyans, but as this was long ago discredited there is no reason to discuss it here. Kendall (1999), whilst not quite reviving the idea of a Theban priestly ancestry for the Kushite kings did suggest that a "band of Theban priestly families" fled to Nubia and that this explained the "sudden infusion" of Egyptian influences at Kurru in his generation 'B'. Kendall goes on to elaborate this notion in a manner worthy of Brugsch, *but* the whole depends on an exact synchronism between Kendall's chronology for the Kurru cemetery and Kitchen's for late Libyan Egypt which, following Aston 1989, if not James *et al.* 1991, is certainly impossible. Whilst rejecting an Egyptian priestly ancestry for the Kushite kings, other writers have assumed a significant role played by the temple of Amun at Gebel Barkal (Adams 1977: 257; Török 1989: 54) which they assume to have continued to function throughout the three hundred years following the end of the Viceregal administration (see James 1991: 680 for a more sceptical view).
10. Firth 1927: 25-28; Adams 1964: 114-15; Trigger 1965: 112-14.
11. Jacquet-Gordon 1982; S.T. Smith 1995: 155.
12. See Adams 1976: 130-132 summarising discussion. A.J.Arkell and J.Desanges favoured political or military motivation whereas the Soviet scholar I.Katznelson not surprisingly attributed it to economic decline.
13. Zibelius-Chen 1989; Morkot 1993 Chapter 10; see also Chapter XI with nn. 43-47 below.
14. Mohamed Ahmed 1992.
15. Griffith 1922; 1923.
16. My thanks to Dr Irene Liverani Vincentelli for information; see now *Nubia and Sudan* (Bulletin of the Sudan Archaeological Research Society) 3 (1999) for report of New Kingdom tombs at the site.
17. G.A. Reisner, *SNR* 2 (1919): 237-54; *JEA* 6 (1920): 28-55; 1921; 1923.
18. Dunham 1950.
19. Kendall 1982: 22-23.
20. Ali Hakem 1988: 253-55.
21. Török 1995.
22. First proposed in James *et al.* 1991: 213 and 376 n 27, the idea was considered only by Kendall 1999.
23. James *et al.* 1991: 377 n 31 (el Kurru); on heirloom theories in east Mediterranaean archaeology generally see James *et al.* 1991: 316-317, also 45-46, 80-81, 251-253.

XI Rivers of Ivory

The attribution to this period of the inscriptions of Menmaetre (Goedicke 1972) and Usermaetre (Morkot 1991; 1992; 1993; 1994; 1995) has not been generally accepted although Kendall (1999) proposes that Ary might be Alara, and O'Connor (1993: 61) acknowledges the likelihood of an indigenous state after the New Kingdom. The evidence presented in this chapter and its intepretation is, therefore, to be understood as a 'not proven' to the satisfaction of the majority of Egyptologists and Nubian scholars.

1.   Temple 'A': Macadam 1955: 12-13, 28-44 pls. 4, I-V, XXXVI-XL.
2.   Temple 'B': Macadam 1955: 17-22, 45-52, pls. 4, VI-VIII, XXXVI, XLI-XLII.
3.   Kawa Inscriptions XIV (see n. 13 below) and XV: Macadam 1949: pl 34.
4.   Adams 1964: 115.
5.   Hintze 1973: 134-35.

6. Macadam 1949: 72-76.
7. Macadam 1949: 90 inscr. XLV.
8. Macadam 1947.
9. Dunham 1970: 34 no. 25 and pl xxxvii.
10. Priese 1977.
11. The episode was discussed by Priese 1997 and Török 1986: 205-06, no.25. My thanks to Peter James for detailing the inconsistencies in Diodoros' account and his comments on the whole episode.
12. Goedicke 1972.
13. Kawa Inscription XIV, now Copenhagen I.N.1708: Macadam 1949, pls. 32-33.
14. Macadam 1955: pls. VI-VIII.
15. The Karimala inscription was discussed by Grapow 1940; photographs and a hand copy of the text were given in Dunham and Janssen 1960: 10-11, pls. 13–14 with a commentary by M.F.L. Macadam who was cautious about its content; a new translation based on the studies of Grapow and Macadam is to be found in *FHN* 1: 35-41. Caminos 1994 offers many preliminary insights, prior to the publication of the authoritative epigraphical edition and study: Caminos 1998: 20-27, pls. 14-17.
16. *ANET*:275-276.
17. *ANET*: 282-284. There has been considerable debate on whether 'Musri' is, in this case, Egypt; most recent writers (eg Kitchen 1986: 327) following the arguments of Tadmor 1961, accept that it is.
18. Postgate 1974: 283-84 (111.1.1).
19. James *et al.* 1991: 247-251.
20. There are good reasons for seeing the reburials of pharaohs as, at least in part, a means of increasing reserves of precious metals.
21. Morkot 1991b; see also R.Morkot, *CRIPEL* 17/3 (1998): 147-154.
22. This idea, proposed by Morkot (1999) was received with very mixed reactions, but has now been adopted by Török (1995: 212 cf. pp. 207-08 for his acceptance of continuity of elite power and other features).
23. The most recent translation into English is by Pierce in *FHN* II: 471–94.
24. See Shinnie 1955; Welsby 1996: 50 draws attention to the (possibly late Kushite) defence of this site.
25. The translations here are adapted from Macadam 1949: 14-21 (Kawa IV); 32-41 (Kawa VI) and *FHN* I 135-143 (Kawa IV); 164-75 (Kawa VI).
26. Macadam 1949: 50-67 (Kawa IX); *FHN* II: 400-420.
27. Dunham 1950: 86-90; stela *FHN* I: 119-120.
28. The reconstruction of the royal genealogy by Macadam (1949) and Macadam and Dunham (1949) was closely examined in Morkot 1993, Appendixes 5 and 6; cf. Morkot 1999.
29. Dunham 1950: fig 7c, pl.XXXII.C found in Kurru 1 although Reisner suggested Kurru 8 as the possible tomb.
30. Leclant 1963: fig 1; Vercoutter *et al.* 1976: 91, fig 67; *FHN* I: 45.
31. Leclant 1963: 78-81, figs 2-5.
32. Priese 1970: 18. The more recent publication of the texts by J.-M.Kruchten (*Les annales des prêtres de Karnak* (XXI et XXIII*mes* Dynasties) *et autres textes contemporains relatifs à l'initiation des prêtres d'Amon. Orientalia Lovaniensia Analecta* 32, Leuven, 1989: 126) does not add any weight to Priese's interpretation.
33. With the exception of Adolf Erman (1897), the late 19th and early 20th century writers generally misinterpreted the role of the God's Wives and their familial relationships, regarding them as royal wives and heiresses (see n.8 to Chapter II above). The position of Kashta as protaganist was argued by Zeissl 1944: 68 and continued in the literature until Adams 1977: 260 and Priese (in *Africa in Antiquity* I: 78).
34. Kitchen 1986: 151 and n 289 following brother-succession theory of Macadam; he has been followed by, eg, Bierbrier 1975: 103; Trigger 1976: 145; T.G.H.James 1991: 682-83 and n 31.
35. Certainly, on inscriptional evidence, the GWA Isis, Shepenwepet I, Shepenwepet II, Amenirdis II, Neitiqert and Ankhnasneferibre. This was discussed in detail by Morkot 1999: 194-96.

36. The inscription on the celebrated alabaster statue (Cairo CG 565; Leclant 1965: pl.LXI) found in the chapel of Osiris-neb-ankh in the enclosure of Monthu at north Karnak specifically states this relationship. On Amenirdis generally, see Leclant *LdA* I: 196-99.

37. Although there is no direct evidence, this was the assumption of Dunham and Macadam 1949 and most other scholars have followed them. Some confusion has been caused by the inscriptions which refer to Pa-abt-ta-mer (also read as Piebtetemery) which several scholars (such as Zeissl 1944: 73) attributed to a separate individual.

38. Oxford, Ashmolean Mus. E 3922, of Pebatjma herself; and the broken stela of Peqatror, Chicago OIM 6408 with Moscow Pushkin Mus. I.l.b37 see now Leahy 1995: 182-87; Wenig 1990.

39. Priese argued that the title Great King's Wife was used only during the lifetime of the husband, but cf Leahy 1995: 182, 187. We are still uncertain of the implications of many royal titles such as 'King's Sister'.

40. Wenig 1990, also see Leahy 1995: 182-83.

41. Morkot 1993: 256-265; 1995, 237-38. The same conclusion was indepently reached by Lisa Heidorn in a paper presented at the Nubian Conference in Lille 1994.

42. Vernus 1975: 26-59; see also Spalinger 1978: 22.

43. See Kitchen 1986: 65-66, 275-76; Reisner 1920: 53; objects from her burial detailed in PM I.2: 664-666.

44. Kaiser *et al. MDAIK* 38 (1982): 331-34.

45. F. Junge *Elephantine XI ... Kampagne, 1969-1976.* DAIK AV 49 (1987): 62-3 (5.2), Taf. 38a.

46. Aston and Taylor 1990: 147-48.

47. Leahy 1990: 171-72; 1992: 147-48.

48. There is some possibility that the region designated *Dodekaschoinos* was already in existence by the 26th Dynasty, and may have been created as a result of the Egyptian withdrawal from Nubia at the end of the 20th Dynasty.

49. Horton 1991.

50. P. Rowley-Conwy *JEA* 74 (1988): 245-48.

51. Whilst it is still very difficult to give a retrospective calculation, the work of Aston and Taylor on the families of Osorkon III and Takeloth III clearly indicate a lowering of the dates for those kings (and probably by more than those writers would allow).

52. Aston and Taylor 1990: 143.

53. See n. 7 to Chapter VIII, above.

XII The Mighty Bull, Arising in Napata

1. Cairo JE 48862, 47086-47089. A new edition of the text, with commentary, was made by Grimal 1981a; translations are numerous; the most recent and reliable are those of Lichtheim 1980: 66-80; and by R.Pierce in *FHN* I: 62-112 (no.9).

2. Richard Parker suggested that the king's name "Py" or "Piye"found in papyrus documents written in abnormal hieratic was actually that of the king known from the hieroglyphic texts as "Piankhy". This was confirmed by the text of the lesser Dakhla Stela (Janssen 1968: 172). That "Py" or "Piye" was the original Kushite form of the name was argued by Leclant (*OLZ* 61, 1966, 552) and Priese (1968); see also G. Vittmann *Orientalia* 43 (1974) 12-16; Beckerath *MDAIK* 24 (1969): 58-62.

3. The stela was excavated and published by Reisner (1931). A new translation may be found in *FHN* I: 55-60. Reisner (1931) discusses the titulary and its Thutmoside prototype (see also Kitchen 1986: 359).

4. Reisner 1931: 94-100 documented the changes of titulary. Reisner had originally acknowledged two kings called Piankhy, but following his excavations at el Kurru proposed that there was only one. He was followed in this by Macadam 1949: 119; Dunham and Macadam 1949; Leclant and Yoyotte 1952: 35 and n 3. Most early Egyptologists had assumed that there were two, or more, kings called 'Piankhy', eg de Rougé (in 1863), Brugsch etc. Mariette (in *Aperçu de l'histoire d'Egypte ...* Paris 1867: 49, 100-101) placed Piankhy after Taharqo.

5. The Louvre stela was acquired by the museum in 1826 from the Salt collection, first illustrated by Prisse d'Avennes in 1847 as 18th Dynasty (on the evidence of the name Menkheperre); referred to by de Rougé etc as 25th Dynasty, attributed by Petrie to Piye see Kitchen 1986: 137, 371 (less certainly). see now Yoyotte 1989 who details reasons for attributing the monument to King "Iny".

6. See Dunham 1970 55 fig 40. The name Piye is always accompanied here by the epithets favoured by Osorkon II, "beloved of Amun" and "son of Bastet". Despite the names of Ramesses II at Barkal, the writing of the prenomen Usermaetre in the columned hall is typical of the Libyan period.

7. B 501, Reisner 1931: 96; B 801, Reisner *JEA* 4 (1917): 258 and pl.XXXIV; a bandage from western Thebes (London BM EA 6640) on which see further n. 9 below.

8. For the lesser Dakhla stela (Oxford, Ashmolean Museum 1894.107b) see Janssen 1968.

9. Redford 1985 discusses the possibility of a reign of 40 years on the evidence of the British Museum bandage (n.7 above) with a regnal-year date ("20 + X", but not "30", perhaps "40") although retains year 24 as its limit; Kitchen (1973: 152) had argued for a reading of "year 30" on the bandage and reign of around 31 years. The problems and uncertainties of this document negate its value as a source. On the basis of the sed-festival scenes in B501 T.Kendall assumes a reign-length of over 30 years (see following note). The length and internal chronology of the reign was discussed in Morkot 1993: 238-49.

10. These were copied and partially published by T .Kendall (in his Berlin conference paper) who describes them as "elaborate".

11. These are still mostly unpublished in any accessible form but see the Reisner photographs in Dunham 1970: pls L, LI (also Smith and Simpson 1981: 397, fig 390) and Kendall 1999

12. Loukianoff 1926. A translation and commentary may be found in *FHN* I: 118-19 no 10, where the problems of dating the fragment are noted.

13. Priese 1972: 5. This reconstruction seems very unlikely, a view also held by the authors of *FHN* I: 60.

14. Yoyotte 1989. The second inscription was on the roof terrace of the temple of Khonsu at Karnak.

15. Wilson 1951: 293; Gardiner 1961: 340 see also Adams 1977: 262-63.

16. Wilson 1951: 293.

17. Gardiner 1961: 340.

18. cf. Adams 1977: 247-48.

19. Adams 1977: 261.

20. For scientific theories of cultural decadence see Pick 1989. These racial theories were fundamental to the work of Grafton Elliot Smith, Douglas Derry and others who worked with human remains from Egypt (eg Flinders Petrie). That they had continuing validity is implicit in the interpretations of Gardiner and Wilson cited in the preceding notes, and perhaps also in the work of Arnold Toynbee quoted by Adams.

21. Priese 1970.

22. *FHN* I: 119-20, no 11.

23. Kawa Inscriptions IV and VI (Macadam 1949); see also Morkot 1999: 189-91.

24. Priese 1968: 177-79; Leahy 1995: 182.

25. Kendall describes and comments on this scene in his Berlin conference paper.

26. Published by Leahy 1995: 178-82, pls.XXIV-V.

27. M. Gitton, *Rde* 19 (1967): 161-63..

28. Dunham 1950: 30-37; Kendall 1982: 26-30, nos. 6-24.

29. Kendall 1982: 28-30, nos. 11-24.

30. Kurru 52; Dunham 1950: 81-85.

31. See above p. 112 fig 52. The amulet (Boston MFA 24.928) from the tomb of Nefrukekashta is illustrated in Wenig 1978: 181, no. 95; cf the menat of Taharqo, Wildung 1996: 196, no 221, and the relief inWenig 1978: 162 no. 71.

32. M.B. Reisner 1934; Dunham 1970: 33, no. 21; *FHN* I: 268-76, no. 40.

XIII   Uniter of the Two Lands

1. See Chap XII n. 3 above. *FHN* I p.58; the epithets "king of kings" and "ruler of the rulers" are also typically New Kingdom, particularly 18th Dynasty.

2. As the king had followed Thutmose III in all other aspects of the titulary, it seems most likely that he adopted Menkheperre as his prenomen. Usermaetre and Sneferre can be shown to be associated only with much later phases of the reign.

3. Khartoum SNM 1851: Reisner 1931: 89-94, pls V, VI; Dunham 1970: 29 no 13; *FHN* I: 55-60.- Discussions are to be found in Reisner 1931: 94-100; Kitchen 1986: 359; Priese 1970; Morkot 1995: 231-32.

4. Priese 1972: 5, I do not accept this reconstruction (so also *FHN* I: 60, see above Chap XII n 13) although the events recounted certainly belong to a very early point in the reign. It would not be unreasonable to expect this inscription to refer to year 1 or 2.

5. Reisner published an account of B800-900 in *JEA* 6 (1920): 247-64; cf Dunham 1970: 77-81. Reisner's original excavations of B 1200 were unpublished (but see Dunham 1970: 95-98). Kendall's re-excavation of part of the structure and re-assessment of Reisner's surviving plans and records allowed him to suggest that the earliest phase of building belonged to the time of Piye or one of his immediate predecessors, with several later rebuildings down to the Meroitic period (Kendall 1991).

6. On the western Delta in the Libyan period and the rise of Sais see Yoyotte 1961; Priese 1970; Kitchen 1986: 145-47, 350-51, 355; Ray 1974; Morkot 1993: 212-215.

7. Yoyotte 1960.

8. The Abemayor stela from Tell Farain, Yoyotte 1961: 153; Kitchen 1986: 355.

9. Yoyotte 1961: 151-53, pl. I.1.

10. The translation of sections of the Victory Stela of Piye is based upon those of Lichtheim 1980 and Pierce in *FHN* I: 62-112. On the progress and specific aspects of the campaign see Spalinger 1979; Grimal 1981a; Kessler 1981; Kitchen 1986.

11. Purem is given no Libyan titles such as Chief of the Ma, but given his role as a Kushite general, that is to be expected. On the name see Leahy 1984.

12. There has been some dispute over the rendering of this name: Lemersekny seems preferable to "Ru(ma)sekny" or "Shenasekny". Parallels can be found in other texts of the Napatan period such as the stela of Aspelta (Louvre E257; *FHN* I: 259-65) Amani-sekny and Amani-talhakny. The name could be considered to be "Meroitic", but that does not necessarily indicate that this man came from the central Sudan.

13. Ideally 1 *akhet* 1 fell on the 19/20 July, but, if the calendar did revolve and become out of synch as most Egyptologists believe, it probably fell in late December by the reign of Piye. For a discussion of the calendrical problems see James *et al.* 1991: 225-228.

14. Such, at least, is conventional Egyptological wisdom see preceding note.

15. See Roberts 1995.

16. Or he may have chosen to do this on his victorious return to Thebes at the end of the campaign, an appropriate time to consolidate his position with new appointments.

17. St.Petersburg Hermitage 220: Graefe 1981: 109, n85; Cairo JE 43653 refers to the God's Wife Shepenwepet daughter of king Osorkon ..., the Hand of the God Amenirdis daughter of king [Kashta] and the Adorer of the God Shepenwepet daughter of [name erased] see Graefe 1981: 20-21 j55.

18. A large number of such Osiris statues survives, many from Medinet Habu see eg PM II: 480-481.

19. See n 5 to Chap XII above and Yoyotte 1989.

20. See also Roberts 1995: 61-2 for another translation and comments on the significance of this fulsome description of the princess.

21. Published by Mariette. Another object which perhaps belonged to the princess is the carnelian amulet of Horus the child in the Hermitage Museum, St Petersburg, inscribed on its reverse with a cartouche carrying the name Mutirdis. The amulet was attributed by Jens Lieblein to the 26th Dynasty.

22. The officials named Pediamen-neb-nesut-tawy were originally differentiated as 'A' and 'B' (Kitchen 1986: 226-28), but Vittmann's (1978: 89) argument that these were the same individual has now been generally accepted (Kitchen 1986: 563-65; Aston and Taylor 1990: 134-35). Pediamen-neb-nesut-tawy A/B married a king's daughter (probably of Takeloth III, see Aston and Taylor 1990: 134).

23. Griffith 1922.

24. The faience panels, reputedly (see Leahy 1992: 237 n. 88) from Karnak, are now in Edinburgh and Brooklyn (59.17);cf. comments of Leahy 1992, 238. A stela from Tell el Rub'a of year 21 of Iuput is in Geneva see J.-L. Chappaz *Genava* 30 (1982): 71-81.

25. The statue of Takushit, Athens 110, see Smith and Simpson 1981: 391 fig. 385. Yoyotte (1961: 160-61 and n. 5) suggested that the name meant "the Kushite" and that there was marriage between Akunosh and the Kushites. Takushit's sister Nesbastetrud is known from a statue of Osiris which gives her the title "king's wife".

26. Yoyotte 1961: 161-62, pl II/3.

27. The scholarly opposition to identification with Osorkon III is based upon chronological reconstructions eg Kitchen (1986: 178) who dismisses the idea that Piye's campaign

"would fall into the 27th year of Osorkon III" with an exclamation mark! Most commentators have assumed the ruler in question to have been that "powerless shadow pharaoh" (Kitchen) or "pliant weakling" (Redford), Osorkon "IV". This ruler was, until quite recently, virtually without monuments, but now attributed to him are the aegis, Louvre E7167 (J.Berlandini in *Hommages Sauneron* IFAO BdE LXXX.1: 1979, 98-109), the seal, Leiden A010a and relief, Leiden F 1971/9.1 (Schneider, also in *Hommages Sauneron*: 264-66).

28. Patjenfy's possible kushite marriage suggested by the stela of Shebitqo (n. 8 to Chap.XVI below) on which he is given the title "king's son".

XIV The Bull, ruler of Egypt

1. Louvre E 3915: Leclant 1962: 203-07, pl 68-9.
2. Of these sculptures, Lepsius removed to Berlin one ram and the falcon image of Sopd; the other rams remain *in situ*. Reisner acquired a number of statues for Boston Museum of Fine Art depicting Horus of Nekhen, Serqet, Thutmose III, Amenhotep III and the Viceroy Dhutmose. The statues of the Viceroy Merymose and of Bekenwer and Heqaemsasen are in Khartoum SNM (for all see Dunham 1970). There was also a colossal vulture and other serpent figures.
3. Six stone "sockets" for stelae survive in the first court (B 501), four of them flanking the entrances to the central kiosk. The date of completion is only assumption, but since the scenes illustrating the campaign occur in 502, the court clearly postdates that and the only scenes of Piye in the court 501 are of the sed-festival. The year-date, 21, on the stela indicates only the date of the text, *not* of the events narrated.
4. Most writers assume that the reliefs of the sed-festival do indicate a celebration of that event, and have assumed that this happened according to convention in year 30. Such an event would have been an ideal time for changes of titulary (as happened with Amenhotep III, Ramesses II and others): Sneferre, perhaps to be understood "the one whom Re perfects" and "the one who brings Re to perfection", being an appropriate choice.
5. The discovery of the obelisk fragment at Kadakol is not sufficient evidence to claim that Piye built a temple at this site.
6. This bizarre assumption is stated or implicit in eg Wilson 1951: 293; Gardiner 1961: 340; Adams 1977: 262; Kitchen 1986: 372 and many secondary historical works.
7. el-Sayed 1975: 37-53, pl. VII; Kitchen 1986: 371-72.
8. Priese 1970: 19, n.19.
9. The existence of a Tefnakht "II", to be identified with the *Stephinates* of Manetho as a local Saite ruler, has been quite generally assumed since Petrie 1905: 318-19 (see Kitchen 1986: 145-47, 395). Wolfgang Helck suggested the equation of Manetho's *Stephinates* with the Tefnakht of the Piye stela. The late tradition of Diodoros 1.45.1-2 and Plutarch *De Iside et Osiride* 8 recounts an episode relating to "Tnephachtos the father of Bocchoris the wise".
10. Kitchen 1986: 139-41.
11. For the Khaliut stela see Dunham 1970: 33 no21; M.B. Reisner 1934; a new translation in *FHN* I: 268-279, no. 40. The possibility of some sort of opposition to Piye is perhaps raised again by the newly published evidence of the Tang-i Var inscription (Frame 1999) which indicates that Shebitqo was ruling in Kush *before* his accession as pharaoh in Egypt. Clearly this period of Kushite-expansion was far more complex than we have readily acknowledged.
12. Year 21, pLeiden F 1942/5.15: Vleeming, *OMRO* (1980): 61; Menu *RdE* 36 (1985): 74; Year 22, pVatican 10574: Malinine *RdE* 5 (1946): 119-31; Menu *RdE* 36 (1985): 75. For the lesser Dakhla stela, Oxford, Ashmolean Museum 1894, see Janssen 1968.
13. For the chronology of the dynasty see Morkot 1999: 202-210. Dates for Piye's campaign against Tefnakht (generally assumed to have taken place in his regnal years 19 and 20) vary from (all *circa*) 734 (Lichtheim 1980); 730 (Gardiner 1961: 335); 728 (Petrie 1905; Grimal 1981: 216-19; Kitchen 1986; *FHN* I 114); 720 (Albright 1953); 716 (Redford 1985; 1992); to 712 or 709 (Depuydt 1993: 271, 272 n. 26).
14. For the text Oppenheim in *ANET* (1969), 286, 287; Luckenbill 1927: II, 31-2. For the correct reading see Spalinger 1973: 97. This problem is discussed by Kitchen (1986: 583) who, whilst acknowledging the correct translation claims that his high dates "are

still a valid option"; see also Kitchen 1986: 143-144, 380, 552; Redford 1985: 1986, 322-324 and Depuydt 1993: 271-72 particularly n. 24.

15. Redford 1985; 1992: 346 n 129 opts for after January 711; Depuydt 1993 gives a minimal chronology and places Shabaqo's invasion in 705; see also Morkot 1999: 207-208.

16. The Annals from Khorsabad: Luckenbill 1927: II 13-14 § 30; Oppenheim *ANET*, 286b. The Display Inscriptions: Luckenbill 1927: II 31-2 §§ 62-63; Oppenheim *ANET*: 286a-b. The Display Inscription of Salon XIV: Luckenbill 1927 II: 40-1 §§ 79-80; Oppenheim *ANET*: 285a. Prism A inscription: Luckenbill 1927 II: 105; Oppenheim *ANET* 287a.

17. Although some argue that he was an Asiatic; see most recently Frame 1999 for the incident.

18. Kitchen originally argued (in 1973 = 1986: 143-44) that Pi'ru was Shabaqo and used the evidence of the Yamani incident as an anchor-date for the 25th Dynasty (with a myriad chronological and historical assumptions dependent upon it). Spalinger (1973: 100) argued that Pi'ru had to be a Delta ruler, rather than a Kushite. This was accepted by Kitchen (1986: 552, 583) who thus identified him with Osorkon IV, but retained his chronology (see n. 14 above).

19. Bakenranef certainly had some control of Memphis (the burial of Apis, see n 5 to Chap XV below) and Djanet (Tanis) (see n 8 to Chap XV below) and might therefore be the likeliest candidate, even if there was another ruler in Djanet.

20. In Assyria the years were identifed by designated officials (called *limmu*). The best-preserved Eponym (or *Limmu*) Chronicle was discovered by Henry Rawlinson in 1862. It names every eponym official of the Late Assyrian empire from the reign of Adad-nirari II to that of Assurbanipal, ie from 911-660 BC. The lists name the eponymous official, his rank, and an event (often military) of the year. On the eponym lists and the initial hostility to Rawlinson's reconstruction see James *et al.* 1991: 265-269. For a composite list see Luckenbill 1927: II 427-39.

21. Meluhha is understood by Assyriologists as a variant of *Kusu* "Kush" at this period.

22. el-Amin *Sumer* 9 (1953): 35 *ff.*, figs. 2-6; Reade *JNES* 35 (1976): 100 *ff.* The reliefs are further discussed by Redford (1992: 347-48) who suggests that the depiction of Kushites may be anachronistic detail if the reliefs were carved much later. He further questions whether Kushites would be present among Egyptian forces prior to Shabaqo's conquest. However, with Kushite control of Thebes and Upper Egypt it is possible that contingents of troops were sent by Piye.

XV The Broken Reed

At the final stages of editing this volume, the Tang-i Var inscription of Sargon II was published by Grant Frame (1999) with additional comments by Donald Redford. This text casts a completely new light on the events of the period following 711 BC and, as too often happens, raises more questions than it answers.

1. Tabakenamun is recorded on a fragment of a statue of the High Priest of Amun, Haremakhet (Cairo JE 49157), from the temple of Mut at Karnak, although their relationship is nowhere stated and his sarcophagus appears to give his mother's name as Mesbat.

2. Mesbat is attested only on the sarcophagus of Haremakhet (Cairo JE 55194).

3. For Qalhata see Chapter XXII, p 293 with fig 113 below.

4. For Istemkheb see p. 224 below, and Leahy 1984.

5. The ancient traditions consistently associate Bocchoris with legal affairs and the reign may have seen some important legislation; on the evidence of Diodoros (i.65, 79,1; 94,5) these related to contracts and commerce. Neither of the important studies of the tradition is easily accessible: Alexandre Moret, *De Bocchori Rege* (1903) and J.M.A. Janssen 'Over farao Bocchoris' in *Varia Historica... A.W. Byvanck*(1954)17-29. The episode of the courtesan is reported in Plutarch's *Life of Demetrius*, 27.

6. For the Apis stelae see Malinine, Posener and Vercoutter 1968; also for this period Vercoutter 1960. Of the stelae with the cartouches of Bakenranef (nos 91-117), some carried the year date, 6, specified (on stela no 102) as 1 *akhet* 5. The reports of Mariette and Maspero and more recent accounts on the year-date of Shabaqo are contradictory.

There are also indications that the chamber had been used for the burial of an Apis bull in year 37 of Sheshonq V. The material has been discussed by Vercoutter 1960: 65-7; Redford 1985: 8; Kitchen 1986: 141-42 n 247, 377, 489; James *et al.* 1991: 236-38; Morkot 1993: 249-51.

7. Karnak NT 30, Beckerath 1966: 52; Horbeit stela (Louvre E 10571), Yoyotte 1961.
8. J.Yoyotte *Kêmi* 21 (1971): 35-45.
9. Stela from Sau of year 4 : Moscow, Pushkin Museum; I.1.a.54646: Hodjash and Berlev 1982: 165, no.108, pl.p.163. Stela from Buto of year 6: New York MMA 55.144,6; Yoyotte 1961: 172.
10. Unlike the other Kushite pharaohs, many of Shabaqo's female relatives have typically Egyptian names, and some of their titles (such as those of Tabakenamun) also suggest an Egyptian origin. The likelihood of Libyan/Kushite diplomatic marriages has generally been ignored in the scholarly literature and sometimes even considered deemed unlikely.
11. Kitchen 1986: 378.
12. London BM 84527, 84884 (excavated by Layard) see H.R. Hall, *Catalogue of scarabs... British Museum* I 290 nos 2775, 2776.
13. Postgate 1974: 283-84 (111.1.1).
14. Toronto ROM 910.28.1, reputedly from Jerusalem; see Kitchen 1986: 379 and n 767 and Leclant in *LdA* V (Schabaka) 503 and nn 93-94. The dating is disputed (but usually ascribed to years 1 or 2) as is its validity as a record of real military activities in Sinai rather than 'propaganda' recording his conquest of Egypt.
15. Kuhrt 1995 II Chapter 9.
16. 2 *Kings* 20.12-19 and almost identical *Isaiah* 39.1-8. For the folly of seeking help in Egypt, *Isaiah* 30.1-5 and following, also *Isaiah* 31.1-3. The episode of the embassy of Merodach-baladan to Hezekiah is anachronistic being placed after the campaign of Sennacherib and in *Kings* after the death of Sennacherib. This should be another sign that the text is far from reliable (see n 17 following and text).
17. Kitchen 1986: 157-61, 383-86 (with nn 823, 824), 552-554 and 584-85 for all facets of the episode. Kitchen 1986: 154-56, 557-58 gives his reasons (not accepted here) why he thinks that Shebitqo rather than Shabaqo was reigning. Also see Redford 1992: 351, 353 who argues for a lower chronology than Kitchen and that, consequently, Shabaqo was reigning. Redford (1992: 353-54, nn.163, 165) is as forceful as Kitchen in refuting the idea that Taharqo was reigning and that there was a second campaign.
18. Grayson *CAH* III.2 (1992).
19. Mitchell 1982.
20. The reliefs, now in the British Museum are widely illustrated, e.g.Pritchard *The Ancient Near East in Texts and Pictures* (ANET) and J. Reade *Assyrian Sculpture* 1983: figs. 65-73.
21. Herodotos II.141 states that Sethos who had been high priest of Hephaestus (ie Ptah), led his army against Sennacherib.
22. Kitchen 1983.
23. The evidence gives no clear date but perhaps between year 12 and 15.
24. M. Jones and A. Milward Jones published slabs of a door of Shabaqo reinscribed for Psamtik II; *JARCE* 22: 23 and 26; *JARCE* 25: 105-16, on 111-13 and fig. 7. On the history of the building see M.Jones 'The temple of Apis in Memphis' *JEA* 76 (1990): 141-47 (144 for Shabaqo).
25. The cartouches were recut for Psamtik II who did not bury an Apis either, although this reign saw extensive *damnatio memoriae* of the Kushite pharaohs (best documented at Thebes see Yoyotte 1951.
26. F.Junge 'Zur Fehldatierung des sog. Denkmals memphitischer Theologie' *MDAIK* 29 (1973): 195-204.
27. For an emphatic attribution of the phenomenon to the early Saites and the view that the kushites "merely aped a fad" see Redford 1992: 345, n. 125.
28. Leclant 1981; Berlandini *BSEG* (1984-85).
29. For the reliefs of Gemenefkhonsubak see pp.284-85 and fig.111 below.
30. Munich S 4859; Russmann 1974: 45-6 no 2 and fig 2; Russmann 1968-69: 90-1 figs. 1-3; Wildung 1996: 176-77 no. 169. Despite its battered state has close similarities with the small faience head of Shabaqo in the Louvre which was also crowned with a sun-disk (see Russmann 1968-69: 92 figs 4-6, 93). For the fragment of the small green schist

statue of Shabaqo "beloved of Ptah South of his Wall" (Louvre N.2541) see Russmann 1968-69: 100-01, figs. 13-14. Russmann with due caution indicates the possibility that the splendid head in Brooklyn (60.74: Russmann *BMA* 10, (1968-69): 97-100, figs. 10-12) might belong to this statue.

31. Cairo JE 44665: Leclant 1954: 31-42, pl. 7.
32. Leclant 1965: 134-37, pls. LXXVII-IX.
33. C. Van Siclen made a reconstruction using Taharqo's colonnade at North Karnak as a parallel. A different reconstruction, based on new evidence from the area preceding the pylon has now been proposed by Christian Loeben. My thanks to him for information on the colonnade and a copy of his paper. For the blocks of the colonnade reused as the flooring see Leclant 1965: 137-39, pl. LXXX.
34. Parker, Leclant, Goyon 1979: 5-9, 80, 86, pls 2E, 3A-C; Leclant 1965: 77-78, pls. XLI, XLV.
35. Leclant 1965: 19, pl. VI A.
36. Leclant 1951: *RdE* 8 101-120; 1965: 17; J.Yoyotte, 'Un porche doré: La porte du IV*e* pylône au grand temple de Karnak' *CdE* 55 (1953): 28-38.
37. Leclant 1965: 19-23, pl. VII.
38. Leclant 1965: 36-41, pls. XII-XVI.
39. Leclant 1965: 94-98.
40, Couyat and Montet 1912: 98, no. 187, pl 35; Graefe 1981: 70.
41. The closest parallel is perhaps the relief block in Berlin (AS. 1480) depicting Shebitqo.
42. Macadam 1955: 14, 45, 46, 47 (fig 14), 48 213 pl. XLII CVII.
43. Leclant in *Kush* 1 (1952): 47, pl. xvi.b.
44. Dunham 1950.

XVI   Enduring of Epiphanies

1. Morkot 1999:191-92, 205-206.
2. Kawa Inscription V; Macadam 1949, 15
3. Morkot 1999: 191-94.
4. An inscription on the statue of the HPA Haremakhet (JE 49157) reads "king's wife (of) Shebitqo king's daughter Piye Arty" with Piye written within a cartouche. The formulation is read by some (as here) as meaning "king's daughter of Piye, Arty" and by others as "king's daughter, Piye-Arty". Dunham and Macadam 1949 no 16 (following Lefebvre) thought that she was the same as the wife of Tanwetamani. See also Morkot 1993: 373-74 no 18.
5. The material fully discussed in Leahy 1984; Morkot 1993: 381, no 36.
6. The vexed issue of a possible co-regency between Shabaqo and Shebitqo must be again considered following the evidence of the Tang-i Var inscription (Frame 1999). Previously its existence (or not) has been argued on chronological premises. A co-regency, argued by Macadam 1949: 19, 20 on the evidence of NT 33 (see n 9 below), was rejected by Leclant and Yoyotte 1952; Kitchen 1986: 170-71; Beckerath 1993: 8; but advocated by Spalinger 1973; Murnane 1977: 189-90, 235-36; Yurco 1980: 225; and Redford 1985; 1992: 354, cf. now Redford 1999: 58-9.
7. The highest year so-far recorded is year 3 of Nile Text 33; Kitchen 1986: 551 comments that this "is nowhere near his real length of reign on any calculation", thereby clearly revealing his premises for reconstructing chronology (similarly on p.154).
8. The stela MMA 65.45 has been cited by Leclant (*LdA* V: 515, 516 n 1, citing Gomaà 1974: 98 n 27 who gives no date) and Redford (1985: 13 table 1) presumably on a mis-reading of Meeks 1979 673 (25.5.00) where the date is given as "*x*" for year-unknown. My thanks to Dr. Catherine Roehrig of the Metropolitan Museum for confirming my suspicions about the year-date (in a letter of 13 March 1991) and for supplying me with a photograph and hand copy of the text.
9. NT 33; Beckerath 1966: 53; Beckerath 1993; Redford 1992: 354 n. 166 understands it as Shebitqo's coronation. There is nothing in the text which explicitly states that Shebitqo had not been in Egypt earlier than year 3. There is no month given, although some writers assume "1st month" is indicated see eg Kitchen 1986: 170 and n. 369.
10. The actual date of the Feast of the Valley was dictated by the appearance of the new moon during the second month of Shomu. Kitchen 1986: 170 and n. 373 points out

that Shebitqo's presence might be associated with the festival of Amun which took place at Karnak in the 1st month of Shomu, days 1-5.

11. Changes of policy do not necessarily indicate changes of ruler, but of circumstances (eg Assyrian threat to Egyptian trading interests in Palestine).

12. See n.21 to Chapter XV above.

13. MMA 65.45, on which see n. 8 preceding.

14. Cairo CG 1291 (now Aswan, Nubian Museum); Russmann 1974: 53 no. 29, fig. 7; it is unlike the statues of Shabaqo, Taharqo or Tanwetamani and has its closest parallels in the reliefs of Shebitqo.

15. Leclant 1965: 47-54, pls XXI-XXVIII; Redford *JEA* 59 (1973): 16-30.

16. Leclant 1965: 59-61 pl. XXXVI-VII; the block in Yale illustrated in pl XXXVII is not Shebitqo (perhaps pre-New Kingdom) see Leahy 1995: 192 n 37.

17. Dunham 1950.

XVII The City of Amun

1. Caminos 1963.

2. Various higher dates have been proposed following from the assumption that Piye was dead by 715 BC, which (of course) would make Taharqo older at his accession and death.

3. Kawa V, l.15; Macadam 1949: 22-32; *FHN* I:145-55, no 22.

4. e.g. Macadam (1949:128) who thought that Taharqo usurped the right of prince Khaliut.

5. Kwasman 1988: 384-85, no. 333.

6. Mosul Museum: Russmann 1974: 47 nos 7-8; Simpson, *Sumer* X (1954): 193-4; Vikentiev, *Sumer* XI (1955): 111-116.

7. Vercoutter 1960; accepted by Kitchen 1986: 156, 489. The assumption being that the (relatively short-lived) bull which succeeded that buried in year 2 of Shabaqo (= 6 Bakenranef) died at the end of Shabaqo's reign; that installed in year 14 of Shabaqo spanned the postulated 12 year reign of Shebitqo, dying at the 'average age' of 16 years. However, if a short chronology for the dynasty (with a short reign for Shebitqo) is followed, only one bull is necessary: installed in year 2 of Shabaqo, such a bull would have been between 20 and 26 years old at death, an age well-documented at this period for Apis bulls.

8. NT 34 and NT 35, Beckerath 1966: 47-48; Kitchen 1986: 388 n 839. The flood is referred to in Kawa inscription V, Macadam 1949: 22-32; FHN I, with parallel texts from Koptos, Mataana and Tanis (Macadam 1949: pls 9-10); Leclant and Yoyotte 1949.

9. In years 7 (NT 36), 8 (NT 37), and 9 (NT 38). Beckerath 1966: 48, 53-54.

10. On the marvels (Kawa V, 10-13) see Macadam 1949: 19-20 corrected by Leclant and Yoyotte 1952:16, 22-4; and Kitchen 1986: 168-70.

11. Grayson *CAH* III.2 (1992).

12. The whole subject of the Kushites and their activities in Libya and the Oases of the Western Desert needs further research. The original chapel in the fortress at Qasr el-Ghueida is not 25th Dynasty, but of the reign of Darius. However, note the reference to a record of Libyan conflict in Redford 1992: 355, n. 175; the presence of an Amun cult at Siwa could be interpreted as a Kushite inspiration and classical sources clearly associated Taharqo, metamorphosed into "Etearchos king of the Ammonians" (Herodotos II.32) with Siwa; "Etearchos" appears again (Herodotos IV.153) as the name of a Cretan ruler who was grandfather of Battus founder of Cyrene.

13. Sau objects; weights London Petrie Museum UC 2398 "beloved Osiris *hry ib* Sau" see Petrie, *Ancient Weights and Measures* (1926): X pl. 29.

14. "Ammeris the Aithiops" is often assumed to have been a Kushite governor, but Priese 1970 argued that he should be identified with Kashta on the basis of his own (speculative) reading of Kashta's prenomen as Nemaetre; Ammeris has also been understood as a corruption of Usermaetre (ie Piye). Some earlier writers thought *Ammeris* should be identified with the cartouches of Amonaso (ie Amanislo) found on the Soleb lion (see Chap.I).

15. Often identified with a Tefnakht "II", but there are dissenting voices, see Chap.XIV n. 9 above.

16. Published in 1886 and accepted by many scholars since (eg Petrie 1905); Kitchen 1986, n 267 amends Manetho's reign length to 16 years; but see Ray *JEA* 60 (1974): 255-56.

17. Spalinger 1974a: 298 n. 17; Kitchen 1986: 145-146.

18. The stela is discussed in Leclant 1949; the statue; Russmann 1974: 51 no. 21.

19. The monuments of Pedubast; Montet 1966; Habachi *ŹÄS* 93 (1966): 69-74; Kitchen 1986.
20. Montet 1966.
21. What might have happened in Perbastet in the late Libyan-Kushite-Early Saite periods has been reconstructed very largely from the assumptions about the identity of Osorkon III and the 'Theban 23rd Dynasty' - there is virtually nothing archaeological. Most scholars would bring the line to an inglorious end with Piye's Osorkon (usually Osorkon 'IV') and it is perhaps possible that he should be identified with the HPA Osorkon son of Takeloth III. The surviving material for rulers such as Gemenefkhonsubak is difficult to place precisely chronologically.
22. Ruszczyc 1977: 391-85 pl 59-64; Habachi *BIFAO* 82 (1982): 216, 230.
23. Leclant in *Mélange Mariette* (IFAO *BdE* XXXII) (1961): 251-84 on 272-73, fig 6.
24. The head from Akhmim, now Florence 7655: Russmann 1974: 54 no 31 fig 1.
25. London Petrie Mus. UC 15812; see also Leahy 1979 for the vizier and Tjeny.
26. From a Ramesside hymn to Amun.
27. Leclant 1965: 216-19, 262-85, 318-19.
28. For the monuments and genealogies of these families see Kitchen 1986 (with references to older literature) and Bierbrier 1975; there have been numerous additions, emendations and corrections to these genealogies see significantly Vittmann 1978; Aston and Taylor 1990.
29. This seems likely from the evidence but the precise dating is difficult. Also note that new material is constantly being brought to light.
30. Eigner 1984: 40-41.
31. R.Fazzini and W.Peck 'The precinct of Mut during Dynasty XXV and early Dynasty XXVI, a growing picture' *SSEAJ* 11 (1981): 115-26; R.A.Fazzini 'A sculpture of King Taharqa (?) in the precinct of the goddess Mut at South Karnak' in *Mélanges Mokhtar* (IFAO *BdE* XCVII) (1985): 293-306.
32. Sarcophagi of Haremakhet, Cairo JE 55194: Leclant 1954: 180; Pasker1962.
33. Cairo CG 42203: Leclant 1957: 171.I
34. The broken statue in Sydney, Nicholson Museum, carries the name of Taharqo.
35. Rosalind Moss, 'The statue of an ambassador to Ethiopia at Kiev,' *Kush* 8 1(960): 269-71.
36. The pylon has been attributed by some Egyptologists to the 30th Dynasty. For the court and colonnade see Leclant 1965: 8-17, pl I, V; Laufray 1970 *Karnak III* [= *Kêmi* 20]; Lauffray 1975 *Karnak V.*
37. Parker, Leclant, and Goyon 1979.
38. Leclant 1965: 59-61, pl XXXVI-VII.
39. Leclant 1965: 78-80, 109.
40. Leclant 1965: 54-56 pl XXX (re-used Kushite blocks).
41. Leclant 1965: 56-58, pl.XXXI-V.
42. Cairo CG 560 (now in the Nubia Museum, Aswan): Russmann 1974: 47, figs 8-9; Wenig 1978: 167-no 76; Smith and Simpson 1981: 402-03, figs 396-97 (and compare figs 394-95).
43. Leclant 1965: 41-47, pl XVII-XX.
44. Leclant 1965: 23-26, pl.VIII-XI.
45. Leclant 1965: 85-108.
46. Cairo JE 39403, 39404: Leclant 1965: 103, pls LXIV-LXV; Russmann 1974: 48 nos 12-13.
47. Leclant 1965: 85-88.
48. Leclant 1965: 131-33; recently unearthed blocks of Shepenwepet II see *Karnak V*, 18.
49. Leclant 1965: 84; now *Karnak VI.*
50. Leclant 1965: 110-13.
51. Leclant 1965: 114-18.
52. Berlin 17271 see Lichtheim 1980: on Monthuemhat see Leclant 1961 and n. 64 below.
53. Leclant 1965: 143 no 41 *bis*, pl LXXVI.
54. Hölscher *Excavations at Medinet Habu* V (Chicago OIC LXVI) (1954).
55. Leclant 1965: 161, B,C pl LXXXI, B; one names Amenirdis.
56. My thanks to Prof. Jean Jacquet for a copy of his article 'Medinet Habou: Les additions tardives à l'est du temple de la XVIIIe dynastie' from *Egyptological Studies in honor of Abdel Aziz Sadek*, and to Dr.Helen Jacquet-Gordon and Dr. W. R.Johnson for information.
57. Hölscher (as n. 54).
58. Leclant 1965: 154-59 and Hölscher (as n. 54).

59. Hölscher (as n. 54)

60. Eigner 1984.

61. C.Kuentz 'Remarques sur les statues de Harwa' *BIFAO* 34 (1934): 143-63.

62. Leclant 1965: 175-76, pl LXXXVI (Ramose) and 176-77 (Kelbasken); Eigner 1984; 40-3.

63. Manfred Bietak *Theben-West (Luqsor) Vorbericht über die ersten vier Grabungskampagnen (1969-1971)* Wien, 1972. Osterreichische Akademie der Wissenschaften: 33-35, pls XVIII-XXIII.

64. For the tomb of Tjesreperet see Leclant 1965, 179; for that of Monthuemhat, Leclant 1961; J.D.Cooney, *JARCE* 3 (1964) 79-87, pls XVI-XX; and see n.12 to Chap.XX below.

XVIII *The Throne of the Two Lands*

1. *Orientalia* 56 (1987): Tab. XLIII-XLV.

2. The closest parallels seem to be reliefs of Shebitqo from Karnak (see n.41 to Chap. XV) and newly uncovered blocks from Medinet Habu (see n.56 to Chap. XVII).

3. F.Ll. Griffith, 'Four granite altar stands at Philae' *BIFAO* 30 (1930): 128-132. For blocks recovered from the foundations of the Ptolemaic temple of Isis see Farag *OrAnt* 18 (1979): 281-289, pls. 18-20. For 25th Dynasty burials at Shellal, Williams 1990: 31.

4. For the temple of Taharqo at Qasr Ibrim see *JEA* 51 (1965): 28, pl. 12.2; *JEA* 56 (1970): 17-18, pl. 25.3; *JEA* 61 (1975): 16 pl. 9; *JEA* 63 (1977) pl. 6, 3; Horton 1991. Near Qasr Ibrim a rock inscription of Taharqo of year 19 marking the cattle road also recorded by inscriptions west of Tafa (Roeder 1911: 211 pl. 93.a, 127.b) and at Khor Hanushiya (Roeder 1911: 215-16, pls. 94, 127.a; Weigall 1908: 68 pl. xxvii.4). At Aniba, opposite Ibrim, New Kingdom tombs were reused during the 25th Dynasty see Williams 1990: 34).

5. Smith 1976: 217; Caminos 1974: I, 57-60, 82-86, pls. 69-71, 99-102; II, 11, 54, pls. 13-14. New Kingdom tombs were re-used see Williams 1990: 47 n 46.

6. At Mirgissa 27 tombs of Third Intermediate-25th Dynasty date were exacavated: Geus in Vercoutter 1975: 479-501. Most notably a group of Sakhmet amulets in yellow and blue faience (Vercoutter 1975: 496, fig. 24.24, 25) is identical to a group from Sanam (Oxford Ash. Mus. 1921.712-713; Griffith 1923: pl. XXII.4).

7. The temple of Taharqo; Dunham and Janssen 1960: 12-13, pls 35-38 (lintel and altar), 32-45 plan VII (mud brick structure of same date); lintel and jambs, Khartoum SNM 449, Budge 1907 I: opp. 483. The cemetery contained re-used New Kingdom graves Dunham and Janssen 1960: 74-105, graves 500, 515, 520, 523, 552, 553.

8. The Taharqo blocks from WT1 were published by M. Schiff-Giorgini, *Kush* 13 (1965): 116-123, figs. 2-5; *Orientalia* 53 (1984) pls. 31-32; J.Leclant 'Taharqa à Sedeinga' *Studien zu Sprache und Religion Ägyptens* (Festschrift W. Westendorf), Göttingen 1984: 1113-20; A. Labrousse in C.Bonnet ed *Etudes Nubiennes (Conférence de Genève)* II (1994): 131-32.

9. For Kawa see principally Macadam 1949 (inscriptions) and 1955 (temple and other excavated remains of town). The altar of Taharqo found re-used in the Church of the Granite Columns at Dongola certainly came from Kawa (where no altar was found); Jakobielski and Krzyzaniak *Kush* 15 (1967-68): 161-62, pl. 32 a-b.

10. Ali Hakem 1988: 109-118.

11. Macadam 1955: 63-4, pls. I a-b, XLIX.

12. London BM EA 1770: Russmann 1974: 18, 50 no 18, fig 12; Wenig 1978: 50 fig. 24, 168 no. 77.

13. For the excavated remains of the temple see Jacquet Gordon *et al.* (*JEA* 55 (1969): 103-11) where it was suggested that the site of Tabo was to be identified with ancient Pnubs (an idea generally accepted), this was questioned by the discovery at Kerma of a priest of Pnubs (Bonnet and Valbelle *BIFAO* 80 (1980): 1-12 . There are other Napatan remains at Kerma; Bonnet *Genava*, ns 36 (1988): 19-20, VI; Bonnet and Mohamed Ahmed *Genava*, ns 32 (1984): 35-42, XVII-XX.

14. Griffith 1922 (temple and town), 1923 (cemetery).

15. Barque stand: Dunham 1970: 21 no 14 91 pl. 19 29.

16. Boston MFA 21.3096; Dunham 1970: 43 pl. XLVII.E; Russmann 1974: 59-60.

17. There are no new publications of the reliefs or architecture of the rock-cut temples at Gebel Barkal, but see the study of Christian Robisek, *Das Bildprogramm des Mut-Tempels am Gebel Barkal*, Beiträge zur Ägyptologie 8, Wien, 1989.

18. The earliest burials in the elite cemeteries are dated to the early 25th Dynasty. The Amun temple has close affinities with Barkal 500 and may have its origins in this period. Similarly

M 250 could be of 25th Dynasty origin. For a complete assessment of the archaeological material from Meroe and its interpretation see Török 1997: 15-40.

19. Gerharz 1994 (English summary: 329-342), see 145-85, Exkurs F, for imported beads and amulets.

XIX War

1. Kuhrt 1995.
2. see Grayson 1975: 8-28 for discussion of texts. The relevant text here is Chronicle 1 which covers the period from Nabu-nasir (747-734 BC) to Shamash-shuma-ukin (668-648 BC), see Grayson 1975: 69-87.
3. Grayson *CAH* III.2 (1992).
4. Simo Parpola, 'The murderer of Sennacherib' in B. Alster (ed) *Death in Mesopotamia* (Copenhagen 1980): 171-182.
5. *ANET*: 289-290 (9).
6. Many of these have been re-published in Starr 1990.
7. Grayson 1970: 82: Chronicle 1.iii. 40-42.
8. ND 2715: Saggs 1955: 127 no XII, a letter from Qurdi-Assur-lamur to the king, probably reign of Tiglathpileser III.
9. Mnm C Dog River Stela ll. 31-34: Borger 1956: 102; Zeissl 1944: 40f.
10. see Tadmor *BibAr* 29 (1966): 97ff.
11. Esarhaddon Chronicle 7 (Kitchen 1986 391 n.869 says uncertain whether 677 or 674) and Tadmor. *ANET*: 290a, b; Borger 1956: 33, 50-51, 86, 111B. For identification of Arza see Weissbach *ZA* 38 (1929): 108-110. Quotes from Heidel 1956:14, ll.57-63.
12. see inscriptions Borger 1956, 8 para 5:2 f; p.33:15; pp 48-50; p.101 para 66:25; p.111 para 72:13 p.111 para 74 iii 9, iv 7.
13. Chronicle 1.iv.6-7: Grayson 1970: 83.
14. cf. Borger 1956: 50, 32-34; 49f; 111 para 72 r.14; Heidel 1956; *ANET* 290-291 c.
15. *ANET* 533f and Parpola 1988.
16. *ANET*: 302b cf Grayson 1970: 84, Chronicle 1.iv.16.
17. BM 25091 (98-2-16, 145) published by Grayson 1970: 125-128, as Chronicle 14.
18. Chronicle 14.20: Grayson 1970: 126; Fecht 1968; Redford 1992.
19. The two stelae from Tell Ahmar in Aleppo Museum and the stela from Sam'al (Zenjirli) in Berlin, Vorderasiatische Museum, VA 2708: F. von Luschan, *Ausgrabungen in Sendchirli, I*, Berlin 1893: 11ff, 30ff Taf.I-V.
20. Every combination of the likely candidates has been suggested: Taharqo and Baal (by von Luschan); Taharqo and Abdimilkutti (by Unger); Ushanukhuru and Baal (by Weissbach; and Spalinger 1974a: 304 and n.39); and Ushanukhuru and Abdimilkutti (by Thureau-Dangin, *Syria* 10 (1929): 185-205 on 192). Helene von Zeissl (1944: 36) and Kenneth Kitchen (1986: § 353 and n.872) plump for Taharqo.
21. The most recent publication in Starr 1990: 94-97, nos. 81 and 82. see also no. 83.
22. Starr 1990: 104-105 no. 89.
23. Starr 1990: 98-104, no. 84, with fragments of similar texts, nos. 85, 86, 87, and no. 88.
24. ANET 292.
25. There is a possibility that this fragmentary text might refer, not to the crossing of Sinai, but to a campaign into Nubia itself; there is, as yet, no direct evidence to support this; see also Redford 1992: 360 and n 199.
26. BM 80-7-19,15: *ANET* 293:4. Redford 1992: 360 n 200 on the identity of Ishkhupri as "(Mansion of) Was-Khupri" to be associated with Sety II, which he locates near modern Faqus, ie in the vicinity of Per-Ramesses, but cf comments of Spalinger 1974: 302 n 37 on reading of name. Clearly the location depends on how many days were spent in battle and its preparation, rather than marching.
27. *ANET* 293.
28. Chronicle 1.iv.23-28: Grayson 1970: 85-86; cf Chronicle 14.25: Grayson 1970.
29. W.G. Lambert *Journal of Jewish Studies* 33 (1982): 61-70.
30. Chronicle 1.iv.27: ANET 303a.
31. BM 91-5-9, 218 Borger's Frt J see Oppenheim ANET 293f.
32. Fales and Postgate 1992, 32-34, No.24.
33. K 1577: Fales and Postgate 1992: 55-56, no.47.

34. The meaning of the Assyrian term, generally understood as 'eunuch' has been questioned by Stephanie Dalley.

35. Cairo JE 38018 (now in the Nubia Museum, Aswan): Wenig 1978: 172 no 83; Aldred 1980: 219-220, fig 183.

36. *Jeremiah* 38.7-13.

37. Parpola 1993: 91-93 (no. 112), for dating and discussion Parpola 1983.

XX Assyria in Egypt

1. On Assyrian policy in Egypt see Spalinger 1974 and Onasch 1994. Many other writers gloss over this period, referring primarily to the installation of, or resistance by, the Libyan dynasts (eg Kitchen 1986: 392-93; James 1991).

2. The Rassam Cylinder (with parallel text of Prism A): Luckenbill 1927, 293-94; *ANET* 295; Spalinger 1974a; 1974b; Onasch 1994: 30-59, 116-23.

3. Fecht 1958; Kitchen 1986: 395-97.

4. Leahy 1983. For the location of Natho see Kitchen 1986: 397 n 906; perhaps near Tell el-Yahudiyeh or Leontopolis.

5. He is Bakennefi 'C' of Kitchen 1986, 'II' of Spalinger 1974; a statue of him Cairo 22-10-48-16 was published by Habachi 1957 along with other monuments; see also Yoyotte 1961: 161-65, 173-79; and Vittmann 'Zur Familie der Fürsten von Athribis in der Spätzeit', *SAK* 10 (1983): 333-39.

6. For Pedubast 'II' see L.Habachi in *ZÄS* 93 (1966): 69-74; A.R.Schulman 'A problem of Pedubasts' *JARCE* 5 (1966): 33-41; Kitchen 1986: 396. For Djedu (Busiris) and its rulers see Yoyotte 1961: 126 no 23, 165-66; Gomaà 1974: 63-7.

7. Priese 1970: 19 n 18 identifies Punubu with Per-neb, part of the territory of Piye's opponent (Victory Stela, line 3). He equates Per-neb with el Santa where a statue of a Tefnakht of the reign of Psamtik I was discovered in 1968. Priese makes this Tefnakht 'III' a brother of Nekau I. Yoyotte understood the Assyrian Punubu as 'Per-Inbu' (cf Kitchen 1986: 397 n 908). Priese identifies Bukurninip of Pahnuti of the Assyrian list as a Bakenranef - 'Bocchoris II' suggesting him to have been a son of Tefnakht 'II' and brother of Nechepsos/Nekauba.

8. Fecht 1958.

9. Amongst those who assume a Nimlot 'II': Fecht 1958; Kitchen 1986: 397.

10. Fecht (1958: 114-16) identified Taini with Aswan, but see Leahy 1979; also De Meulenaere *CdE* 53-4 (1978) 230-31.

11. Leahy 1979; Graefe 1981:41-2.

12. Leclant 1961; for recent work in the tomb of Monthuemhat see Russmann in *JARCE* 31 (1994): 1-19; *JARCE* 32 (1995): 117-26; and *JARCE* 34 (1997): 21-39.

13. Spalinger 1974a: 314-16.

14. Because of his titles, Ankh-Sheshonq father of Pediese, is said by Kitchen (1986: 236 n 178) to have been a Theban priest, but cf the comments of Leahy 1992:150, 21a-b.

15. Starr 1990: 102-104, no 88.

16. Chronicle 1.iv.29; Chronicle 14.27; Chronicle 15.11: Grayson 1970: 86, 127, 129. cf *JCS* 18 (1964):12 ii 15.

17. Hunger 1992: 281 no 505 [80-7-19,63; RMA 44] dated to Mar 29 668.

18. The Rassam Cylinder (Luckenbill 1927: 290-323) was compiled in the eponymy of Shamash-dan-inanni, following Assurbanipal's 9th campaign; see Spalinger 1974.

19. Apis buried year 24, 4 *Peret*, day 23: Vercoutter 1960: 71; Malinine *et al.* 1968 I: 99-103, 122-24, nos 125-28, 158-60. Vercoutter assumed the bull's age at "about 20 years". The successor was installed in year 26 and died in year 20, 4 *Shomu* day 20 of Psamtik I aged 21 years. This bull was the first recipient of an official stela (IM 3733: Parker in *Kush* 8 1960: 268, pl. 38; Malinine *et al.*1968 I: 146 no 192, pl. 52 with private stelae nos 193-262 on pp 146-192). This burial is one of the decisive chronological links between the 25th and 26th Dynasties. The few minor problems are discussed by Vercoutter (1960: 72-76) and Kitchen (1986: 161-63).

20. The Cylinder B cf Thompson *Iraq* 7 1941: 103 f no 104 on pl 14 and no 25 on pl 15.

XXI The Osiris Taharqo

1. Principally Dunham 1955, with many individual objects in the exhibition catalogues *Africa in Antiquity* (Wenig 1978) and *Sudan* (Wildung 1996).

2. see n 8 to Chap XVIII above.
3. See the generally judicious survey of T.G.H.James 1991: 738-47. For a balance to Redford's (1992: 345 and n.125) arguments for a western Delta (principally Saite) origin in the late Libyan period see the reasoned judgement of Leahy 1992: 234-39. While, as Leahy comments, the late Libyan period is no longer seen as the artistic nadir claimed by an earlier generation, there is much art historical research still to be done. The problems surrounding the political-historical framework do not aid appraisals of artistic development. On the terms *archaising* and *archaistic* see Bothmer 1960: xxxvii-viii.
4. James 1991: 742.
5. Bothmer 1960: xxxviii; Aldred 1980: 219; James 1991: 745.
6. All that survives of this statue is the base and feet. This fragment is, however, closely similar to the almost complete statue of Queen Amanimalel from Barkal (Khartoum SNM 1843: Dunham 1970: 21 no 9, pls. XVII-VIII; Wildung 1996: 222-23 no. 231). Just as the statues of Taharqo found at Barkal had their Egyptian parallels and served as prototypes for later royal images, so undoubtedly there were statues of Kushite queens in Egypt and Kush which were also copied later.
7. Hall 1925; on architecture in the 25th Dynasty see Leclant 1965: 199-228.
8. The rock crystal amulet with Hathor head: Wenig 1978: 180 no 93. For the pebbles from the tomb of Khensa see p 177 and n. 29 to Chap XII above. The cloisonne ram: Wenig 1978: 180 no. 94. A ram on greenstone column: Wildung 1996: 180 no. 172.
9. Winged goddess of Kushite type: Wenig 1978: 187-188 no. 104; Kendall 1982:31 no. 27; similar with lioness head, Wenig 1978: 186 no. 103; Egyptian and Kushite types, Wildung 1996: 182-183: nos. 178-181;
10. The Kushite regalia is discussed in detail by Russmann 1974 and her further comments in *Meroitica* 5 (1979): 49-53; see also the valuable study of Leahy 1992.
11. Macadam 1955: pl LXIV, e, f-g; Queen Tekahatamani in B 300, Robisek 1989 (n. 17 to Chap. XVIII above): 114; for the reliefs of B 700 see Griffith 1929; stela of princess Amenirdis, Habachi 1977.
12. Russmann (1974: 57-69, Appendix II) catalogues the known bronze images of kings of this period, cf the comments on 12-13, 19-21, figs. 1, 14-20, 25-26. For the image of Taharqo with Hemen see Russmann 1974: 19-20.
13. Aldred 1980: 222-23, Smith and Simpson 1981: 411, fig. 405.
14. The use of Egyptian (specifically Theban) religious and astonomical texts in the Napatan burials is discussed by Susan Doll in *Meroitica* 6 (1982): 276-80 and Janice Yellin in *Meroitica* 7 (1984): 577-82. Parker, Leclant and Goyon 1979: 84-86 discuss the theology of Amun in the edifice of Taharqo by the sacred lake at Karnak. Although they are reticent in accrediting this to a "new" theology created under the Kushite pharaohs, it is clear that the period sees some very significant religious developments parallel to its artistic and literary inspiration.
15. For Taniy see M.A.Leahy 'A Seventh century lady (Cairo CG 20564 + Vienna 192)' *GM* 108 (1989): 45-55; for Abydos stelae see Munro 1973 (and here fig 112).
16. James 1991: 738-41. For economic texts see Malinine 1953; 1983 and in *RdE* 6 (1951): 157-78; *RdE* 34 (1983-84): 93-100; Menu *JEA* 74 (1988) 165-81; 1989.
17. Spalinger1979.
18. For royal women see Morkot 1999.
19. Brother succession was argued in detail by Macadam 1949, Appendix; followed by eg Adams 1977; Kitchen 1986; T.G.H. James 1991. A matrilineal system was argued by Priese 1981 but is not generally accepted (see O'Connor 1983; Török 1999) The whole issue was discussed in great detail by Morkot 1999 and the contributing papers of E. Kormysheva and L.Török.

XXII The triumph of Sau

1. Luckenbill 1927: §§ 775-8; *ANET* 295.
2. Cairo JE 48863: Grimal 1981: pls I-IV; the most recent English language translation is *FHN* I:193-207, no 29.
3. Morkot 1999: 210-214.
4. For the Assyrian texts see Luckenbill 1927: 295 § 775; 351 § 906; 366 § 944; 405 § 1117; *Onasch* 1994. Macadam (1949, 124-25) argued for the emendation, and has generally

been followed (see Kitchen 1986, 150). Leahy 1984b has argued in favour of following the Assyrian texts.

5. The co-regency was argued by Schäfer *ZÄS 35* (1897): 67-70 and accepted by Zeissl 1944: 48. Kitchen (1986, 173) and Murnane (1977, 193-96, 236) have observed that there is no decisive evidence, but that it would have lasted no more than a few months.

6. Herodotos 2.152.1, states that Psamtik fled from *Sabakos*, to Syria.

7. The Rassam Cylinder, Luckenbill 1927: 295-96 §§ 776-78, with parallel and abbreviated texts of Prisms C, E, and building tablets §§ 877, 892, 894, 906-08. Also Spalinger 1976; Onasch 1994.

8. *Nahum* 3, 8-10.

9. W.M.F. Petrie, *Six Temples at Thebes, 1896* (1897).

10. Installation texts dated to years 4 and 9: Vittmann, *SAK* 10 (1983) 327, 329 n 11.

11. The process, not clearly documented, probably saw the reduction in status of dynasts (or perhaps their successors) to the rank of 'Mayors' see Yoyotte 1961; Spalinger 1976.

12. Burstein1984.

13. Caminos 1964.

14. Benson and Gourlay 1899, 257-58 and plates. The presence of the "ship of Piye" in the flotilla has caused some confusion in the dating of the reliefs, and an attribution by Benson and Gourlay to the early 25th Dynasty. The blocks certainly belong to scenes depicting the arrival and installation of Neitiqert, see Kitchen 1986: 236-39 with discussion and bibliography.

15. Caminos 1964, 75, lines 15-17.

16. Caminos 1964, 74, lines 2-3.

17. The death of Neitiqert is recorded on the stela of Ankhnasneferibre, see A.Leahy 'The adoption of Ankhnasneferibre at Karnak' *JEA* 82 (1996), 145-65.

18. Habachi 1977 published a stela in Cairo depicting the princess and her husband, and other monuments of the couple. The identification of this Amenirdis with the Divine adoratrix has been widely accepted (eg Vittmann 1978, 145; cf comments of Leclant *LdÄ* VI, 182 n 234). It seems more likely that the wife of the Vizier Monthuhotep was not daughter of Taharqo, but perhaps of Shabaqo, Morkot 1993: 371-72.

19. Cairo JE 48866 Grimal 1981b pls V-VII recent English language translation *FHN* I, 232-44; the genealogy and its interpretation was discussed by Morkot 1999:196-200.

BIBLIOGRAPHY

Abbreviations for periodicals and series

ASAE	*Annales du Service des Antiquités de l'Égypte*. Cairo.
BIFAO	*Bulletin de l'Institut française d'Archéologie orientale du Caire*. Cairo.
BzS	*Beiträge zur Sudanforschung*. Vienna.
CdE	*Chronique d'Égypte*. Brussels.
CRIPEL	*Cahiers de Recherches de l'Institut de Papyrologie et d'Égyptologie de Lille*.
FHN	*Fontes Historiae Nubiorum*. Bergen
GM	*Göttinger Miszellen*. Göttingen.
JARCE	*Journal of the American Research Centre in Egypt*. Cairo.
JEA	*Journal of Egyptian Archaeology*. London.
JNES	*Journal of Near Eastern Studies*. Chicago.
Kush	*Journal of the Sudan Antiquities Organization*. Khartoum.
LdÄ	*Lexicon der Ägyptologie*.
LAAA	*Annals of Archaeology and Anthropology*. Liverpool
MDAIK	*Mitteilungen des Deutschen Archäologischen Instituts, Abteilung Kairo*.
SAA	*State Archives of Assyria*. Helsinki.
SAK	*Studien zur Altägyptischen Kultur*. Hamburg.
SSEAJ	*Journal of the Society for the Study of Egyptian Antiquities*. Toronto.
ZÄS	*Zeitschrift für Ägyptische Sprache und Altertumskunde*. Berlin (old abbreviation *ÄZ*).

Abdalla, Abdelgadir M.
1989 Meroitic Kush, Abyssinia and Arabia. A contribution to the Hauptreferat: L. Török, Kush and the external world. *Studia Meroitica 1984* (= *Meroitica* 10: 383-387).

Adams, William Y.
1964 Post-pharaonic Nubia in the light of archaeology, 1. *JEA* 50: 102-120.
1977 *Nubia: corridor to Africa*. Princeton University Press.
1985 Doubts about the lost pharaohs. *JNES* 44: 185-192.

Aldred, C.
1979 More light on the Ramesside tomb robberies in J.Ruffle, G.A.Gaballa and K.A.Kitchen eds. *Glimpses of Ancient Egypt. Studies in honour of H.W. Fairman*. Warminster, 92-99.
1980 *Egyptian art*. London.

Ali Hakem, A.M.
1988 *Meroitic architecture. A background of an African civilization*. Khartoum.

Andrae, Walter
1977 *Das wiedererstandene Assur*. Munich (reprint of 1st edn. Leipzig 1938).

Arkell, Anthony J.
1950 Varia Sudanica. *JEA* 36: 24-42.

Aston, David A.
1989 Takeloth II - a king of the 'Theban Twenty-third Dynasty'? *JEA* 75: 139-153.

Aston, David A. and Taylor, John H.
1990 The family of Takeloth III and the 'Theban' Twenty-third Dynasty, in Leahy ed. 1990: 131-154.

Benson, Margaret and Gourlay, Janet
1899 *The Temple of Mut in Asheru*. London.

Bernal, Martin

1987   *Black Athena*. London.

1989.   Response to Professor Snowden. *Arethusa* Special Fall Issue: 30-32.

Bierbrier, Morris L.

1975.   *The Late New Kingdom in Egypt (c.1300-664 B.C.)*, Warminster.

Bietak, Manfred

1968   *Studien zur Chronologie der nubischen C-Gruppe: Ein beitrag zur Frühgeschichte Unternubiens zwischen 2200 und 1550 vor Chr*. Vienna.

1987   The C-Group and Pan-Grave culture in Nubia, in Hägg ed. *(1987)*: 113-128.

Bonnet, Charles

1987   Kerma, royaume africaine de Haute Nubie, in Hägg ed. (1987): 87-111.

1990   *Kerma, royaume de Nubie*, Genè ve.

Borger, R.

1956   *Die Inschriften Asarhaddons, Königs von Assyrien* (AfO Beiheft 9). Graz.

Bothmer, B.V.

1960   *Egyptian sculpture of the Late Period*. The Brooklyn Museum, New York.

Breasted, James H.

1905   *A history of Egypt from the earliest times to the Persian conquest*. (2nd edn London 1927*)*.

Brugsch, Heinrich (translated by Mary Brodrick)

1891   *Egypt under the Pharaohs. A history derived entirely from the monuments*. London.

Burstein, Stanley M.

1984   Psamtek I and the end of the Nubian domination of Egypt. *SSEAJ* 14: 31-34.

Caminos, Ricardo A.

1958   *The Chronicle of Prince Osorkon*. Analecta Orientalia, 37. Rome.

1964   The Nitocris Adoption Stele. *JEA* 50: 71-101.

1994   Notes on Queen Katimala's inscribed panel in the temple of Semna in *Hommages à Jean Leclant. vol. 2 Nubie, Soudan, Ethiopie. IFAO Bib. d'Étude* 106/2. Le Caire. 73-80.

1998   *Semna-Kumma I The Temple of Semna*. London.

Celenko, Theodore, ed.

1996   *Egypt in Africa* Indianapolis Museum of Art in cooperation with Indiana University Press.

Cerny, Jaroslav

1965   Egypt from the death of Ramesses III to the end of the Twenty-first Dynasty. *CAH* 2nd edn II-chapter 35.

Dalley, Stephanie

1985   Foreign chariotry and cavalry in the armies of Tiglath-pileser III and Sargon II. *Iraq* 47: 31-48.

Davies, W.V. ed.

1991   *Egypt and Africa. Nubia from prehistory to Islam*. London.

Depuydt, Leo

1993   The date of Piye's Egyptian campaign and the chronology of the Twenty-fifth Dynasty. *JEA* 79: 269-274.

Dewachter, Michel

1976   Un fonctionnaire préposé aux marches méridionales à l'époque d'Amenophis II: (Pa)-Hekaemsasen. *CRIPEL* 4, 53-60

Drews, Robert

1993   *The end of the Bronze Age. Changes in warfare and the catastrophe ca. 1200 B.C.* Princeton University Press.

Dunham, Dows

1950   *Royal cemeteries of Kush. I. el Kurru*. Cambridge, Mass.

1955   *Royal cemeteries of Kush. II. Nuri*. Boston.

1967   *Second Cataract Forts II: Uronarti, Shalfak, Mirgissa*. Boston.

1970   *The Barkal temples*. Boston.

Dunham, Dows and Janssen, J.M.A.

1960   *Second Cataract Forts I. Semna Kumma*. Boston.

Dunham, Dows and Macadam, M.F.Laming

1949   Names and relationships of the royal family of Napata. *JEA* 35: 139-149.

Eigner, D.

1984   *Die monumentalen Grabbauten der Spätzeit in der thebanischen Nekropole*. Vienna.

Emery, W.Bryan

1948   *Nubian Treasure. An account of the discoveries at Ballana and Qustul.* London.

1965   *Egypt in Nubia* [USA edn. *Lost land emerging*, 1967].

Emery, W.B., Smith, H.S., Millard, A.

1979   *Buhen: the archaeological report.* London.

Eph'al, I.

1982   *The ancient Arabs. Nomads on the borders of the fertile crescent 9th-5th centuries B.C.* The Magnes Press, the Hebrew University, Jerusalem. E.J.Brill, Leiden.

Erman, Adolf

1892   Historische Nachlese 3. Eine äthiopische Königin, *ZÄS* 30: 47-49.

Fales F.M. and J.N. Postgate

1992   *Imperial administrative records, part I. Palace and temple administration. SAA.* 7. Helsinki University Press.

Fecht, Gerhard

1958   Zu den Namen ägyptischer Fürsten und Städte in den Annalen des Assurbanipal und der Chronik des Asarhaddon. *MDAIK* 16: 112ff.

Firth, Cecil M.

1927   *Archaeological survey of Nubia: Report for 1910-11.* Cairo.

Fischer, Henry G.

1961   The Nubian mercenaries of Gebelein during the First Intermediate Period. *Kush* 9: 44-80.

Frame, Grant

1999   The inscription of Sargon II at Tang-i Var. *Orientalia* 68: 31-57.

Frandsen, Paul

1979   Egyptian imperialism. in M.T.Larsen ed., *Power and Propaganda. A Symposium on ancient empires* (= *Mesopotamia* 7), Copenhagen. pp.167-190.

Gardiner, Alan H.

1961   *Egypt of the Pharaohs.* Oxford.

Gerharz, Rudolf

1994   *Jebel Moya.* (*Meroitica* 14). Berlin.

Goedicke, Hans

1972   Review of Dunham 1970 in *AJA* 89.

1981   The campaign of Psammetik II against Nubia. *MDAIK* 37: 187-198.

Gomaà, Farouk

1974   *Die libyschen Fürstentümer des Deltas vom Tod Osorkons II. bis zur Wiedereinigung Ägyptens durch Psametik I. TAVO* Reihe B, Nr.6. Wiesbaden.

Graefe, Erhart

1981   *Untersuchungen zur Verwaltung und Geschichte der Institution der Gottesgemahlin des Amun vom Beginn des Neuen Reiches bis zur Spätzeit. ÄA* 37. Wiesbaden.

Grapow, Hermann

1940   Die Inschrift der Königin Katimala am Tempel von Semne. *ZÄS* 76, 24-41.

Grayson, A.Kirk

1975   *Assyrian and Babylonian chronicles.* Texts from Cuneiform sources. vol V. Locust Valley, NY.

1982   Assyria: Ashur-dan II to Ashur-nirari V (934-745 B.C.) *CAH III*.1 238-281.

Griffith, Francis Ll.

1922   Oxford excavations in Nubia. [Sanam] *LAAA* 9: 67-124.

1923   Oxford excavations in Nubia: xviii. the cemetery of Sanam. *LAAA* 10: 73-171.

1929   Scenes from a destroyed temple at Napata. *JEA* 15: 26-28.

Grimal, Nicholas-C.

1981a   *Le stèle triomphale de Pi(ankh).* Cairo. *MIFAO* 105, Cairo.

1981b   *Quatre stèles napatéens au Musée du Caire.* JE49963-48866. *MIFAO* 106, Cairo.

Grzymski, Kryzstof

1997   The Debba Bend in the New Kingdom. *Warsaw Egyptological Studies* I: 93-100.

Habachi, Labib

1977   Mentuhotep, the Vizier and son-in-law of Taharqa, in E. Endesfelder *et al.* eds. *Ägypten und Kusch. Schriften zur Geschichte und Kultur des Alten Orients* 13 (Fs.F. Hintze).Berlin.

1980   The military posts of Ramesses II on the coastal road and the western part of the Delta. *BIFAO* 80: 13-30.

1981   *Sixteen Studies on Lower Nubia. ASAE* Cahier 23.

Hägg, Tomas, ed.

1987 *Nubian culture past and present*. [= Konferenser 17] Stockholm.

Hall, H.R.

1925 The Ethiopians and Assyrians in Egypt. *CAH* 1st edn III: 270-288.

Heidel, Alexander

1956 A new hexagonal prism of Esarhaddon (676 BC). *Sumer* 12, 9-37.

Heidorn, Lisa A.

1994 Historical implications of the pottery from the earliest tombs at El Kurru. *JARCE* 31: 115-20.

Hintze, F.

1973 Meroitic chronology: problems and prospects. *Sudan im Altertum* (= *Merotica* 1). Berlin: 127-44.

Hintze, F. and W.-F. Reineke

1989 *Felsinschriften aus dem Sudanesischen Nubien*. Berlin.

Hodjash, S.I. and O. Berlev

1982 *The Egyptian reliefs and stelae in the Pushkin Museum of Fine Arts, Moscow*. Leningrad.

Horton, Mark

1991 Africa in Egypt: new evidence from Qasr Ibrim. In Davies, W.V. ed., 1991: 264-277.

Hoskins, George

1835 *Travels in Ethiopia, above the Second Cataract of the Nile; exhibiting the state of that country, and & its various inhabitants under the dominion of Mohammed Ali; and illustrating the antiquities, arts, and history of the ancient kingdom of Meroe*. London.

Hunger, H.

1992 *Astrological reports to Assyrian Kings*. SAA 8. Helsinki.

Jacquet-Gordon, Helen

1982 Review of W.Y. Adams, *Meroitic North and South* (= *Meroitica* 2) *OLZ* 77: 451-454.

James et al.

Peter J.James, I.J.Thorpe, Nikos Kokkinos, Robert G.Morkot, John A.Frankish

1991 *Centuries of Darkness*. London. (American edition: Rutgers University Press, 1993).

James, T.G.H.

1991 Egypt: the twenty-fifth and twenty-sixth dynasties. *CAH* III.2. Chapter 35.

Jansen-Winkeln, Karl

1992 Das Ende des Neuen Reiches. *ZÄS* 119, 22-37.

1995 Historische probleme der 3.Zwischenzeit. *JEA* 81, 129-149.

Janssen, Jac J.

1968 The lesser Dakhla Stela *JEA* 54

Kemp, Barry J.

1978 Imperialism and empire in New Kingdom Egypt (c.1575-1087 BC). in P.D.A. Garnsey and C.R.Whittaker eds., *Imperialism in the ancient world*. Cambridge 1978. pp. 7-57.

Kendall, Timothy

1982 *Kush, Lost kingdom of the Nile*. Brockton, Mass.

1997 *Kerma and the kingdom of Kush, 2500-1500 BC*. Washington, D.C.

1999 The origin of the Napatan State: el Kurru and the evidence for the Royal ancestors. *Studien zum antiken Sudan* (= Meroitica 15): 3-117. Berlin.

Kessler, Dieter

1981 Zu den Feldzügen des Tefnachte, Namlot und Pije in Mittelägypten. *SAK* 9: 227-51.

Kitchen, Kenneth A.

1986 *The Third Intermediate Period in Egypt (1100-650 BC)*. Warminster. (1st edn. 1973).

1990 The arrival of the Libyans in late New Kingdom Egypt, in Leahy ed 1990, 15-27.

Kozloff, A.P. and Bryan, B.M.

1992 *Egypt's dazzling sun. Amenhotep III and his world*. Cleveland Museum of Art and Indiana University Press.

Kuhrt, Amélie T.L.

1987 Usurpation, conquest and ceremonial: from Babylon to Persia, in D. Cannadine and S. Price *Rituals of royalty. Power and ceremonial in traditional socities*. Cambridge, 20-55

1995 *The Ancient Near East c.3000-330 BC*. London and New York.

Kwasman, Theodore

1988 *Neo-Assyrian legal documents in the Kouyunjik collection of the British Museum*. Studia Pohl: Series Maior 14. Roma.

Lacovara, Peter
1987   The internal chronology of Kerma. *BzS* 2: 51-74.
1991   The stone vase deposit at Kerma. in Davies ed *Egypt and Africa*: 118-128.
Leahy, M.Anthony
1979   Nespamedu, "King" of Thinis. *GM* 35: 31-39.
1984   The name P3-wrm. *GM* 76: 17-23.
1984   Tanutamon, son of Shabako? *GM* 83: 43-45.
1985   The Libyan Period in Egypt: an essay in interpretation. *Libyan Studies* 16: 51-65.
1990   Abydos in the Libyan Period, in Leahy ed., 1990: 155-200.
1992   Royal iconography and dynastic change, 750-525 BC: the blue and cap crowns. *JEA* 78, 223-240.
1995   Kushite monuments at Abydos. *The Unbroken Reed. Studies in the culture and heritage of ancient Egypt in honour of A.F.Shore* (London): 171-92.
Leahy, A. ed
1990   *Libya and Egypt c1300-750 BC*. SOAS/The Society for Libyan Studies, London.
Leclant, Jean
1954   *Enquêtes sur les sacerdoces et les santuaires égyptiens à l'époque dite <éthiopiennes> (XXVᵉ Dynastie)*. Cairo, IFAO BE 17.
1961   *Montouemhat. Quatrième prophète d'Amon, prince de ville*. Cairo. IFAO BE 35.
1962   Deux monuments de la reine Kensa. *Kush* 10: 203-210.
1963   Kashta, pharaon en Egypte. *ZÄS* 98: 16-32.
1965   *Recherches sur les monuments thébains de la XXVᵉ dynastie dite Ethiopienne*. Cairo.
Leclant, J. and Yoyotte, J.
1949   Nouveaux documents relatifs à l'an VI de Taharqa. *Kêmi* 10: 28.
1952   Notes d'histoire et de civilisation éthiopiennes. A propos d'un ouvrage récent. *BIFAO* 51: 1-39.
Lefkowitz, Mary R. and Guy M.Rogers, eds.
1996   *Black Athena revisited*. The University of North Carolina Press.
Lichtheim, Miriam
1973   *Ancient Egyptian Literature. A book of readings. vol 1: The Old and Middle Kingdoms*. University of California Press. Berkeley, California and London.-
1976   *Ancient Egyptian Literature. A book of readings. vol 2: The New Kingdom*. University of California Press. Berkeley, California and London.-
1980   *Ancient Egyptian Literature. A book of readings. vol 3: The Late Period*. University of California Press. Berkeley, California and London.
Lie, A.G.
1929   *The inscriptions of Sargon II, King of Assyria. Part I. The annals*. Paris.
Linant de Bellefonds, L.M.A.
1958   *Journal d'un voyage à Méroé dans les années 1821 et 1822*. ed. Margaret Shinnie. *Sudan Antiquities Service, Occasional Papers No. 4*. Khartoum.
Liverani, Mario
1987   The collapse of the Near Eastern regional system at the end of the Bronze Age: the case of Syria. In Rowlands, M., M.T.Larsen, and K.Kristiansen, eds *Centre and periphery in the ancient world*. Cambridge: 66-73.
Lloyd, Seton
1980   *Foundations in the dust*. London.
Loukianoff, Gr.
1926   Nouveaux fragments de la stèle de Piankhi. *Ancient Egypt* 11: 86-89.
Luckenbill, D.D.
1927   *Ancient records of Assyria and Babylonia*. Chicago.
Macadam, M.F.Laming
1949   *The temples of Kawa. I. The inscriptions*. London.
1955   *The temples of Kawa. II. History and archaeology of the site*. London.
Malinine, M.
1953   *Choix de textes juridiques en hiératique 'anormal' et en démotique (XXV-XXVII Dynasties)*. Paris.
1983   *Choix de textes juridiques en hiératique 'anormal' et en démotique (deuxième partie)*. Cairo.
Malinine, M., G. Posener an J. Vercoutter
1968   *Catalogue des stèles du Sérapeum de Memphis*. Paris.

Menu, Bernadette

1989 Women and business life in Egypt in the first millenium BC in B. Lesko (ed) *Women's earliest records: from ancient Egypt to Western Asia:* 193-205. Atlanta.

Mitchell, Terence C.

1982 Israel and Judah until the revolt of Jehu (931-841 B.C.) and Israel and Judah from Jehu until the period of Assyian domination. *CAH* III.1 442-510.

Mohamed Ahmed, Salah el-Din

1992 *L'agglomération napatéene de Kerma. Enquête archéologique et ethnographique en milieu urbain.* Paris.

Mohamed Aly, Fouad Abdel-Hamid and M. Dewachter

1967 *Le Temple d'Amada.* IV. Centre de Documentation et d'Etudes sur l'ancienne Egypt. Le Caire.

Montet, Pierre

1966 *Le lac sacré de Tanis.* Paris.

Moorhead, Alan

1972 *The Blue Nile.* Harmondsworth.

Moran, W.L.

1992 *The Amarna Letters.* Johns Hopkins University Press, Baltimore and London.

Morkot, Robert G.

1991a Nubia in the New Kingdom: the limits of Egyptian control in Davies, W.V. ed 1991: 294-301.

1991b H. Sancisi-Weerdenburg and A. Kuhrt eds., *Achaemenid History VI. Asia Minor and Egypt: Old cultures in a new empire:* 321-336.

1993 Economic and cultural exchange between Kush and Egypt, PhD dissertation. University of London (unpublished).

1994 The Nubian Dark Age. in Bonnet ed *Etudes Nubiennes* (Genève) II: 45-47.

1995 The economy of Nubia in the New Kingdom. *Actes de la VIIIe Conférence internationale des études nubiennes. I. Communications principales. CRIPEL* 17: 175-189.

1995 The foundations of the Kushite state. *Actes de la VIIIe Conférence internationale des études nubiennes. I. Communications principales. CRIPEL* 17: 175-189.

1999 Kingship and kinship in the empire of Kush. *Studien zum antiken Sudan* (= *Meroitica* 15): 179-229.

Munro, P.

1973 *Die spätägyptischen Totenstelen. Äg. Forschungen* 25. Gluckstadt.

Nordström, Hans-Ake

1972 *Neolithic and A-Group Sites.* SJE 3:1. Uppsala-Lund.

O'Connor, David

1986 The locations of Yam and Kush and their historical implications. *JARCE* 23: 27-50.

1987 The location of Irem. *JEA* 73: 99-136.

1990 The nature of Tjehemu (Libyan) society in the later New Kingdom, in Leahy ed. 1990 29-113.

1991 *Early states along the Nubian Nile,* in Davies, W.V. ed, 1991: 145-165.

1993 *Ancient Nubia. Egypt's rival in Africa.* The University Museum of archaeology and Anthropology. University of Pennsylvania. Philadelphia.

Onasch, Hans-Ulrich

1994 *Die Assyrischen Eroberungen Ägyptens. ÄAT (Ägypten und Altes Testament)* 27/1. Wiesbaden.

Parker, Richard A.

1962 *A Saite Oracle Papyrus from Thebes.* Providence.

Parker, R.A., J. Leclant, and J.-C. Goyon

1979 *The edifice of Taharqa by the Sacred Lake of Karnak.* Providence and London.

Parpola, Simo

1970 *Letters from Assyrian scholars to the Kings Esarhaddon and Assurbanipal.* Part I: Texts. AOAT 5/1. Neukirchen-Vluyn.

1983 *Letters from Assyrian scholars to the Kings Esarhaddon and Assurbanipal. Part II: Commentary and appendices.* AOAT 5/2. Neukirchen-Vluyn.

Parpola, S. and K. Watanabe,

1988 *Neo-Assyrian treaties and loyalty oaths.* SAA 2. Helsinki.

Petrie, W.M.F.

1905 *A History of Egypt from the XIXth to the XXXth Dynasties.* London.

Pfeiffer, R.H.

1935 *State-letters of Assyria. A transliteration and translation of 355 official Assyrian letters dating from the Sargonid Period 722-626 BC.* American Oriental Series vol 6. New Haven, Connecticut.

Pick, Daniel

1989   *Faces of degeneration: a European disorder, c.1848-c.1918*, Cambridge.

Pitard, W.T.

1987   *Ancient Damascus. A historical study of the Syrian city-state from the earliest times until its fall to the Assyrians in 732 B.C.E.* Winona Lake, Indiana.

Posener, G.

1940   *Princes et pays d'Asie et de Nubie.* Bruxelles.

Postgate, Nicholas J.

1974   *Taxation and conscription in the Assyrian empire. Studia Pohl: Series maior* 3. Roma.

Priese, Karl-Heinz

1970   Der Beginn der kuschitischen Herrschaft in Ägypten. *ZÄS* 98: 16-32.

1977   Eine verschollene Bauinschrift des frühmeroitischen Königs Aktisanes (?) vom Gebel Barkal, in E. Endesfelder *et al.* eds. *Ägypten und Kusch. Schriften zur Geschichte und Kultur des Alten Orients* 13: (Fs. F. Hintze): 343-67. Berlin.

1981   Matrilineare Erbfolge im Reich von Napata. *ZÄS* 108: 49-53.

Redford, Donald B.

1985   Sais and the kushite invasions of the eighth century BC. *JARCE* 22: 5-15.

1992   *Egypt, Canaan, and Israel in ancient times.* Princeton.

1999   A note on the chronology of dynasty 25 and the inscription of Sargon II at Tang-i Var. *Orientalia* 68: 58-60.

Reisner, George

1920   The Viceroys of Ethiopia. *JEA* 6: 28-55.

1923   Kerma Parts I-III *Harvard African Studies* vol 5; and Parts IV-V *Harvard African Studies*, vol. 6.

1931   Inscribed monuments from Gebel Barkal. *ZÄS* 66: 76-100.

Reisner, G.A. and M.B.Reisner,

1933   Inscribed monuments from Gebel Barkal. 2 The granite stela of Thutmosis III. *ZÄS* 69: 24-39.

Richardson, Arzinia

1990   Nefertiti was black. *Biblical Archaeology Review* 16 (2): 67, 70.

Roberts, Alison M.

1995   *Hathor rising. The serpent power of ancient Egypt.* Northgate Press.

Russell, Michael

1833   *Nubia and Abyssinia: comprehending their civil history, antiquities, arts, religion, literature, and natural history.* 2nd edn.Edinburgh and London.

Russmann, E.R.

1974   *The representation of the king in the XXVth Dynasty.* MRE 3. Bruxelles-Brooklyn.

1997   Mentuemhat's Kushite wife (further remarks on the decoration of the Tomb of Mentuemhat, 2).-*JARCE* 34: 21-39.

Ruszczyk, Barbara

1977   Taharqa à Tell Atrib, in E. Endesfelder *et al.* eds. *Ägypten und Kusch. Schriften zur Geschichte und Kultur des Alten Orients* 13 (Fs. F. Hintze). Berlin: 391-95.

Säve-Söderbergh, Torgny

1941   *Ägypten und Nubien.* Lund.

1960   The paintings in the tomb of Djehutyhetep at Debeira. *Kush* 8: 25-44.

1963   The tomb of the prince of Teh-khet. *Kush* 11: 159-174.

1987   *Temples and Tombs of ancient Nubia.* UNESCO Paris and London.

1991   Te-khet, the cultural and sociopolitical stucture of a nubian princedom in Tuthmoside times, in Davies ed. 1991: 186-194.

Säve-Söderbergh, T. and Lana Troy,

1991   *New Kingdom pharaonic sites* SJE 5:2. Copenhagen, Oslo, Stockholm and Helsinki.

Saggs, H.W.F.

1955   The Nimrud Letters, 1952 - Part II: Relations with the West. *Iraq* 17: 126ff.

Sauneron, S. and Yoyotte, J.

1950   La campagne nubienne de Psammétique II et sa signification historique. *BIFAO* 50: 157-207.

Shinnie, Peter L.

1955   A note on Ast-Reset. *JEA*: 128-29.

1967   *Meroe. A civilization of the Sudan.* (Ancient peoples and places). London.

1996   *Ancient Nubia*. London and New York.

Simpson, W. Kelly
1963   *Hekanefer and the dynastic material from Toshka and Arminna*. New Haven and Yale.

Smith, H.S.
1966   The Nubian B-Group. *Kush* 14 69-124.
1976   *The fortress of Buhen. The inscriptions*. London.
1991   The development of the "A-Group" culture in northern Lower Nubia, in Davies, W.V. ed. 1991: 92-111.
1994   The princes of Seyala in Lower Nubia in the predynastic and protodynastic periods. in *Hommages à Jean Leclant*. vol. 2 *Nubie, Soudan, Ethiopie. IFAO Bib. d'Étude* 106/2. Le Caire. 361-376.

Smith, H.S. and A.L. Smith
1976   A reconsideration of the Kamose texts. *ZÄS* 103: 48-76.

Smith, Stuart Tyson
1995   *Askut in Nubia*. London and New York.

Smith, W. Stevenson and W. Kelly Simpson
1981   *Art and architecture of ancient Egypt*. Harmondsworth.

Snowden, F.M.
1970   *Blacks in antiquity. Ethiopians in the Greco-Roman experience*. Harvard University Press.
1983   *Before color prejudice. The ancient view of blacks*. Harvard University Press.
1989   Bernal's 'blacks,' Herodotus, and other classical evidence. *Arethusa* Special fall issue: 83-95.
1990   Did Herodotus say the Egyptians were black? *Biblical Archaeology Review* 16 (2): 72-74.

Spalinger, A.J.
1973   The year 712 BC and its implications for Egyptian history. *JARCE* 10: 95-101.!
1974   Esarhaddon and Egypt: an analysis of the first invasion of Egypt. *Orientalia* 43: 295-326.
1976   Psammetichus, King of Egypt: I. *JARCE* 13: 133-147.
1978   The foreign policy of Egypt preceding the Assyrian conquest. *CdE* 53 (105): 22-47.
1979   The military background of the campaign of Piye. *SAK* 7: 273-302.

Spiegelberg, W.
1921   *Ägyptische und andere Graffiti aus der thebanischen Nekropolis*. Heidelberg

Starr, I.
1990   *Queries to the Sungod: divination and politics in Sargonid Assyria*. SAA 4. Helsinki.

Steindorff, G.
1937   *Aniba II*. Service des Antiquités de l'Égypte. Mission archéologique de Nubie, 1929-1934. Glückstadt and Hamburg.

Tadmor, Hayim
1958   The campaigns of Sargon II of Assur: a chronological-historical study. *JCS* 12 22-40 and 77-100.
1961   Que and Musri. *IEJ* 11: 143-50.
1975   Assyria and the west: the ninth century and its aftermath; in H. Goedick and J.J.M. Roberts eds., *Unity and Diversity. Essays in the history, literature and religion of the ancient Near East*. Johns Hopkins University Press, Baltimore and London: 36-48.

Topozada, Z.
1988   Les deux campagnes d'Amenhotep III en Nubie. *BIFAO* 88: 153-164.

Török, L.
1986   *Der meroitischen Staat 1*. (= *Meroitica* 9). Berlin.
1995   The emergence of the Kingdom of Kush and her myth of the state in the first millenium BC. *Actes de la VIIIe Conférence internationale des études nubiennes. I. Communications principales. CRIPEL* 17: 203-228.
1999   The origin of the Napatan state: the long chronology of the el-Kurru cemetery. *Studien zum antiken Sudan (= Meroitica* 15) 149-159.

Trigger, B.
1976   *Nubia under the Pharaohs*. (Ancient peoples and places). London.
1978   Nubian ethnicity: some historical considerations. *Etudes Nubiennes* (Chantilly): 317-323.
1982   The reasons for the construction of the Second Cataract forts. *SSEAJ* 12: 1-6

Trigger et al.
B.G.Trigger, B.J. Kemp, D. O'Connor, A.B. Lloyd
1983   *Ancient Egypt. A Social History*. Cambridge.

UNESCO ed. Gamal Mokhtar
1981 *General History of Africa. II. Ancient Civilizations of Africa.* Heinemann and University of California Press.

Vercoutter, Jean
1960 Napatan kings and Apis worship. *Kush* 8: 62-76.
1975 *Mirgissa II. Les nécropoles.* CNRS. Paris.

Vercoutter et al.
J.Vercoutter, J. Leclant, F.M.Snowden, J.Desanges.
1976 *The image of the black in western art. I From the Pharaohs to the fall of the Roman empire.* New York, Menil Foundation.

Vittmann, G.
1978 *Priester und Beamte im Theben der Spätzeit. Genealogische und prosopographische Untersuchungen zum thebanischen Priester-und Beamtentum der 26. Dynastie.* Beiträge zur Ägyptologie 1. Wien.

Weinstein, J.M.
1981 The Egyptian empire in Palestine: a reassessment. *BASOR* 241: 1-28.

Welsby, D.A.
1996 *Kingdom of Kush.* London.

Wenig, Steffen
1978 *Africa in Antiquity. The arts of ancient Nubia and the Sudan II. The Catalogue.* The Brooklyn Museum.
1990 Pebatma - Pekareslo - Pekar-tror. Ein Beitrag zur Frühgeschichte der Kuschiten. *Studia in honorem Fritz Hintze* (= *Meroitica* 12): 333-352.

Wente, E.F.
1966 On the suppression of the High-Priest Amenhotep. *JNES* 25 73-87.

Wildung, D.
1996 *Sudan. Antike Königreiche am Nil.* Tübingen. (English and French editions).

Williams, B.B.
1980 The lost pharaohs of Nubia. *Archaeology* 33: 12-21.
1986 *The A-group royal cemetery at Qustul: Cemetery L* OINE III. Chicago.
1992 *New Kingdom remains from cemeteries R, V, S, and W at Qustul and cemetery K at Adindan.* OINE VI. Chicago.

Wilson, John
1951 *The culture of ancient Egypt.* Chicago. (Original title: *The Burden of Egypt*).

Yellin, Janice W.
1995 Egyptian religion and its ongoing impact on the formation of the Napatan state. *Actes de la VIIIe Conférence internationale des études nubiennes. I. Communications principales. CRIPEL* 17: 243-263.

Yoyotte, Jean
1951 Le martelage des noms royaux éthiopiens par Psammtique II. *CdE* 8: 215-239
1961 Les principautés du Delta au temps de l'anarchie libyenne. *Mélanges Maspero* I.4 Cairo pp.121-181.
1989 Pharaon Iny. Un roi mystérieux du VIIIe siècle avant J.-C. *RdE* 40: 113-131.

Yurco F.J.
1989 Were the Egyptians black or white? *Biblical Archaeology Review* 15 (5): 24-29, 58
1990 Reply to Anderson. *Biblical Archaeology Review* 16 (2): 14, 64-65.
1990 Reply to Richardson. *Biblical Archaeology Review* 16 (2): 70, 72.

Zeissl, Helene von
194 *Äthiopen und Assyrer in Ägypten. Beiträge zur Geschichte der Ägyptischen Spätzeit.* (*ÄF* 14) Glückstadt/Hamburg.

Zába, Zbynek
1974 *Rock inscriptions of Lower Nubia.* Prague.

Zibelius, K.
1972 *Afrikanische Orts- und Volkernamen in hieroglyphischen und hieratischen Texten.* TAVO Beiheft Reihe B/1. Wiesbaden.

Zibelius-Chen, K.Ã
1989 Uberlegungen zur Ägyptischen Nubienpolitik in der Dritten Zwischenzeit. *SAK* 16 329-345.

INDEX

Abbreviations : OK - Old Kingdom; MK - Middle Kingdom; NK - New Kingdom; HPA - High Priest of Amun; GWA - God's Wife of Amun; k - king; Ch - Chief.

italic numeral indicates an illustration on that page.